T0189654

Requirements Engineering for Service and Cloud Computing

Muthu Ramachandran · Zaigham Mahmood
Editors

Requirements Engineering for Service and Cloud Computing

 Springer

Editors
Muthu Ramachandran
School of Computing, Creative
 Technologies, and Engineering
Leeds Beckett University
Leeds
UK

Zaigham Mahmood
University of Derby
Derby
UK

and

North-West University
Potchefstroom
South Africa

ISBN 978-3-319-84616-3   ISBN 978-3-319-51310-2   (eBook)
DOI 10.1007/978-3-319-51310-2

Printed on acid-free paper

This Springer imprint is published by Springer Nature
The registered company is Springer International Publishing AG
The registered company address is: Gewerbestrasse 11, 6330 Cham, Switzerland

Preface

Overview

Requirements Engineering (RE) is the process of discovering, documenting, and managing the requirements for a computer-based system. The goal is to produce a set of specifications, as the first stage in the system development process, to form the basis for further design and development of the required system. Since the production of a complete, correct, and unambiguous set of requirements has numerous inherent issues, RE has become an important research topic in the field of software engineering. Additionally, with the emergence of the cloud computing paradigm, developments in social media and service computing, inherent challenges of the RE process have grown in numbers and complexity. This is because the new software systems are expected to be scalable, operable on all varieties of diverse platforms, sustainable, fail safe, and, in general, suitable for distributed computing environments. Now, software is being deployed as Web services and as software-as-a-service (SaaS) to be consumed by users on a wide variety of diverse smart devices, via the Internet protocols.

The current approaches to developing SaaS, embedded systems and enterprise applications, using methodologies such as service orientation and component-based design, have their focus on meeting the increasing levels of demands for distributed software as a service that is more accessible, configurable (over a distributed large-scale global network), and shareable for multi-tenancy. In the recent past, we have known software as functions, objects, classes, components, and even frameworks. However, the concept of a *software service* is new and different from the traditional software engineering perspective. In this context, the notion of a software product has changed considerably.

Unfortunately, there is a distinct lack of systematic approaches and methodologies to identify, define, visualize, specify, and validate requirements for such services, although there are some developments underway by way of new products and methodologies to cater for the needs of the industry. Also, the current software systems are beyond the traditional stakeholder concept. In respect to the newer approaches, the user base is now much wider and data and applications are shared through social media and other networked mobile technologies.

With this background, there is an urgent need for properly integrated solutions, taking into account the requirements of scalability, flexibility, sustainability, and operability for distributed computing environments. In this respect, the current text is probably the first book on the topic of RE for service and cloud computing.

This book, *Requirements Engineering for Service and Cloud Computing,* aims to capture the state of the art of the current advances in requirements engineering. Majority of the contributions in this book focus on: requirements elicitation; requirements specifications; requirements classification and requirements validation and evaluation. In this book, 36 researchers and practitioners of international repute have presented latest research developments, methodologies, current trends, state-of-the-art reports, case studies, and suggestions for further understanding, development and enhancement of subject area of requirements engineering for software systems for distributed environments.

Objectives

The aim of this volume is to present and discuss the state of the art in terms of methodologies, trends and future directions for requirements engineering for the service and cloud computing paradigm. The objectives include:

- Capturing the state-of-the-art research and practice relating to requirements engineering for the service and cloud computing;
- Discussing developments, tools, technologies, and trends in the subject area of software requirements engineering;
- Analyzing the relevant theoretical frameworks, practical approaches, and methodologies for service requirements;
- In general, advancing the understanding of the emerging new methodologies relevant to requirements engineering for the service and cloud computing.

Organization

There are 13 chapters in *Requirements Engineering for Service and Cloud Computing.* These are organized in three parts, as follows:

- *Part I: Requirements Elicitation for Service and Cloud Computing.* Requirements elicitation is the first key component of requirements engineering that involves various stakeholders to identify and clarify requirements for services' development. This section has a focus on various approaches, research, and practices towards requirements elicitation. There are five chapters in this part. Chapter 1 discusses experiences gained from participation in a number of large, commercial information system development projects in both public and private sectors in which the traditional way of handling the requirements has proven to be insufficient. Chapter 2 presents cloud dimensions that are graphically presented via conceptual models, as each dimension has specific entities, properties, and relationships. Chapter 3 presents approaches to requirements engineering for cloud-based environments; whereas Chap. 4 presents an overall aggregated effective quality of service (OAEQoS) model for capturing non-function requirements. Chapter 5 probes further into requirements engineering for software-defined cloud environments.

- *Part II: Requirements Specification for Service and Cloud Computing*. This part of the book comprises three chapters that focus on requirements specification. The first chapter presents an abstraction layer for SaaS architecture with a focus on multi-agent based inter-cloud environment, called enterprise cloud bus system (ECBS), to conceptualize the different behavioral facets of software systems in service and cloud computing paradigm. The next chapter discusses an approach on how BPMN nodes are mapped to services and presents an algorithm for dynamic discovery of appropriate services. The final contribution in this section suggests a framework for requirements classification and change management focusing on distributed platform-as-a-service (PaaS) and software-as-a-service (SaaS) systems as well as complex software ecosystems that are built using PaaS and SaaS, such as tools-as-a-service (TaaS).
- *Part III: Requirements Validation, Evaluation, and QoS for Service and Cloud Computing*. There are four chapters in this section that focus on requirements validation, evaluation, and quality of service (QoS). The first three chapters present appraisal and analysis of inherent security requirements, and discuss ways to make transition from information systems to Web services. The fourth contribution in this part addresses an approach to simulating composite Web services for predicting the QoS parameters. The final contribution presents a set of distributed agile requirements engineering patterns after several validation process.

Target Audiences

The current volume is a reference text aimed at supporting a number of potential audiences, including the following:

- *Software engineers* and *project managers* who wish to adopt the newer approaches to ensure the accurate and complete system specifications.
- *Students and lecturers* who have an interest in further enhancing the knowledge of technologies, mechanisms, and frameworks relevant to requirements engineering for distributed environments.

- *Researchers* in this field who require up-to-date knowledge of the current practices, mechanisms, and frameworks relevant to systems' requirements engineering.

Leeds, UK   Muthu Ramachandran
Derby, UK and Potchefstroom, South Africa   Zaigham Mahmood

Acknowledgements

The editors acknowledge the help and support of the following colleagues during the review, development, and editing phases of this text:

- Dr. S. Parthasarathy, Thiagarajar College of Engineering, Tamil Nadu, India
- Dr. Pethuru Raj, IBM Cloud Center of Excellence, Bangalore, India
- Prof. Andrea Zisman, Open University
- Prof. Bashar Nuseibeh, Open University
- Prof. T.R.G. Nair, Raja Rajeswari College of Engineering, India.

We would also like to thank the contributors to this book: 34 authors and co-authors, from academia as well as industry from around the world, who collectively submitted 12 chapters. Without their efforts in developing quality contributions, conforming to the guidelines and meeting often the strict deadlines, this text would not have been possible.

October 2016

Muthu Ramachandran
Zaigham Mahmood

Acknowledgements

Contents

Part I   Requirements Elicitation for Service and Cloud Computing

1   **What We Say We Want and What We Really Need: Experiences
    on the Barriers to Communicate Information System Needs**   3
    Aapo Koski and Tommi Mikkonen

2   **Cloud Dimensions for Requirements Specification**   23
    Ana Sofia Zalazar, Luciana Ballejos and Sebastian Rodriguez

3   **Analyzing Requirements Engineering for Cloud Computing**   45
    Ana Sofia Zalazar, Luciana Ballejos and Sebastian Rodriguez

4   **Classification of Non-functional Requirements of Web Services
    from Multiperspective View**   65
    Maya Rathore and Ugrasen Suman

5   **The Requirements Elicitation Approaches for Software-Defined
    Cloud Environments**   89
    Pethuru Raj, Parvathy Arulmozhi and Nithya Chidambaram

**Part II   Requirements Specification for Service and Cloud
           Computing**

6   **Formal Modeling of Enterprise Cloud Bus System: A High
    Level Petri-Net Based Approach**   121
    Gitosree Khan, Sabnam Sengupta and Anirban Sarkar

7   **Requirements to Services: A Model to Automate Service
    Discovery and Dynamic Choreography from Service Version
    Database**.   151
    Swapan Bhattacharya, Ananya Kanjilal, Sabnam Sengupta,
    Jayeeta Chanda and Dipankar Majumdar

**8   Architecturally Significant Requirements Identification,
      Classification and Change Management for Multi-tenant
      Cloud-Based Systems** 181
      Muhammad Aufeef Chauhan and Christian W. Probst

**Part III   Requirements Validation, Evaluation, and QoS
             for Service and Cloud Computing**

9   Cyber Security Requirements Engineering 209
      Christof Ebert

**10 Appraisal and Analysis of Various Self-Adaptive
      Web Service Composition Approaches** 229
      Doaa H. Elsayed, Eman S. Nasr, Alaa El Din M. El Ghazali
      and Mervat H. Gheith

**11 Transition from Information Systems to Service-Oriented
      Logical Architectures: Formalizing Steps
      and Rules with QVT** 247
      Nuno Santos, Nuno Ferreira and Ricardo J. Machado

**12 Improving the QoS of a Composite Web Service
      by Pruning its Weak Partners** 271
      Kuljit Kaur Chahal, Navinderjit Kaur Kahlon
      and Sukhleen Bindra Narang

**13 Using Distributed Agile Patterns for Supporting
      the Requirements Engineering Process** 291
      Maryam Kausar and Adil Al-Yasiri

Index 317

About the Editors

Dr. Muthu Ramachandran is a Principal Lecturer in the Computing, Creative Technologies, and Engineering School as part of the Faculty of Arts, Environment and Technology at Leeds Beckett University in the UK. Previously, he spent nearly eight years in industrial research (Philips Research Labs and Volantis Systems Ltd, Surrey, UK) where he worked on software architecture, reuse, and testing. His first career started as a research scientist where he worked on real-time systems development projects. Muthu is an author of books including: Software Components: Guidelines and Applications (Nova Publishers, NY, USA, 2008) and Software Security Engineering: Design and Applications (Nova Publishers, NY, USA, 2011). He has also widely authored and published nine books, over hundreds of journal articles, over 50 book chapters and over 200 conferences papers on various advanced topics in software engineering, software security, cloud computing, and education. Muthu has been leading conferences as chairs and as keynote speakers on global safety, security and sustainability, emerging services, IoT, big data, and software engineering. Muthu is a member of various professional organizations and computer societies: IEEE, ACM, Fellow of BCS, and a Senior Fellow of HEA. He has also been an invited keynote speaker on several international conferences. Muthu's research projects have included all aspects of software engineering, SPI for SMEs (known as Prism model), emergency and disaster management systems, software components and architectures, good practice guidelines on software developments, software security engineering, and service and cloud computing. Projects details can be accessed at www.se.moonfruit.com and at www.software-research.com.

Muthu can be reached at m.ramachandran@leedsbeckett.ac.uk and re.for.cloud@gmail.com

Prof. Dr. Zaigham Mahmood is an author/editor of 19 books, six of which are dedicated to electronic-government and the other thirteen focus on the subjects of cloud computing, data science, Internet of Things, and software project management, including: *Cloud Computing: Concepts, Technology & Architecture* which is also published in Korean and Chinese languages; *Cloud Computing: Methods and*

Practical Approaches; Software Engineering Frameworks for the Cloud Computing Paradigm; Cloud Computing for Enterprise Architectures; Cloud Computing Technologies for Connected Government; Continued Rise of the Cloud: Advances and Trends in Cloud Computing; Cloud Computing: Challenges, Limitations and R&D Solutions; Data Science and Big Data Computing: Frameworks and Methodologies; Connectivity Frameworks for Smart Devices: The Internet of Things from a Distributed Computing Perspective; and *Software Project Management for Distributed Computing: Life-Cycle Methods for Developing Scalable and Reliable Tools.* Additionally, he is developing two new books to appear later in 2017. He has also published more than 100 articles and book chapters and organized numerous conference tracks and workshops.

Professor Mahmood is the Editor-in-Chief of *Journal of E-Government Studies and Best Practices* as well as the Series Editor-in-Chief of the IGI book series *E-Government and Digital Divide.* He is a Senior Technology Consultant at Debesis Education UK and Associate Lecturer (Research) at the University of Derby UK. He further holds positions as Foreign Professor at NUST and IIU in Islamabad Pakistan and Professor Extraordinaire at the North West University Potchefstroom South Africa. Professor Mahmood is also a certified cloud computing instructor and a regular speaker at international conferences devoted to cloud computing and e-government. His specialized areas of research include distributed computing, project management, and e-government.

Other Springer Books by the Editors

Strategic Systems Engineering for Cloud and Big Data

By Muthu Ramachandran

This reference text provides state of the approaches on strategic approaches to cloud computing and big data.

Enterprise Security

By Muthu Ramachandran

This book provides state-of-the-art approaches on enterprise security, cloud security, and big data security issues.

Cloud Computing: Challenges, Limitations and R&D Solutions

By Zaigham Mahmood

This reference text reviews the challenging issues that present barriers to greater implementation of the cloud computing paradigm, together with the latest research into developing potential solutions. This book presents case studies and analysis of the implications of the cloud paradigm, from a diverse selection of researchers and practitioners of international repute. ISBN: 978-3-319-10529-1.

Continued Rise of the Cloud: Advances and Trends in Cloud Computing

By Zaigham Mahmood

This reference volume presents latest research and trends in cloud-related technologies, infrastructure, and architecture. Contributed by expert researchers and practitioners in the field, this book presents discussions on current advances and practical approaches including guidance and case studies on the provision of cloud-based services and frameworks. ISBN: 978-1-4471-6451-7.

Cloud Computing: Methods and Practical Approaches

By Zaigham Mahmood

The benefits associated with cloud computing are enormous; yet the dynamic, virtualized, and multi-tenant nature of the cloud environment presents many challenges. To help tackle these, this volume provides illuminating viewpoints and case studies to present current research and best practices on approaches and technologies for the emerging cloud paradigm. ISBN: 978-1-4471-5106-7.

Software Engineering Frameworks for the Cloud Computing Paradigm

By Zaigham Mahmood

This is an authoritative reference that presents the latest research on software development approaches suitable for distributed computing environments. Contributed by researchers and practitioners of international repute, the book offers practical guidance on enterprise-wide software deployment in the cloud environment. Case studies are also presented. ISBN: 978-1-4471-5030-5.

Cloud Computing for Enterprise Architectures

By Zaigham Mahmood

This reference text, aimed at system architects and business managers, examines the cloud paradigm from the perspective of enterprise architectures. It introduces fundamental concepts, discusses principles, and explores frameworks for the adoption of cloud computing. The book explores the inherent challenges and presents future directions for further research. ISBN: 978-1-4471-2235-7.

Data Science and Big Data Computing: Frameworks and Methodologies

By Zaigham Mahmood

This reference text focuses on data science and provides practical guidance on methodologies and frameworks for big data analytics. Expert perspectives are provided by an authoritative collection of 36 researchers and practitioners, discussing latest developments, emerging trends; and innovative approaches suggesting best practices for efficient data analytics. ISBN: 978-3-319-31859-2.

Connectivity Frameworks for Smart Devices: The Internet of Things from a Distributed Computing Perspective

By Zaigham Mahmood

This is an authoritative reference that focuses on the latest developments on the Internet of Things. It presents state of the art of the current advances in the connectivity of diverse devices; and focuses on the communication, security, privacy, access control, and authentication aspects of the device connectivity in distributed environments. ISBN: 978-3-319-33122-5.

Part I
Requirements Elicitation for Service and Cloud Computing

Chapter 1
What We Say We Want and What We Really Need: Experiences on the Barriers to Communicate Information System Needs

Aapo Koski and Tommi Mikkonen

Abstract Information system requirements are meant to communicate the relevant needs and intention to a wide range of stakeholders. The requirements form the basis on which the tenders are issued, projects are agreed upon, and service-level agreements are made. However, as the requirements state what the system owners—or the ones who are willing to pay for the system—want the system to achieve, they reflect the owners' views and understanding. This setup is plagued by many weaknesses. First, the system owners are seldom experts in the information system design and therefore they may be unable to state all the relevant requirements comprehensively. Second, no matter how much energy and time is invested in the requirement definition and elicitation, many aspects of the requirements are only revealed during the development and deployment, and remain unforeseen until later on, when the development is well under way. Finally, the required system architecture cannot be appropriately designed, if we do not know the requirements at a sufficient level. In this chapter we reflect our experiences from participating in a number of large, commercial information system development projects in both public and private sectors in which the traditional way of handling the requirements has proven to be insufficient. With the software as a service (SaaS) business model, where the goal is frequent releases and continuous delivery of ever-improved services, the associated weaknesses become even more prominent. We propose better practices for specifying systems and suggest concentrating a lot more on the true communication and discussion, focusing always on the most important issues and most important stakeholders only and keeping the vision updated and clear for the whole duration of a system development project and also the system maintenance period.

A. Koski (✉)
Basware Oyj, Tampere, Finland
e-mail: aapo.koski@iki.fi

T. Mikkonen
Tampere University of Technology, Tampere, Finland
e-mail: tommi.mikkonen@tut.fi

© Springer International Publishing AG 2017
M. Ramachandran and Z. Mahmood (eds.), *Requirements Engineering for Service and Cloud Computing*, DOI 10.1007/978-3-319-51310-2_1

Keywords Requirements specification · Requirements management · System architecture · External quality · Internal quality · Process quality · Communication · Software as a service · Continuous delivery

1.1 Introduction

When referring to requirements related to an information system, we usually mean requirements originating from customer-side stakeholders. These requirements represent the views and needs of the people at the business or enterprise operations level, covering end-users, acquirers, customers, and a number of other stakeholders. The requirements are recorded to solve the stakeholders' problems. These problems to be solved vary in their nature, and often the different stakeholders perceive the situation in very different ways. To further complicate the matter, the set of requirements for fulfilling stakeholders' needs typically has a strong connection not just to the domain the stakeholders represent, but also to the history and to the environment in which the system is to be operational.

In addition to stakeholder's needs, we have system requirements, which should unambiguously specify how the system is to be developed as well as define the basis for system architecture design and technology selections. System requirements are naturally closely related and connected to the customer-side requirements, but they ought to be written in a language that is fully and unambiguously understood by system designers, architects, developers, testers, as well as other people that work on the system provider's side. Ideally, system requirements complement the original end-user requirements and provide deeper understanding on what the system needs to be capable of doing. Making stakeholder and system requirements meet—so-called requirements elicitation—appears to be the hardest and the most critical part of the development of any larger information system. Furthermore, the situation gets even more complex as new boundaries emerge over time, for instance when the business model changes. Today, the most dramatic change is when installable systems operated in full in customer premises are being replaced by software that is provided as a service.

This chapter reflects industrial experiences gained from a number of large, commercial, software as a service(SaaS) information system development projects for both public and private sectors during the last decade. As we, the authors of the chapter, represent the system providers, we look at the information system projects from the system provider's point of view, from which it is not always quite clear where the customer-side requirements originate, what kind of a history the requirements have and what kind of real needs are hiding behind the stated requirements. In particular, we address the dependencies and overlaps between requirements, which require extensive effort to understand properly, but if left not fully understood, pose a significant threat to the success of the system development project. While a prominent attribute throughout the information system projects has been that the bigger the project, the larger the number of requirements is, it is equally clear that the traditional way of handling the requirements has proven inadequate in several respects. Having had the first-hand opportunity to observe this has thought us valuable lessons for later use.

The rest of this chapter is structured as follows. In Sect. 1.2, we discuss the characteristics of the requirements and their diverse role in the information system domain. In Sect. 1.3, we provide an insight to the actual requirements we have encountered in the projects and discuss the possible reasons why the requirements often are like they are: far from optimal. In Sect. 1.4, we present our understanding on the nature of the true needs of the system owners and how the true needs are reflected in the written requirements. In Sect. 1.5, we discuss the barriers to communication which, based on our experiences, are the main reason for low-quality requirements and requirement management. In Sect. 1.6, we discourse the relation between the requirements and the system architecture. Finally, in Sect. 1.7, we draw some final conclusions and present better ways to collaborate and communicate, thus enhancing the quality of the requirements.

1.2 The Challenging Role of the Requirements

With requirements, we aim at specifying what a computer system or service should do [1]. The requirements are important in a number of ways in the development [2], including typically at least the following views:

- They form the basis of the system requirements and various activities related to the system design;
- They form the basis of system validation and stakeholder acceptance;
- They act as a reference for all the integration and verification activities;
- They serve as means of communication between all the stakeholders, like the technical staff, management, and the stakeholder community.

Based on our industry experiences, especially the final view is often overlooked and misinterpreted. Yet the role of the requirements as a means of communication to a vast audience is pivotal in any development effort where contracting plays a role, because the requirements form the basis on which the tenders are issued [3], projects are agreed upon [4], and service-level agreements are made [5]. Altogether, the requirements are fundamental to the economic context in the software development: if the quality of the requirements is not good enough or the requirements are not managed properly, the projects' risk to fail increase significantly, the total cost of ownership of the systems increase, and the overall user satisfaction will not be as good as could have been expected. As reported in, e.g., [6, 7], low-quality requirements are the most common reason for the failure of software projects.

The setup where a predefined, fixed set of requirements to satisfy the user needs exists has many weaknesses [8, 9]. Firstly, the people involved in the requirement creation, the system owner and other stakeholders, are seldom experts in the information system design and are thus unable to state all the requirements—especially the nonfunctional ones—with enough detail and rigor to be unambiguous and comprehensive. Requirements that remain ambiguous will be misunderstood, their effect will not be reliably estimated, and they cause a lot of waste in the form of lost time and resources as they are re-specified, detailed and unfortunately also expanded many times in course of a project. Secondly, no matter how much energy and time is put into the creation of the requirements, for any larger information system, many of the true requirements are only fully revealed during the development and deployment of the system itself [10]. Finally, the system architecture, which has the important role to describe how the system will be organized and therefore also to define what the system can or cannot do, cannot be appropriately designed if we do not know the requirements at a sufficient level. Especially, if architecture design is based on assumptions made solely by the system provider side designers and architects, it will be highly unlikely that the architecture will behave in a way that fulfills all the true customer-side requirements.

An important factor that should not be forgotten is that requirements are not only limited to the functionality of the system, as often supposed, but include other aspects as well. Different authors have presented various definitions, but in general functional and nonfunctional (or quality) requirements are separated. For the purposes of this chapter we may take into use the classification by Davis [11]:

- *Functional requirements*: These include statements regarding the services which the system should provide, how the system should react to particular inputs and how the system should behave in particular situations.
- *Nonfunctional requirements*: Constraints related to the services or functions offered by the system, such as timing constraints, security issues, constraints on the development process and so on.
- *Performance and reliability requirements*: Requirements that specify the speed or operational effectiveness of a capability that must be delivered by the system architecture.
- *Interface-related requirements*: Requirements that come from the environment of the system and that reflect characteristics of the integrability of the system.
- *Design constraints*: Requirements that come from the application domain of the system. Typically, such reflect all kinds of constraints that need to be taken into account in that specific domain.

In addition, there often are domain or system specific requirements, for example associated with applicable standards or laws. For instance, developing medical devices or aerospace systems typically have special requirements that are associated with the development of the system rather than the eventual outcome. The problem here is that a service provider cannot always trust that all the relevant domain and system-specific requirements are stated by the system owners as the original requirements that need to be fulfilled and taken into account. This aspect is further emphasized in the SaaS environment, as the end-users who may or may not be aware of the laws and standards, not necessarily verify that the service provided is standard compliant or legal. The unawareness of the end-users, however, does not naturally acquit the service provider from the responsibilities.

1.3   What We Say We Want and Why

To identify possible reasons why the requirements are as they are, we next look at what the stakeholders' requirements of a large-scale information system specification typically contain and what the typical process resulting in the specific set of requirements is. In the scope of experiences presented here, all the projects have started from the system providers' point of view with a request for proposal (RFP) or request for quotation (RFQ) process [12, 13]. While both mark a request for describing a project and sometimes the difference is only in the eye of the beholder, the principal difference between the RFP and the RFQ processes is that commonly the RFP is used when the stakeholders concentrate on describing the problem they have and want to hear in which ways it should be solved. In contrast, the RFQ is used when the stakeholders know what they want but need information on how potential vendors would meet the requirements and how much it will cost. The goal of both the RFP and RFQ is that the potential suppliers are informed that certain service is needed in a way that enables the suppliers to respond factually to the identified requirements. Often, prior to the issuing of the RFQ or RFP to the potential providers, a round of the standard business process of request for information (RFI) [14] is also executed, where the potential vendors are asked to determine what kind of services are available to meet the described needs.

Both RFP and RFQ processes of information systems, disregarding if their domain is public or private sector and also almost regardless of the target and characteristics of the system itself, have taken the habit of starting with a comprehensive specification phase, possibly including also a round of a RFI process. In this phase, the representatives of the future owner of the system (and often also a hired group of consultants) spend a considerable period of time trying to determine the exact needs of the owner as precisely as possible. Typically, the specification phase results in hundreds or even thousands of requirements, written carefully in, e.g., IEEE 830 requirement format [15]. These requirements are reviewed many times, over and over again, and usually they are finally accepted by all the stakeholders, although usually only after a number of refinements and iterations. However, for the potential system providers the details of these processes remain mostly unknown, due to the common reckoning that by giving any of the potential system provider information on the work-in-progress would introduce unfairness in the tender to build the system based on the RFP or the RFQ.

Nevertheless, after the competition based on the RFP or RFQ has been decided and an agreement on the development of the system is signed with a company, this defined, refined, iterated, and finally accepted set of requirements serves as the most valuable artifact for the following steps in the information system design and development process. The requirements are treated in various occasions as the final "truth" to which one can safely refer to when discussing system features or characteristics and by which the customer assesses the progress and the quality of the created system. As anyone involved with information system design and development can verify, the fixed set of requirements is already a problem in itself, and, if not adjusted and refined in a continuous manner, leads often to system implementation that does not correspond to the actual needs of the system owner. Moreover, even if the requirements itself were at some point of the system development process complete and able to reflect the true needs of the system owner, the form and the language used in the writing of the requirements leaves typically a lot of freedom to the interpretation of the requirement. This problem is emphasized when the project is large in size, related to multiple organizations and lasting for a long time, because then the same requirements can be interpreted differently in different phases of the project, when considered by different people playing different roles in the development.

The requirement gathering and specification phase commonly overlooks the architecture of the system to be developed. Although some of the requirements can be categorized as architecturally significant [16], the main features and required characteristics of the system architecture largely remain unspecified and vague. Especially at the present era of agile development methods, where room is typically left for later fine-tuning and revisions, requirements that are specified upfront in the project easily lead to a so-called emerging architecture [17]. Emergent architecture in itself sounds acceptable—and indeed is acceptable for various projects—but for long-lasting, dependable systems and as well as for systems provided by SaaS model, such an approach means that the system architecture has to be rethought many times during the project [18] as we learn more of the system we are developing. This in turn costs money, makes the system development slower, limits the options, and causes a lot of confusion as several, incompatible views to the architecture are simultaneously under consideration by various stakeholders.

The requirements, the architecture, and the original needs or vision of the system to be developed and taken into use give us three points of view into the system. These views are not necessarily similar, however. Ideally, these three elements, complemented with the acceptance testing criteria or test cases, should support and complement each other and together give any stakeholder a clear view on what are we developing and how well it satisfies the needs we have.

When specifying the requirement in the fashion described above, we make, partly unconsciously, partly fully consciously, assumptions, some of which are almost too bold, namely:

- The representatives selected or set to specify the system have all the knowledge required to do the specification job.
- The understanding on the needs we have will not change during the specification process.

Table 1.1 Examples of functional and nonfunctional requirements in industrial projects

Requirement	Type	Comment
"The system shall provide the user the time she has been handling her task"	Functional	Requirement does neither specify what is meant by the time nor give any indication why the time is important to the user
"The system shall support the addition of new ways to communicate"	Functional	Requirement does not limit in any way what kind of ways of communication should be supported and what supporting really means
"The system shall support high availability"	Nonfunctional	Requirement is far too generic and does not succeed in communicating any true need to the reader
"The system shall present all the required information stored in the system to the user in real time"	Non-functional	Requirement cannot be truly met in any distributed information system as there always are delays in the transferring, handling and visualizing the information. The requirement does not give any indication in what scale the system needs to be a real-time system

- The representatives are capable of expressing the needs in a written format that cannot be understood in a wrong or incomplete way by other people and the written down needs leave as little space as possible for vagueness.
- The requirements can be written in the same way regardless of whether a requirement specifies a functional feature or a quality issue.
- The requirements are expressed in such detail that the potential vendors can reliably estimate the time and costs required to implement each requirement.
- Since information systems are nowadays created in an agile—although the most appropriate term in connection with tender projects is agilish—way, the requirements need to be written in a way that allows incremental development. Ideally, the requirements should thus be independent of each other, and therefore implementable in any order.
- Related closely to the previous assumption, the requirements can be written in a way that allows iterative development: the implementation of a feature related to a requirement can be tested, verified, and accepted after an iterative development phase (like sprint), although the need that the requirement reflects is not necessarily fully satisfied by the iterative step in question.

To highlight the points given above, let us take a look at some real-life requirements[1] that we have encountered. These requirements demonstrate the typical qualities and unambiguousness of the requirements (Table 1.1). As can be clearly seen in the examples, even if elaborated with the system owner in project

---

[1]Requirements are taken out of their context to protect the identity of the system in question.

negotiations or other such meetings, the requirements are easily understood differently by different stakeholders, and the estimates on the effort needed to fulfill the requirements are next to impossible to make reliably. The original system owner's intention and the interpretation of the requirement by a developer can easily be totally two different things.

Furthermore, it seems that the bigger the program is and the longer the specification period has been, the greater and bolder the assumptions are, and, consequently, also the greater are the risks involved. This at least partly false feeling of certainty of a comprehensive specification project leads to requirements that are actually neither correct nor comprehensive. Ironically, it seems that almost everybody who has been involved in a public tender projects' specification phase is ready to admit that the produced set of final requirements is not comprehensive, contains contradictory and dependent requirements, is not written in a way that allows iterative and incremental development (i.e., requirements cannot be easily prioritized and split) and does not fully reflect the original vision of the system to be developed.

It also seems that the system requirements—the ones that should specify in a detailed way what the system should do—are often totally forgotten. Instead, an attempt is made to create a system that matches the original system owners' requirements, the ones that never truly were in a form that could be used for verifying whether the original needs were satisfied.

1.4 What We Truly Need

With the requirements specification process explained above, the five main problem areas emerge that are almost inevitably encountered when a project to build the information system starts:

- Problems related to the scope of the developed system.
- Problems related to the volatility of the already specified requirements defining the system.
- Problems related to differences in the expected and the observed quality of the functional and nonfunctional aspects of the system.
- Problems related to the sheer large number of the requirements.
- Problems related to the communication of the true contents of the requirements between the customer representatives and the system provider as well as between the different groups of people, like architects, designers, developers, testers, and management at the system provider side.

When we are aiming at providing an information system as a service—in other words, using the SaaS model—the problems listed above become more prominent than with more traditional system delivery models. With SaaS we are able to provide easily frequent releases for the end-users to use, to easily monitor the user behavior and to give the users effective feedback channels. Thus with SaaS the problems that otherwise may not have been detected, surface early in the system development phase and need to be addressed already during the early phases of the collaboration with all the stakeholders.

We will briefly discuss the first four problem areas in the remainder of this section. In addition, we will address the fourth one—communication—with a more extensive discussion in Sect. 1.5.

1.4.1 Problems of Scope

Requirement elicitation must begin with an organizational and context analysis to determine the boundary of the target system as well as the objectives of the system. Less ambitious elicitation techniques, not fully addressing this concern, introduce the risk of producing requirements that are incomplete and potentially unusable, because they do not adhere to the users' or organizations' true goals for the system. Performing an organizational and context analysis allows these goals to be captured, and then later used to verify that the requirements are indeed usable and correct.

Elicitation techniques can be overambitious as well. In projects that have inspired this paper, elicitation processes were executed several times during the duration of the system development project and almost every time the goal was set to do proper work this time to find to real requirements. We ended up with a new set of requirements, but it was hard to say if this new set was any better in quality.

Elicitation must focus on the creation of requirements and not design activities in order to adequately address users' concerns. Elicitation strategies which produce requirements in the form of high-level designs run the risk of creating requirements which are ambiguous to the user community. These requirements may not be verifiable by the users because they do not adequately understand the design language. Also, requirements expressed as a design are much more likely to incorporate additional decisions not reflecting user or sponsor needs, in which case the requirements will not be precise or truly necessary for the development.

1.4.2 Problems of Volatility

One of the primary causes of requirements volatility is that user needs evolve over time [19]. The requirements engineering process of eliciting, specifying, and validating the requirements should not therefore be executed only once during system development. We should return to these processes frequently and with low threshold, so that the requirements can reflect the new knowledge gained during specification, validation, and subsequent activities. To this end, any requirements engineering methodology should be iterative in nature, enabling refining existing solutions and creating new ones as knowledge increases [20].

Another cause of requirements volatility is that the requirements are the product of the contributions a number of individuals, with different backgrounds and having most often conflicting needs and goals [21].

Volatility also arises when the users and other customer representatives do not fully understand the capabilities and limitations of the technology and architecture already designed for the system. The lack of understanding leads to unrealistic expectations of either the functionality that can be provided, or the time scale of the development. These expectations should be corrected as early as possible in the requirements elicitation process.

1.4.3   Problems of Observed Quality

When we face huge sets of requirements related to a project or some program aiming for taking an information system into operative use, we rarely seem to verify the comprehensiveness of the requirement set.

The quality of an information system is a complex thing, the quality is experienced by different people in a different way and as the quality consists of a number of diverse aspects, the different people on the customer side observe the quality on totally different basis and also differently at different times.

When defining the quality of an information system, we must understand that there exist at least two important categories of qualities, namely the external qualities and the internal qualities.

External quality. When assessing the external quality, the one that the system users and owners face, at least the following items must be taken into account:

- Observed functional quality of the system.
- Observed usability by real end-users.
- Observed performance of the system, under normal load and under some heavier load during times of congestion.
- Observed reliability of the system in diverse but foreseen conditions.
- Observed maintainability of the system during version upgrades or system patching.
- Observed integrability with the system's true environment.

Above, the word *observed* bears particular significance. One cannot be satisfied with any quality aspect of the system, if the aspect is not validated by measuring or observing it. This requirement makes all the quality aspects above to classify as external quality aspects. The external quality aspects are the ones the acceptance criteria must deal with—and not just some of them, but all.

Internal quality. The quality of an information system is not just external quality observed by an end-user or some other stakeholder. When considering an information system of this scale, the internal quality aspects become as important as the external quality aspects when judging the overall quality of the system in the long run. The internal quality consists of the following aspects:

- Testability. The time of manual testing as a major way to test almost any real-life software system has long gone. Testing needs to be automated to enable functional tests with good coverage and repeatability. With automated tests we can perform hard enough stress testing, long-lasting load testing and even fuzzy testing. Manual testing has its place, though. Nothing can replace a human tester in exploratory testing task.
- Maintainability. A critical system has a long life span. The maintenance of the system, in form of patches, updates, and repairs will form a major expenditure.
- Portability. During the long lifetime the system needs to live through all kinds of environments. Non-portability and lack of robustness will become easily suicidal for the system.
- Supportability. The critical system's configuration needs to be identifiable and we must be able to diagnose behavior and performance and debug it.

Without high quality of these aspects, the pace of the development gradually slows soon down to a halt. In addition, to ensure the high quality of the above-mentioned aspects, one needs to be capable of giving constant attention to the aspects. This again requires a considerable amount of time and energy.

1.4.4 Problems of Expected Quality

With the SaaS paradigm gaining popularity, in addition to the problems related to the observed quality by the users and customers of the provided service, one needs to rethink also how the expectations related to the service have changed because of SaaS.

To be able to benefit from the SaaS, the services need to be designed to be provided as services and delivered in the way SaaS model requires. This means at least that the services fulfill the following requirements:

- Provide easy and maintainable ways for integration with a multitude of customer-specific systems
- Allow customer-specific maintainable configuration
- Support true multi-tenancy
- Provide enough scalability
- Allow regular updates
- Allow fast deployment
- Allow customer-specific upgrade schedules
- Provide world-class security the customers can count on.

Failing to meet these requirements hinders us from capitalizing the benefits made possible by the SaaS model.

Furthermore, as the SaaS model is still for many customers a relatively new thing, we cannot even expect the customer to be able to state these requirements in any RFQ or alike, as these quality attributes are more or less assumed ones in the era of the SaaS.

1.4.5 Problems of Quantity

There also seems to exist a common problem of confusion with the requirements when the number of the requirements describing the system in question becomes high. When the total number of requirements is in many hundreds or close to thousand, the functional and nonfunctional requirements tend to become mixed up and it begins to be extremely hard to tell apart the nonfunctional part of the requirement from the functional one. Several different requirements may also be expressed together or depend on each other in a way that makes the fulfillment and verification of the single requirement almost impossible.

To the problem of the management of a large number of requirements the available modern requirement management tools provide a partial solution but there still seems to be a human factor that cannot be overlooked: only information systems up to certain size can be understood by single human beings and when the size increases the comprehensive understanding is gradually lost.

1.5 Barriers to Communication

When we have started new information system projects with some totally new or partially unknown group of customer representatives, the first problem faced is always communications. The customer side has typically been involved with the specification process for already some years and in addition to that, has a vast experience on the domain. The system providers, on the other hand, are typically experts in information system creation and not deeply knowledgeable on the specific details or conventions intrinsic to the domain in question. Now, with SaaS all these stakeholders need to understand the customer domain as well, since otherwise providing suitable service level can simply be impossible. Moreover, it is not in clients' interests to continuously educate the staff that runs the service for them—instead, it should be a primary goal of the service provider that they learn domain specifics as rapidly and as effectively as possible.

1.5.1 Barriers at the Customer Interface

A Savant Institute study found that 56% of errors in installed systems were due to poor communication between user and analyst in defining requirements and that these types of errors were the most expensive to correct using up to 82% of available staff time [22]. Problems of understanding during elicitation can lead to requirements that are ambiguous, incomplete, inconsistent, and even incorrect because they do not address the requirements elicitation stakeholders' true needs. Lack of user input arises when users are not fully aware of their needs or are unable to communicate them. It also arises when analysts and developers fail to ask the necessary questions.

When a system needs to be defined, a series of meeting needs to be held consisting of stakeholders. These stakeholders include clients, users, software engineers, system analysts, domain experts, managers, etc. It has been assumed that having a larger number of people in a meeting helps refining the system requirements and brainstorming becomes much effective and easier. But there is also a potential problem having superfluous and extra stakeholders in a meeting. Furthermore, when we are to deliver possibly tailor-made information system for the customer only once, the meetings make sense and are affordable, but with the SaaS model, arranging constant meetings to define and refine the system requirements may easily become too expensive. Instead, more effective means for getting feedback are required by, e.g., monitoring the service [23].

The language barrier is considered to be a major problem. When there is no proper common protocol to communicate the whole purpose of meeting together is defeated. Different stakeholders may speak literally different languages, e.g., Chinese and English. But even within the same language, it is notorious that stakeholders from different domains (such as management, manufacturing, marketing, and technical) use the same words with different meanings. When literally different languages are used, there is the additional task of translating the relevant documents. When figuratively different "languages" are used, the problem may not even be recognized.

Of course, the lack of clarity in the written down documents also poses a problem if not managed appropriately. Although both the customer and the system provider representatives may have a common understanding on a requirements true content, the precision of the description is difficult to reach without making the requirement document difficult to read.

In the customer interface, according to our experiences, we also seem to play the broken telephone game all too much. The game is played inadvertently when information is passed from customers to consultants or business analysts and only from there to designers, developers and testers.

1.5.2 Internal Barriers

Within the system provider organization, the same barriers to communication exist. Within the development teams we always have some kind of communication problems, being either just lack of discussion or the blind reliance on the information on an issue tracking system's issue instead of asking for better information. The development organization's culture is here in a crucial role: if the culture encourages people to raise issues and do critical thinking, the barriers to communication can at least partly be overcome.

However, it should be always kept in mind that every time we pass information on, it may get changed and misinterpreted, leading to increased project costs and the delivery of the wrong solutions to our customers and users.

1.5.3 Human Barriers

Wiio's laws [24] are observations about how human communication usually fails, except by accident, formulated in a humoristic way. Since the Wiio's laws point out that the communication always fails, anyone who does understand part of your message will miss the other parts. Consequently, the only way to ensure that the essential information has been communicated is through feedback, which is a necessary part of human communication. However, with feedback we cannot be satisfied if we only get positive and encouraging feedback—only getting positive and negative feedback together indicates that there are people who truly have been trying to understand the communicated issue and are interested enough in it to ensure that what she understood was correct.

An important part of one's reflection is thus also an issue of misunderstanding and its sources [25]. The main point here is that when we are communicating and talking to each other we are rather building a common view of what we are really talking about [25]. Accepting this while handling the requirements of an information system would help us a lot in the process: the starting point should be that the dialogue neither enforces one's opinion against the other's one, nor does it add one's opinion to the other's one—the dialogue will change both of the opinions if the communication is successful.

1.6 Requirements and Architecture

A dual relation exists between requirements and architecture. On one hand, requirements specify what a system must do. On the other hand, architecture describes how a system will be organized and how it will behave in order to fulfill these requirements. As requirements describe the problem and architecture describes the solution, it is easy to think that the requirements naturally precede the architecture. Following this line of thought results in the conclusion that the requirements can be defined without any input from the architecture. However, in any larger scale information system project, all the stakeholders are nowadays ready to admit that the requirements cannot really be specified in detail before the system development starts. This means that the required system architecture, which describes how the system will be organized and determines how it will behave, cannot be appropriately designed. This leaves us with the traditional chicken and the egg problem: we cannot design the architecture without the requirements and on the other hand, we cannot find the requirements without some form of architecture.

Without the architecture in the picture, high-level external outcomes and constraints often bubble down to use cases, functional specifications, and wireframe UI models. Without architecture, the detailed requirements easily become conflicting and incomplete. Thus the requirement specification and elicitation process without the specification of the architecture does not really make sense. With every set of requirements offered to the potential system providers, there should also be a description of the architecture of the system to be created—and not just some reference architecture, but an architecture the system owners are committed to and which is not be changed easily as requirements evolve.

To generate such architecture—or maybe more realistically a minimum viable architecture (MVA) [26]—a group of architects and domain experts should look for the biggest challenges in the system at hand, especially from the points of view of the deployment environment, the technical issues and the project teams on both sides of the table, the customer and system provider side. The task for this group is to prioritize the identified challenges, find solutions and also debate and lay out alternative solutions. The architects should be able to point out where some approach has potential side effects on other areas and refine the approaches with the domain experts based on the new information.

At the end of the MVA process, the architects and domain experts have collaborated on finding a solution to a problem at hand that would not have been possible to find without the contribution of both the architects and the domain experts. However, while the MVA is not the solution to the entire set of problems encountered during any larger scale information system project, it defines the architecture strategy, the framework and skeleton for the eventual solution.

To make the concept of the MVA a bit more concrete, let us take a look at the steps taken to create a real-life MVA. This example is related to an information system the main purpose of which is to receive, process, refine, relay and store incident-related data[2]:

- We created the most likely scenario of the process the service needs to handle and identify the most critical part of this scenario.
- We analyzed carefully the roles of the users using the service first and their behavior—what kind of users we expect the service to have and without what features these users can still manage?
- We outlined the simplest possible way to achieve an architectural structure, which allows the service to provide the users the functionalities needed for the most likely scenario, the MVA.
- We made sure we understand all the nonfunctional requirements related to this most typical scenario, like performance, scalability, security, reliability and integrability related requirements. For the security and the performance

---

[2]The MVA is taken out of its context to protect the identity of the system in question.

requirements a good and realistic understanding of the number of users and the amount of expected data is needed—no guesses.

- We wrote down a list of what identified functional and nonfunctional requirements cannot be met with the architecture outlined—all these related to other than the most likely usage scenario. We tried to identify the hardest potential problem areas in the MVA but did not try to solve them in this early phase of the development process.
- We accepted the fact that the MVA will not be the final architecture, but it will be good enough to start with and to get the development process moving on.

1.7 Guidelines for the Transformation

Based on our experiences, we do not assume that any quick changes will happen in the fashion private and public sector information systems will be procured. Instead, we acknowledge that we must deal with the IEEE 830 styled requirements, or "questions" as the requirements are sometimes disguised as, in the foreseeable future. Accepting this, we next start to look for ways to reduce the damage or at least the harm the suboptimal way of expressing the system owner needs the requirements typically cause.

Insisting to know why. We need to understand and accept the fact that the requirements are just sentences written by some people at some point of time with some level of understanding of the situation. If the requirements do not experience transformations and we do not dispose or create new ones during the system development project, we are not responding to the actual needs of the system owner. Especially, the nonfunctional requirements may be very difficult to state precisely. On the other hand, imprecise requirements are not of use, they easily become expensive to implement and are almost impossible to verify reliably. Some simple techniques, like the Five Whys [27], could be employed in the discussion with the system owner's to promote deeper thinking through questioning and is easily adaptable to most problems.

Maintaining agreed practices. No matter how hard the customer and the system or service provider both wish to execute a program or project in an agile fashion, joint practices and processes must be carefully agreed upon. Agility does not mean that we should invent the ways of working every day. Any larger information system project needs to have fully agreed and also documented ways of working related to all interaction between the customer and the system provider. This does not mean naturally that the processes should be inflexible and bureaucratic—they just need to be agreed, known and followed by all the stakeholders in a disciplined way.

Listening the right way. One of the buzzwords in the information system domain has been for long already that the system provider should be customer driven. This means that the system providers should always be aware and respond to customer problems swiftly. However, this approach can also be fatal when the communicated requests from the customer side at different points in time have varying and differing views of how the system should be developed. Cooper [28] stresses the difference between listening to and following a customer. While listening to a customer is good, following a customer by merely doing what a customer tells you to do is not. The customer that the system provider hears best—"the loudest voice"—may not be the most important customer: it may even be that we should not even have this customer!

Importance of continuous interaction. The relationship between the customer and the system provider may not always be easy and all kinds of adversities will be encountered during a long-lasting project. Nevertheless, despite the situation, the communication channels should always be open and utilized on a daily basis. In our experience, no information system project has failed due to excessive communication. If nothing else, the customer representatives should be regularly contacted by the system provider representatives to ask them how they are and how they feel about the project at hand. It should also be kept in mind that a feature management system or a bug or issue tracking system is never a replacement for interactions with end-users and other stakeholders at the customer side. The actuality of human communication lies in the fact that the communication neither enforces one's opinion against the other's one, nor does it add one's opinion to the other's one. The result of the communication is that both of them are changed [25].

Identifying the most valuable features. One of the downsides the continuous interaction with the customers and the end-users has it that along with wideband and frequent communication we inevitably also talk about features and qualities that the customer representatives or the end-users think they would like to have, the so called nice-to-have features and qualities. New features are extremely easy to invent and fun to discuss about. However, each feature should be associated with explicit stakeholder value and prioritized accordingly.

Strict no to feature creep. Since the information system projects are nowadays typically executed in a close co-operation with the end-users and other customer-side stakeholders, the system provider receives easily a lot of feedback on the functional quality aspects of the system under development. When receiving the feedback, the system provider should be very careful to avoid the feature creep [29]. However, the responsibility on keeping the scope set by the system owner should not be on the development teams solely but on the customer representatives and end-users. It seems to be somehow many times forgotten that keeping the feature creep under control is of the highest interest for all stakeholders. In case feature creep takes place, the whole project is immediately in danger and in the worst case no system will be ever created.

To avoid feature creep, one needs to perform rigorous and visible change management. Learning to say "No" in a nice way to customers and end-users is obligatory.

1.8   Conclusions

Although a considerable amount of work has been put into creating and refining the requirements for all kinds of information systems, there still seems to be a lot to do in order to make the development processes produce what is truly needed in an effective way. We have problems with the scope, volatility and quality of the requirements and in particular, problems with the communication related to the requirements. The problems result in misunderstandings, a lot of confusion and eventually waste of time and resources.

To overcome the requirement related problems in system development efforts, no silver bullet exists. However, critical thinking and willingness to truly understand the customer, strict prioritization and disciplined ways of working with the requirements and wideband frequent communication help a lot.

In our opinion, system owners and stakeholders are not to blame for the shortcomings that can be traced back to bad or missing requirements, encountered during the design and development of an information system. The people who are experts in the system design, development, and deployment are responsible for educating the system owners and all other stakeholders regarding how to identify and express the true needs in a form that enables more error-free communication and full comprehension of the issues involved on both sides.

In addition, starting from quality needs instead of functional requirements gives us better chances to find the right solutions to the true needs. One crucial step toward being able to specify the nonfunctional requirements would be the usage of minimum viable architecture (MVA), as an intrinsic part amending the functional and other customer requirements. Doing such architecture requires a lot of trust between the service providers and the system owners, but motivation for this change should be clear: with better quality of requirements and better communication we would be seeing better new information systems, longer information system life span, and eventually happier customers.

References

1. Leffingwell, D., & Widrig, D. (2000). Managing software requirements: a unified approach. Addison-Wesley Professional.
2. Stakeholder Needs and Requirements. (2015, December 18). in BKCASE Editorial Board, Guide to the Systems Engineering Body of Knowledge (SEBoK), version 1.5.1, R.D. Ad-cock (EIC), Hoboken, NJ: The Trustees of the Stevens Institute of Technology ©2015. Retrieved 14 Mar 2016 from http://sebokwiki.org/w/index.php?title=Stakeholder_Needs_and_Requirements&oldid=51430.
3. Hochstetter, J., & Cares, C. (2012, November). Call for Software Tenders: Features and Research Problems. In Proceedings of the 7th International Conference on Software Engineering Advances (ICSEA (Vol. 12).
4. Jurison, J. (1999). Software project management: the manager's view. Communications of the AIS, 2(3es), 2.

5. Marilly, E., Martinot, O., Betgé-Brezetz, S., & Delègue, G. (2002). Requirements for service level agreement management. In IP Operations and Management, 2002 IEEE Workshop on (pp. 57–62). IEEE.
6. Hofmann, H. F., & Lehner, F. (2001). Requirements engineering as a success factor in software projects. IEEE software, 18(4), 58.
7. Jones, C. (2008). Applied software measurement: global analysis of productivity and quality. McGraw-Hill Education Group.
8. Munassar, N. M. A., & Govardhan, A. (2010). A comparison between five models of software engineering. IJCSI, 5, 95–101.
9. Abrahamsson, P., Salo, O., Ronkainen, J., & Warsta, J. (2002). Agile software development methods: Review and analysis.
10. Ralph, P. (2013). The illusion of requirements in software development. Requirements Engineering, 18(3), 293–296.
11. Davis, A. M. (1993). Software requirements: objects, functions, and states. Prentice-Hall, Inc.
12. Wikipedia contributors. "Request for proposal." Wikipedia, The Free Encyclopedia. 7 Feb. 2016. Web. 14 Mar. 2016.
13. Wikipedia contributors. "Request for quotation." Wikipedia, The Free Encyclopedia. 2 Feb. 2016. Web. 14 Mar. 2016.
14. Wikipedia contributors. "Request for information." Wikipedia, The Free Encyclopedia. 20 Feb. 2016. Web. 14 Mar. 2016.
15. IEEE Std 830-1998 (Revision of IEEE Std 830-1993), IEEE Recommended Practice for Software Requirements Specifications.
16. Chen, L., Babar, M. A., & Nuseibeh, B. (2013). Characterizing architecturally significant requirements. IEEE software, 30(2), 38–45.
17. Frakes, W. B., & Kang, K. (2005). Software reuse research: Status and future. IEEE transactions on Software Engineering, (7), 529–536.
18. Kramer, J., & Magee, J. (2007, May). Self-managed systems: an architectural challenge. In Future of Software Engineering, 2007. FOSE'07 (pp. 259–268). IEEE.
19. Brooks, FP Jr. "No Silver Bullet Essence and Accidents of Software Engineering." Computer 4 (1987): 10–19.
20. Christel, Michael G. and Kang, Kyo C. "Issues in Requirements Elicitation", CMU/SEI-92-TR-12, 1992.
21. Ebenau, B. and Strauss, S., Software Inspection Process. McGraw-Hill, 1994.
22. Goodrich, V., & Olfman, L. (1990, January). An experimental evaluation of task and methodology variables for requirements definition phase success. In System Sciences, 1990. Proceedings of the Twenty-Third Annual Hawaii International Conference on (Vol. 4, pp. 201–209). IEEE.
23. Koski, A., Kuusinen, K., Suonsyrjä, S., & Mikkonen, T. (2016). Implementing Continuous Customer Care: First-hand Experiences from an Industrial Setting. In Proceedings of the 42nd Euromicro Conference on SEAA.
24. Wiio, O. A. (1978). Wiion lait—ja vähän muidenkin (Wiio's laws—and some others'). Weilin +Göös.
25. Klimova, B. F., & Semradova, I. (2012). Barriers to communication. Procedia-Social and Behavioral Sciences, 31, 207–211.
26. Erder, M., & Pureur, P. (2015). Continuous Architecture: Sustainable Architecture in an Agile and Cloud-centric World. Morgan Kaufmann.
27. Serrat, Olivier. "The five whys technique." (2009).
28. Cooper, A. (1999). The inmates are running the asylum: [Why high-tech products drive us crazy and how to restore the sanity] (Vol. 261). Indianapolis: Sams.
29. Elliott, B. (2007, July). Anything is possible: Managing feature creep in an innovation rich environment. In Engineering Management Conference, 2007 IEEE International (pp. 304–307). IEEE.

Chapter 2
Cloud Dimensions for Requirements Specification

Ana Sofia Zalazar, Luciana Ballejos and Sebastian Rodriguez

Abstract Cloud computing is a business paradigm that changes the way to evaluate information systems and computing resources. Cloud requirements can rapidly change and new service capabilities are often requested in order to adapt to new business scenarios. The existing works are generally focused in a limited number of requirements and capabilities. The aim of this contribution is to understand the multifaceted components of a service and to give guidelines towards requirements engineering for cloud computing. Thus, cloud services are analyzed by different aspects called dimensions and five dimensions are proposed (i.e., Contractual, Financial, Compliance, Operation, and Technical). Cloud dimensions are graphically presented in conceptual models, because each dimension has specific entities, properties, and relationships. Different specialists and experts may be requested to evaluate particular dimensions in the service level agreement and cloud service adoption, and this approach can guide those activities, support requirements specification, and guide system analysis for cloud computing.

Keywords Cloud computing · Requirements engineering · Requirements specification · Cloud dimension · Service level agreement · Conceptual model · System analysis

A.S. Zalazar (✉) · S. Rodriguez
GITIA (UTN-FRT), CONICET, Rivadavia 1050, 4000 Tucumán, Argentina
e-mail: ana.zalazar@gitia.org

S. Rodriguez
e-mail: sebastian.rodriguez@gitia.org

L. Ballejos
CIDISI (UTN-FRSF), Lavaisse 610, 3000 Santa Fe, Argentina
e-mail: lballejo@frsf.utn.edu.ar

© Springer International Publishing AG 2017
M. Ramachandran and Z. Mahmood (eds.), *Requirements Engineering for Service and Cloud Computing*, DOI 10.1007/978-3-319-51310-2_2

2.1 Introduction

Cloud Computing is a business paradigm, where cloud service providers offer services (e.g., software, storage, computing, and network) managed in their physical infrastructure and cloud service consumers pay per- use after accepting to the service level agreement. Consumers usually move the functionality of their legacy systems to cloud computing or acquire new functionality contracting cloud service to minimize costs of maintenance and to get the advantages of rapidly adaptation to changes.

The NIST introduces a cloud definition framework [17], where there are five main characteristics (i.e., broad network access, rapid elasticity, measured service, on-demand self-service, and resource pooling), five roles (i.e., consumer, provider, auditor, carrier, and broker), three service models (i.e., Software as a Service, Platform as a Service, and Infrastructure as a Service), and four deployment models (i.e., public cloud, private cloud, community cloud, and hybrid cloud). In this paper, the NIST cloud definition framework is extended and five cloud dimensions are added (i.e., contractual, financial, compliance, operational, and technical).

The five proposed cloud dimensions link static properties (e.g., contractual aspects) and dynamic requirements (e.g., technical and operational aspects). Some dimensions may be separately analyzed by domain experts (e.g., compliance dimension is analyzed by lawyers in small- and medium-sized enterprises). The final purpose is to bind different service perspectives in order to manage cloud service adoption. The contribution aims to consolidate different cloud aspects to fluidly satisfy consumer dynamic requirements. Requirements must be clear and interpreted in one way, so this approach proposes an alternative to carry on cloud contracts and manage requirements in a simple and concise manner. In conclusion, cloud consumers (i.e., organizations and users) are provided with accurate information to address their requirements to service offers and cloud providers are fitted with precise attributes to offer service capabilities. This avoids potentially ambiguous terms.

Cloud service agreements may change often according to the service business context, so this type of contract has to be modifiable. Consumers may often require changing quality of service and scalability values. However, dimensions make possible to specify requirements and capabilities for creating cloud contracts. In this paper, requirements specification, dimensions, metrics, and service level agreements are explained in cloud context.

The rest of the paper is organized as a follows. In Sect. 2.2, the background is explained. In Sect. 2.3, the proposed dimensions and some models are proposed in order to facilitate cloud requirements specification and to understand contracts. Section 2.4 is focused on the application and integration of cloud dimensions in service contracts using a sample scenario. Finally, Sect. 2.5 concludes this contribution.

2.2 Background

Cloud computing has been defined by multiple authors [1, 7, 25], and the National Institute of Standard and Technology (NIST) proposes a definition that encompasses general aspects of cloud environment [17]: *"Cloud computing is a model for enabling ubiquitous, convenient, on-demand network access to a shared pool of configurable computing resources (e.g., networks, servers, storage, applications, and services) that can be rapidly provisioned and released with minimal management effort or service provider interaction"*.

This definition introduces also five essential characteristics attributed to Cloud Computing [17]: (a) *On-demand self-service*: cloud consumers automatically access to cloud capabilities according to their needs without human interaction; (b) *Broad network access*: cloud capabilities are available in the network and accessed through heterogeneous client platforms; (c) *Resource pooling*: cloud provider resources are shared to serve multiple cloud consumers using virtualization and tenancy mechanisms; (d) *Rapid elasticity*: cloud provider resources are added and released according to cloud consumers demand, so cloud capabilities appears unlimited; and (e) *Measured service*: cloud resources are measured at a granular level in a transparent manner for both cloud provider and cloud consumer of the used service.

The different deployment models defined by NIST [17] are: (a) *Private cloud*: Under this model, cloud services delivered from a data center are accessed by a single organization with multiple internal users, while preserving management and control of the resources; (b) *Public cloud*: cloud services are allocated under the providers or third parties control, and the underlying infrastructure is shared by multiple consumers and open for public use, using multi-tenancy mechanism; (c) *Community cloud*: physical and virtual resources are shared between several users and organizations from a specific community with common concerns, so this model may require specific policies among users; and (d) *Hybrid cloud*: this type of model is a combination of two or more clouds, which safeguards sensitive data and applications on restricted manner and it takes advantage of the rapid provisioning of other models.

Cloud service models indicate the level of control and abstraction in cloud services. There are three principal service models, and other models can be derived from them [17]: (a) *Software as a Service (SaaS)*: cloud providers offer software applications over the Internet, and users can access them from any location using a computer or mobile device that has Internet access, without managing any infrastructure and platform where the application runs; (b) *Platform as a Service (PaaS)*: this type of services are containers within programming environments, libraries, database, and tools that support development in virtual platforms, so consumers can develop and run their software applications without the cost and responsibility of buying and maintaining the underlying hardware and software; and (c) *Infrastructure as a Service (IaaS)*: cloud service providers offer virtual server instance and storage, and abstract the consumer from the details of infrastructure taking responsibility of all resource physical maintenance, workload balance, technical staff, connectivity devices, and virtual machine (VM) management.

Service characteristics have to be well-defined and specified in order to identify the consumer requirements and to compare different service offers. However, requirements specification approaches in the cloud domain are mostly focused on quality of service [5], pricing and costing [16], access control, privacy, and security [10, 18, 19]. Since the term cloud computing includes other aspects and perspectives, the existing approaches also need to be extended.

2.3 Cloud Dimensions, Requirements, and Capabilities

In order to understand cloud computing, the NIST cloud definition framework [17] is extended and five dimensions are proposed in this contribution, presented in Fig. 2.1. Each proposed dimension represents a specific aspect of cloud computing, and cloud adoption process should consider those dimensions in order to completely satisfy service requirements.

The proposed dimensions support the integration of requirements specifications raised by consumers and capabilities owned by providers into cloud computing. *Requirement* is what cloud consumers want from cloud service and *capability* is what cloud providers offer related to their competences in cloud services. SLA can be used as a specification artifact to assist the selection of cloud service considering consumer requirements and service capabilities. The SLA is a legal format [2] that

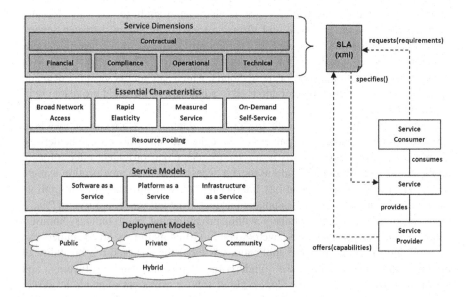

Fig. 2.1 Cloud computing definition framework [17]

helps to negotiate agreements. Cloud consumer hopes to see all his requirements in the corresponding SLA, and cloud provider makes sure that only capabilities that they can meet in his service are included in the agreement. Due to the dynamic nature of the cloud, continuous monitoring on SLA is requested in these contexts [20].

However, practitioners also deal with other requirements and capabilities. For example, IT contracts include terms regarding technical properties, financial factors, compliance restrictions, operational responsibilities, and contractual aspects in cloud computing. The idea of cloud computing as a multidimensional paradigm is not new [21, 22]. This approach grouped cloud aspects in the following dimensions based on the academic community and the practitioners' concerns:

1. *Contractual Dimension* covers all organizational aspects of cloud service level agreement. It includes actors, time periods, and objects like binding service level agreements (SLA), similar to the information of business contractual headlines. Communication between actors is very important, thus contractual dimension also specifies roles, responsibilities, and relations between actors.
2. *Financial Dimension* is defined considering cloud computing as a utility [7], where economic and financial capabilities play a central role in cloud adoption [8]. Cloud service provider employs pricing plan (i.e., renting, usage-based pricing), in which cloud service consumers pay proportionally to the amount of time or resource they use [4]. This dimension considers all aspects of cloud agreements for billing and accounting, such as pay methods, credit management, and cost variables.
3. *Compliance Dimension* describes all legal and regulatory restrictions for cloud service adoption [3], and it also specifies government regulation, business standards, security policy, and privacy certifications which cloud service should be compliant with [15]. The restrictions are strictly imposed in order to respect laws and regulations in the jurisdiction where data resides or is collected.
4. *Operational Dimension* is based on usual events (such as restore, maintain, configuration, and backups) and unusual events (such as incident management and recovery). By considering operational aspects, the cloud providers must have efficient means to support resource allocation and scheduling decisions to remain competitive [13]. Simultaneously, it is important to ensure the confidentiality of cotenants who share the same infrastructure by monitoring virtual behavior. Operative dimension explains all aspects to keep the service running and meet the changes in runtime.
5. *Technical Dimension* encompasses functional properties and measurable aspects of cloud service. Values, units, functions, and methods are requested to define cloud services. Some key performance indicators are measured using a set of measureable properties. Technical aspects are specified in SLAs to understand, compare, and control SLAs.

There is a number of overlapping properties within the five dimensions, such as monitoring and auditing aspects. Audits are requested to ensure that cloud services do not break the laws and regulations in the jurisdiction where data resides or is collected, simultaneously ensuring the confidentiality of cotenants who share the same infrastructure [21]. Thus, frequent audits should be performed on the dimensional properties to monitor compliance with security terms and to ensure adherence to SLA terms, performance standards, procedure, and regulations [6, 23]. Most of the time services are like "*black boxes*" to cloud consumers, so services are evaluated by their behavior (i.e., comparing its inputs, outputs, and performance level) with the expected results [27].

In this contribution, cloud service dimensions are considered the basis for building dynamic SLAs and specifying cloud requirements and capabilities. In the next subsection, more details about each dimension are presented and all aspects related to cloud dimensions are introduced in a conceptual framework for capturing and integrating cloud requirements and capabilities.

2.3.1 Contractual Dimension

Contractual Dimension specifies general information of SLAs and cloud contracts, such as supporting parties, policy of contracting third parties, agreed time, and term conditions. Contractual properties are mostly static during service runtime. Figure 2.2 presents the conceptual model for *Contractual Dimension*, and it is based on SLA services presented by Patel et al. [20]. The shadowy entities in the

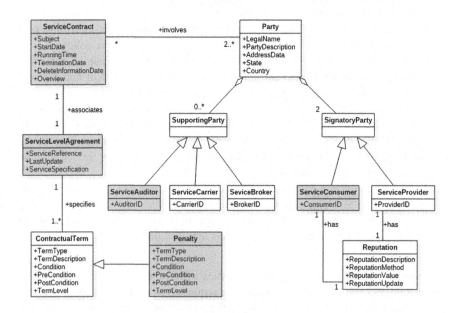

Fig. 2.2 Conceptual model of cloud computing dimension

proposed models represent classes which appear in more than one dimension (e.g., Service Contract and Service Level Agreement).

This dimension also introduces involved parties ("Party" in Fig. 2.2) and their roles during the contract duration. The five cloud roles proposed by the NIST are included in the model [17]: (a) *Provider*: entity that owns the deployed service in its physical servers, and it is responsible for service maintenance and availability; (b) *Consumer*: entity that use the service for completing its business process; (c) *Carrier*: intermediary that provides data transportation and service connectivity; (d) *Broker*: intermediary that is involved in the business contract and the relation between other roles; and (e) *Auditor*: external agent responsible for keeping track all business process, reporting failures, and analyzing the quality of services considering the SLA. *"Signatory Party"* is mandatory and involves *"Service Consumer"* and *"Service Provider"*. The mandatory roles have *"Reputation"* that represents a big impact on organization credibility and trust, and it is also about confidentiality, integrity, and resilience of the service actors. *"Supporting Party"* is optional and involves third parties such as *"Service Auditor"*, *"Service Carrier"*, and *"Service Broker"*.

"Service Contract" presents all information about contract starting time, termination date, service overview, and definitive delete information date that is when the provider must destroy all information about the use of service (consumer data and workload). The terms and conditions within the contract that would cause the termination of the service agreement are presented in *Compliance Dimension*.

"Contractual Term" is probably the most important entity in this model, because it involves all policies and clauses about SLA. It describes expressions and implied terms in the contract [12]. *"Term Type"* defines contractual clauses about termination, modification, suspension, disclaimer, indemnification, remedy, warranty, guarantee, obligation, money refund, support, notification, government request, collecting information, limitation of liability, etc. *"Penalty"* is a category of *"Term Type"* and it is a term used for compensation of non-delivery of service or inadequate service level.

The differences between *"Service Contract"* and *"Service Level Agreement"* are that the former generally describes contracting parties and dates, and the latter describes service parameters, quality of service, agreement terms, and service level.

2.3.2 Financial Dimension

Financial Dimension involves all economic factors of cloud services and contracts, and Fig. 2.3 shows the most relevant classes and their relationships in this dimension. It is universally acknowledged that *"Service Consumer"* associates his *"Billing Account"* to the *"Payment"* processes of the *"Service Contract"*. *"Billing"* is defined by the sum of *"Service Charging"* (cardinality is *"*"* which means *"many"*) that is refines by *"Cost Description"* of different resources (i.e. *"Storage Cost"*, *"Processing Cost"*, *"Network Cost"*, etc.) related to a *"Service Description"*. *"Billing Frequency"* is regarding the cost calculation and it can be daily, weekly,

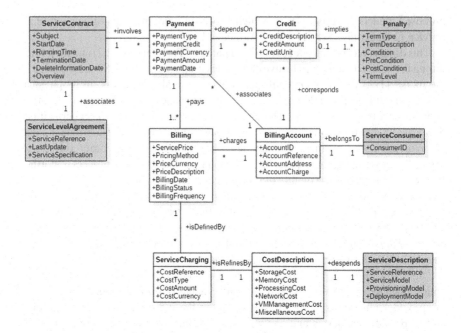

Fig. 2.3 Conceptual model of cloud financial dimension

biweekly, monthly, semi-annual, and annual. Billing processes may use metering mechanisms on the consumption of cloud resources in order to calculate the cost. *"Cost Type"* is related to service adoption phases, and the resource costs can be calculated during service acquisition, service on-going, service composition, and service contract termination. *"Payment Type"* is concerning to payment methods such as debit card, credit card, electronic note, bank transfer, Bitcoins, Pay-Pal, and other credit mechanisms.

From the early years of cloud computing, most of the interest was focused on service pricing of cloud computing [4], and cost reduction was a central factor to the uptake of cloud services. This business paradigm is considered as a fifth utility [7], where resource optimization, pricing models, and virtualization were fundamentals to introduce cloud computing into the market. Therefore, *"Pricing Method"* is probably the most studied attribute of *Financial Dimension*. *"Service Consumer"* can freely choose a service provider with better *"Pricing Method"* and more favorable *"Billing"* terms. Youseff et al. [26] present three models for calculating prices: (a) *tiered pricing*: each service tier has a specific price per unit of time; (b) *per-unit pricing*: cost is applied to the usage units during data storing, data processing, and data transferring; and (c) *subscription-based pricing*: the cost is periodically the same. Other authors [3, 24] similarly list diverse pricing models: (a) *per-use*: resources are billed per unit of time usage; (b) *subscription*: resources can be reserved and renewed for the same price; (c) *prepaid per-use*: the billing is performed against a prepaid credit; and (d) *combined method*: resources can be rented for a period of time and also requested on demand. Karunakaran et al. [14] divulge four extensive subthemes: pricing schemes, user welfare, pricing elements, and collaborative pricing; and they indicate that the key elements for pricing included, hardware, maintenance, power, cooling, staff, and amortization. However, *"Service Consumer"* may subscribe to free services or dynamically adjust pricing method according to his workload and security requirements.

Any change in prices and payments must be notified to *"Service Consumer"* in advance, according to obligations explained in *Contractual* and *Compliance Dimensions*. It may seem like *Financial Dimension* can be also part of *Compliance Dimension*, but governance is a very wide term that mostly involve more legal, security, and standard aspects. *Financial Dimension* is mainly focused on reducing operative costs by sharing infrastructure instead of investing in physical servers.

"Penalty" can have a direct impact to *"Payment"* process through *"Credit"* application. When there are violations of contractual terms, such as inappropriate service level or non-delivered capabilities, *"Penalty"* implies a *"Credit Amount"* that is discounted to the *"Payment Amount"*. This indemnification mechanism is very important; because it involves a compensation for the negative impact on consumer economy. Monitor algorithms must inform about services level changes and violations of contractual terms, before applying any compensation. Cloud providers know through *"Penalty Level"* about the importance and criticism of cloud capabilities in consumer business processes.

2.3.3 Compliance Dimension

Cloud governance and security can be considered the trend topic nowadays [21]. They are also considered challenges, because users no longer have control over the complete system. *Compliance Dimension* specifies legal information, security methods, and service compliance with standards, agreement terms, procedures, and law. Figure 2.4 shows the conceptual model of *Compliance Dimension*.

"Governance" implies a collection of compliance attributes, norms, and certifications. *"Standard Compliance"* has the information about standards that service contract has to conform in order to attain the agreed service level and quality. *"Standard Type"* details the scope of the standardized norms, and it can be focused on communication, virtualization, security, green computing, cloud federation, data interoperability, and syndication. *"Certification Compliance"* specifies information about international certifications that determine capabilities in cloud computing. Certifications and standards are used to formalize security and technical aspects of a procurement agreement, and they ensure that business objectives are met while meeting compliance requirements (e.g., TOSCA, OCCI, OVF, SOAP, ISO 14000, Green Star, HIPAA, PCI, SAS70, FISMA, SSAE16, SCOC1, SCOC2, ISAE3402, IS027001, etc.,). *"Legal Compliance"* and *"Security Compliance"* are contractual agreements that covers data protection and laws application in cloud computing. Legal experts can infer internal and external security risks by considering those

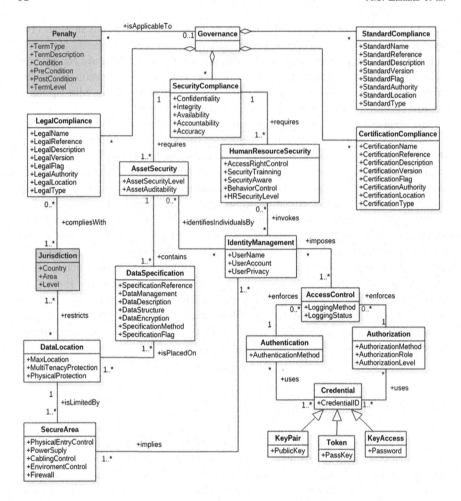

Fig. 2.4 Conceptual model of cloud compliance dimension

compliance terms. *"Legal Type"* specifies terms of uses (ToU), terms of service (ToS), user licensing agreement (ULA), intellectual property clauses, copyright terms, acceptable use, and other legal aspects that limit responsibilities and rights about cloud services. Finally, *"Penalty"* represents the conditions and the compensation when those established governance terms are not met.

"Security Compliance" saves information about levels of confidentiality, integrity, availability, accountability and accuracy, and it requires terms for *"Human Resource Security"* and *"Asset Security"*. *"Human Resource Security"* demands human resources and employers to provide required security level, and some security triggers are created in other to monitor their behaviors. This entity includes all security measures for avoiding internal attacks and unauthorized accesses.

"Identity Management" uses account and name to identify individuals, and it imposes *"Access Control"* to restrict entrance (physically or logically) to the resources and applications.

"Access Control" put into effect *"Authentication"* and *"Authorization"* by granting access based on *"Credential"*. *"Credential"* is a security binding and the most common type of credential are *"Key Pair"*, *"Token"*, and *"Key Access"*. Control algorithms compare credential to an access control list, grant or deny accesses to cloud resources, and keep transaction logs. *"Secure Area"* is a trust location where facilities are installed and capabilities are deployed.

Data are particularly heterogeneous due to the fact the number of databases and files for specific operations [9], thus providers should indicate the efficiency of data management preventing security breaches in runtime [6]. *"Data Specification"* is the entity in the conceptual model that contains all information about data manipulation and management. *"Data Management"* is about data store, data transfer, data regulation, data governance, data portability, data migration, data protection, data controller, data security (i.e., mechanisms for availability, integrity, confidentiality, authentication, and non-repudiation), data access (i.e., mechanism for accounting, credentials, and security logs), data recovery, data backup, data replication, data persistency, data deletion (e.g., right to be forgotten), data sanitization, data preservation, data import and data export.

"Data Location" is limited by *"Secure Area"* and *"Jurisdiction"*. Service consumer and service provider should divide their attention to the jurisdictions over the contract terms (i.e., where signing parties come from) and the jurisdictions over the data is divided, subcontracted, outsourced, collected, processed, and transferred; because each jurisdiction has laws and restrictions. However, *"Jurisdiction"* and its law applications depend on the physical location of the data [21]. If the data is replicated to other countries, *"Legal Compliance"* terms must compliance with one or more *"Jurisdiction"* instances. Before adopting cloud services, *"Service Consumer"* must agree to know and respect jurisdiction laws and legal policy wherein the data is physically stored.

"Support for Forensic" is referenced to *"Legal Compliance"*, and it is the reserved right of the service provider to make available evidences, user data and process to external government and to collaborate with its investigations [2, 21]. Moreover, all compliance terms are guidelines for security, manipulation and visualization of data and workload in cloud environments.

"Data Encryption" is part of *"Data Specification"* and it is increasingly relevant for cloud computing. Data should always be encrypted considering *"Data Structure"* and *"Data Description"* in order to evade external intrusions and data leakages. There are many mechanisms for encryption and *"Service Provider"* generally offers an API for this process [21].

Compliance Dimension represents an analysis of governance terms in cloud contracts. It covers regulations and agreements to ensure that cloud service do not breach security policies and laws imposed by the jurisdictions.

2.3.4 Operational Dimension

Operational Dimension covers requirements about service management and business continuity. This dimension ensures that service workload and data are continuously available or not disrupted for longer than is permissible. Operational tasks are defined in this approach as service maintenance, service recovery, systems powering, systems update, scaling up, and scaling down. Figure 2.5 shows the conceptual model of *Operational Dimension*.

"*Service Description*" is the most important entity in this conceptual model, because it specifies the requirements and capabilities of cloud services. "*Service Description*" indicates relevant information about "*Service Model*" (i.e., Software as a Service, Platform as a Service, and Infrastructure as a Service), "*Deployment Model*" (i.e., Public cloud, Private cloud, Community cloud, and Hybrid cloud) and "*Provisioning Model*" (i.e., on demand, static Provisioning, or dynamic

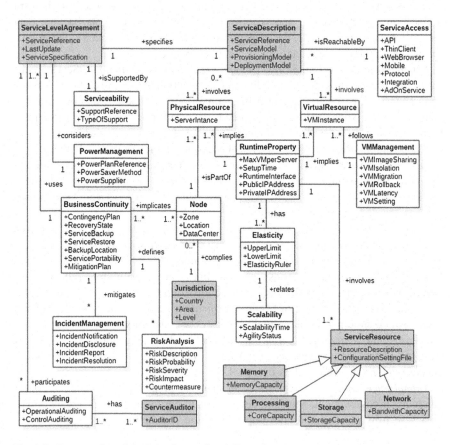

Fig. 2.5 Conceptual model of cloud operational dimension

provisioning of resources). The service is reachable by *"Service Access"* that describes the access mechanisms to use the services.

"Service Level Agreement" specifies *"Service Description"* that involves *"Physical Resource"* (i.e., servers, data center) and *"Virtual Resources"* (i.e., virtual machines). The features of those resources are stored in configuration files, and they indicate the setting of each instance. *"VM Management"* covers the information about virtual machines (VM) with the aim of assurance isolation and scalability.

"Runtime Property" is the entity that contains information about load balance and service runtime. *"Runtime Property"* manages *"Service Resources"* that are specific service features, such *"Storage"* (i.e., database, files), *"Processing"* (i.e., CPU, cores), *"Network"* (i.e., bandwidth, switches), and *"Memory"* (i.e., cache and RAM). Load balancer dynamically distributes data and workloads across multiple computing resources for enhancing the overall performance of service.

Operational Dimension cares about growing the number of resource during period of peak demands and resource updating. Resource capacities change over time due to capability demands. Thus, *"Runtime Property"* has *"Elasticity"* properties that are related to *"Scalability"*, and those entities specify the *"Upper Limit"*, *"Lower Limit"*, *"Scalability Time"*, and *"Elasticity Ruler"* (i.e., triggers and events that change service capacity). In case of peak demands, *"Elasticity"* indicates *"Upper Limit"* of provisioning resources to meet the current need. After the peak load, *"Elasticity"* indicates *"Down Limit"* of decreasing unused resources. Unused resources are released and available in the resources pool that keeps resources active and ready to be used anytime.

Operational Dimension aims to keep the service running and available. Thus, disruption, disaster, peak loads, and peak demands have to be resolved. Consequently, *"Service Level Agreement"* is supported by *"Serviceability"* that has all information to technically support tasks and operations in the cloud. *"Power Management"* is also considered and it administrates power energy and saver methods.

Usually, service providers limit their actions and responsibilities in the presence of force majeure, external suspension, or criminal attacks. However, *"Business Continuity"* is attached to *"Service Level Agreement"* and it considers a contingency plan and evaluation of threats and risks. It also implies *"Node"* and *"Jurisdiction"*, because those have impact into *"Risk Analysis"* and *"Incident Management"*. Moreover, services can be allocated in places where natural disasters or cybercrimes often occur, so those location statistics impact risks and threats analysis (e.g., accidents, security attacks, restrictions imposed by public authorities). Finally, *"Auditing"* driven by *"Auditor"* verifies that services and resources are appropriate and adequately controlled to ensure the service level presented in the agreements.

2.3.5   Technical Dimension

Technical Dimension is about technical metrics and measurements. It aims to verify that the results of measurements are over the acceptance values and service level objectives are met, consequently the promised quality of service has been achieved. Figure 2.6 presents the proposed conceptual model for *Technical Dimension*.

In the conceptual model, *"Service Level Agreement"* specifies *"Service Description"* that involves several *"Service Resources"* (cardinality is *"1..*"* and means *"one or more"*). *"Service Resource"* has a *"Configuration Setting File"* that indicates all features and configurations of the resources. This service configuration file can be thought of as "web.config" or "app.config" or "config".

"Service Level Agreement" is associated to *"Service Level Objective"* that contains *"Service Level Target"* of the deployed service. *"Indicator"* is about *"Service Resource"* and it utilizes *"Metric"* to calculate *"Actual Value"*. *"Metric"* has a measurement method and measurement scale, which is used in relation to a quantitative service level objective and it can be composed with other metrics, similar to

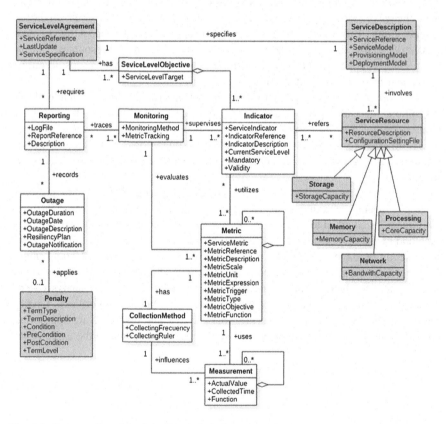

Fig. 2.6 Conceptual model of cloud technical dimension

"Measurement". *"Collection Method"* specifies the *"Collection Frequency"* (e.g., every day, after processing data, etc.) and *"Collection Ruler"* (e.g., when an external event occurs, metric collects value). Each service can have associated one or more metrics, and metrics can be associated to a simple value or a collection of values.

"Monitoring" supervises *"Indicator"* instances of the measured service, and *"Reporting"* records *"Outage"*. When *"Outage Notification"* is critical, *"Penalty"* is applied, because service is under the *"Service Level Objective"* and the *"Service Contract"* is violated. Service provider should offer adequate access to carry on measuring and monitoring of services deployed into his infrastructure. There are many service key indicators (e.g., performance, availability, reliability, agility, etc.) and diverse metrics for measuring indicator values (e.g., processing throughput, network throughput, bandwidth speed, instance speed, computing speed, response time, recovery time, resolution time, upload time, download time, connecting time, boot time, reboot time, scale up time, scale down time, request per minute, uptime, downtime, etc.,). Metrics provide knowledge about capabilities of a cloud service and it is very important to support decisions in order to satisfy service level requirements.

Key indicators are not explicitly defined in the model, because they mostly depend on service level agreements. Moreover, some authors point out that the indicator *"Performance"* is only measured by the metric *"Service Response Time"* [11] and others specify that the indicator *"Performance"* is calculated by the metric *"Page Down Load Rate"* [5]. Moreover, there are many attributes regarding to quality of service and key performance indicators in cloud computing that express almost same requirements but using different expressions, metrics, and restrictions (e.g., availability and reliability). The list below explains the most common indicators and their associated metrics.

- *Accountability* is a group of quality attributes used to evaluate whether data is handled according to service consumer requirements and is protected in the cloud. It is associated to measure and score services, and it is related to compliance, transparency, control, and auditability of the services [11].
- *Agility* represents how quickly new capabilities are added to adjust the amount of demands and also resources scale. It is related to elasticity, portability, adaptability, and flexibility [11]. It can be measured considering capacity of CPU, memory, and time to scale up and scale down service resources.
- *Assurance* indicates that service is securely delivered in accordance to the SLA and service consumer expectations. It involves availability, stability, serviceability, reliability, and resiliency [11].
- *Availability* is typically measured by the probability that service is active when needed. It is used as an indicator of the percentage uptime, considering the downtime due to faults and other causes, such as planned maintenance and upgrading. It can be also presented as a redundancy method for masking errors and faults. It is measured considering uptime of the service in specific time (e.g., 99.99% uptime per month) [2].

- *Performance* is probably the most common indicator in cloud computing, and there are many solutions to calculate in terms of functionality, time, and resource processing. Depending on the context, performance can be metering by time to complete and receive the process request (service response time), amount of data that can be recuperated from the system in specific unit of time (throughput), or capability to meet deadlines (timeliness) [2].
- *Scalability* describes the aptitude and the time to increase or decrease storage space, and growth or reduction of workloads. It is associated to Elasticity that is the illusion of unlimited resources. Scalability can also be measured by considering maximum of virtual machines for account (scale up), minimum of virtual machines for account (scale down), time to increase a specific number of resources, and time to decrease a specific number of resources, boot time, suspend time, delete time, and provisioning time [2].
- *Usability* is complex to measure because it indicates how practical is to use and consume cloud services. So it depends of cloud users and subjectivism. It is related to accessibility, learnability, and operability [11].

In summary, the proposed conceptual model is useful to identify relevant information about cloud service, but service provider and consumer should clearly indicate what to consider an indicator and what metrics are relevant to measure it.

2.4   Sample Scenario: The Security Guard Company

The sample scenario about the Security Guard Company was introduced for the first time in this project in the approach about dynamic requirements of cloud computing [27], and it is extended in this contribution for explaining cloud dimensions. The Security Guard Company offers a catalog of real-time security modules to its clients in South America, in order to solve the weakness and vulnerabilities of the local public security services. Moreover, the company significantly reduces clients' on-site staff costs by automating security controls in small and large-scale installations.

The Security Guard Company has deployed an integrated system that enables entrances and exits monitoring of buildings, rooms, and parking lots. The system integrates sophisticated digital video cameras, smoke sensors, motion sensors, temperature sensors, and algorithms of face recognition and car patent recognition. The video cameras and sensors are strategically installed in spots of the client facilities, and the incoming data of those devices are recording in the company data center. The company remotely monitors multiple buildings, and some triggers are executed to send notification to clients, local police office, fire station, and emergency medical services. Additionally, the clients can visualize multiple cameras and sensor status in a single interface. The system notifies relevant events to clients using mobile apps, text messages, and email notifications.

The company has grown exponentially in the last months, and it decides to reduce costs by moving all video records and control data older than 6 months to a cloud server, because those videos are not regularly consulted. It also decides to keep the complex security system on premise into the company data center in order to avoid security threats and to regularly update software modules.

Finally, Amazon Simple Storage Service (Amazon S3) is picked after comparing multiple services to find the best one in regard to cloud dimension in South America. Amazon S3 provides secure, durable, highly scalable cloud storage, and it also takes account of backup, recovery, near-line archive, big data analytics, disaster recovery, and content distribution. The relevant terms are extracted from requirements document file and service offers, in order to pick the best service for the given scenario. Some terms of the cloud dimension are completed during the service specification (e.g., pricing method, price currency, term description) and others, during the service runtime (e.g., storage cost, cost reference, capacity).

In the service specification, some entities of *Contractual Dimension* explained in Fig. 2.2 are clearly identified in Amazon Web Service Agreement (AWS Agreement), Amazon S3 agreement and the consumer requirements. The *"Subject"* of the contract is storage capacity, the *"Service Reference"* is named *"Amazon S3 Standard"* and it is based on the *"Service Level Agreement"* updated on *"September 16, 2015"*, in the provider's website. The information of service provider is *"Amazon Web Services, Inc.,"* and its address is *"410 Terry Avenue North, Seattle, WA 98109-5210, USA"*. Some of the *"Contractual Term"* detected in the SLA are mostly about suspension or termination when maintenance, force majeure events, unavailable internet access, demarcation point, action or inaction of third part and failure of equipments, software or other technology under control of consumer or third part take place. *"Penalty"* is only considered when a claim of outage is sent from the consumer to Amazon Web Service, Inc. Finally, other *"Contractual Term"* specifies the right of the service provider to change any term with no less than 90 days advance notice. It is required 30 days advance notice prior to service termination, and 30 days are required not to erase any content after termination date.

About *Financial Dimension* showed in Fig. 2.3, it is clear that payment method is *"pay-per-use"* and the billing is released *"monthly"*. Penalty terms take places when *"monthly update percent (MUP)"* is less than *"99.95%"* and the refund is about *"10–30% in credit"* to the service consumer. One *"Credit"* is equivalent to *"1 USD"* and the *"Credit Amount"* can only be used in the next payments. All money transactions use credit card accounts in Amazon Web Service, Inc., so the Security Guard Company should indicate a credit card number in the *"Billing Account"* and *"Payment"*. The company credit card will automatically be charged for that month's usage. The service pricing is complex, because it depends on service reference (e.g., Amazon S3 standard, Glacier), region (e.g., South America, USA, Europe), gigabytes per months, data transfer (i.e., IN and OUT) and requests type (i.e., put, copy, post, list, get). However, the provider offers an online calculator for billing calculus (e.g., *"cost reference"* for *"data transfer out from Amazon S3"* in *"South America"* is between *"$0.250 and $0.230 per GB"*). Delete requests are always free.

Entities of *Compliance Dimension* presented in Fig. 2.4 are often referenced in AWS Agreement in different parts, because the provider offers many mechanisms for "*Data Encryption*", "*Access Control*", and "*Data Specification*". Some available options for "*Access Control*" are: (a) "*AWS identity and Access Management (IAM)*" that grant IAM users fine-grained control to bucket or object; (b) "*Access Control Lists (ACLs)*" that selectively grants certain permissions on individual objects; (c) "*Bucket Policy*" that grants permission across some or all of the objects within a single bucket, (d) "*Query String Authentication*" that shares object through URLs on a specified period of time, and (c) "*Virtual Private Cloud (VPC)*" that uses provider network to transfer data in multiple levels of security control. Some "*Data Encryption*" methods are: (a) Server-Side Encryption with Amazon S3 Key Management (SSE-S3) using Advanced Encryption Standard (AES) 256-bit symmetric key, (b) Server-Side Encryption with Customer-Provided Keys (SSE-C) using Advanced Encryption Standard (AES), and (c) Server-Side Encryption with AWS Key Management Service (KMS) (SSE-KMS) that provides an audit trail and control to comply with PCI-DSS, HIPAA/HITECH, and FedRAMP industry requirements. For authentication method, the "*Multi-Factor Authentication (MFA)*" and "*Authentication Device*" are the alternatives in this service. For data transference, SSL encryption of data is the basic method for data in transit using HTTPS protocol, and Bit Torrent Protocol is also available in the cloud provider environment. In "*Multitency Protection*", Amazon S3 uses a combination of Content-MD5 checksums and cyclic redundancy checks (CRCs) for assuring data integrity. The service should also comply with Apache Software License or other open source license.

The contract "*Jurisdiction*" depends on the U.S. government rights respect with federal law. The "*Jurisdiction*" of the consumer is also part of the *Compliance Dimension*, as it is showed in Fig. 2.4, and tax exemption certificates depend on each consumer jurisdiction. The service "*Jurisdiction*" depends on the country on where the data is stored and processed, so Brazil is also a "*Jurisdiction*" implied in the agreements.

In *Operational Dimension* presented in Fig. 2.5, "*Service Description*" is specified as Infrastructure as a Service. The Amazon S3 instance is allocated in Sao Paulo, Brazil (South America Region), because it is the closest data center to the service consumer's facilities. The node is called as "*sa-east-1 (3)*" into Amazon S3 environments. Sao Paulo is closed to the clients and this data center location enables the company to address specific legal and regulatory requirements. However, it is common that available backup is cross-region replication (CRR) and in two provider facilities. Elasticity and scalability are unlimited into this provider offer and "*VM Management*" uses XEN hypervisor in virtualization settings. Finally, the "*Support*" is free of charges, and any suggestion is confidential.

The last but not less important characteristics of the services are in the *Technical Dimension* showed in Fig. 2.6, and there are many instances for the attribute "*Service Level Target*" (e.g., "*durability is equal to 99.999999999% in MUP*", "*availability is equal to 99.99% in MUP*", "*availability SLA is equal to 99.9% in MUP*", "*first byte latency is equal to milliseconds*"). Storage is measured by "*total *byte hour usage*. *"Audit Logs"* are configurable and *"Reporting"* considers event notification and send alerts by Amazon SNS or Amazon SQS.

In conclusion, cloud dimension structure makes requirements specification and service specification more efficient than using other methods. Amazon S3 Standard is considered the best solution to keep copy of files under the pricing model "pay-per-use", especially when clients can ask for old video records anytime, however the company can define rules to automatically migrate Amazon S3 objects to Amazon S3 Standard—Infrequent Access (Standard—IA) or Amazon Glacier based on the age of the data. The Security Guard Company can save money in infrastructure and its clients can access directly to the data stored in the cloud server.

2.5 Conclusions

In this paper, traditional cloud definition framework is extended and five new dimensions are considered: (a) *Contractual Dimension*: contract trails that specify stakeholders, disclaims, and general agreements between parties; (b) *Financial Dimension*: economic aspects of cloud services that are involved in billing, pricing, and costs; (c) *Compliance Dimension*: regulations that restrict cloud services such as legal, standards, and proceedings; (d) *Operational Dimension*: characteristics that cover specifications about service management, deployment, and access control; and (e) *Technical Dimension*: measurable and technical factors that may need functions, values, constraints, metrics, and units.

Because of the stochastic and dynamic nature of cloud contexts, there is not a simple and standard procedure for managing requirements and matching them with service providers offers. Thus, conceptual models about cloud dimensions are presented in order to analyze requirements and capabilities of cloud services, and they can be used to understand them and negotiate agreements with service providers.

In conclusion, considering cloud service as a multifaceted component is a good starting point for handling the dynamism of cloud environment. Different experts can individually analyze those cloud facets and contribute with the contract negotiation. Moreover, the dimensions are very complete and flexible for adding new features, so they can be the bases for future proposals, models, and ontologies. The dimensions are the bases for defining SLA schemas and ontology to create a consistent SLA in machine readable format.

References

1. Abbasov, B. (2014). Cloud computing: State of the art reseach issues. In Application of Information and Communication Technologies (AICT), 2014 IEEE 8th International Conference on (pp. 1–4). IEEE.
2. Alhamad, M., Dillon, T., Chang, E. (2010). Conceptual SLA framework for cloud computing. In 4th IEEE International Conference on Digital Ecosystems and Technologies (pp. 606–610). IEEE.

3. Andrikopoulos, V., Binz, T., Leymann, F., Strauch, S. (2013). How to adapt applications for the Cloud environment. Computing, 95(6), 493–535.
4. Armbrust, M., Fox, A., Griffith, R., Joseph, A.D., Katz, R., Konwinski, A., Lee, G., Patterson, D., Rabkin, A., Stoica, I., Zaharia, M.(2010). A view of cloud computing. Communications of the ACM, 53(4), 50–58.
5. Bao, D., Xiao, Z., Sun, Y., Zhao, J. (2010). A method and framework for quality of cloud services measurement. In 2010 3rd International Conference on Advanced Computer Theory and Engineering (ICACTE) (Vol. 5, pp. V5–358). IEEE.
6. Boampong, P. A., Wahsheh, L. A. (2012). Different facets of security in the cloud. In Proceedings of the 15th Communications and Networking Simulation Symposium (p. 5). Society for Computer Simulation International.
7. Buyya, R., Yeo, C. S., Venugopal, S., Broberg, J., and Brandic, I. (2009). Cloud computing and emerging IT platforms: Vision, hype, and reality for delivering computing as the 5th utility. Future Generation computer systems, 25(6), 599–616.
8. Carroll, M., Van Der Merwe, A., Kotze, P. (2011). Secure cloud computing: Benefits, risks and controls. In 2011 Information Security for South Africa (pp. 1–9). IEEE.
9. Copie, A., Fortiş, T. F., Munteanu, V. I. (2012, August). Data security perspectives in the framework of cloud governance. In European Conference on Parallel Processing (pp. 24–33). Springer.
10. Fabian, B., Gürses, S., Heisel, M., Santen, T., Schmidt, H. (2010). A comparison of security requirements engineering methods. Requirements engineering, 15(1), 7–40.
11. Garg, S. K., Versteeg, S., Buyya, R. (2013). A framework for ranking of cloud computing services. Future Generation Computer Systems, 29(4), 1012–1023.
12. Greenwell, R., Liu, X., Chalmers, K. (2015). Semantic description of cloud service agreements. In Science and Information Conference (SAI) (pp. 823–831). IEEE.
13. Heilig, L., Voß, S. (2014). Decision analytics for cloud computing: a classification and literature review. Tutorials in Operations Research–Bridging Data and Decisions, 1–26.
14. Karunakaran, S., Krishnaswamy, V., Sundarraj, R. P. (2013). Decisions, models and opportunities in cloud computing economics: a review of research on pricing and markets. In Australian Symposium on Service Research and Innovation (pp. 85–99). Springer.
15. Liu, F., Tong, J., Mao, J., Bohn, R., Messina, J., Badger, L., Leaf, D. (2011). NIST cloud computing reference architecture. NIST special publication 500–292.
16. Martens, B., Walterbusch, M., Teuteberg, F. (2012, January). Costing of cloud computing services: A total cost of ownership approach. In System Science (HICSS), 2012 45th Hawaii International Conference on (pp. 1563–1572). IEEE.
17. Mell, P., Grance, T. (2011). The NIST Definition of Cloud Computing (Draft). NIST Special Publication 800–145.
18. Mouratidis, H., Islam, S., Kalloniatis, C., Gritzalis, S. (2013). A framework to support selection of cloud providers based on security and privacy requirements. Journal of Systems and Software, 86(9), 2276–2293.
19. Naveed, R., Abbas, H. (2014). Security Requirements Specification Framework for Cloud Users. In Future Information Technology (pp. 297–305). Springer Berlin Heidelberg.
20. Patel, P., Ranabahu, A. H., Sheth, A. P. (2009). Service level agreement in cloud computing.
21. Pichan, A., Lazarescu, M., Soh, S. T. (2015). Cloud forensics: technical challenges, solutions and comparative analysis. Digital Investigation, 13, 38–57.
22. Repschlaeger, J., Wind, S., Zarnekow, R., Turowski, K. (2012, January). A reference guide to cloud computing dimensions: infrastructure as a service classification framework. In System Science (HICSS), 2012 45th Hawaii International Conference on (pp. 2178–2188). IEEE.
23. Rimal, B. P., Choi, E., Lumb, I. (2010). A taxonomy, survey, and issues of cloud computing ecosystems. In Cloud Computing (pp. 21–46). Springer London.
24. Suleiman, B. (2012). Elasticity economics of cloud-based applications. In Services Computing (SCC), 2012 IEEE Ninth International Conference on (pp. 694–695). IEEE.

25. Vaquero, L. M., Rodero-Merino, L., Caceres, J., and Lindner, M. (2008). A break in the clouds: towards a cloud definition. ACM SIGCOMM Computer Communication Review, 39 (1), 50–55.
26. Youseff, L., Butrico, M., Da Silva, D. (2008). Toward a unified ontology of cloud computing. In 2008 Grid Computing Environments Workshop (pp. 1–10). IEEE.
27. Zalazar, A. S., Rodriguez, S., Ballejos, L. (2015). Handling Dynamic Requirements in Cloud Computing. In Simposio Argentino de Ingeniería de Software (ASSE 2015)-JAIIO 44 (pp. 21–46). SADIO.

Chapter 3
Analyzing Requirements Engineering for Cloud Computing

Ana Sofia Zalazar, Luciana Ballejos and Sebastian Rodriguez

Abstract Cloud computing is a business paradigm, where cloud providers offer resources (e.g., storage, computing, network) and cloud consumers use them after accepting a specific service level agreement. Cloud requirements can rapidly change over time, so organizations need to count with rapid methods to elicit, analyze, specify, verify, and manage dynamic requirements in a systematic and repeatable way. The existing works of this field are generally focused in a limited number of requirements and capabilities for cloud services. This chapter aims to provide a comprehensive and systematic literature review of academic researches done in requirements engineering for cloud computing area. During this study, some approaches for cloud computing were found that considered a limited number of characteristics (e.g., security, privacy, performance) and few activities involving diverse stakeholders. Generally, cloud stakeholders have got neither guidelines nor standards to manage multiple aspects of services in cloud environments. Thus, a literature review was first conducted and five dimensions are discussed (i.e., Contractual, Compliance, Financial, Operational, and Technical) in order to classify cloud characteristics, specify requirements, and support cloud contracts. Different specialists and experts may be requested to evaluate particular dimensions in the service level agreement and cloud service adoption. Finally, a simple sample is given to illustrate how to identify the cloud dimensions.

Keywords Cloud computing · Requirements engineering · Cloud dimension · Requirements specification · Literature review · Information system · Service level agreement

A.S. Zalazar (✉) · S. Rodriguez
GITIA (UTN-FRT), CONICET, Rivadavia, 1050, 4000 Tucumán, Argentina
e-mail: ana.zalazar@gitia.org

S. Rodriguez
e-mail: sebastian.rodriguez@gitia.org

L. Ballejos
CIDISI (UTN-FRSF), Lavaisse 610, 3000 Santa Fe, Argentina
e-mail: lballejo@frsf.utn.edu.ar

© Springer International Publishing AG 2017
M. Ramachandran and Z. Mahmood (eds.), *Requirements Engineering for Service and Cloud Computing*, DOI 10.1007/978-3-319-51310-2_3

3.1 Introduction

Cloud computing is an Internet-based business where service providers offer information and communication technology (ICT) resources by optimizing physical and logical infrastructure, and service consumers pay only those which they use for storing, analyzing, processing, transferring, and managing data in provider's resources. Cloud computing enables organizations to consume ICT resources as a utility (like gas and electricity), rather than having to invest and maintain on-premise computing infrastructures. Thus, cloud computing is changing the way in which companies are doing business and dealing with information technology.

Even though the success of any software solution depends mostly in the identification of requirements in early stages of software development [1], it is shown that there are not well-known foundations and methodologies for handling cloud requirements in the academic community [2, 3]; and no empirical evidence was found about how to elicit and manage requirements in cloud domain [4]. Therefore, a systematic literature review is necessary to compile all the evidences of requirements engineering activities in this context, to synthesize high-level insights from published studies, and to consider the challenges presented in research results. Individual published studies considered in systematic reviews are called primary studies, so systematic reviews are labeled secondary studies [5].

Primary studies have reported experiences and lessons learned from applying diverse methods and techniques for adopting cloud services. The secondary study presented in this chapter is expected to identify, analyze, and interpret those primary researches, in order to contribute to the existing knowledge bases and to improve the state of the practice in requirements engineering for cloud computing.

It is a fact that cloud environments are stochastic and dynamic, so it is complex to manage cloud requirements in a systematic and repeatable way [3], especially when requirements rapidly change in a non-predictive manner. The main causes why cloud requirements change are: (a) organizational policies change the business priorities, so the requirements have to be aligned with the new scope and goals; (b) environment and marketplace change by the addition of competitors or new business targets; (c) legislation changes may request new forms, features, and security algorithms in cloud applications; and (d) new technology solutions appear. Thus, the main objective of this work is to understand and carefully analyze cloud computing domain, considering published researches in the field of requirements engineering, in order to identify and quantify research topics on requirements engineering in cloud computing.

The NIST introduces a cloud definition framework, where there are five main characteristics (i.e., broad network access, rapid elasticity, measured service, on-demand self-service, and resource pooling), five roles (i.e., consumer, provider, auditor, carrier, and broker), three service models (i.e., Software as a Service, Platform as a Service, and Infrastructure as a Service), and four deployment models (i.e., public cloud, private cloud, community cloud, and hybrid cloud) [6]. In this contribution, the NIST cloud definition framework is also extended and five cloud dimensions are added (i.e., contractual, financial, compliance, operational, and technical) after conducting a literature review.

The five proposed cloud dimensions link static properties (e.g., contractual aspects) and dynamic requirements (e.g., technical and operational aspects). Some dimensions may be separately analyzed by domain experts (e.g., compliance dimension is analyzed by lawyers in small and medium-sized enterprises). The final purpose is to bind different service perspectives in order to manage cloud service adoption. This chapter aims to consolidate different cloud aspects to fluidly satisfy consumer dynamic requirements. In conclusion, cloud consumers (i.e., organizations and users) are provided with accurate information to address their requirements to service offers and cloud providers are fitted with precise attributes to offer service capabilities. This avoids potentially ambiguous terms.

The rest of this paper is organized as follows. Section 3.2 introduces some insights about cloud computing and requirements engineering. Section 3.3 presents a brief discussion about the findings and some graphs of the literature review. In Sect. 3.4, the proposed dimensions and some models are proposed in order to facilitate cloud requirements specification. Finally, Sect. 3.5 discuses the final remarks and future works.

3.2 Background

Cloud computing is a paradigm of external arrangement, where third party services are contracted according to *Service Level Agreements* (SLA) between cloud providers and service consumers, by means of Internet protocols. In this way, cloud providers optimize the usability of their own technology infrastructure offering storage solutions (*hosting*) and computer services (*outsourcing*), and cloud consumers pay for cloud services taking into account the type of service charge (i.e., pay per use, subscription, etc.) [6, 7]. The cloud environments are stochastic and dynamic, so it is complex to identify, clarify, and manage cloud requirements in a systematic way [3, 8], especially when services and requirements change in an unpredictable manner.

Requirements engineering is the field of software engineering dedicated to identify, analyze, specify, and validate software requirements [9]. The software requirements represent the needs and constraints considered in the software solution of a real problem.

Requirements engineering is related to software design, software testing, software maintenance, configurations management, quality assurance, and other processes of software engineering. Pohl in his book [10] considers elicitation, analysis, specification, validation/verification, and management of requirements, as requirements engineering processes. In addition, Flores et al. assume that requirements engineering process for general services involve the next activities [11]:

1. *Requirements Specification*: service requirements are identified.
2. *Requirements Analysis*: requirements are analyzed in detail and possible conflicts between them are examined.
3. *Requirements Validation*: requirements consistency and completeness must be evaluated.
4. *Requirements Management*: it supports all activities and solutions during RE process.

Wieger in [1] classifies requirements engineering artifacts in: business requirements, scenarios and uses cases, business rules, functional requirements, quality attributes, external interface requirements, constraints, data definitions, and potential software solutions. Moreover, Pohl specifies goals, scenarios, and requirements oriented to the software solutions, as part of the RE artifacts [10].

In cloud computing, requirements engineering approaches are mostly concentrated in object-oriented artifacts and service-oriented tools. Thus, some authors adjusted existing tools, languages, and methodologies to this paradigm. The biggest challenge in cloud computing is the lack of standard, that help meet the objectives covering many different aspects of cloud services [12]. Existing requirements engineering processes for cloud computing are generally about a limited number of nonfunctional requirements. Moreover, most of the approaches about cloud requirements are focused on particular characteristics, as security [8], privacy [13], availability, and other performance aspects [14, 15].

However, cloud business paradigm is still growing popularity, because cloud offers and cloud demands are rising at the marketplace. Cloud providers optimize their physical infrastructure offering IT resources as cloud services, and consumers outsource solutions adopting cloud models (i.e., Software as a Service, Platform as a Service, and Infrastructure as a Service). In consequence, cloud computing is very complex to administrate because of the dynamism imposed by the context, i.e., elastic resources (released, turned off/on, resized, scaled up/down), stochastic requirements depending of business changes (peak/nonpeak times), heterogeneous consumers from different places and jurisdictions, distributed systems, and remote manage.

Some authors propose frameworks and methods, but there is no available empirical evidence on the elicitation methods utilized by cloud providers [4]. For instance, Repschlaeger et al. [2] present a framework that includes evaluation criteria to adopt cloud services, and Schrödl and Wind [16] propose a framework to validate established process models for RE in regards to the implementation for cloud computing. Schrödl and Wind conclude that none of the common models (V-model, Volere, Extreme Programming, and Rational Unified Process) is suitable to cover the needs of requirements engineering under cloud computing.

Small and medium-sized enterprises also develop projects for adopting cloud services and migrating legacy systems to cloud environments. Besides cloud projects are a major trend in IT solutions [17], little information about frameworks and methods for supporting projects during system development life cycle for this domain is given [18]. In addition, the lack of requirements engineering methods promotes the occurrence of unpredictable risks related with incorrect or unjustified decisions which can be made during project plan developments. There are no standardized processes to manage requirements engineering activities or to decide how they should be performed, and organizations try to adapt existing techniques or create new one for supporting cloud projects, missing suitable, and systematic guidance [3, 4]. Thus, this chapter aims to provide a comprehensive and systematic literature review of the academic research done in requirements engineering for cloud computing, and introduces the main concerns in this area. Having an overview about methods and techniques for handling cloud requirements, providers and consumers can implement existing approaches taking into account different dimensions for cloud services. Regarding this background, different aspects of requirements are considered for cloud computing by identifying and classifying core concepts within existing academia literature. Security is one of the most relevant issues in cloud computing community [18, 19]. Moreover, IT governance, legal, laws, ethical, standards, and managerial issues are not completely considered in the researches done in this area [20, 21].

In order to conduct this review, several reviews and mapping studies about cloud computing were first consulted, because they compile all the evidence about contributions and synthesize high-level insights from primary studies during past years. In fact, there was not found any general peer-reviewed paper on requirements engineering for cloud computing specifically, while secondary researches found showed that academic community is mainly focused on only specific characteristics of cloud services, i.e., security [19, 21–24], technological aspects [17], accounting models [25], quality of services [26, 27], and service composition [28]. The proposed cloud dimensions for requirements engineering are derived from those characteristics.

3.3   Literature Review

Selecting digital libraries and relevant databases was crucial for this secondary research (literature review). Four popular digital libraries were chosen: IEEE Xplore Digital Library, ACM Digital Library, Elsevier ScienceDirect, and SpringerLink. Those libraries covered important works in requirements engineering and cloud computing. However, some considerations were made on the research scope and strategy of this research. First, Google Scholar engine was taken out of the scope, because it returned the largest number of duplicate articles during the search simulations. Second, ACM Digital Library returned similar results offered by IEEE and Springer engines, but it also returned some relevant studies. Third, it was not found relevant evidence of related works about cloud requirements before 2009 during the pilot searches, so the manual search of primary studies in digital libraries published between 2009 and 2015 was planned. Finally, the basic query string was searched within titles and calibrated regarding each engine. Data extraction and selection process was undertaken using the steps described in Fig. 3.1.

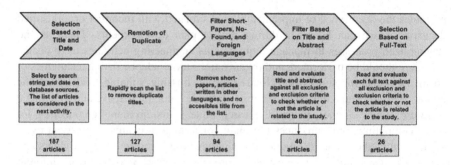

Fig. 3.1 Selection process of the literature review

Advanced search options for each database source were used that allowed to improve the inclusion of articles related to the study. Even though some articles were first picked by title and abstract, they were no precisely about requirements engineering for cloud computing. Thus, some articles were excluded from the set of relevant primary studies after considering the inclusion and exclusion criteria. The inclusion and exclusion criteria which were applied in this literature reviews are listed in Table 3.1. Search engines previously mentioned returned a list of studies as result of the research protocol which also were considered in three phases of manual inspection. First, each paper was scanned to ensure that its contributions were

Table 3.1 Selection criteria of primary studies

Inclusion criteria	Exclusion criteria
The study was published in digital libraries between 2009 and 2015	The primary study did not comply with the inclusion criteria
The full-text of the study was available and written in English	The study was a short paper (less than 6 pages)
The study was published in the form of journal article or conference paper	The study was in form of text book, thesis, book chapter, editorials, paper position, keynotes, opinion, tutorial, poster, or panel
The study was focused on requirements engineering for cloud computing	The study was a duplicated report of the same research (same authors, similar title and results)
The study contained relevant information to answer the proposed research questions	The study paper was a previous version of a more complete paper published about the same topic.
The study was related to requirements engineering processes and it involved explicit activities	The study summarized an existing research work or road-map, so it is considered incomplete
The study was a primary study that included solutions, experiences or evaluations	The study was a secondary study (informal survey, literature review, mapping study)
The study provided a reasonable amount of information, technical characteristics, and details regarding its contribution	The study did not suggest explicitly any method, technique, tool, or artifact to manage cloud requirements

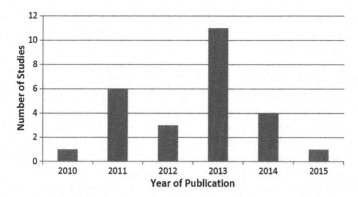

Fig. 3.2 Number of studies per year

related to the scope of this review. Then, some studies were selected after applying the criteria on each title, abstract, keywords, and conclusion. Finally, each full-text was analyzed considering the criteria in order to decide whether or not a study should be involved in this review.

From the list of selected articles, the tendency of publication date was evaluated, and it is showed in Fig. 3.2. The interest in the topic has changed over time, and half of the selected studies put attention to security and privacy aspects of cloud computing. Most of the articles were published in 2013, but only two articles were written by the same authors and two articles were published in the same journal. It seems that cloud computing fundamentals and processes are occasionally considered by researchers in different journals and scientific events. However, several organizations and workgroups were found to be working on standards and processes, such as National Institute of Standards and Technology (NIST),[1] Cloud Standard Customer Council (CSCC),[2] IEEE Cloud Computing Standard Study Group (IEEE CCSSG),[3] and Open Cloud Consortium (OCC).[4]

To conduct the literature review, eight research questions were formulated. The research questions and the findings are graphically evaluated below.

RQ1: What are the main requirements engineering approaches investigated in cloud computing? From the selected primary studies, it can be noted that frameworks and methodologies motivated research activities on the field of cloud computing. Recently, contributions proposed frameworks to evaluate and to handle requirements for cloud computing projects, however there are not well-known tools and automatic techniques supporting cloud adoption. The answer of this question is summarized in Fig. 3.3.

---

[1]http://www.nist.gov/.

[2]http://www.cloud-council.org/.

[3]http://www.computer.org/web/ieee-cloud-computing/standards/.

[4]http://www.cloud-council.org/.

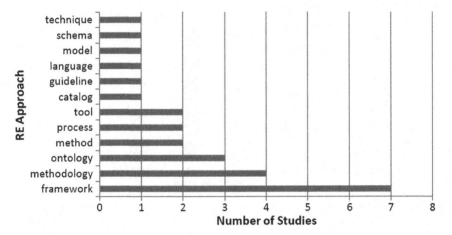

Fig. 3.3 Main requirements engineering approaches (RQ1)

RQ2: What phases and activities of requirements engineering do the approaches support? The results for this question are shown in Fig. 3.4. Requirements engineering activities were listed and answer "*All*" were considered when the contribution was generic and represented all activities in its process. The most studied activities were requirements elicitation and requirements specification, and some authors considered both activities in the same step in requirements engineering process. Requirements validation was not considered in the primary studies, and it was concluded that this activity was difficult to carry on especially because stakeholders have limited control over the services.

RQ3: Who are the actors/stakeholders or roles considered in the approaches? For this question, the roles presented by NIST [29] were considered, i.e., consumer, provider, broker, carrier, and auditor. The results are presented in Fig. 3.5. Most of the selected papers had consumers as main actors during requirements engineering activities. Carrier that supports transportation of service and auditor that evaluates the service provided were explicitly out of the primary study scopes. Developer role was considered in several studies, but analyst, consultant, and manager were not

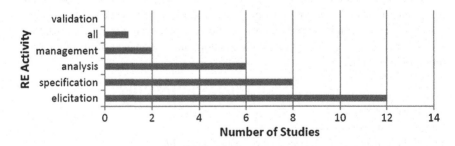

Fig. 3.4 Phases and activities of requirements engineering (RQ2)

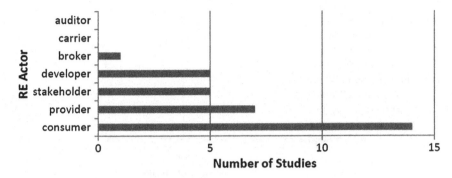

Fig. 3.5 Actors/stakeholders/roles considered in the approaches (RQ3)

implicitly considered. During the research, answer "stakeholder" was selected when the contribution was general, unclear about who were the target actors, or focused on several actors.

RQ4: What are the cloud requirements and attributes covered in the studied literature? Most of the studies were focused on specific attributes and requirements, and the results are shown in Fig. 3.6. Security is the most studied aspect of cloud computing in the field of requirements engineering. Cloud security is a trend topic and many research groups try to find a way for guaranteeing security in cloud services. Privacy, trust, and access control can be considered as part of security aspects.

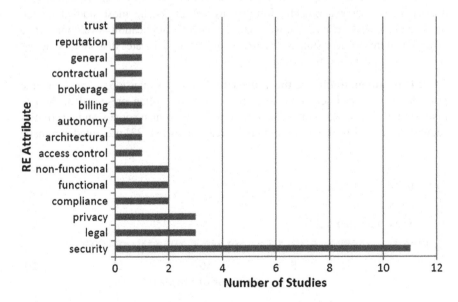

Fig. 3.6 Cloud requirements attributes covered in the studies (RQ4)

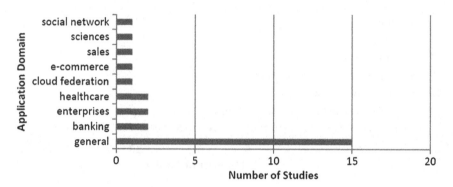

Fig. 3.7 Domains involved in the studies (RQ5)

RQ5: What are the domains involved in the primary studies? Figure 3.7 presents the different domains announced in the studies. The selected approaches were mainly general and with little information about domains and supported areas. Several primary studies considered banking, healthcare, and enterprise scenarios. However, there was strong tendency to integrate many domains in the same solution, *"General"* in Fig. 3.7, so it is concluded that general and generic approaches are needed for handling cloud requirements suitable to all domains.

RQ6: What are the cloud computing models considered in the proposals? Deployment models were not taken into account in the selected papers and most studies did not specify any service model as study scope. Figure 3.8 shows the final results. Only one article [30] considered Platform as a Service and Software as a Service in the same approach. Software as Service is the most studied model, because cloud service adoption was mainly related to application development and programs in the primary studies. *"General"* in Fig. 3.8 indicates that authors did not specify the models and the proposal is generic.

RQ7: How automatable are the approaches? For this question, there were three possible answers and semiautomatic approaches were often presented in the primary studies. There were many contributions that presented some manual activities supported by tools or programs, but only three studies [31–33] presented automatic

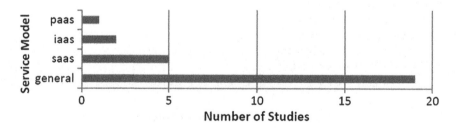

Fig. 3.8 Cloud computing models considered in the studies (RQ6)

Fig. 3.9 Automated approaches in cloud computing

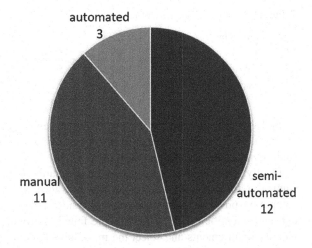

and automatable approaches for requirements engineering in cloud computing. The results are shown in the pie chart presented in Fig. 3.9.

RQ8: What are the open issues and publication trends in requirements engineering for cloud computing? Cloud services are deployed in multiple resources shared by many different stakeholders [34, 35], and the main challenge is how to elicit commonalities and variances of numerous consumer requirements [36]. So far, there was identified a large amount of issues towards legal constraints [37–40], privacy, access control, and security requirements [13, 31–34, 41–46]. However, several approaches were also focused on functional aspects [36, 47], nonfunctional requirements [48], trust and reputation characteristics [35], and other requirements [3]. In the same manner, specific primary studies considered important to analyze separately billing attributes [49], architectural aspects [12], autonomic requirements [50], brokerage regulations [30], and contractual ruling [51].

Quality Assessment. Finally, a quality assessment considering a scale from 0 to 1 was conducted. The goal was to detect those primary studies with low quality or irrelevant contribution. Quality assessment of the studies considered was a significant part into the research protocol, because it helped reviewers to evaluate whether the contribution of each study was relevant for this review or not. In order to detect the level of significance of each study, six quality assessment questions and possible scores based on [52] were defined, and the final checklist was built, as follow:

- QA1: How clear was the approach presented in the study?
- QA2: How relevant and mature was the approach for cloud computing?
- QA3: How detailed were the activities explained in the approach?
- QA4: How clear was the approach applied in the application domain?
- QA5: How complete was the list of goals and requirements considered in the approach?
- QA6: How flexible and extensible was the approach presented in the study?

Table 3.2 Qualitative summary of the studies

Value description	QA1	QA2	QA3	QA4	QA5	QA6
High = 1	18	16	18	14	10	22
Party = 0.5	8	10	8	11	16	4
None/unknown = 0	0	0	0	1	0	0

In Table 3.2, the number of papers that present high, medium, and low values for each of the qualitative questions is summarized. In conclusion, most of the studies were over the medium values.

Finally, it can be concluded that cloud computing is a traversal field and it can be studied in different domains (i.e., health, insurance, financial, etc.). However, cloud computing processes are occasionally considered by researchers in different journals and scientific events. The literature failed to provide a systematic approach to identify requirements and select the most suitable cloud service provider based on such requirements [13]. Nowadays, consumers have to trust providers taking into account functional attributes, price, and provider's reputation and market share [13, 35, 41].

3.4 Discussions

From a set of 187 documents, only 26 relevant works have been selected and some terms were extracted to define the vocabulary of cloud computing. The terms are classified into five cloud dimensions. Each proposed dimension represents a specific aspect of cloud computing, and cloud adoption process should consider those dimensions in order to completely satisfy service requirements. For each dimension, service consumers should also follow the most suitable requirements engineering methods considering the nature of their requirements. The NIST cloud definition framework [6] is presented in Fig. 3.10 and the five dimensions are added.

The proposed dimensions show the semantic connections among such terms, and the cloud domain knowledge can be inferred from it. The dimensions are related to cloud services and SLA, and they can also be used to identify cloud requirements and constraints in natural language documents, such as request for proposal and software specification template. Organizations may also consider having experts in diverse fields (such as accounting manager, lawyer for legal terms, etc.) to elicit specific requirements for each dimension, especially for billing and law regulation.

The idea of cloud computing as a multidimensional paradigm is not new. For instance, Repschlaeger et al. [53] presented six target dimensions based on general objective which stakeholders pursue: (1) service and cloud management; (2) IT security and compliance; (3) reliability and trustworthiness; (4) scope and

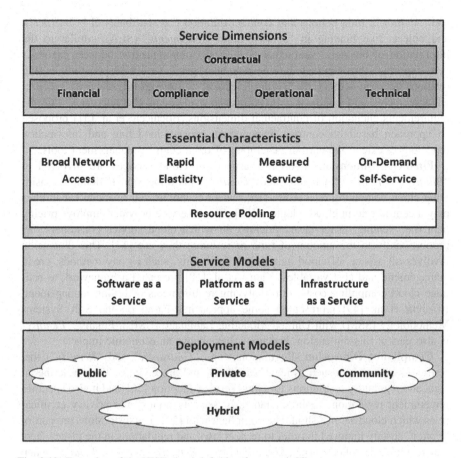

Fig. 3.10 Extension of the NIST cloud definition framework [6]

performance; (5) costs; and (6) flexibility. Pichan et al. [54] considered three dimensions to analyze services in cloud computing: (1) technical; (2) organizational; and (3) legal. However, practitioners also deal with other requirements and capabilities that research question four (RQ4) has showed. For example, IT contracts include terms regarding technical properties, financial factors, compliance restrictions, operational responsibilities, and contractual aspects in cloud computing.

In this contribution, cloud service dimensions are considered the basis for specifying cloud requirements and capabilities. The cloud dimensions are explained below.

Contractual Dimension. Contract trails specify stakeholders, disclaims, and general agreements between parties (i.e., "*Supporting Party*" and "*Signatory Party*"). This dimension covers all organizational aspects of cloud service level agreement. It includes actors (i.e., "*Provider*", "*Consumer*", "*Broker*", "*Carrier*", and "*Auditor*"), time periods and contract duration (i.e., attributes of "*Contract*"), and objects like binding in "*Service Level Agreements*" (SLA), similar to the information of business contractual headlines. Communication between actors is very important, thus contractual dimension also specifies roles, responsibilities, and relations between actors (i.e., "*Term of Service*"). "*Umbrella Agreement*" specifies all agreements and contracts with similar provider and characteristics. For the requirements elicitation of contractual dimensions, Bochicchi et al. [51] proposed an approach based on contract management process modeling and information modeling to extend the current generation of open contract management tools.

Financial Dimension. Economic aspects of cloud services are involved in "*Billing*", "*Pricing*", "*Account*" and "*Credit*". This dimension is defined considering cloud computing as a utility [15], where economic and financial capabilities play a central role in cloud adoption [55]. Cloud service provider employs pricing plan (i.e., renting, usage-based pricing), in which cloud service consumers pay proportionally to the amount of time or resource they use [14]. This dimension involves all aspects of cloud agreements for billing, such as pay methods, credit management, and cost variables. Klems et al. [18] presented a framework to estimate cloud computing costs. For analyzing requirements of billing management, Iwashita et al. [49] represented some approaches based on the Soft Systems Methodology (SSM) with Unified Modeling Language (UML). Finally, "*Penalty*" is also part of this dimension, because it has always an economic impact.

Compliance Dimension. Regulations (i.e., "*Guarantee*" and "*Remedy*") that restrict cloud services such as legal, standards, and proceedings. They describe all legal and regulatory restrictions for cloud service adoption [56], and it also specifies government regulation, business standards, security policy, and privacy certifications which cloud service should be compliant with [57]. The restrictions are part of "*Policy*" strictly imposed in order to respect laws and regulations in the place where data resides or is collected (i.e., "*Jurisdiction*"). "*Remedy*" involves "*Penalty*" when a "*Policy*" is violated. The consumer should pay attention to all requirement dimensions at a given time and describe in details some specifications about security, privacy, data manipulation, performance, and availability under "*Policy*" class. For instances, several approaches may be suitable for analyzing Compliance Dimensions. Mouratidis et al. [13] present a methodology that supports just elicitation and security of privacy requirements in cloud computing, by the understanding of the organizational context (i.e., goals, actors, tasks, resources, and plan) and the analysis of constraints, threats, and vulnerabilities [58]. Beckers et al. [41] contribute a catalog of security and privacy requirement patterns that support engineers in eliciting compliance requirements [31, 37]. Ficco et al. [42] present the development of a methodology that considers security concerns as an integral part of cloud-based applications design and implementation. Humberg et al. [39] developed an approach to represent regulations in the form of ontologies, which can then be used to examine a given system for compliance requirements in cloud computing.

Operational Dimension. All characteristics that cover specifications about service management, deployment, and access control. Operational Dimension is related to "*Service Description*", "*Virtual Resource*" and "*Physical Resource*". It is based on usual events (such as restore, maintain, configuration, and backups) and unusual events (such as incident management and recovery). By considering operational aspects, the cloud providers must have efficient means to support resource allocation and scheduling decisions to remain competitive [59]. Bao et al. [60] proposed a measurement method, which mainly measures availability and performance of cloud services and it supports operational decisions. Simultaneously, it is important to ensure the confidentiality of co-tenants who share the same infrastructure by auditing virtual behavior. Operative Dimension explains all aspects to keep the service running and meet the changes in runtime. In requirements engineering, Rimal et al. [12] classified architectural features according to the requirements of end users and provided key guidelines to software architects and cloud computing application developers for creating future architectures.

Technical Dimension. It encompasses functional properties and measurable aspects of cloud service. Some key performance indicators are measured using a set of measureable properties. Technical aspects are specified in SLA to understand, compare, and control SLA. Measurable and technical factors that need "*Indicator*", "*Metric*", "*Measure*", "*Unit*", "*Collection Method*", and "*Function*". "*Service Level Objective*" is used to compare "*Current Value*" audited by the "*Monitor*". All technical aspects are requested to defined cloud services. For Technical Dimension and application requirements, Sun et al. [47] provided a framework for searching the cloud market for a set of products that meet those requirements, using ontologies. Zardari and Bahsoon [36] also proposed a process for cloud adoption considering cloud requirements and Goal Oriented Requirements Engineering (GORE).

There are a number of overlapping properties and classes within the five dimensions, such as "*Monitor*", "*Account*", and "*Penalty*". "*Monitor*" is requested to ensure that cloud services do not break the laws and regulations in the jurisdiction where data resides or is collected, simultaneously ensuring the confidentiality of co-tenants who share the same infrastructure [54]. Thus, frequent audits should be performed on the dimensional properties to monitor compliance with security terms and to ensure adherence to agreements terms, performance standards, procedure, and regulations [61, 62]. Most of the time services are like "black boxes" to cloud consumers, so services are evaluated by their behavior (i.e., comparing its inputs, outputs, and performance level) with the expected results [58].

The service consumer, as a requirements engineer, may compare different methodologies (BPMN, UML, GoRE, SecureUML, Secure i*, Tropos, KAOS, and SQUARE) and present a conceptual framework with a strong focus on security and compliance for cloud computing. The consumer may also combine the approaches to come to the definition of the requirements, because some approaches may be focused on just few requirements engineering activities and different dimensions.

3.5   Sample Scenario: Sales Company

In this section, there is a sample about how to identify cloud dimensions. For example, a sales company (i.e., *"Consumer"* in Contractual Dimension) has recently shown consistent growth, so it aims to reduce the workload of the organization by migrating the purchase and sales module to cloud computing. The goal is to let suppliers and customers interoperate through this module after exchanging security certificates. The module allows visualizing the available stock and book new orders in real time, without overloading the company infrastructure. This company expects to reduce its total costs by paying a service subscription price (*"Pricing"*) and to gain flexibility considering unlimited storage and network resources (i.e., *"Service Description"*). The requirements engineer uses a natural language description (e.g., something similar to the description just provided) as an input to specify the basic needs of his/her system. The engineer maps the terms of the expressed needs to the proposed conceptual model. Then, the conceptual model shows relationships with other concepts, which can be associated to additional dimensions that were not considered in the needs expressed by the requirements engineer at the beginning. For example, *"Subscription Price"* from the initial description is related to Financial Dimension. *"Storage"* and *"Network"* are related to Operational Dimension.

Other classes are implicit in the initial description, such as "Data Security", *"Ethical"*, and *"Law Regulation"* that are linked to *"Policy"* in Compliance Dimension. At this stage, the requirements engineer can realize that other concepts (e.g., *"Measure"*, *"Unit"*, *"Current Value"*, etc.) in the model are related to his/her needs, and those concepts may have a relevant impact during the cloud service adoption, so he/she should pay considerable attention to them.

Finally, the company relies on the requirements engineering deliverable (e.g., supporting documents and descriptions) produced as a result of the proposed conceptual model. This deliverable helps the company to document initial requirements, to understand cloud services, to manage its dynamic requirements, to find inconsistency and risks, to compare cloud offers of different providers, and to contract the best cloud solution according to the company business goals and mission.

3.6   Conclusions

Summarizing, requirements engineering for cloud computing was investigated. Some primary studies were selected between 2009 and 2015, and only 26 filtered studies answered the proposed research questions. The literature review presented an overview about the topic and created new concerns about cloud requirements.

Cloud computing may be considered as a multidimensional paradigm, where different activities (i.e., elicitation, analysis, specification, validation/verification, and management), roles (i.e., consumer, provider, broker, auditor, carrier, user, analyst, consultant, manager, engineer, developer), and service dimensions (i.e., contractual, operational, technical, compliance, and financial) are integrated.

The cloud dimensions are explained in this chapter and a conceptual model integrated all of them. It is considered that the service consumer still needs to do some initial modeling and specification, because requirements have to be documented to ensure that the service provider offers exactly what is needed by the consumer. The service consumer should describe the required services, components, or applications using the dimensions. The dimensions are very complete and flexible for adding new features, so they can be the bases for future proposals, models, and ontologies.

Because the requirements change frequently, a streamline is needed. They should be monitored and traced using some traceability mechanisms (i.e., backward-from, forward-from, backward-to, or forward-to). Consequently, the requirements can undergo changes over the time and are normally covered under change management. A simple change in a requirement implies modifications in the parameters, configuration, and components, and the solution may no longer support the necessary functionality. In our future work, the objective is to give support to the complete requirement engineering process for cloud computing, by offering a framework to manage requirements in all dimensions and also support cloud adoption.

References

1. Wiegers, K., Beatty, J. (2013). Software requirements. Pearson Education.
2. Repschlaeger, J., Zarnekow, R., Wind, S., Turowski, K. (2012). Cloud Requirement Framework: Requirements and Evaluation Criteria to Adopt Cloud solutions. In European Conference on Information Systems (ECIS) (p. 42).
3. Zardari, S., Bahsoon, R. (2011). Cloud adoption: a goal-oriented requirements engineering approach. In Proceedings of the 2nd International Workshop on Software Engineering for Cloud Computing (pp. 29–35). ACM.
4. Todoran, I., Seyff, N., Glinz, M. (2013). How cloud providers elicit consumer requirements: An exploratory study of nineteen companies. In 2013 21st IEEE International Requirements Engineering Conference (RE) (pp. 105–114). IEEE.
5. Kitchenham, B. (2004). Procedures for performing systematic reviews. Keele, UK, Keele University, 33(2004), 1–26.
6. Mell, P., Grance, T. (2011). The NIST Definition of Cloud Computing (Draft). NIST Special Publication, 800–145:1–6, 145.
7. Vaquero, L. M., Rodero-Merino, L., Caceres, J., Lindner, M. (2008). A break in the clouds: towards a cloud definition. ACM SIGCOMM Computer Communication Review, 39(1), 50–55.
8. Iankoulova, I., Daneva, M. (2012). Cloud computing security requirements: A systematic review. In 2012 Sixth International Conference on Research Challenges in Information Science (RCIS) (pp. 1–7). IEEE.
9. Abran, A., Bourque, P., Dupuis, R., Moore, J. W. (2001). Guide to the software engineering body of knowledge-SWEBOK. IEEE Press.

10. Pohl, K. (2010). Requirements engineering: fundamentals, principles, and techniques. Springer Publishing Company, Incorporated.
11. Flores, F., Mora, M., Álvarez, F., Garza, L., Duran, H. (2010). Towards a systematic service-oriented requirements engineering process (S-SoRE). In International Conference on ENTERprise Information Systems (pp. 111–120). Springer Berlin Heidelberg.
12. Rimal, B. P., Jukan, A., Katsaros, D., Goeleven, Y. (2011). Architectural requirements for cloud computing systems: an enterprise cloud approach. Journal of Grid Computing, 9(1), 3–26.
13. Mouratidis, H., Islam, S., Kalloniatis, C., Gritzalis, S. (2013). A framework to support selection of cloud providers based on security and privacy requirements. Journal of Systems and Software, 86(9), 2276–2293.
14. Armbrust, M., Fox, A., Griffith, R., Joseph, A.D., Katz, R., Konwinski, A., Lee, G., Patterson, D., Rabkin, A., Stoica, I. and Zaharia, M. (2010). A view of cloud computing. Communications of the ACM, 53(4), pp. 50–58.
15. Buyya, R., Yeo, C. S., Venugopal, S., Broberg, J., Brandic, I. (2009). Cloud computing and emerging IT platforms: Vision, hype, and reality for delivering computing as the 5th utility. Future Generation computer systems, 25(6), 599–616.
16. Schrödl, H., Wind, S. (2011). Requirements engineering for cloud computing. Journal of Communication and Computer, 8(9), 707–715.
17. Sriram, I., Khajeh-Hosseini, A. (2010). Research agenda in cloud technologies.
18. Klems, M., Nimis, J., Tai, S. (2008). Do clouds compute? a framework for estimating the value of cloud computing. In Workshop on E-Business (pp. 110–123). Springer Berlin Heidelberg.
19. Mazher, N., Ashraf, I. (2014). A Systematic Mapping Study on Cloud Computing Security. International Journal of Computer Applications, 89(16):6–9.
20. El-Gazzar, R. F. (2014). A literature review on cloud computing adoption issues in enterprises. In International Working Conference on Transfer and Diffusion of IT (pp. 214–242). Springer Berlin Heidelberg.
21. Pfarr, F., Buckel, T., Winkelmann, A. (2014). Cloud Computing Data Protection–A Literature Review and Analysis. In 2014 47th Hawaii International Conference on System Sciences (pp. 5018–5027). IEEE.
22. Benslimane, Y., Plaisent, M., Bernard, P., Bahli, B. (2014). Key Challenges and Opportunities in Cloud Computing and Implications on Service Requirements: Evidence from a Systematic Literature Review. In Cloud Computing Technology and Science (CloudCom), 2014 IEEE 6th International Conference on (pp. 114–121). IEEE.
23. Latif, R., Abbas, H., Assar, S., Ali, Q. (2014). Cloud computing risk assessment: a systematic literature review. In Future Information Technology (pp. 285–295). Springer Berlin Heidelberg.
24. Zapata, B. C., Alemán, J. L. F., Toval, A. (2015). Security in cloud computing: A mapping study. Comput. Sci. Inf. Syst., 12(1), 161–184.
25. da Silva, F. A. P., Neto, P. A. D. M. S., Garcia, V. C., Assad, R. E., Trinta, F. A. M. (2012). Accounting models for cloud computing: A systematic mapping study. In Proceedings of the International Conference on Grid Computing and Applications (GCA) (pp. 3–9). The Steering Committee of The World Congress in Computer Science, Computer Engineering and Applied Computing (WorldComp).
26. Abdelmaboud, A., Jawawi, D. N., Ghani, I., Elsafi, A., Kitchenham, B. (2015). Quality of service approaches in cloud computing: A systematic mapping study. Journal of Systems and Software, 101, 159–179.
27. Lehrig, S., Eikerling, H., Becker, S. (2015). Scalability, elasticity, and efficiency in cloud computing: A systematic literature review of definitions and metrics. In Proceedings of the 11th International ACM SIGSOFT Conference on Quality of Software Architectures (pp. 83–92). ACM.
28. Jula, A., Sundararajan, E., Othman, Z. (2014). Cloud computing service composition: A systematic literature review. Expert Systems with Applications, 41(8), 3809–3824.

29. Grance, T., Patt-Corner, R., Voas, J. B. (2012). Cloud Computing Synopsis and Recommendations. NIST Special Publication, 800–146.
30. Kourtesis, D., Bratanis, K., Friesen, A., Verginadis, Y., Simons, A. J., Rossini, A., Schwichtenberg, A. and Gouvas, P. (2013). Brokerage for quality assurance and optimisation of cloud services: An analysis of key requirements. In International Conference on Service-Oriented Computing (pp. 150–162). Springer International Publishing.
31. Beckers, K., Côté, I., Goeke, L., Güler, S., Heisel, M. (2014). A structured method for security requirements elicitation concerning the cloud computing domain. International Journal of Secure Software Engineering (IJSSE), 5(2), 20-43.
32. Jhawar, R., Piuri, V., Samarati, P. (2012). Supporting security requirements for resource management in cloud computing. In Computational Science and Engineering (CSE), 2012 IEEE 15th International Conference on (pp. 170–177). IEEE.
33. Muller, I., Han, J., Schneider, J. G., Versteeg, S. (2011). Tackling the Loss of Control: Standards-based Conjoint Management of Security Requirements for Cloud Services. In Cloud Computing (CLOUD), 2011 IEEE International Conference on (pp. 573–581). IEEE.
34. Clarke, R. (2010). User requirements for cloud computing architecture. In Cluster, Cloud and Grid Computing (CCGrid), 2010 10th IEEE/ACM International Conference on (pp. 625–630). IEEE.
35. Moyano, F., Fernandez-Gago, C., Lopez, J. (2013). A framework for enabling trust requirements in social cloud applications. Requirements Engineering, 18(4), 321–341.
36. Zhou, X., Yi, L., Liu, Y. (2011). A collaborative requirement elicitation technique for SaaS applications. In Service Operations, Logistics, and Informatics (SOLI), 2011 IEEE International Conference on (pp. 83–88). IEEE.
37. Beckers, K., Heisel, M., Côté, I., Goeke, L., Güler, S. (2013). Structured pattern-based security requirements elicitation for clouds. In Availability, Reliability and Security (ARES), 2013 Eighth International Conference on (pp. 465–474). IEEE.
38. Gordon, D. G., Breaux, T. D. (2011). Managing multi-jurisdictional requirements in the cloud: towards a computational legal landscape. In Proceedings of the 3rd ACM workshop on Cloud computing security workshop (pp. 83–94). ACM.
39. Humberg, T., Wessel, C., Poggenpohl, D., Wenzel, S., Ruhroth, T., Jürjens, J. (2013). Using Ontologies to Analyze Compliance Requirements of Cloud-Based Processes. In International Conference on Cloud Computing and Services Science (pp. 36–51). Springer International Publishing.
40. Kousiouris, G., Vafiadis, G., Corrales, M. (2013). A Cloud provider description schema for meeting legal requirements in cloud federation scenarios. In Conference on e-Business, e-Services and e-Society (pp. 61–72). Springer Berlin Heidelberg.
41. Beckers, K., Côté, I., Goeke, L. (2014). A catalog of security requirements patterns for the domain of cloud computing systems. In Proceedings of the 29th Annual ACM Symposium on Applied Computing (pp. 337–342). ACM.
42. Ficco, M., Palmieri, F., Castiglione, A. (2015). Modeling security requirements for cloud based system development. Concurrency and Computation: Practice and Experience, 27(8), 2107–2124.
43. Guesmi, A., Clemente, P. (2013). Access control and security properties requirements specification for clouds' seclas. In Cloud Computing Technology and Science (CloudCom), 2013 IEEE 5th International Conference on (Vol. 1, pp. 723–729). IEEE.
44. Kalloniatis, C., Mouratidis, H., Islam, S. (2013). Evaluating cloud deployment scenarios based on security and privacy requirements. Requirements Engineering, 18(4), 299–319.
45. Liccardo, L., Rak, M., Di Modica, G., Tomarchio, O. (2012). Ontology-based Negotiation of security requirements in cloud. In Computational Aspects of Social Networks (CASoN), 2012 Fourth International Conference on (pp. 192–197). IEEE.
46. Naveed, R., Abbas, H. (2014). Security Requirements Specification Framework for Cloud Users. In Future Information Technology (pp. 297–305). Springer Berlin Heidelberg.

47. Sun, Y. L., Harmer, T., Stewart, A. (2012). Specifying cloud application requirements: an ontological approach. In International Conference on Cloud Computing (pp. 82–91). Springer International Publishing.
48. Tariq, A., Khan, S. A., Iftikhar, S. (2014). Requirements Engineering process for Software-as-a-Service (SaaS) cloud environment. In Emerging Technologies (ICET), 2014 International Conference on (pp. 13–18). IEEE.
49. Iwashita, M., Tanimoto, S., Fujinoki, Y. (2013). Approaches to analyze requirements of billing management for cloud computing services. In Computer and Information Science (ICIS), 2013 IEEE/ACIS 12th International Conference on (pp. 17–22). IEEE.
50. Vassev, E., Hinchey, M. (2014). Autonomy requirements engineering for self-adaptive science clouds. In Parallel & Distributed Processing Symposium Workshops (IPDPSW), 2014 IEEE International (pp. 1344–1353). IEEE.
51. Bochicchio, M. A., Longo, A., Mansueto, C. (2011). Cloud services for SMEs: Contract Management's requirements specification. In 12th IFIP/IEEE International Symposium on Integrated Network Management (IM 2011) and Workshops (pp. 145–152). IEEE.
52. Brereton, P., Kitchenham, B. A., Budgen, D., Turner, M., Khalil, M. (2007). Lessons from applying the systematic literature review process within the software engineering domain. Journal of systems and software, 80(4), 571–583.
53. Repschlaeger, J., Wind, S., Zarnekow, R., Turowski, K. (2012). A reference guide to cloud computing dimensions: infrastructure as a service classification framework. In System Science (HICSS), 2012 45th Hawaii International Conference on (pp. 2178–2188). IEEE.
54. Pichan, A., Lazarescu, M., Soh, S. T. (2015). Cloud forensics: technical challenges, solutions and comparative analysis. Digital Investigation, 13, 38–57.
55. Carroll, M., Van Der Merwe, A., Kotze, P. (2011). Secure cloud computing: Benefits, risks and controls. In 2011 Information Security for South Africa (pp. 1–9). IEEE.
56. Andrikopoulos, V., Binz, T., Leymann, F., Strauch, S. (2013). How to adapt applications for the Cloud environment. Computing, 95(6), 493–535.
57. Liu, F., Tong, J., Mao, J., Bohn, R., Messina, J., Badger, L., Leaf, D. (2011). NIST cloud computing reference architecture. NIST special publication, 500(2011), 292.
58. Zalazar, A. S., Rodriguez, S., Ballejos, L. C. (2015). Handling Dynamic Requirements in Cloud Computing. In Simposio Argentino de Ingeniería de Software (ASSE 2015)-JAIIO 44 (Rosario, 2015).
59. Heilig, L., Voß, S. (2014). Decision analytics for cloud computing: a classification and literature review. Tutorials in Operations Research–Bridging Data and Decisions, 1–26.
60. Bao, D., Xiao, Z., Sun, Y., Zhao, J. (2010). A method and framework for quality of cloud services measurement. In 2010 3rd International Conference on Advanced Computer Theory and Engineering (ICACTE) (Vol. 5, pp. V5–358). IEEE.
61. Boampong, P. A., Wahsheh, L. A. (2012). Different facets of security in the cloud. In Proceedings of the 15th Communications and Networking Simulation Symposium (p. 5). Society for Computer Simulation International.
62. Rimal, B. P., Choi, E., Lumb, I. (2010). A taxonomy, survey, and issues of cloud computing ecosystems. In Cloud Computing (pp. 21–46). Springer London.

Chapter 4
Classification of Non-functional Requirements of Web Services from Multiperspective View

Maya Rathore and Ugrasen Suman

Abstract With the rapid growth of functionally identical web services, Quality of Service (QoS) plays vital role for deciding the most suitable services for consumers. Although, QoS for web services has gained extensive attention in the literature, most of the existing efforts are unable to consider the multiperspective QoS of web services. Unlike conventional software paradigms, web services are provided, developed and used by different users such as provider, consumer and broker. As a result, QoS requirements vary from user to user. Existing researches are unable to provide standard solution, which can deal with what service providers, consumers and broker should expose in service description as QoS parameters. Therefore, in this book chapter, a multiperspective PCB-QoS classification of non-functional parameters along with new QoS parameters, i.e. access rate and Overall Aggregated Effective Quality of Service (OAEQoS) is presented. Due to the extensible nature of PCB-QoS classification, it can be extended to accommodate more number of QoS parameters. This QoS classification is based on the idea of partitioning the generic QoS parameters according to multi-user's perspective. An Average Real Value Sum Method (ARSM) based on default priority constraints is also proposed for ranking of web services that uses the presented QoS classification. With the help of proposed approach, the user can specify the service requirements without taking the hurdle of specifying the weights for each QoS parameter during web service operations. It also prevents the services from malicious service provider to publish the incorrect and inaccurate QoS information. Experimental evaluation shows the effectiveness of proposed approach over the existing approach.

M. Rathore (✉) · U. Suman
School of Computer Science and IT, Devi Ahilya University (DAVV),
Indore, Madhya Pradesh, India
e-mail: mayarathore114@gmail.com

U. Suman
e-mail: ugrasen123@yahoo.com

M. Ramachandran and Z. Mahmood (eds.), *Requirements Engineering for Service and Cloud Computing*, DOI 10.1007/978-3-319-51310-2_4

Keywords Qos · Web services · SLA · SOA · Collaborative filtering ·
Non-functional requirements · Multi-attribute decision mechanism · QoS broker ·
Weighted sum method · QoS model

4.1   Introduction

With the rapid development of functionally identical web services available on the
web, QoS plays essential role in determining the most suitable services for consumers. QoS parameters can be considered as the distinctive criteria for web service
operation. In order to ensure the QoS of web services, service-level agreement
(SLA) is negotiated as a contract between service provider and service consumer
[1]. The SLA can also contain other agreed details such as, cost and some functional properties. In traditional software development paradigm, different users are
involved at various stages of application development life cycle and play significant
role in expressing the non-functional requirements explicitly or implicitly. As a
result, QoS requirements vary from user to user. Unlike traditional software paradigms, web services are created, provided and used by different users, such as
provider, consumer and broker. However, many service consumers are not involved
in any of the service development phase and do not have access to their predefined
logic or implementation. Hence, service consumers cannot easily evaluate the
non-functional aspects of web services until they actually invoke them [2]. Also,
service providers must have to provide a detailed service description for each
service.

Moreover, among the various phases of service development, most of the current
efforts classify the QoS parameters from consumer's perspective for web service
selection [3, 4, 5, 6, 7]. Web service selection based on QoS parameters is a
multi-attribute decision mechanism (MADM). It uses weighted sum method
(WSM) to transform the multidimensional parameters of QoS of web services into a
single-goal function [2, 5]. In this, a utility function is used, which maps the quality
vector into a single real value, to enable sorting and ranking of service candidates.
In this method, each parameter should have a predefined weight or priority
according to its importance for web service discovery request, which is very difficult when service consumers do not know which parameter is more/or less
important. Therefore, an approach can be designed that can automatically decide
the priority of each QoS parameter during service selection and registration by
service consumer and provider. At the same time, it can evaluate the overall QoS
score of a web service.

In this book chapter, a multiperspective PCB-QoS classification of
non-functional parameters along with new QoS parameters, i.e. access rate and
OAEQoS, is presented [8]. Due to the extensible nature of PCB-QoS classification,
it can be extended to accommodate more number of QoS parameters. This QoS
classification is based on the idea of partitioning the generic QoS parameters
according to multi-user's perspective. PCB-QoS classifies QoS parameters at the

level of web service operation, which are performed by service consumer, provider and broker during service request, service publish and service discovery of atomic as well as composite web services. In this chapter, an average real value sum method (ARSM) approach is also proposed for the computation of overall quality score (OQS) of each candidate web service that uses PCB-QoS classification. With the help of proposed approach, service broker and consumer can rank services based on their OQS. Experimental evaluation shows the effectiveness of proposed approach over the existing approach.

The remainder of the chapter is organized as follows. Section 4.2 provides the related work and literature review of various QoS classification models and ranking methods used by existing QoS-based web service selection approaches. A comparative study of various QoS models is presented in Sect. 4.3. An extensible multiperspective PCB-QoS classification along with its parameters is proposed in Sect. 4.4. In this section, an algorithm for the evaluation of proposed parameters is also presented. Section 4.5 presents an ARSM approach for aggregating different QoS parameters into a single unit. The implementation of proposed approach is presented in Sect. 4.6. Section 4.7 shows the experimental evaluation of proposed approach. Finally, summary of the chapter is provided in Sect. 4.8.

4.2   Literature Review

Currently, discovering the most appropriate services based on QoS for a simple or complex task requires continuous monitoring for trustworthiness of published QoS information and the reputation of involved web services. Assuring the quality of selected web services has been discussed in various research proposals [6, 9–11]. Various QoS models have been proposed in the literature in which QoS parameters are evaluated by third-party broker [6, 9–11, 12, 13, 14]. A third-party broker can be a software, web service or application through which service provider and consumer interact to each other for publishing and discovering the web services [15]. A third-party broker also performs monitoring and updation of QoS database to guarantee that the discovered services based on QoS are reliable and trustable 9–11, 13]. The QoS service broker helps service consumers to select the best services for the composite service before invocation. The consumer uses the required service and provides a feedback about that web service to the QoS broker. The QoS broker collects feedback and updates reputation parameter for future uses of service by consumer. Generally, QoS broker assigns and stores rank for all accessed services according to this reputation value.

A QoS-aware middleware for web service composition is proposed in which the non-functional parameters are defined for atomic services including execution price, completion time, reputation, successful execution rate and availability [16]. A generic QoS model is proposed, which includes response time, price, reliability and throughput [16]. Web service quality model includes six QoS properties, i.e. execution price, execution duration, reliability, reputation, availability and a new parameter, i.e. composability [13]. A QoS-aware model for web service discovery contains cost, response time and availability [7]. These approaches deal with generic QoS parameters of web services from consumers' perspective such as, price, execution duration, availability and reliability [6, 7, 9–11, 12, 13, 14–17]. Moreover, these approaches rely on service providers to advertise their QoS information or provide an interface to access the QoS values, which is subject to manipulation by the providers. Obviously, service providers may not advertise their QoS information in an impartial way, for example, execution duration, reliability, etc. The approaches only obtain quality supplied by providers and unable to obtain quality experienced from consumers.

A collaborative filtering method based on combining the user-based and item-based approaches automatically predicts the QoS values of the current user by collecting information from other similar users. Similar service users are the users, who have the same previous QoS experience on the same set of commonly invoked web services with the current user [18]. This approach requires no web service invocations and at the same time, it helps service users to discover suitable web services by analyzing QoS information from similar users. It uses response time and failure rate QoS parameters for web services. The approach is unable to construct the runtime QoS information of web services and considers only consumers perspective for service selection.

There exists a classification of QoS parameters for distributed heterogeneous system [19]. The QoS parameters are classified into absolute, relative and computed category. A tree structure to represent the composite service providers requirements, which is defined on the multiple QoS properties and service offers is proposed with varied consumer preferences [20]. The QoS requirements are classified into QoS category and context category, which are often divided into execution, security, environmental and business categories [21]. On web service management, a trusted quality of web service management framework is based on multidimensional qualities of web service model and end-to-end monitoring [22]. These approaches have a high dependency on the service provider to publish non-functional parameter values, which may be malicious and inaccurate.

A policy-centred metamodel (PCM) is proposed that provides developers, providers and users with a frame to describe non-functional parameters (NFP) aiming to support the web service selection and composition [23]. The approach is based on the explicit distinction between NFP offered by service provider and requested by service consumer, concept of policy that aggregates NFP descriptions into single entity with an applicability condition, and finally, on a set of constraint operators, which is particularly relevant for NFP requests. A QoS model is proposed that allows service providers to advertise the QoS offered and service consumers to specify QoS requirements [1]. A catalogue of generic QoS parameters is considered when service descriptions are developed and non-functional parameters that are relevant from consumer's perspective [2]. A quality model classifies non-functional parameters based on the different stakeholders' requirements [3]. In this model, the web services qualities from three different perspectives, namely; developer, provider and consumer are discussed. The presented model also contains metrics for some of the identified quality parameters.

The literature contains a large number of approaches dealing with QoS classification and management at the consumer side. This is reasonable, as many QoS requirements are important mostly from the consumer point of view. However, customer-level requirements should be considered along with provider and broker level, which are quite different. A successful QoS management strategy should consider all these point of views. Also, there are various generic and domain specific QoS models for web service selection in which the overall quality score is computed using the traditional WSM method. The limitation with WSM method is that it requires user preferences in terms of weights to be specified with each non-functional parameter at design time, which is not always possible with inexperienced users. Therefore, an approach can be proposed, which is able to construct the weights for each non-functional parameter automatically, if user is unable to decide.

4.3   Comparison of Various QoS Models

Various research works have been discussed in the literature to address the QoS for web services from different users' perspective. Most of the existing work considers only generic QoS parameters from consumer's perspective in their QoS models [6, 7, 13, 16]. Table 4.1 shows the comparative analysis of existing QoS models of web services. These QoS models are compared on the basis of various parameters such as, QoS parameters, QoS evaluation and monitoring method, runtime QoS aggregation, QoS model extensibility, inclusion of consumers' ranking, inclusion of brokers' ranking and perspectives. The strength and weakness of various QoS models are evaluated on the basis of these parameters, which are discussed as follows:

- *QoS parameters used*: It can be classified into generic and domain-specific QoS parameters. With the help of this parameter, it will be easy to determine whether the approach uses the generic or domain-specific QoS parameters in their QoS models.
- *QoS evaluation and monitoring*: It helps in analyzing whether or not the existing approach supports runtime evaluation and monitoring of QoS parameter for composed process.
- *Runtime QoS aggregation*: It can be helpful to determine whether the approach is able to aggregate non-functional parameters to generate overall score at runtime using the suitable aggregation function. On the basis of the generated score, rank of the service can be decided by the broker.
- *QoS model extendibility*: An approach can be analyzed for the extendibility of their QoS model so that new QoS parameters can easily be accommodated depending on the different application domains.

Table 4.1 Comparative analysis of existing QoS models

Parameters Approach	QoS parameter	QoS evaluation and monitoring	Runtime QoS aggregation	QoS model extendibility	Inclusion of consumers ranking	Inclusion of brokers ranking	User perspectives
Trust and reputation [24]	Generic	No	No	No	Yes	No	Consumer
UDDI extension and certifier [6, 13] [16] [20] [25]	Generic	No	No	No	Yes	No	Consumer
Broker [7]	Generic	No	No	No	No	No	Consumer
Analytic hierarchy process [20]	Generic	No	No	No	No	No	Consumer
User and item based collaborative filtering approach [1]	Generic	No	No	No	Yes	No	Consumer
PCM metamodel [23]	Generic	No	No	Yes	No	No	Provider, developer and consumer

- *Inclusion of consumers' ranking*: Different service consumers have diverse and changeable preferences for the non-functional parameters depending on the situation. This parameter helps in determining whether or not the approaches involve the consumer preferences during service discovery request.
- *User perspectives*: This parameter helps in analyzing whether or not the existing approach considers requirements of different users at various stages of service development while designing the QoS models.
- *Inclusion of brokers' ranking*: Runtime evaluation of QoS parameter after the verification of providers' service by broker should be recorded as brokers' feedback. The broker generates the ranking of particular web service before publishing on web. This parameter helps in determining whether or not the approach involves brokers' ranking for web service during service registration.

From the comparative analysis of various existing QoS models, it has been observed that most of the existing work only focus on consumers' perspective QoS for web service selection [5, 6, 7, 16, 20, 24, 25]. Some considers non-functional parameters from both consumer and provider perspective while others include broker, consumer and developer perspectives [1, 2, 3]. Apart from the existing work, there can be a multiperspective classification of QoS parameters, which can classify non-functional parameters from the consumer, broker and provider perspective at the level of web service operation. Also, developing a mechanism through which the computation of rank value can be performed without taking the hurdle of specifying the weights for each QoS parameter. In this book chapter, an extensible multiperspective classification of QoS parameters, PCB-QoS classification is presented, which considers some new QoS parameters, i.e. access rate and overall aggregated effective QoS (OAEQoS) parameter [8]. An approach for the computation of overall quality score of web services that uses presented classification is also proposed. Unlike traditional WSM approach, the ARSM approach computes the overall quality score using default priority constraints, which is associated with each QoS parameter of PCB-QoS classification.

4.4 PCB-QoS Classification

Generally, web service requirements are classified into functional and non-functional categories. Functional requirements describe the specific function of a web service, which includes inputs, operations and outputs. Non-functional requirements describe the additional features associated with each web service related to the operation. An extensible multiperspective PCB-QoS classification of non-functional parameters of web services is proposed and it is shown in Fig. 4.1. This classification is based on the idea of partitioning generic non-functional parameters from different perspective. This type of classification can be helpful for the explicit distinction between requested, offered and monitored non-functional parameters from the perspective of service provider, consumer and broker. Also, it

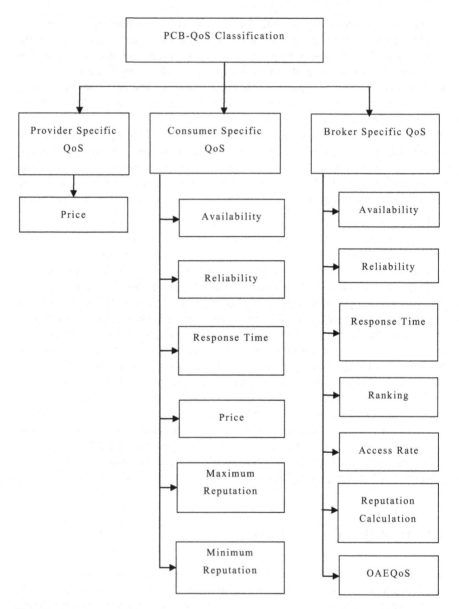

Fig. 4.1 PCB-QoS classification for web services

can be helpful to specify non-functional requirements for different types of operations performed on web services such as, web service monitoring, discovery and publish to be performed by various parties involved at runtime.

4.4.1 Perspectives of PCB-QoS Classification

The parameters of PCB-QoS classification can be viewed from three perspectives, i.e. provider, consumer and broker, which are discussed in subsequent paragraphs.

Service Consumers' Perspective. From service consumers' perspective, non-functional properties can be classified as mandatory and optional. Service consumer uses QoS parameter with functional requirements during service discovery request, which includes price, response time, availability, reliability, minimum reputation score and maximum reputation score. The service consumer requires the knowledge and representation of various non-functional parameters for service discovery request, which is not always possible. The presented PCB-QoS classification automatically predicts non-functional parameters value with a default priority constraint on behalf of service consumers' to avoid aforementioned problem.

Service Broker's Perspective. Since the internal logic of the services is hidden from service consumers; therefore, actual QoS is unknown until the service is invoked. Hence, quality management of services before publishing is important in SOA environment. Defining metrics is a precondition to evaluate the QoS, which ensures that the high quality service is published [8]. Exposing non-functional parameters from brokers' perspective is essential during web service monitoring, publishing and service discovery request. From consumers' perspective, the broker can automatically consider the non-functional parameter for service discovery request, if they are unable to explicitly specify these parameters. Since, there can be situations where the service consumers do not have appropriate knowledge about the importance and values for different non-functional parameters to be specified during service request. A priority can be used to control the order in which QoS parameters have to be considered at various web service operations. Non-functional parameters from broker's perspective include availability, reliability, response time, ranking, access rate and OAEQoS. The broker also works on behalf of service provider in order to ensure the correctness and accuracy of published QoS information.

Service Providers' Perspective. From the providers' point of view, non-functional parameters are those parameters that web service provider require to be guaranteed after publishing the web service. A provider can publish two types of non-functional parameters along with functional requirements, which are static and dynamic. The PCB-QoS model prevents the services from publishing the malicious and wrong information of non-functional parameters by service provider. Some static parameters such as price can be obtained from the service providers directly. However, other QoS attributes' values like response time, availability and reliability need to be monitored and published by reliable third-party broker. Here, service provider registers the services to broker and then broker publishes the services along with static and dynamic QoS parameters.

4.4.2 PCB-QoS Parameters

The parameters of PCB-QoS classification are explained as follows:

Access Rate. Access rate is an accessibility parameter that requires continuous monitoring of web services through broker to provide updated QoS information. It is directly related with the availability from the host location. Before publishing a new service on the server, the broker invokes and monitors the particular service in its own operating environment for a specific time period. The purpose of monitoring the web service is to evaluate the access rate and other QoS parameter, so that the consumer can always access web service with updated QoS information.

Access rate (A_r) can be defined as the rate of total number of web service requests which are requested by the service consumer through broker interface. It is the sum of successfully invoked web services, failed web services and bounced web services without invocation. These three types of request can be represented by success access rate, i.e. $(S(A_r))$, failure access rate, i.e. $(F(A_r))$, and bounce access rate, i.e. $(B(A_r))$. Access rate can be calculated as follows:

$$A_r = \sum (S(A_r)) + \sum (F(A_r)) + \sum (B(A_r)) \tag{4.1}$$

Bounce access rate. It is the rate at which the service consumer discovers the particular service and return back without invoking it through broker interface. The bounce access rate can be calculated as the ratio of total number of bounces for a web service (W_b) and access rate A_r. $B(A_r)$ can be calculated as follows:

$B(A_r)$ = Total number of bounced web services/(total number of bounced web services + total number of invoked web services)

$$= B(A_r) = \frac{\sum W_b}{\sum W_b + \sum W_i} \tag{4.2}$$

Thus, the percentage of $B(A_r)$ can be calculated as

$$B(A_r) = \frac{\sum W_b}{A_r} * 100 \tag{4.3}$$

Failure access rate. It is the ratio between the number of times a web service request failed (W_{failed}) to perform its operation for any reason and the number of times the web service was called for execution; i.e. failed executions/called for execution. It is the relationship between the number of times the web service failed after execution and the number of times the web service is successfully invoked. Failure access rate can be represented by $F(A_r)$ and can be calculated using the following formula:

$F(A_r)$ = Failed web services/(failed web services + successfully invoked web services + bounced web services).

Thus, the percentage of $F(A_r)$ can be calculated as

$$F(A_r) = \frac{\sum W_{failed}}{A_r} * 100 \qquad (4.4)$$

Successful access rate. It is the ratio between the number of times a web service is successfully invoked to perform its operation and the number of times the web service was called for execution, i.e. successful executions/called for execution. It is the relationship between the number of times the web service is successfully invoked and the number of times the web service was called for execution. Successful access rate $S(A_r)$ can be calculated using the following formula:

$$S(A_r) = \frac{\sum W_{successful}}{A_r} * 100 \qquad (4.5)$$

The sum of the probability of $S(A_r)$ and the probability of $F(A_r)$ will always be unity. It can be expressed as follows:

$$S(A_r) + F(A_r) = 1 \qquad (4.6)$$

$$S(A_r) = 1 - F(A_r) \qquad (4.7)$$

Reliability. Reliability is the probability in which the provider correctly answers a request within a maximum expected time. It is measured as the number of success request divided by the number of request. It is denoted by $W_{reliability}$ and can be expressed as follows:

$$W_{reliability} = S(A_r) \qquad (4.8)$$

Availability. is the probability that the web service is in its expected functional condition, and therefore, it is capable of being used in a stated environment. Availability deals with the duration of uptime for web service operations. It is often expressed in terms of uptime and downtime of web service. Uptime refers to a capability to perform the task and downtime refers to not being able to perform the task. It is dented by availability and can be expressed as follows:

$$W_{availability} = \frac{\sum S(A_r)}{A_r} \qquad (4.9)$$

Response Time. Response time is the total time duration spent between the request from service consumer to broker ($T_{sc\_request}$, $T_{sb\_request}$) and response from service broker to service provider ($T_{sb\_response}$, $T_{sp\_response}$) for a particular web service from the side of service consumer, broker and service provider It is denoted by W_{rt} and can be calculated as

$$W_{rt} = \left(T_{sc\_request} + T_{sb\_request}\right) - \left(T_{sb\_response} + T_{sp\_response}\right) \qquad (4.10)$$

Effective Service Access Time. It is the total time required to serve the consumers' request for particular service through broker. It can be denoted by TESA. The broker access time (T_{BA}) and service access time (T_{SA}) can be evaluated through broker for TESA. T_{BA} and T_{SA} can be calculated as

$$T_{BA} = T_{sc\_request} - T_{sb\_response} \qquad (4.11)$$

$$T_{SA} = \left(T_{sc\_request} + T_{sb\_request}\right) - \left(T_{sb\_response} + T_{sp\_response}\right) \qquad (4.12)$$

Therefore,

$$T_{ESA} = (F(A_r) * T_{BA}) + (F(A_r) * T_{SA}) \qquad (4.13)$$

Overall Aggregated Effective QoS. Overall aggregated effective QoS (OAEQoS) parameter is an aggregated quality score of a web service that requires the values of all non-functional parameters obtained through monitoring and evaluation performed by third-party broker. With the help of this parameter, the broker can easily obtain the overall quality score and rank of a web service by combining all the non-functional parameter of registered web service before publishing it on server. Also, the consumer can select the best services for simple as well as complex task with provided rank.

In OAEQoS parameter, each non-functional parameter should have a priority assigned according to their importance during service selection and registration. Most of the times, service consumers are not experienced enough in deciding priorities to non-functional parameters for web service selection; therefore, a default priority constraint can be assigned to non-functional parameters according to their importance. The priority value can vary from 1 to 5. The priority value 1 is the lowest priority assigned to a parameter, which is less important and 5 means highest priority assigned to a parameter, which is more important during service selection and registration and so on.

OAEQoS requires that the values of non-functional parameters should be in exactly the same measurable unit. It is calculated at runtime as an average aggregated sum of real values of response time, availability, reliability, etc., by the number of non-functional parameters. OAEQoS for each web service can be computed as follows:

$$OAEQoS(WS) = \sum\nolimits_{i,j=0}^{n,m} w_i q_j / x, \qquad (4.14)$$

where q_j is the monitored QoS value of each non-functional parameter of web service, w_i is the default priority value of a parameter, and x is the number of non-functional parameters. The values of each QoS parameter q_j for every web service are calculated at runtime by third-party broker during service registration.

Although, the number of QoS parameters discussed in the presented classification is limited, but due to the extensible nature of the PCB-QoS, it is possible to extend the classification to integrate other non-functional parameters without altering the basic one.

4.4.3 *Monitoring and Evaluation Algorithm for PCB-QoS Parameters*

An algorithm is proposed for monitoring and evaluation of different non-functional parameters and overall quality score at broker's operating environment. With the help of proposed algorithm, broker can monitor the non-functional parameters of each web service before publishing on host location and the consumers of service can retrieve up-to-date web services with QoS information. In this algorithm, invoke and monitor procedure invokes the particular web service for a specified time period for finding the number of successful request (success_req), failed request (failed_req) and bounced request (bounced_req). The obtained values of success_req, failed_req and bounced_req can further be used to construct the values of other non-functional parameters. The tot_req is the count of total number of request arrived for a particular web service. The s_rate, f_rate and b_rate represents the rate of percentage of successful, failed and bounced requests. OAEQoS is the average of all the evaluated QoS parameters. The update_old_QoS_dataset updates the old QoS data with the new QoS data after every invocation.

The algorithm for monitoring and evaluation of proposed QoS parameters, i.e. INVOKE_&_MONITOR_WEB_SERVICE performed at broker's operating environment is discussed in Algorithm 1 below.

Algorithm 1 INVOKE_&_MONITOR_WEB_SERVICE (WSName, WSUrl, N). WSName is the name of web service to be invoked and WSUrl is the destination URL, where the service is actually located. N is the total number of QoS parameters used for the evaluation of average score of all QoS parameters.

Input: WsName, WSUrl, N.

Output: successful_req, failed_req, bounced_req, tot_req, s_rate, f_rate, b_rate, reliability, availability, response_time, OAEQoS.

1. [Initialize]
   success_req=0
   failed_req=0
   bounced_req=0
2. [Retrieve old successful request, failed request and bounced request from web service QoS dataset]
   Read&Store (WSName, old_succ_request, old_failed_request, old_bounced_request)
3. [Invoke the specified web service]

If invoked_success=true then
End if
If invoked_bounced=true then
success_req=success_req +1
End if
If invoked_failed=true then
failed_req =failed_req +1
End if
If invoked_bounced=true then
bounced_req =bounced_req +1
End if

4. [Evaluate other parameters]
   tot_req=success_req+failed_req+bounced_req
   s_rate=success_req/ tot_req
   f_rate=failed_req/ tot_req
   b_rate=bounced_req/tot_req
   reliability=s_rate
   availability=s_rate/ (s_rate+f_rate)
   response_time=avg (resp_time)
   OAEQoS=(reliability+availability+response_time)/ N

5. [Update the old QoS values into the dataset]
   update_old_QoS_Dataset (success_req, failed_req, bounced_req, tot_req, s_rate, f_rate, b_rate, reliability, availability, response_time, OAEQoS)

6. [Display the QoS values]
   Print availability, reliability, response_time, OAEQoS.

7. [Finished]
   Return.

The INVOKE_&_MONITOR_WEB_SERVICE algorithm monitors and evaluates non-functional parameters. The procedure EVALUATE_WEB_SERVICES calls INVOKE_&_MONITOR_WEB_SERVICE to evaluate non-functional parameters for each web service and it is described as follows:

Algorithm 2 EVALUATE_WEB_SERVICES (WSName s). Given WSName is the name of web service; WSUrl is the destination url of web service and N is the number of QoS parameters. Algorithm Evaluate_WS shows the list of similar web services that fulfils the required functionality. This algorithm evaluates the QoS parameters for each service s in service list service_list.

Input: Web service name
Output: Web service with QoS

1. [Read the number of non-functional parameters]
   Read N

2. [Select web service from service_list for QoS evaluation]
   For each service s in service_list
   Begin

   CALL INVOKE_&_MONITOR_WEB_SERVICE

   End.

This algorithm can be helpful in evaluating the values of different non-functional parameters through access rate and provide the aggregated QoS score of each web service during service discovery and publish. The obtained quality score can be used for ranking and selecting the appropriate service for composition, which has highest score. In spite of the aforesaid advantages, the proposed algorithm can be considered to evaluate the values of non-functional parameters of different units.

4.5 ARSM Approach

An ARSM approach is a rank-value computational approach for computing the rank value of a service. It uses the PCB-QoS classification for the computation of overall quality score. It is based on the concept of MADM approach for the calculation of overall quality score. In ARSM approach, each non-functional parameter is assigned a default priority implicitly as a weight. An ARSM approach is an enhancement over traditional WSM approach, where each non-functional parameter is assigned a specific weight explicitly between 0 and 100 % [5]. It is an averaging method in which the monitored values of different non-functional parameters are multiplied with corresponding weights, summed up and finally it is divided by the number of non-functional parameters. The ARSM approach helps to determine the values of non-functional parameters of PCB-QoS classification model. Among the various non-functional parameters, the OQS can be computed in three steps using ARSM approach, namely; scaling QoS parameters values, assigning default priority constraint and computation of OQS. These steps are discussed in following subsections.

4.5.1 Scaling QoS Parameters Value

Scaling QoS parameter values to allow a uniform measurement of the multidimensional service qualities requires independent units and range. Since, QoS parameters could be either positive or negative in scaling, some QoS values need to be maximized, i.e. higher value provides higher quality, for example availability and reliability. Whereas, other values have to be minimized, i.e. higher value provides lower quality. This includes parameters such as, execution time and price. In this situation, the QoS parameters need to be normalized according to the formulas [5]. The values of negative attributes are normalized by expression (4.15) and the values of positive attributes are normalized by expression (4.16).

$$q_{i,j} = \begin{cases} (q_{i,j}^{max} - q_{i,j})/(q_{i,j}^{max} - q_{i,j}^{min}) & \text{if } q_{i,j}^{max} - q_{i,j}^{min} \neq 0; \quad i,j = 1,2,\ldots,n \\ 1 & \text{if } q_{i,j}^{max} - q_{i,j}^{min} = 0 \end{cases}$$

(4.15)

$$q_{i,j} = \begin{cases} (q_{i,j} - q_{i,j}^{min})/(q_{i,j}^{max} - q_{i,j}^{min}) & \text{if } q_{i,j}^{max} - q_{i,j}^{min} \neq 0; \quad i,j = 1,2,\ldots,n \\ 1 & \text{if } q_{i,j}^{max} - q_{i,j}^{min} = 0 \end{cases}$$

(4.16)

In the scaling process, each QoS attribute value, $q_{i,j}$, is transformed into a value between 0 and 1, by comparing it with the minimum($q_{i,j}$) and maximum($q_{i,j}$) possible values according to the available QoS information of service candidates.

4.5.2 Assigning Default Priority Constraints

Scaling process is followed by a priority assignment process for representing user priorities and preferences. The ARSM approach requires that each non-functional parameter should have assigned default priority according to their importance during service selection and registration such as WSM method. Unlike WSM method, ARSM approach is able to automatically incorporate the priority with each non-functional parameter, if it is not specified by the service consumer. Since there can be situations, where the service consumers do not know which non-functional parameter is more or less important for web service discovery. Therefore, on behalf of service consumer, a default priority is assigned to each non-functional parameter according to their importance by the service broker. The priority value varies from 1 (less important) to 5 (more important). The default priority can be used at the time of service selection as well as services registration.

4.5.3 Computation of OQS

Computation of OQS requires transforming the multidimensional parameters of QoS of web service into a single real value, to enable sorting and ranking of service candidates. OQS parameter is an overall quality score of a web service that requires the values of all non-functional parameters obtained through monitoring and evaluation performed by a third-party broker. This parameter can be helpful to obtain the overall quality score and rank of a web service, which is to be published later onto server. Also, on the basis of provided rank, the consumer can also be able to select the best services for simple as well as complex task. OQS requires that the values of all non-functional parameters should be in the same measurable unit. It is calculated at runtime as an average aggregated sum of real values of response time, availability, reliability, etc., by the number of non-functional parameters. The following formula can be used to compute OQS for each web service:

$$OQS(WS) = \sum_{i,j=0}^{n,m} w_i q_j / x \qquad (4.17)$$

4.6 Implementation

The monitoring and evaluation of PCB-QoS parameters can be implemented through a set of functionally similar web services stored into database. These web services have been collected from different sources such as service-repository.com, xmethod.net, theserverside.com, visualwebservice.com, webservicex.com and webservicex.net. The WSdatabase for these web services is created in SQL Server 2008 R2, which includes approximately 1385 web services with their web service id (WSID), web service name (WSname) and URLs. These web services were invoked several times for a period of 1 month. All the web services were tested to initially determine the number of successful, failed and bounced request. The total_request, success_rate, failure_rate, bounce_rate, availability, reliability, response_time and rating can be calculated after finding the success, failed and bounced requests.

Out of 1385 web services, a weather forecasts web service having WSDL URL; http://www.webservicex.net/WeatherForecast.asmx? and web service ID 8 is accessed directly from remote location around 80 times to determine successful, failed and bounced request. The results after invoking the web services have stored in SQL Server 2008 R2. The value of OAEQoS parameter can be evaluated using these evaluated values of non-functional parameter as shown in Table 4.2.

A graphical user interface (GUI) is developed as shown in Fig. 4.2, to implement the monitoring and evaluation mechanism for the proposed parameters on Windows 2007 server platform using Microsoft Visual Studio .NET 2012 development environment and ASP.NET, C#.NET as a programming language. The interface helps to evaluate the values of above parameters such as, total_request, success_rate, failure_rate, bounce_rate, availability, reliability, response_time and OAEQoS for weather forecast web service.

Table 4.2 Values of non-functional parameters

ID	WSName	WSURL	Success Access Rate	Failure Rate	Average Success Access	Availability	Response Time	Reliability	OAEQoS
1	Calculator service	#http://localhost:5	100	30	0.76	0.7058824	0.041	0.7058824	0.484255
2	calculator service	#http://localhost:5	59	45	0.59	1	0.001	0.8023	0.6011
3	calculator service	#http://localhost:5	90	20	0.81	1	0.001	0.5	0.500333
4	Translate service	#http://www.web	79	15	0.84	0.8723	0.441	0.45	0.587767
5	Whether forcast se	http://www.webse	50	18	0.74	0.8727	0.041	0.7	0.5379
6	Stock Quote	#http://www.web	30	45	0.4	0.8749	0.041	0.7	0.538633
7	Send SMS service	#http://www.web	20	5	0.7	0.81	0.003	0.84	0.551
8	Whether forcast se	#http://www.web	50	10	0.5	0.84	0.003	0.74	0.527667
9	Whether forcast se	#http://www.restf	67	15	0.45	0.74	0.005	0.4	0.381667
10	US Address verifc	#http://www.web	90	20	0.7	0.4	0.008	0.7	0.369333
11	Calculate	http://www.deept	89	30	0.7	0.7	0.015	0.67	0.461667
12	AutoCompleteSer	http://www.hydro	90	50	0.5	0.5	0.002	0.7	0.400667
13	ASP_x0020_to_x	http://fullerdata.co	78	10	0.76	0.45	0.002	0.6	0.350667
14	showmyip	http://www.ippag	89	10	0.47	0.7	0.002	0.5	0.400667
15	PingService	http://216.33.67.1	89	10	0.6	0.7	0.002	0.74	0.460667
16	Dilbert	http://gcomputer.n	90	4	0.5	0.5	0.041	0.4	0.313667
17	Trans	http://www.sarma	98	7	0.42	0.67	0.041	0.7	0.470333
18	Artists	http://sixteencolor	95	9	0.37	0.7	0.041	0.5	0.413667
19	Comments	http://adamkinney	45	10	0.8	0.6	0.003	0.8727	0.4919
20	captchaWebServi	http://www.axiseb	67	15	0.77	0.5	0.003	0.8749	0.4593
21	AutoCompleteSer	http://www.brend	60	10	0.8	0.42	0.005	0.81	0.411667
22	ExtractWS	http://cluuz1.cluuz	55	10	0.8	0.37	0.008	0.84	0.406
23	IpToLocationWS	http://www.conne	34	10	0.9	0.8	0.015	0.8727	0.562567
24	GuestBook	http://www.dotne	69	25	0	0.77	0.002	0.8749	0.548967
25	Crop	http://crop.goofyt	40	1	0	0.8	0.003	0.81	0.537667
26	sendmailWSDL	http://www.nhuyn	32	1	0	0.8	0.003	0.84	0.547667
27	HashProviderServ	http://web8.secur	60	1	0	0.9	0.005	1	0.635
28	Calculator_x0020	http://www.ecs.sy	20	1	0	0.8	0.008	1	0.602667
29	soapCheckUserR	http://www.trixbo	40	1	0	0.77	0.015	0.8723	0.552433
30	SessionService1	http://aspalliance.c	45	1	0	0.8	0.002	0.8727	0.558233
31	CasGroups	http://skyservice.p	45	1	0	0.8	0.002	0.8749	0.558967
32	RecipeService	http://oscar.snapp	50	1	0	0.9	0.002	0.7	0.534
33	EktronAsyncProc	http://www.capito	68	1	0	0	0.002	0.66	0.220667

Fig. 4.2 Evaluation of non-functional parameters and OAEQoS

For example, for weather web service, which is having ID 8, the value of OAEQoS will be 0.4631, when the observed real values of reliability, availability and response time are considered as 0.7058824, 0.7058823 and 0.041, respectively, as shown in Table 4.2. Similarly, the non-functional parameters can be evaluated for other web services. With the help of interface as shown in Fig. 4.2, the broker can evaluate the value of OAEQoS parameter by aggregating different non-functional parameters value. Through the value of OAEQoS parameter, the broker can rank web service before publishing on the host location from where it is accessible by the service consumers. The service consumer can select the best services for discovery and composition of services with the help of published OAEQoS score.

4.7   Experimental Evaluation

The experimental evaluation of ARSM approach have been conducted and compared with the WSM method used by most of the existing service selection approaches for ranking candidate services. Out of these 1385 services, 20 web services were invoked and tested several times for a period of 8 days to determine the value of access rate, availability, reliability, response time, and reputation of service. The overall quality score can be computed with the help of five non-functional parameters, which are response time, availability, reliability, cost and reputation. The functional requirements of a service and the QoS constraints are provided as input for the service selection process.

The validity of proposed ARSM approach can be analyzed by applying it on a set of generic QoS parameters such as, response time, throughput, availability, reliability and cost considered by most of the existing service selection approaches [5, 6, 7, 13, 16]. Here, the performance of ARSM approach is compared against WSM approach using the QoS parameters and their values specified in Table 4.3. Empirical results of the proposed ARSM approach against the existing service selection approaches, which uses WSM, are shown through the graphical representation in Fig. 4.3. It shows that the performance of proposed ARSM approach is 10% better than WSM method used in existing approaches for calculation of overall quality score of around 1385 services [5, 6, 13]. Thus, it is easier to rank and select the candidate web service with highest quality score using the proposed approach for composition without specifying weights for non-functional parameters explicitly.

Table 4.3 Values of non-functional parameters in WSM and ARSM [5]

Services	Response time	Throughput	Availability	Reliability	Cost	Rank value using $WSM = \sum W_i * Q_i$	Rank value using $ARSM = \sum (W_i * Q_i)/x$
S1	0.6783	0.6448	1	0.95	0.99	0.72148	0.85262
S2	0.5778	0.5058	1	0.99	0.96	0.70153	0.80672
S3	0.402	0.4585	0.98	0.98	0.97	0.65534	0.7581
S4	0.2512	0.5669	0.99	0.99	0.98	0.65478	0.75562
S5	0.2702	0.598	0.97	0.97	0.99	0.65470	0.75964
S6	0.4772	0.567	0.97	0.96	0.98	0.69783	0.79084
S7	0.5512	0.5667	0.99	0.94	0.99	0.70758	0.80758
S8	0.2512	0.5669	0.99	0.99	0.9901	0.65734	0.75764
S9	0.3512	0.009	0.99	0.98	0.97	0.56704	0.66004
S10	0.2512	0.5669	0.99	0.99	0.9901	0.65840	0.75764

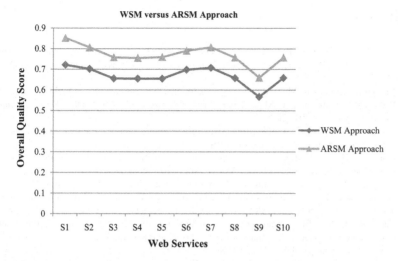

Fig. 4.3 WSM versus ARSM Approach

4.8 Summary

The classification of generic QoS parameters from the multi-user perspective is required at different levels of web service operations such as, service discovery request, publishing, monitoring and evaluation. In most of the service selection approaches, QoS models are designed from consumers' point of view. Since the QoS requirements are different at various stages of service development, still there is a lack of standard solution, which can deal with different users' QoS requirements. In this chapter, an extensible multiperspective PCB-QoS classification is presented in which non-functional parameters are classified with various perspective considering web service consumers, providers and broker at various stages of service development. This classification can reduce the overhead to specify QoS parameters during web service discovery and registration. PCB-QoS classification is helpful in situation, where the service consumers have little or no knowledge about the description of QoS of web service. It also prevents the services from malicious service provider to publish the incorrect and inaccurate QoS information.

Apart from the PCB-QoS classification, an ARSM approach is proposed to compute the overall quality score for ranking candidate services with the help of presented QoS classification. Unlike WSM approach, the ARSM approach uses the default priority constraints associated with each QoS parameter of PCB-QoS classification. An algorithm is also presented for monitoring and evaluation of PCB-QoS parameters. Experiments have been conducted to show the effectiveness of proposed approach. In spite of the above advantages, the proposed ARSM approach is unable to consider the non-functional parameter values of different units.

References

1. Choi, S. W., Her, J. S., Kim, S. D.: QoS Metrics for Evaluating Services from the Perspective of Service Providers. IEEE International Conference on e-Business Engineering, pp. 622–625 (2007).
2. Balfagih, Z., Hassan, M. F.: Quality Model for the Web Services from Multi-stakeholders' Perspective. Information Management and Engineering (ICIME'09), Kuala Lumpur, Malaysia, pp. 287–291 (2009).
3. Becha, H. and Daniel, A.: Non-functional Properties in Service Oriented Architecture—A Consumer's Perspective. Journal of Software, Vol. 7, No. 3 (2012).
4. Hong, L., Hu, J.: A Multi-dimension QoS based Local Service Selection Model for Service Composition. Journal of Networks, Vol. 4, No. 5, pp. 351–358 (2009).
5. Guoping, Z., Huijuan, Z., Zhibin, W.: A QoS-based Web Services Selection Method for Dynamic Web Service Composition. First International Workshop on Education Technology and Computer Science (ETCS'09), IEEE Computer Society, Vol. 3, pp. 832–835 (2009).
6. Thirumaran, M., Balasubramanie, P.: Architecture for Evaluating Web Services QoS Parameters using Agents. International Journal of Computer Applications (IJCA), Foundation of Computer Science, USA, Vol. 10, No. 4, (2010).
7. Zheng, Z., et al.: QoS Aware Web Service Recommendation with Collaborative Filtering. Published in IEEE Transactions on Services Computing, Vol. 4, No. 2, pp. 140–152 (2011).
8. Rathore, M., Suman, U.: Evaluating QoS Parameters for Ranking Web Services. 3rd IEEE International Advance Computing Conference(IACC-2013), IEEE Computer Society, Ghaziabad (UP), February 22–23, (2013).
9. Rajendran, T., Balasubramanie, P.: An Efficient WS-QoS Broker based Architecture for Web Service Selection. International Journal of Computer Applications (IJCA), Foundation of Computer Science, USA, Vol. 1, No. 9, (2010).
10. Rajendran, T., Balasubramanie, P.: An Optimal Broker based Architecture for Web Service Discovery with QoS Characteristics. International Journal of Web Services Practices (IJWSP), Korea, Vol. 5, No. 1, pp. 32–40 (2010).
11. Rajendran, T.: Flexible and Intelligent Architecture for Quality based Web Service Discovery with an Agent based Approach. International Conference on Communication and Computational Intelligence (INCOCCI), Erode, pp. 617–622 (2010), 27-29 December.
12. Esfahani, R. K. M.: Reputation Improved Web Service Discovery based on QoS. Journal of Convergence Information Technology (JCIT), Vol. 5, No. 9, (2010).
13. Ye, G.: A QoS Aware Model for Web Service Discovery. First International Workshop on Education, Technology and Computer Science (ETCS '09), IEEE Computer Society, Wuhan, Vol. 3, pp. 740–744 (2009).
14. Rajendran, T., Balasubramanie, P.: An Efficient Architecture for Agent based Dynamic Web Services Discovery with QoS. Journal of Theoretical and Applied Information Technology (JATIT), Pakistan, Vol. 15, No. 2, (2010).
15. Rathore, M., Suman, U.: A Quality of Service Broker based Process Model for Dynamic Web Service Composition. Science Publications, Journal of Computer Science, USA, Vol. 7, No. 8, pp. 1267–1274 (2011).
16. Rajendran, T.: Efficient Approach towards an Agent-Based Dynamic Web Service Discovery Framework with QoS Support. Proc. of CSIT International Symposium on Computing, Communication, and Control (ISCCC 2009), Singapore, Vol. 1, pp. 74–78 (2009).
17. Zeng, L., et al.: QoS aware Middleware for Web Services Composition. IEEE Transactions on Software Engineering, Vol. 5, No. 30, pp. 311–327 (2004).
18. Vinek, E., et al.: Classification and Composition of QoS Parameters in Distributed, Heterogeneous System. 11th IEEE/ACM International Symposium on Cluster, Cloud and Grid Computing (CCGrid), IEEE Computer Society, Washington, pp. 424–433 (2011).
19. Yu, T., et al.: Efficient Algorithms for Web Services Selection with End to-End QoS Constraints. ACM Transaction on Web (TWEB), ACM New York, Vol. 1, No. 1, (2007).

20. Chaari, S., et al.: Framework for Web Service Selection Based on Non-functional Properties. International Journal of Web Services Practices (IJWSP), Korea, Vol. 3, No. 2, pp. 94–109 (2008).

21. Guo, N., et al.: A Trusted Quality of Web Service Management Framework based on Six Dimensional QOWS Model and End to End Monitoring. Proc. of the 11th APNOMS, Springer. pp. 437–440 (2008).

22. Kim, Y.: QoS Aware Web Services Discovery with Trust Management. Journal of Convergence Information Technology (JCIT), Vol. 3, No. 2, pp. 67–73 (2008).

23. Paoli, F. D., et al.: A Meta-model for Non-functional Property Description of Web Services. Proc. of IEEE International Conference on Web Services (ICWS), (2008).

24. Wang, H.: Reputation based Semantic Service Discovery. Fourth International Conference on Semantics, Knowledge and Grid (SKG'08), Beijing, pp. 485–486 (2009), 3–5 December.

25. Sha, L., Shaozhong, G., Xin, C., Mingjing, L.: A QoS based Web Service Selection Model. International Forum on Information Technology and Applications, IEEE Computer Society, Vol. 3, pp. 353–356 (2009).

Chapter 5
The Requirements Elicitation Approaches for Software-Defined Cloud Environments

Pethuru Raj, Parvathy Arulmozhi and Nithya Chidambaram

Abstract Without an iota of doubt, the overwhelming domain of requirements elicitation and engineering has been continuously and consistently evolving in order to catch up and match with the tricky and terrific expectations of producing and sustaining next-generation systems, solutions, and services. Especially in the hot and happening IT space and considering the growing complications of systems of engagements (SoE)-like applications, the aspect of requirements engineering is garnering a lot of attention and attraction. IT industry professionals and academic professors are working in unison in charting out easy-to-implement and use methods toward simplified requirements-gathering platforms, procedures, and practices. In this chapter, we would like to dig deeper and deal with the concept of software-defined clouds. Further on, the readers can read how requirements are being solicited and subjected to a variety of investigations before getting selected as sound and rewarding requirements for the right formation of software-defined clouds. We will also register the proven and promising approaches and articulations to speed up the process of simplifying and streamlining up the tasks associated with the requirements engineering activity.

Keywords Software-defined networks · Requirements elicitation · Systems of engagements (SoE) · Software-defined clouds

P. Raj (✉)
Infrastructure Architect, Global Cloud Center of Excellence, IBM India,
Bangalore, India
e-mail: peterindia@gmail.com

P. Arulmozhi · N. Chidambaram
School of Electrical & Electronics Engineering, SASTRA University,
Thanjavur 613401, India
e-mail: parvathy@ece.sastra.edu

N. Chidambaram
e-mail: cnithya@ece.sastra.edu

© Springer International Publishing AG 2017
M. Ramachandran and Z. Mahmood (eds.), *Requirements Engineering for Service and Cloud Computing*, DOI 10.1007/978-3-319-51310-2_5

5.1 Recollecting the Requirements Engineering Process

The field of software requirements engineering has been positively evolving in order to fulfill the varying expectations of building new-generation software products and packages. The quality of requirements collection has a direct impact on the mandated success of software engineering. It enables software developers, programmers, and engineers, to gain a deeper and decisive understanding about the problems to resolve and the functionalities to implement. Building a competent software-based solution is good but if it does not meet the customers' expectations, then it is bound to doom. Precisely and perfectly capturing both business expectations and end users' needs and constructing the software accordingly are the most crucial things for the intended success of software engineering. In short, producing and refining proven and promising techniques for efficient and effective requirements elicitation and engineering is, therefore, an important ingredient for software engineering. With the arrival and articulation of powerful technologies (cloud, mobile, analytics, social, embedded, etc.), there have to be improvements and innovations in requirements gathering and application construction in consonance.

Typically, the requirements engineering process begins with the inception phase and then moves on to elicitation, elaboration, negotiation, problem specification, and ends with review or validation of the requirements specification. There are several techniques, templates, tables, patterns, and other methods to unambiguously share the requirements understanding across geographically distributed software development team. Use cases, scenarios, functionality and feature lists, model diagrams, and written specifications. Different methods are being followed for different situations. The first and foremost stage of inception is described as follows. Software engineers use context-free and common questions to establish the nitty-gritty of the problem, the people who want a solution, the nature of the solution, and the effectiveness of the collaboration between customers and developers

The second phase is requirements elicitation that involves identifying and understanding directly from customers and end users what the foremost objectives and end-goals of software productions are, how the product ultimately fits into the brewing business needs, and how the product is to be used on a day-to-day basis, etc. The elaboration phase focuses on developing a refined technical model of software functions, features, and constraints using the information obtained during inception and elicitation. The negotiation step includes the refined requirements are further categorized and organized into subsets, the intrigued relations among the requirements identified, requirements reviewed for correctness and get prioritized based on customer needs, etc.

The specification stage represents the production of work products describing the functional as well as the nonfunctional requirements. Finally, it is validating the recorded requirements with different stakeholders. Typically a comprehensive feasibility study covering the various aspects such as the financial implications, technical competency, resource availability, etc. is initiated to get to know whether there is any kind of risks toward fulfilling the project implementation. There are integrated platforms and tools galore for requirements management and tracking, change management, etc. However considering the complexity of software applications, the requirements engineering step goes through a variety of beneficial and strategically sound transformations peppered with a few distinct disruptions. In this chapter, we would like to focus on the ways and means of doing requirements engineering for next-generation cloud environments. As accentuated below, the cloud paradigm is traversing through a number of inspiring and innovation-filled transformations.

5.2 The Literature Survey

The field of requirements engineering is definitely a matured one but with the consistent arrival and availability of newer technology paradigms, the need for unearthing fresh and flexible techniques and tools for facilitating accurate and auditable requirements elicitation is being insisted everywhere. In this survey section, we are to see some of the well-known research papers on this critical yet challenging topic.

Holger Schrödl and Stefan Wind [1] evaluate a few selected requirements engineering methods in terms of their applicability to the specific requirements of cloud-based solutions. Armed with that knowledge, the authors have prepared a comparison framework containing the features of cloud computing for a structured comparison of different requirements engineering methods. This comparison framework is applied to four established process models for requirements engineering followed by recommendations for a requirements engineering system adapted to cloud computing. *Shreta Sharma and S.K. Pandey* [2] have attempted to cover all the major elicitation techniques along with their significant aspects at one place. The intention of the authors is that such a comprehensive review would enable the concerned stakeholders and readers to understand and select the most appropriate technique to be used for their impending projects. *Lori MacVittie* [3] has written a white paper and titled it as *"Controlling the Cloud: Requirements for Cloud Computing."* The author has articulated the various requirements to setup and sustain cloud environments. *Bhaskar Prasad Rimal, Admela Jukan, Dimitrios Katsaros,* and *Yves Goeleven* [4] have explored the architectural features of cloud computing and classified them according to the requirements of end users, enterprises that use the cloud as a platform, and cloud providers themselves. They have also shown that several architectural features will play a major role in the adoption of the cloud paradigm as a mainstream commodity in the enterprise world. This paper also provided a few key guidelines to software architects and cloud application developers.

The *white paper* [5] outlines the top ten critical requirements of cloud service providers (CSPs) to worldwide corporates in order to confidently and cogently embrace the various cloud offerings. There are a variety of service providers and it is pertinent and paramount to have a firm grip of what are being offering, how they are being packaged and delivered, etc. There are certain minimum expectations out of these fast-flourishing cloud service providers. There are well-articulated risks and this paper has listed the important ingredients of CSPs in order to lessen the headaches of cloud consumers and customers.

Pericles Kouropoulos [6] has clearly articulated the urgent need for the state-of-the-art mechanisms to extract traceable and trendy requirements for building and hosting enterprise-grade application software on cloud environments. As enlisted below, cloud environments, whether private, public or hybrid, are being preferred to host and deliver enterprise-class applications. Thus the requirements are definitely different for cloud-native as well as cloud-enabled applications. The point here is that the appropriate changes need to be embedded in the ways and means of performing requirements engineering in order to match up with the latest trends and transitions happening in the hot IT space. This paper has laid down a set of viable and venerable procedures and practices in order to emerging software.

Todoran, Irina; Seyff, Norbert; Glinz, Martin [7] has detailed a lot about requirements elicitation in his seminal paper. It is a well known and widely accepted fact that requirements elicitation is a crucial step toward delivering successful software. In the context of emerging cloud systems, the question is whether and how the elicitation process differs from that used for traditional systems, and if the current methods suffice. The authors have prepared value-enabling questionnaire and interviewed 19 cloud providers to gain an in-depth understanding of the state of practice with regard to the adoption and implementation of existing elicitation methods. The results of this exploratory study show that, whereas a few cloud providers try to implement and adapt traditional methods, the large majority uses ad hoc approaches for identifying consumer needs. There are various causes for this situation, ranging from consumer reachability issues and previous failed attempts, to a complete lack of development strategy. The study suggests that only a small number of the current techniques can be applied successfully in cloud systems, hence showing a need to research new ways of supporting cloud providers. The primary contribution of this paper lies in revealing what elicitation methods are used by cloud providers and clarifying the challenges related to requirements elicitation posed by the cloud paradigm. Further on, the authors have identified some key features for cloud-specific elicitation methods.

Iliana Iankoulova and Maya Daneva [8] have exclusively focussed on the security requirements. There are many publications dealing with various types of security requirements in cloud computing but not all types have been explored in sufficient depth. It is also hard to understand which types of requirements have been under-researched and which are most investigated. This paper's goal is to provide a comprehensive and structured overview of cloud computing security requirements and solutions. The authors have carried out a systematic review and identified security requirements from previous publications that they have classified in nine subareas: access control, attack/harm detection, non-repudiation, integrity, security auditing, physical protection, privacy, recovery, and prosecution. The authors have found that

(i) the least researched subareas are non-repudiation, physical protection, recovery and prosecution, and that (ii) access control, integrity, and auditability are the most researched subareas.

There is an *executive's guide* [9] to the software-defined data center (SDDC) published by TechRepublic, USA. This document details and describes the nitty-gritty of next-generation cloud centers. The motivations, the key advantages, and the enabling tools and engines along with other relevant details are being neatly illustrated there. An SDDC is an integrated abstraction layer that defines a complete data center by means of a layer of software that presents the resources of the data center as pools of virtual and physical resources and allows their composition into arbitrary user-defined services. A modern SDDC deployment is defined by virtualized, software-defined resources that can be scaled up or down as required and can be deployed as needed in a number of distinct ways. There are three key components to the SDDC:

1. Software-defined computing
2. Software-defined networking
3. Software-defined storage

There are a several useful links in the portal [10] pointing to a number of resources on the software-defined cloud environments. The readers are encouraged to visit the portal to get the links for highly beneficial information on SDDCs.

5.3   Reflecting the Cloud Journey

The cloud journey is rigorously on the right track. The principal objective of the hugely popular cloud paradigm is to realize highly organized and optimized IT environments for enabling business automation, acceleration, and augmentation. Most of the enterprise IT environments across the globe are bloated, closed, inflexible, static, complex, and expensive. The brewing business and IT challenges are therefore how to make IT elastic, extensible, programmable, dynamic, modular, and cost-effective. Especially with the worldwide businesses are cutting down their IT budgets gradually year after year, the enterprise IT team has left with no other option other than to embark on a meticulous and measured journey to accomplish more with less through a host of pioneering and promising technological solutions. Organizations are clearly coming to the conclusion that business operations can run without any hitch and hurdle with less IT resources through effective commoditization, consolidation, centralization, compartmentalization (virtualization and containerization), federation, and rationalization of various IT solutions (servers, storage appliances, and networking components). IT operations also go through a variety of technologies-induced innovations and disruptions to bring in the desired rationalization and optimization. The acts of simplification and standardization for achieving IT industrialization are drawing a lot of attention these days. The various IT resources such as memory, disk storage, processing power, and I/O consumption are critically and cognitively monitored, measured and managed toward their utmost utilization. The pooling and sharing of IT solutions and services are being given the prime importance toward the strategic IT optimization.

Even with all the unprecedented advancements in the cloud landscape, there are opportunities and possibilities. The concept of software-defined clouds (SDCs) is, therefore, gaining a lot of accreditation these days. Product vendors, cloud service providers, system integrators, and other principal stakeholders are looking forward to having SDCs. The right and relevant technologies for the realization and sustenance of software-defined cloud environments are fast maturing and stabilizing, and hence, the days of SDCs are not too far away. This chapter is specially crafted for expressing and exposing all the appropriate details regarding the elicitation and engineering of various requirements (functional as well as nonfunctional).

5.4 Elucidating the Cloudification Process

The mesmerizing cloud paradigm has become the mainstream concept in IT today and its primary and ancillary technologies are flourishing. The cloudification movement has blossomed these days and most of the IT infrastructures and platforms along with business applications are being remedied to be cloud-ready in order to reap all the originally envisaged benefits of the cloud idea.

The virtualization technique has put in a firm and fabulous foundation for the runaway success of cloud computing. Especially server machines are being logically partitioned to carve out a few highly insulated virtual machines (VMs). Then there are a number of standards-compliant and industry-strength automation tools for resource provisioning, configuration, orchestration, monitoring, and management, software deployment and delivery. A 360° view of IT infrastructural components through an integrated dashboard is the new normal. Thus powerful tools play out a very interesting and inspiring role in making cloud pervasive, persuasive, and penetrative. Most of the manual activities associated with the establishment of IT infrastructures, software installation, IT administration and operation, IT services management and maintenance are being automated through a variety of technologies. The concept of DevOps is very enticing these days in order to ensure the incredible requirements of IT agility, adaptivity, and affordability. Automation through templates, patterns, and tools is becoming a common affair in IT lately and to substantially reduce human errors. The productivity of IT systems is being remarkably increased through various ways and means. The processes are synchronized to be lean yet efficient. Domain-specific languages (DSLs) are being brought into bring the required automation. Platforms are being readied to accelerate IT management, governance, and enhancement. There are standards, such as OpenStack and their optimal implementations in order to enforce resource portability, interoperability, accessibility, scalability, live-in migration, etc. That is, the distributed deployment of compute instances and storage appliances under the centralized management is the key differentiator for the prodigious success of cloud computing.

Technology Choice is Critical—There are several competent yet contrasting technologies in the IT space today and hence the selection of implementation technologies has to be strategically planned and carefully played out. Not only the technologies but also the methodologies need to be smartly carried out. In other words, the technology embarkation and usage have to be done with all seriousness and sagacity otherwise, even if the technologies chosen might be sound yet projects would not see the originally emphasized success. Further on, the history clearly says that many technologies emerged and disappeared from the scene without contributing anything substantial due to the lack of inherent strengths and sagacity. Very few technologies could survive and contribute copiously for a long time. Primarily the intrinsic complexity toward technologies' all-around utilization and the lack of revered innovations are being touted as the chief reasons for their abject and abysmal failure and the subsequent banishment into the thin air. Thus, the factors, such as the fitment/suitability, adaptability, sustainability, simplicity, and extensibility of technologies ought to be taken into serious consideration while deciding technologies and tools for enterprise-scale, transformational and mission-critical projects. The cloud technology is being positioned as the best-in-class technology in the engrossing IT domain with all the necessary wherewithal, power, and potential for handsomely and hurriedly contributing for the business disruption, innovation, and transformation needs. Precisely speaking, the cloud idea is the aggregation of several proven techniques and tools for realizing the most efficient, elegant, and elastic IT infrastructure for the ensuing knowledge era.

5.5   The IT Commoditization and Compartmentalization

The arrival of cloud concepts has brought in remarkable changes in the IT landscape that in turn lead in realizing big transitions in the delivery of business applications and services and in the solid enhancement of business flexibility, productivity, and sustainability. Formally cloud infrastructures are centralized, virtualized, automated, and shared IT infrastructures. The utilization rate of cloud infrastructures has gone up significantly. Still, there are dependencies curtailing the full usage of expensive IT resources. Employing the decoupling technique among various modules to decimate all kinds of constricting dependencies, more intensive and insightful process automation through orchestration and policy-based configuration, operation, management, delivery, and maintenance, attaching external knowledge bases are widely prescribed to achieve still more IT utilization to cut costs remarkably.

Lately, the aroma of commoditization and compartmentalization is picking up. These two are the most important ingredients of cloudification. Let us begin with the commoditization technique.

- The Commoditization of Compute Machines—The tried and time-tested abstraction aspect is being recommended for fulfilling the commoditization need. There is a technological maturity as far as physical/bare metal machines getting commoditized through partitioning. The server commoditization has reached a state of semblance and stability. Servers are virtualized, containerized, shared across many clients, publicly discovered and leveraged over any network, delivered as a service, billed for the appropriate usage, automatically provisioned, composed toward large-scale clusters, monitored, measured, and managed through tools, performance tuned, made policy-aware, automatically scaled up and out based on brewing user, data and processing needs, etc. In short, cloud servers are being made workloads-aware. However, that is not the case with networking and storage portions.
- The Commoditization of Networking Solutions—On the networking front, the propriety and expensive network switches, and routers and other networking solutions in any IT data centers and server farms are consciously commoditized through a kind of separation. That is, the control plane gets abstracted out and hence, the routers and switches have only the data forwarding plane. That means, there is less intelligence into these systems thereby the goal of commoditization of network elements is technologically enabled. The controlling intelligence embedded inside various networking solutions are adroitly segregated and is being separately developed and presented as a software controller. This transition makes routers and switches dumb as they lose out their costly intelligence. Also, this strategically sound segregation comes handy in interchanging one with another one from a different manufacturer. The vendor lock-in problem simply vanishes with the application of the widely dissected and deliberated abstraction concept. Now with the controlling stake is in pure software form, incorporating any kind of patching in addition to configuration and policy changes in the controlling module can be done quickly in a risk-free and rapid manner. With such a neat and nice abstraction procedure, routers, and switches are becoming commoditized entities. There is fresh business and technical advantages as the inflexible networking in present-day IT environments is steadily inching toward to gain the venerable and wholesome benefits of the commoditized networking.
- The Commoditization of Storage Appliances—Similar to the commoditization of networking components, all kinds of storage solutions are being commoditized. There are a number of important advantages with such transitions. In the subsequent sections, readers can find more intuitive and informative details on this crucial trait. Currently, commoditization is being realized through the proven abstraction technique.

Thus commoditization plays a very vital role in shaping up the cloud idea. For enhanced utilization of IT resources in an affordable fashion and for realizing software-defined cloud environments, the commoditization techniques are being given more thrusts these days.

The compartmentalization is being realized through the virtualization and containerization technologies. There are several comprehensive books on Docker-enabled containerization in the market and hence, we skip the details of containerization, which is incidentally being touted as the next best thing in the cloud era.

As indicated above, virtualization is one of the prime compartmentalization techniques. As widely accepted and articulated, virtualization has been in the forefront in realizing highly optimized, programmable, managed, and autonomic cloud environments. Virtualization leads to the accumulation of virtualized and software-defined IT resources, which are discoverable, network-accessible, critically assessable, interoperable, composable, elastic, easily manageable, individually maintainable, centrally monitored, and expertly leveraged. The IT capabilities are being given as a service and hence we often come across the word "*IT as a Service.*" There is a movement toward the enigma of granting every single IT resource as a service. With the continued availability of path-breaking technologies, resource provisioning is getting automated and this will result in a new concept of "resource as a service (RaaS)."

Bringing in the much-discoursed modularity in order to enable programmable IT infrastructures, extracting and centralizing all the embedded intelligence via robust and resilient software, distributed deployment, centralized management, and federation are being touted as the viable and venerable course of actions for attaining the originally envisaged success. That is, creating a dynamic pool of virtualized resources, allocating them on demand to accomplish their fullest utilization, charging them for the exact usage, putting unutilized resources back to the pool, monitoring, measuring, and managing resource performance, etc. are the hallmarks of next-generation IT infrastructures. Precisely speaking, IT infrastructures are being software-defined to bring in much-needed accessibility, consumability, malleability, elasticity, and extensibility.

On-demand IT has been the perpetual goal. All kinds of IT resources need to have the inherent capable of preemptively knowing of users' as well as applications' IT resource requirements and accordingly fulfill them without any instruction, interpretation, and involvement of human resources. IT resources need to be scaled up and down based on the changing needs so that the cost can be under control. That is, perfect provisioning of resources is the mandate. Overprovisioning raises up the pricing whereas underprovisioning is a cause for performance degradation worries. The cloud paradigm transparently leverages a number of software solutions and specialized tools in order to provide scalability of applications through resource elasticity. The expected dynamism in resource provisioning and de-provisioning has to become a core and concrete capability of clouds.

That is, providing right-sized IT resources (compute, storage, and networking) for all kinds of business software solutions is the need of the hour. Users increasingly expect their service providers' infrastructures to deliver these resources elastically in response to their changing needs. There is no cloud services infrastructure available today capable of simultaneously delivering scalability, flexibility, and high operational efficiency. The methodical virtualization of every component of a cloud center ultimately leads to software-defined environments.

5.6 The Emergence of Software-Defined Infrastructures (SDI)

We have discussed the commoditization tenet above. Now the buzzword of software-defined everything (SDE) is all over the place as a fulfilling mechanism for next-generation cloud environments. As widely accepted, software is penetrating into every tangible thing in order to bring in decisive and deterministic automation. Decision-enabling, activating, controlling, routing, switching, management, governance, and other associated policies and rules are being coded in software form in order to bring in the desired flexibilities in product installation, administration, configuration, customization, etc. In short, the behavior of any IT products (compute, storage, and networking) is being defined through software. Traditionally, all the right and relevant intelligence are embedded into IT systems. Now those insights are being detached from those systems and run in a separate appliance or in virtual machines or in bare metal servers. This detached controlling machine could work with multiple IT systems. It is easy and quick to bring in modifications to the policies in software controller rather on the firmware, which is embedded inside IT systems. Precisely speaking, deeper automation and software-based configuration, controlling, and operation of hardware resources are the principal enablers behind the longstanding vision of software-defined infrastructure (SDI).

A *software-defined infrastructure* is supposed to be aware and adaptive to the business needs and sentiments. Such infrastructures are automatically governed and managed according to the business changes. That is, the complex IT infrastructure management is automatically accomplished in consonance with the business direction and destination. Business goals are being literally programmed in and spelled in a software definition. The business policies, compliance and configuration requirements, and other critical requirements are etched in a software form. It is a combination of reusable and rapidly deployable patterns of expertise, recommended configurations, etc. in order to run businesses on the right path. There are orchestration templates and tools, cloud management platforms, such as OpenStack, automated software deployment solutions, configuration management, and workflow scheduling solutions, etc. in order to accelerate and automate resource provisioning, monitoring, management, and delivery needs. These solutions are able to absorb the above-mentioned software definitions and could deliver on them perfectly and precisely. The SDI automatically orchestrates all its resources to meet the varying workload requirements in near real-time. Infrastructures are being stuffed with real-time analytics through additional platforms, such as operational, log, performance, and security analytics.

As enunciated above, the SDI is a nimble, supple, highly optimized and orga-nized, and workload-aware. The agility gained out of SDI is bound to propagate and penetrate further to bring the much-needed business agility. The gap between the business expectations and the IT supplies gets closed down with the arrival of software-defined infrastructures. SDI comprises not only the virtualized servers but also virtualized storages and networks. There are a few other names for SDI. VMware calls it software-defined data centers (SDDCs), while others call it software-defined environments (SDEs), software-defined clouds (SDCs), cloud-enabled data centers (CeDCs). We can settle for the name *software defined clouds (SDCs)."*

5.7   The Major Building Blocks of Software-Defined Clouds (SDCs)

Software-defined infrastructures are the key ingredients of SDCs. That is, an SDC encompasses software-defined compute, storage, and networking components. The substantially matured server virtualization leads to the realization of software-defined compute machines. Highly intelligent hypervisors (alternatively recognized as virtual machine monitors (VMMs) act as the perfect software solution to take care of the creation, provisioning, de-provisioning, live-in migration, decommissioning of computing machines (virtual machines and bare metal servers), etc. Most of the servers across leading cloud centers are virtualized and it is clear that the server virtualization is reaching a state of stability. In a sense, the SDC is simply the logical extension of server virtualization. The server virtualization dramatically maximizes the deployment of computing power. Similarly, the SDC does the same for all of the resources needed to host an application, including storage, networking, and security.

In the past, provisioning a server machine to host an application took weeks of time. Today a VM can be provisioned in a few minutes. Even containers can be provisioned in a few seconds. That is the power of virtualization and containeriza-tion. This sort of speed and scale being made possible through virtualization plat-forms is being extended to other IT resources. That is, the whole cloud center is getting fully virtualized in order to tend towards the days of software-defined clouds.

In SDCs, all IT resources are virtualized so they can be automatically configured and provisioned and made ready to install applications without any human inter-vention, involvement, and interpretation. Applications can be operational in min-utes thereby the time to value has come down sharply. The IT cost gets reduced significantly. There are a number of noteworthy advancements in the field of server virtualization in the form of a host of automated tools, design, and deployment patterns, easy-to-use templates, etc. The cloud paradigm became a famous and fantastic approach for data center transformation and optimization because of the unprecedented success of server virtualization. This riveting success has since then penetrated into other important ingredients of data centers. IT resources are virtualized thereby are extremely elastic, remotely programmable, easily consumable, predictable, measurable, and manageable. With the comprehensive yet compact virtualization sweeping each and every component of data centers, the goals of distributed deployment of various resources but centrally monitored, measured, and managed is nearing the reality. Server virtualization has greatly improved data center operations, providing significant gains in performance, efficiency, and cost-effectiveness by enabling IT departments to consolidate and pool computing resources. Considering the strategic impacts of 100% virtualization, we would like to focus on network and storage virtualization methods in the sections to follow.

Network Virtualization—Server virtualization has played a pivotal and paramount role in cloud computing. Through server virtualization, the goals of on-demand and faster provisioning besides the flexible management of computing resources are readily and rewardingly fulfilled. Strictly speaking, server virtualization also includes the virtualization of network interfaces from the operating system (OS) point of view. However, it does not involve any virtualization of the networking solutions such as switches and routers. The crux of the network virtualization is to derive multiple isolated virtual networks from sharing the same physical network. This paradigm shift blesses virtual networks with truly differentiated capabilities to coexist on the same infrastructure and to bring forth several benefits toward data center automation and transformation. Further on, VMs across geographically distributed cloud centers can be connected to work together to achieve bigger and better things for businesses. These virtual networks can be crafted and deployed on demand and dynamically allocated for meeting differently expressed networking demands of different business applications. The functionalities of virtual networks are decisively varying. That is, virtual networks come handy in fulfilling not only the basic connectivity requirement but also are capable of getting tweaked to get heightened performance for specific workloads. The Fig. 5.1 vividly illustrates the difference between server and network virtualization.

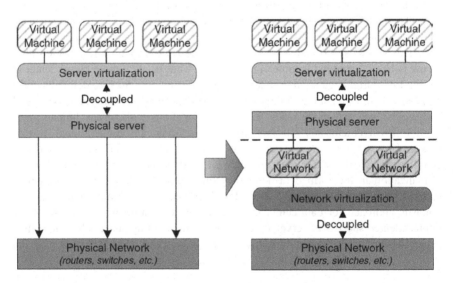

Fig. 5.1 Depicting the differences between server and network virtualization

5.8   Network Functions Virtualization (NFV)

There are several network functions, such as load balancing, firewalling, routing, switching, etc. in any IT environment. The idea is to bring forth the established virtualization capabilities into the networking arena so that we can have virtualized load balancing, firewalling, etc. The fast-emerging domain of network functions virtualization aims to transform the way that network operators and communication service providers architect and operate communication networks and their network services.

Network Functions Virtualization (NFV) is getting a lot of attention these days and network service providers have teamed up well to convince their product vendors to move away from special-purpose equipment and appliances toward software only solutions. These software solutions run on commodity servers, storages, and network elements, such as switches, routers, application delivery controllers (ADCs), etc. By embracing the NFV technology, communication, and cloud service providers could bring down their capital as well as operational costs significantly. The power consumption goes down, the heat dissipation too goes down sharply, the cost of employing expert resources for administering and operating special equipment is bound to come down significantly, and time-to-market for conceiving and concretizing newer and premium services. Due to its software-driven approach, NFV also allows service providers to achieve a much higher degree of operational automation and to simplify operational processes such as capacity planning, job scheduling, workload consolidation, VM placement, etc.

In an NFV environment, the prominent operational processes such as service deployment, on-demand allocation of network resources, such as bandwidth, failure detection, on-time recovery and software upgrades, can be easily programmed and executed in an automated fashion. This software-induced automation brings down the process time to minutes rather than weeks and months. There is no need for the operational team to personally and physically visit remote locations to install, configure, diagnose, and repair network solutions. Instead, all kinds of network components can be remotely monitored, measured, and managed.

In short, it is all about consolidating diverse network equipment types (firewall, switching, routing, ADC, EPC, etc.) onto industry-standard x86 servers using virtualization. The immediate and strategic benefits include the operational agility, which could empower business agility, autonomy, and affordability.

Software-Defined Networking (SDN)—The brewing technology trends indicate that networks and network management are bound to change once for all. Today's data centers (DCs) extensively use physical switches and appliances that haven't yet been virtualized and are statically and slowly provisioned. Further on, the current environment mandate for significant and certified expertise in operating each vendor's equipment. The networking solutions also lack an API ecosystem towards facilitating remote discovery and activation. In short, the current situation clearly points out the absence of programmable networks. It is quite difficult to bring in the expected automation (resource provisioning, scaling, etc.) on the currently running inflexible, monolithic and closed network and connectivity solutions. The result is the underutilization of expensive network equipment. Also, the cost of employing highly educated and experienced network administrators is definitely on the higher side. Thus besides bringing in a bevy of pragmatic yet frugal innovations in the networking arena, the expressed mandate is for substantially reducing the capital as well as the operational expenses being incurred by the traditional network architecture is clearly playing in the minds of technical professionals and business executives.

As the virtualization principle has been contributing immensely to server consolidation and optimization, the idea of network virtualization has picked up in the recent past. The virtualization aspect on the networking side takes a different route compared to the matured server virtualization. The extraction and centralization of network intelligence embedded inside all kinds of network appliances, such as routers, switches, etc. into a centralized controller aesthetically bring in a number of strategic advantages for data centers. The policy-setting, configuration, and maneuvering activities are being activated through software libraries that are modular, service-oriented, and centralized in a controller module and hence the new terminology "software-defined networking" (SDN) has blossomed and hugely popular. That is, instead of managing network assets separately using separate interfaces, they are controlled collectively through a comprehensive, easy-to-use, and fine-grained interface. The application programming interface (API) approach has the intrinsic capability of putting a stimulating and sustainable foundation for all kinds of IT resources and assets to be easily discoverable, accessible, usable and composable. Simplistically speaking, the aspect of hardware infrastructure programming is seeing the reality and thereby the remote manipulations and machinations of various IT resources are gaining momentum.

The control plane manages switch and routing tables while the forwarding plane actually performs the Layer 2 and 3 filtering, forwarding and routing. In short, SDN decouples the system that makes decisions about where traffic is sent (the control plane) from the underlying system that forwards traffic to the selected destination (the data plane). This well-intended segregation leads to a variety of innovations and inventions. Therefore, standards-compliant SDN controllers provide a widely adopted API ecosystem, which can be used to centrally control multiple devices in different layers. Such an abstracted and centralized approach offers many strategically significant improvements over traditional networking approaches. For instance, it becomes possible to completely decouple the network's control plane and its data plane. The control plane runs in a cluster setup and can configure all kinds of data plane switches and routers to support business expectations as demanded. That means data flow is regulated at the network level in an efficient manner. Data can be sent where it is needed or blocked if it is deemed a security threat.

A detached and deft software implementation of the configuration and controlling aspects of network elements also means that the existing policies can be refurbished whereas newer policies can be created and inserted on demand to enable all the associated network devices to behave in a situation-aware manner. As we all know, policy establishment and enforcement are the proven mechanisms to bring in the required versatility and vitality in network operations. If a particular application's flow unexpectedly needs more bandwidth, SDN controller proactively recognizes the brewing requirement in real time and accordingly reroute the data flow in the correct network path. Precisely speaking, the physical constraints are getting decimated through the software-defined networking. If a security appliance needs to be inserted between two tiers, it is easily accomplished without altering anything at the infrastructure level. Another interesting factor is the most recent phenomenon of "bring your own device (BYOD)." All kinds of employees' own devices can be automatically configured, accordingly authorized and made ready to access the enterprise's network anywhere anytime.

The Key Motivations for SDN—In the IT world, there are several trends mandating the immediate recognition and sagacious adoption of SDN. Cloud-enabled data centers (CeDCs) are being established in different cool locations across the globe to provide scores of orchestrated cloud services to worldwide businesses and individuals over the Internet on a subscription basis. Application and database servers besides integration middleware solutions are increasingly distributed whereas the governance and the management of distributed resources are being accomplished in a centralized manner to avail the much-needed single point of view (SPoV). Due to the hugeness of data centers, the data traffic therefore internally as well as externally is exploding these days. Flexible traffic management and ensuring "bandwidth on demand" are the principal requirements.

The consumerization of IT is another gripping trend. Enterprise users and executives are being increasingly assisted by a bevy of gadgets and gizmos such as smartphones, laptops, tablets, wearables etc. in their daily chores. As enunciated elsewhere, the *"Bring Your Own Device (BYOD)"* movement requires enterprise networks to inherently support policy-based adjustment, amenability, and amelioration to support users' devices dynamically. Big data analytics (BDA) has a telling effect on IT networks especially on data storage and transmission. The proprietary nature of network solutions from worldwide product vendors also plays a sickening role in traditional networks and hence there is a clarion call for bringing in necessary advancements in the network architecture. Programmable networks are therefore the viable and venerable answer to bring in the desired flexibility and optimization in highly complicated and cumbersome corporate networks. The structural limitations of conventional networks are being overcome with network programming. The growing complexity of traditional networks leads to stasis. That is, adding or releasing devices and incorporating network-related policies are really turning out to be a tough affair at the current setup.

As per the leading market watchers, researchers and analysts, SDN marks the largest business opportunity in the networking industry since its inception. Recent reports estimate the business impact tied to SDN could be as high as $35 billion by 2018, which represents nearly 40% of the overall networking industry. The future of networking will rely more and more on software, which will accelerate the pace of innovation incredibly for networks as it has in the computing and storage domains (explained below). SDN has all within to transform today's static and sick networks into calculative, competent and cognitive platforms with the intrinsic intelligence to anticipate and allocate resources dynamically. SDN brings up the scale to support enormous data centers and the virtualization needed to support workloads-optimized, converged, orchestrated, and highly automated cloud environments. With its many identified advantages and astonishing industry momentum, SDN is on the way to becoming the new norm and normal for not only for cloud but also corporate networks. With the next-generation hybrid and federated clouds, the role of SDN for fulfilling network function virtualization (NFV) is bound to shoot up.

In short, SDN is an emerging architecture that is agile, adaptive, cheaper, and ideal for network-intensive and dynamic applications. This architecture decouples the network control and forwarding functions (routing) enabling the network control to become directly programmable and the underlying infrastructure to be abstracted for applications and network services, which can treat the network as a logical or virtual entity.

The Need of SDN for the Cloud—Due to a number of enterprise-wide benefits, the adoption rates of cloud paradigm have been growing. However, the networking aspect of cloud environments has typically not kept pace with the rest of the architecture. There came a number of enhancements, such as network virtualization (NV), network function virtualization (NFV) and software-defined networking (SDN). SDN is definitely the comprehensive and futuristic paradigm. With the explosion of computing machines (both virtual machines as well as bare metal servers) in any cloud centers, the need for SDN is sharply felt across. Networks today are statically provisioned, with devices that are managed at a box-level scale and are underutilized. SDN enables end-to-end based network equipment provisioning, reducing the network provisioning time from days to minutes, and distributing flows more evenly across the fabric allowing for better utilization.

On summarizing, SDN is the definite game-changer for next-generation IT environments. SDN considerably eliminates network complexity in the midst of multiple and heterogeneous network elements. All kinds of network solutions are centrally configured and controlled to eliminate all kinds of dependencies-induced constrictions and to realize their full potential. Network capabilities are provisioned on demand at the optimal level to suit application requirements. In synchronization with other infrastructural models appropriately, the on-demand, instant-on, autonomic, and smart computing goals are easily delivered.

5.9 Accentuating Software-Defined Storage (SDS)

We are slowly yet steadily getting into the virtual world with the faster realization of the goals allied with the concept of virtual IT. The ensuing world is leaning toward the vision of anytime anywhere access to information and services. This projected transformation needs a lot of perceivable and paradigm shifts. Traditional data centers were designed to support specific workloads and users. This has resulted in siloed and heterogeneous storage solutions that are difficult to manage, provision newer resources to serve dynamic needs, and finally to scale out. The existing setup acts as a barrier for business innovations and value. Untangling this goes a long way in facilitating instant access to information and services.

Undoubtedly storage has been a prominent infrastructural module in data centers. There are different storage types and solutions in the market. In the recent past, the unprecedented growth of data generation, collection, processing, and storage clearly indicates the importance of producing and provisioning of better and bigger storage systems and services. Storage management is another important topic not to be sidestepped. We often read about big, fast, and even extreme data. Due to an array of technology-inspired processes and systems, the data size, scope, structure, and speed are on the climb. For example, digitization is an overwhelming worldwide trend and trick gripping every facet of human life thereby the digital data is everywhere and continues to grow at a stunning pace. Statisticians say that every day, approximately 15 petabytes of new data is being generated worldwide and the total amount of digital data doubles approximately every 2 years. The indisputable fact is that machine-generated data is larger compared to man-generated data. The expectation is that correspondingly there have to be copious innovations in order to cost-effectively accommodate and manage big data.

Software-defined storage (SDS) is a relatively new concept and its popularity is surging due to the abundant success attained in software-defined compute and networking areas. As explained above, SDS is a part and parcel of the vision behind the establishment and sustenance of software-defined data centers (SDDCs). With the virtualization concept penetrating and piercing through every tangible resource, the storage industry also gets inundated by that powerful trend. Software-defined storage is a kind of enterprise-class storage that uses a variety of commoditized and, therefore, cheap hardware with all the important storage and management functions being extricated and performed using an intelligent software controller. With such a clean separation, SDS delivers automated, policy-driven, and application-aware storage services through an orchestration of the underlining storage infrastructure. That is, we get a dynamic pool of virtual storage resources to be picked up dynamically and orchestrate them accordingly to be presented as an appropriate storage solution. Unutilised storage resources could be then incorporated into the pool for serving other requests. All kinds of constricting dependencies on storage solutions simply vanish with such storage virtualization. All storage modules are commoditized and hence the cost of storage is to go down with higher utilization. In a nutshell, storage virtualization enables storage scalability, replaceability, substitutability, and manageability.

An SDS solution remarkably increases the flexibility by enabling organizations to use nonproprietary standard hardware and, in many cases, leverage existing storage infrastructures as a part of their enterprise storage solution. Additionally, organizations can achieve massive scale with an SDS by adding heterogeneous hardware components as needed to increase capacity and improve performance in the solution. Automated, policy-driven management of SDS solutions helps drive cost and operational efficiencies. As an example, SDS manages important storage functions including information lifecycle management (ILM), disk caching, snapshots, replication, striping, and clustering. In a nutshell, these SDS capabilities enable you to put the right data in the right place, at the right time, with the right performance, and at the right cost automatically.

Unlike traditional storage systems such as SAN and NAS, SDS simplifies scale out with relatively inexpensive standard hardware, while continuing to manage storage as a single enterprise-class storage system. SDS typically refers to software that manages the capture, placement, protection, and retrieval of data. SDS is characterized by a separation of the storage hardware from the software that manages it. SDS is a key enabler modernizing traditional, monolithic, inflexible, costly, and closed data centers toward software-defined data centers that are highly extensible, open, and cost-effective. The promise of SDS is that separating the software from the hardware enables enterprises to make storage hardware purchase, deployment, and operation independent from concerns about over or underutilization or interoperability of storage resources.

Cloud-based Big Data Storage—Object storage is the recent phenomenon. Object-based storage systems use containers/buckets to store data known as objects in a flat address space instead of the hierarchical, directory-based file systems that are common in the block and file-based storage systems. Nonstructured and semi-structure data are encoded as objects and stored in containers. Typical data includes emails, pdf files, still and dynamic images, etc. Containers stores the associated metadata (date of creation, size, camera type, etc.) and the unique Object ID. The Object ID is stored in a database or application and is used to reference objects in one or more containers. The data in an object-based storage system is typically accessed using HTTP using a web browser or directly through an API like REST (representational state transfer). The flat address space in an object-based storage system enables simplicity and massive scalability. But the data in these systems cannot be modified and every refresh gets stored as a new object. Object-based storage is predominantly used by cloud services providers (CSPs) to archive and backup their customers' data.

Analysts estimate that more than 2 million terabytes (or 2 exabytes) of data are created every day. The range of applications that IT has to support today spans everything from social computing, big data analytics, mobile, enterprise, and embedded applications, etc. All the data for all those applications has got to be made available to mobile and wearable devices, and hence, data storage acquires an indispensable status. As per the main findings of Cisco's global IP traffic forecast, in 2016, global IP traffic will reach 1.1 zettabytes per year or 91.3 exabytes (1 billion gigabytes) per month, and by 2018, global IP traffic will reach 1.6 zettabytes per year or 131.9 exabytes per month. IDC has predicted that cloud storage capacity will exceed 7 Exabytes in 2014, driven by strong demand for agile and capex-friendly deployment models. Furthermore, IDC had estimated that by 2015, big data workloads will be one of the fastest-growing contributors to storage in the cloud. In conjunction with these trends, meeting service-level agreements (SLAs) for the agreed performance is a top IT concern. As a result, enterprises will increasingly turn to flash-based SDS solutions to accelerate the performance significantly to meet up emerging storage needs.

The Key Characteristics of Software-Defined Storage—SDS is characterized by several key architectural elements and capabilities that differentiate it from the traditional infrastructure.

Commodity Hardware—With the extraction and centralization of all the intelligence embedded in storage and its associated systems in a specially crafted software layer, all kinds of storage solutions are bound to become cheap, dumb, off-the-shelf, and hence, commoditized hardware elements. Not only the physical storage appliances but also all the interconnecting and intermediate fabric is to become commoditized. Such segregation goes a long way in centrally automating, activating, and adapting the full storage landscape.

Scale-Out Architecture—Any SDS setup ought to have the capability of ensuring fluid, flexible, and elastic configuration of storage resources through software. SDS facilitates the realization of storage as a dynamic pool of heterogeneous resources thereby the much-needed scale-out requirement can be easily met. The traditional architecture hinders the dynamic addition and release of storage resources due to the extreme dependency. For the software-defined cloud environments, storage scalability is essential to have a dynamic, highly optimized and virtual environment.

Resource Pooling—The available storage resources are pooled into a unified logical entity that can be managed centrally. The control plane provides the fine-grained visibility and the control to all available resources in the system.

Abstraction—Physical storage resources are increasingly virtualized and presented to the control plane, which can then configure and deliver them as tiered storage services.

Automation—The storage layer brings in extensive automation that enables it to deliver one-click and policy-based provisioning of storage resources. Administrators and users request storage resources in terms of application need (capacity, performance, and reliability) rather than storage configurations, such as RAID levels or physical location of drives. The system automatically configures and delivers storage as needed on the fly. It also monitors and reconfigures storage as required to continue to meet SLAs.

Programmability—In addition to the inbuilt automation, the storage system offers fine-grained visibility and control of underlying resources via rich APIs that allows administrators and third-party applications to integrate the control plane across storage, network and compute layers to deliver workflow automation. The real power of SDS lies in the ability to integrate it with other layers of the infrastructure to build end-to-end application-focused automation.

The maturity of SDS is to quicken the process of setting up and sustaining software-defined environments for the tactic as well as the strategic benefits of cloud service providers as well as the consumers at large.

5.10 The Key Benefits of Software-Defined Clouds (SDCs)

The new technologies have brought in highly discernible changes in how data centers are being operated to deliver both cloud-enabled and cloud-native applications as network services to worldwide subscribers. Here are a few important implications (business and technical) of SDCs.

The consolidation and centralization of commoditized, easy-to-use and maintain, and off-the-shelf server, storage, and network hardware solutions obviates the need for having highly specialized and expensive server, storage, and networking components in IT environments. This cloud-inspired transition brings down the capital as well as operational costs sharply. The most important aspect is the introduction and incorporation of a variety of policy-aware automated tools in order to quickly provision, deploy, deliver and manage IT systems. There are other mechanisms such as templates, patterns, and domain-specific languages for automated IT setup and sustenance. Hardware components and application workloads are being provided with well-intended APIs in order to enable remote monitoring, measurement, and management of each of them. The APIs facilitate the system interoperability. The direct fallout here is that we can arrive at highly agile, adaptive, and affordable IT environments. The utilization of hardware resources and applications goes up significantly through sharing and automation. Multiple tenants and users can avail the IT facility comfortably for a cheaper price. The cloud technologies and their smart leverage ultimately ensure the system elasticity, availability, and security along with application scalability.

Faster Time to Value—The notion of IT as a cost center is slowly disappearing and businesses across the globe have understood the strategic contributions of IT in ensuring the mandated business transformation. IT is being positioned as the most competitive differentiator for worldwide enterprises to be smartly steered in the right direction. However, there is an insistence for more with less as the IT budget is being consistently pruned every year. Thus enterprises started to embrace all kinds of proven and potential innovations and inventions in the IT space. That is, establishing data centers locally or acquiring the right and relevant IT capabilities from multiple cloud service providers (CSPs) are heavily simplified and accelerated. Further on, resource provisioning, application deployment, and service delivery are automated to a greater extent and hence it is easier and faster to realize the business value. In short, the IT agility being accrued through the cloud idea translates into business agility.

Affordable IT—By expertly pooling and assigning resources, the SDCs greatly maximize the utilization of the physical infrastructures. With enhanced utilization through automation and sharing, the cloud center brings down the IT costs remarkably while enhancing the business productivity. The operational costs come down due to tools-supported IT automation, augmentation, and acceleration.

Eliminating Vendor Lock-in—Today's data center features an amazing array of custom hardware for storage and networking requirements, such as routers, switches, firewall appliances, VPN concentrators, application delivery controllers (ADCs), storage controllers, intrusion detection, and prevention components. With the storage and network virtualization, the above functions are performed by software running on commodity x86 servers. Instead of being locked into the vendor's hardware, IT managers can buy commodity servers in quantity and use them for running the network and storage controlling software. With this transition, the perpetual vendor lock-in issue gets simply solved and surmounted. The modifying source code is quite easy and fast, policies can be established and enforced, software-based activation and acceleration of IT network and storage solutions are found to be simple, supple and smart, etc.

Less Human Intervention and Interpretation—SDCs are commoditized and compartmentalized through abstraction, virtualization and containerization mechanisms. As accentuated above, there are infrastructure management platforms, integration and orchestration engines, integrated brokerage services, configuration, deployment and delivery systems, service integration, and management solutions, etc. in order to bring in deeper and decisive automation. That is, hitherto manually performed tasks are getting automated through toolsets. This enablement sharply lessens the workloads of system, storage, and service administrators. All kinds of routine, redundant, and repetitive tasks are getting automated on a priority basis. The IT experts, therefore, can focus on their technical expertise to come up with a series of innovations and inventions that subsequently facilitate heightened business resiliency and robustness.

Hosting a range of Applications—All kinds of operational, transactional, and analytical workloads can be run on SDCs, which is emerging as the comprehensive yet compact and cognitive IT infrastructure to ensure business operations at the top speed, scale, and sagacity. Business continuity, backup and archival, data and disaster recovery, high availability, and fault-tolerance are the other critical requirements that can be easily fulfilled by SDCs. As we expectantly move into the era of big data, real-time analytics, mobility, cognitive computing, social networking, web-scale systems, the Internet of Things (IoT), artificial intelligence, deep learning, etc., the SDCs are bound to play a very stellar and sparkling role in the days ahead.

Distributed Deployment and Centralized Management—IT resources and business applications are being extremely distributed these days by giving considerations for cost, location, performance, risk, etc. However, a 360° view through a single pane of glass is required in order to have a firm and fine grip on each of the assets and applications. The centralized monitoring, measurement, and management is the most sought-after feature for any SDC. The highly synchronized and unified management of various data center resources is getting fulfilled through SDC capabilities.

Streamlined Resource Provisioning and Software Deployment—There are orchestration tools for systematic and swift provisioning of servers, storages, and network components. As each resource is blessed with RESTful or other APIs, the resource provisioning and management become simpler. Policies are the other important ingredient in SDCs in order to have intelligent operations. As we all know, there are several configuration management tools and in the recent past, with the culture of DevOps spreads widens overwhelmingly, there are automated software deployment solutions. Primarily orchestration platforms are for infrastructure, middleware, and database installation whereas software deployment tools take care of application installation.

Containerized Platforms and Workloads—With the unprecedented acceptance of Docker-enabled containerization and with the growing Docker ecosystem, there is a wave of containerization across the data centers and their operations. Packaged, home-grown, customized, and off-the-shelf business applications are being containerized, IT platforms, database systems, and middleware are getting containerized through the open-source Docker platform and IT infrastructures are increasingly presented as a dynamic pool of containers. Thus SDCs are the most appropriate one for containerized workloads and infrastructures.

Adaptive Networks—As inscribed above, SDC comprises network virtualization that in turn guarantees network function virtualization (NFC) and software-defined networking (SDN). Network bandwidth resource can be provisioned and provided on demand as per the application requirement. Managing networking solutions such as switches and routers remains a challenging assignment for data center operators. In an SDC, all network hardware in the data center is responsive to a centralized controlling authority, which automates network provisioning based on defined policies and rules. A dynamic pool of network resources comes handy in fulfilling any varying network requirements.

Software-defined Security—Cloud security has been a challenge for cloud center professionals. Hosting mission-critical applications and storing customer, confidential, and corporate information on cloud environments are still a risky affair. Software-defined security is emerging as the viable and venerable proposition for ensuring unbreakable and impenetrable security for IT assets, business workloads, and data sources. Policy-based management, the crux of software-defined security, is able to ensure the much-required compliance with security policies and principles. SDC is innately stuffed with software-defined security capabilities.

Green Computing—SDCs enhance resource utilization through workload consolidation and optimization, VM placement, workflow scheduling, dynamic capacity planning, and management. Energy-awareness is being insisted as the most vital parameter for SDCs. When the electricity consumption goes down, the heat dissipation too goes down remarkably thereby the goal of green and lean computing gets fulfilled. This results in environment sustainability through reduced release of harmful greenhouse gasses.

In summary, applications that once ran on static, monolithic and dedicated servers are today hosted in software-defined, policy-aware, consolidated, virtualized, automated, and shared IT environments that can be scaled and shaped to meet brewing demands dynamically. Resource allocation requests that took days and weeks to fulfill now can be accomplished in hours or even in minutes. Virtualization and containerization have empowered data center operations, enabling enterprises to deploy commoditized and compartmentalized servers, storages, and network solutions that can be readily pooled and allocated to fast-shifting application demand.

5.11 The Requirements Gathering Steps for Software-Defined Clouds

Typically there are two major types of requirements. The first one is functional requirements (FR). That is, what the system will provide to users. The second one is nonfunctional requirements (NFR), which is being termed as the quality of service (QoS) or quality of experience (QoE) attributes. That is, how the functionality is being provided to users. The key activities associated with the cloud idea are as follows

1. Enterprise-wide Assessment for cloud journey
2. IT Rationalization and Modernization and Cloud Migration
3. Cloud Compute, Storage, and Network Provisioning
4. Cloud-based Application Development, Deployment, and Delivery
5. Cloud Management and Security
6. Cloud Backup and Disaster Recovery

There are different requirements for different enterprises. There are several types of cloud environments ranging from private, public, hybrid, and community clouds. There are specific cloud options, such as storage, knowledge, sensor, device, science, and mobile clouds. As explained above, we are stepping into the era of software-defined clouds. There are not only cloud infrastructures but also cloud platforms and software. Thus the full IT stack is incrementally cloudified. It is predicted that most of the business workloads are to find their new residence in multiple clouds. There are technologically sound solutions in order to enable and establish a seamless connectivity between different and distributed cloud environments. Cloud integration, orchestration, and federation are being simplified and streamlined through a host of powerful tools.

Let us focus on software development and deployment in Cloud Environments.

Software applications can be fully or partially moved to clouds. That is, some components can be kept locally and the remaining ones can be migrated to remote clouds. Similarly, applications can be fully developed using cloud-based platforms (PaaS). There are greatly popular PaaS solutions, such as the open-source Cloud Foundry, IBM Bluemix, GE Predix, etc. Some application components can be replaced by highly advanced software from third-party software vendors. So there are a number of possibilities and opportunities. That is, with the arrival of local and remote IT environments and the seamless connectivity between them, there are more viable and venerable options for software developers, business executives, IT architects, etc. However, this emergence of two key and fast-expanding landscapes brings forth new set of concerns and challenges,

Modernization and migration of legacy/local/on-premise applications to empower them to run in cloud environments comfortably are an on-going activity. The legacy application is referred to as a tightly coupled and massive package of software and hardware solutions whose programming languages, technologies, and tools belong to the past decades. Then the multi-tier/distributed architecture applications, such as JEE and .NET came along and shone for some time. These days, everything is service-oriented, centric and software-defined. With clouds emerging as the most competitive and cognitive IT environment, the modernization, and migration of old as well as recent applications are initiated and subjected to a variety of investigations in order to clearly understand the risks, the opportunities, the challenges, the dependencies, etc. There are articulations by research scholars and scientists that there has to be a set of tasks to be performed as a part of cloud migration preparation. Some of them are being given below.

Organizational Analysis—An organization-wide business, offering, social, and financial details of the organization have to be studied and gathered. That is, the business strategy in place needs to be thoroughly understood and validated with the concerned executives and stakeholders in order to gain a deeper knowledge of the various business offerings, operations, and outputs. The business capabilities, processes, architecture, and other decision-enabling details need to be carefully collected and classified.

The Technical Team Analysis—On the other side, how the business expectations are being accomplished by the enterprise IT team. The application portfolio, the platform details, and the underlying infrastructure, the security and the governance mechanisms in place, etc. need to be consciously captured and verified with all the sincerity and sagacity. The team's technical capabilities ought to be analyzed deeply to gain whether the cloud migration can be fast-tracked in a hassle-free manner. The other prominent analyses need to be planned and performed in the direction of unearthing any other show-stoppers. There are several persistent questions such as whether application workloads getting modernized and migrated to the cloud can produce the same performance as they were giving in the local environment?

Requirement Analysis—Gathering requirement is an important aspect for attaining the intended success of cloud migration. There are certain distinct advantages cloud consumers and customers can easily and quickly avail and accrue out of the raging and mesmerizing cloud paradigm. Depending on the job at hand, the requirements need to be elicited from various stakeholders with all the care.

Cloud Opportunity Assessment—This is the first and foremost activity to understand whether the impending engagement is opening up a sustainable cloud opportunity through a few basic questions. The business strategy and planning details can throw the right and relevant information for cloud service providers to incisively and decisively to understand what sort of opportunity is in the hand. Accordingly, further queries and clarifications can be sent out to the prospective client to gather more decision-enabling information. The details such as what is the current IT state of the client, where the corporate wants to be in, how it wants to reach the planned state, etc. can definitely lead to zero down the exact route to be considered and capitalized. A template for cloud opportunity assessment is given below.

International deal (Yes/no)
Name of the customer/project code
Lead IMT country
Sector**
Sales connect #
Opportunity type (New logo/base growth)
Deal stage (NBIE/NBP/FIRM/BAFO)
Lead business unit
Contract duration (years)
Total TCV $M
Cloud TCV $M
Bid submission date
Customer down select date
Expected contract signature date
Expected boarding start date
Expected service start date (Go Live)
Competitor/s

Functional Requirements—Once it is clearly understood that the deal is all about the cloud-enablement, the cloud architects, consultants, and project executives have to prepare a set of questions to probe the client to extract as much as possible to formulate a comprehensive requirements document. Typically the functional requirements explain about the facilities, features, and functionalities to be provided to the client and its users by the cloud and communication service providers, security, and storage service providers, etc. Functional requirements are being documented and well-understood through the leverage of use case and scenario concepts. Use cases can be further subdivided into primary, secondary, and tertiary use cases. The traceability need gets easily accomplished through the classification of use cases. There are integrated development platforms enabling the requirements management.

Nonfunctional Requirements—This set of requirements is tough to implement. Still, there are pioneering technologies and tools to realize the quality of service (QoS) attributes/nonfunctional requirements (NFRs). Generally, there can be scalability of application workloads through elastic cloud infrastructures, high availability through clustering of resources, fault-tolerance through clustering and redundant systems, security through a bevy of mechanisms, algorithms, industry-strength standards, certifications, improved processes, practices, security patterns, etc. A sample template for capturing nonfunctional requirements is given below.

Non-functional requirements
Availability
Scalability
Security
Data privacy
Single sign-on
Vendor lock-in
Energy efficiency
Modifiability/maneuverability
Accessibility
Consumability
Simplicity and sustainability
Auditability

The non-functional requirements are relatively tough but mandatory to fulfill the agreed SLA comfortably to earn the customer delight. There are additional requirements for the cloud arena. For example, they are migration, integration, orchestration, BUR strategy, etc.

5.12   Integration Requirements

The customer's cloud requirements go beyond the originally anticipated. New public, as well as private cloud companies providing newer offerings, are emerging on the planet, and hence, the cloud integration needs are bound to grow consistently. The cloud solution architecture has to be prepared based on the current and future requirements.

Multiple public cloud service providers (CSPs)
Traditional IT
Private clouds
SaaS and PaaS providers
Identity management
Service management
Approval management
Configuration management DB
Management/billing
Security management providers

The cloud characteristics checklist

Technical area	Description
Architectural control	(a) Can the workload be relocated to a Cloud center? (b) Does the client require the architectural control? If yes, list the details in the deck (c) Mention the cloud deployment pattern: IaaS/PaaS/SaaS/Service Provider (SP)
Integration	(a) Is there integration with multiple clouds/legacy infrastructure/other cloud providers? (b) Is there a requirement of cloud broker services? Specify
Provisioning	(a) Does the client accept the standard SLO for provisioning services? (b) Who will operate the cloud portal for provisioning of services? (c) Is there a requirement of unified portal for multiple clouds and non-cloud environments? (d) Is there a requirement for a software-defined environment? (E.g.), SDN/NFV, SDS, etc. (e) Does the solution include business continuity services— HA/DR/Backup/Archive? Has client detailed on any specific failure scenarios to be considered for resiliency? If Yes, has a solution arrived for addressing the same?
Service catalog	(a) Who will develop and manage the custom service catalog? (b) Does the solution include reusable patterns? List details in the deck. (c) Mention the portal used for placement of the service catalog for unified operation
Metering and elasticity	(a) Does the client ask to pay only for the services consumed with high volatility of capacity requirements? If so, does the proposed solution outline the associated billing solution? (b) Does the proposal entail on-demand scaling of resources? If yes, explain the bursting requirements and modalities for scaling the solution
Migration	(a) What are the T&T/Migration elements that are part of the deal? E.g., DC relocation, System Migration, Server consolidation, Server refresh, Move existing images to the cloud, etc. (b) Mention which elements—New install/Rapid migration/Re-platforming. (c) If migration is in proposal scope, add the implementation details. Which team is engaged for the migration services?
Security and regulatory compliance	(a) Does the customer have any additional security or compliance requirements for Industry or Country specific? E.g., FDA, PCI etc. If yes, list the details. (b) Are there special security or compliance requirements that will drive the "local delivery" of the cloud service (e.g., Data residency/privacy, ITAR, NHS, specific design requirements etc.)? If yes, list the details. (c) Who is responsible for defining and delivering the security policies?

(continued)

(continued)

Technical area	Description
	(d) Which security services team is engaged to solution these additional/special security requirements?
Service Management (SM)	(a) For Private/Hybrid cloud, list the SM process and tools. Describe how it is realized in the solution. (b) Is there a requirement of the SM bridge—Cloud and non-cloud and Client managed environments? Describe the integration points with a list of tools. (c) Who is responsible for steady state delivery (d) Who will provide service management (Client)—(1) OS-and-below (2) MW&DB (3) Application? (e) Is the client willing to use global resources for managed services? (f) Does the client accept standard SLAs of the cloud service provider?
DevOps	(a) Is DevOps in scope for the cloud solution? What capabilities are being expected from the cloud—E.g., Release Management, Quality Management, Collaborative Life Cycle Management, etc. (b) Does the client have DevOps capability in their existing environment? Enumerate the tools and DevOps solution used in the existing environment in the deck. (c) Is the cloud solution expected to deliver DevOps by re-using the client's existing tooling landscape?

5.13　Conclusion

The aspect of IT optimization is continuously getting rapt and apt attention from technology leaders and luminaries across the globe. A number of generic, as well as specific improvisations, are being brought into make IT aware and adaptive. The cloud paradigm is being touted as the game-changer in empowering and elevating IT to the desired heights. There have been notable achievements in making IT being the core and cost-effective enabler of both personal as well as professional activities. There are definite improvements in business automation, acceleration, and augmentation. Still, there are opportunities and possibilities waiting for IT to move up further.

The pioneering virtualization technology is being taken to every kind of infrastructures, such as networking and storage to complete the IT ecosystem. The abstraction and decoupling techniques are lavishly utilized here in order to bring in the necessary malleability, extensibility, and serviceability. That is, all the configuration and operational functionalities hitherto embedded inside hardware components are now neatly identified, extracted, and centralized and implemented as a separate software controller. That is, the embedded intelligence is being developed now as a self-contained entity so that hardware components could be commoditized. Thus, the software-defined compute, networking, and storage disciplines have become the hot topic for discussion and dissertation. The journey of data centers (DCs) to software-defined environments (SDEs) is being pursued with vigor and rigor. In this chapter, we have primarily focused on the industry mechanism for capturing and collecting requirements details from clients.

References

1. Holger Schrödl and Stefan Wind, *"Requirements Engineering for Cloud Computing"* Journal of Communication and Computer 8 (*2011*)
2. Shreta Sharma and S. K. Pandey, *"Revisiting Requirements Elicitation Techniques"*, International Journal of Computer Applications, August *2013*
3. Lori MacVittie, a white paper on the title *"Controlling the Cloud: Requirements for Cloud Computing"* *2014*
4. Bhaskar Prasad Rimal, Admela Jukan, Dimitrios Katsaros and Yves Goeleven, *"Architectural Requirements for Cloud Computing Systems: An Enterprise Cloud Approach"* J Grid Computing (*2011*)
5. Critical Requirements for Cloud Applications—How to Recognize Cloud Providers and Applications that Deliver Real Value, a white paper by Workday *2014*
6. Pericles Loucopoulos, Requirements Engineering for Emergent Application Software J. Cordeiro et al. (Eds.): ICEIS *2012*, LNBIP, Springer-Verlag Berlin Heidelberg *2013*
7. Todoran, Irina; Seyff, Norbert; Glinz, Martin, How cloud providers elicit consumer requirements: An exploratory study of nineteen companies, In: 21st IEEE International Requirements Engineering Conference, Rio de Janeiro, Brazil, *15 July 2013*
8. Iliana Iankoulova & Maya Daneva, *"Cloud Computing Security Requirements: a Systematic Review"* Sixth International Conference on Research Challenges in Information Science (RCIS), *2012*
9. Executive's guide to the software defined data center, published by TechRepublic, USA, *2016*
10. www.peterindia.net An Information Technology Portal

Part II
Requirements Specification for Service and Cloud Computing

Chapter 6
Formal Modeling of Enterprise Cloud Bus System: A High Level Petri-Net Based Approach

Gitosree Khan, Sabnam Sengupta and Anirban Sarkar

Abstract The chapter focuses on an abstraction layer of SaaS architecture for multi-agent-based inter-cloud environment, called Enterprise Cloud Bus System (*ECBS*) to conceptualize the different behavioral facets of such system in service and cloud computing paradigm. The model is formalized using a set of high level Petri-net-based formal constructs called High Level Enterprise Cloud Bus Petri-net (*HECBP*) with varieties of relationship types among participation cloud bus components. It is accompanied with a rich set of Petri-net graphical notations and those are used to specify the effective toward modeling interactions among the heterogeneous agent present within the cloud bus of *ECBS* at conceptual level design of multi cloud system. The approach facilitates to analyze the behavioral features of inter-cloud architecture and modeled its dynamics at the conceptual level. The *HECBP* is also able to ensure correctness and performance of the system at design time by focusing on meeting the increasing demands for distributed software as a service and making the system functionality more scalable, configurable, and shareable. This chapter includes modeling of several behavioral facets like, fairness, boundedness, liveliness, safeness, etc., in a dead lock-free way. Moreover, this chapter provides a discussion on state-space analysis study, which further validates the theoretical analysis of *HECBP* model and future research scope in this area.

Keywords Cloud computing · Service-Oriented architecture · Enterprise cloud bus system · Multi-agent system · Behavioral analysis · High-level enterprise cloud bus Petri-net · Colored Petri-net · Boundedness · Liveness · Reachability · Safeness

G. Khan (✉) · S. Sengupta
B.P. Poddar Institute of Management & Technology, Kolkata, India
e-mail: khan.gitosree@gmail.com

S. Sengupta
e-mail: sabnam_sg@yahoo.com

A. Sarkar
National Institute of Technology, Durgapur, India
e-mail: sarkar.anirban@gmail.com

© Springer International Publishing AG 2017
M. Ramachandran and Z. Mahmood (eds.), *Requirements Engineering for Service and Cloud Computing*, DOI 10.1007/978-3-319-51310-2_6

6.1 Introduction

Service-Oriented Computing is an emerging computing paradigm for requirement engineering that utilizes service as software as the basic constructs to support the development of rapid and low-cost composition of software applications. Growing complexity of Enterprise Software applications and increasing numbers of clouds throughout the world have increased the challenges for Software as a Service (*SaaS*) in the recent trends of requirement engineering. Therefore, the need for Cloud computing has evolved as an important key areas of software engineering research and practices, which identifies functional requirements from users along with its benefits of cost effectiveness and global access. By providing on demand access of services to a distributed environment of computing resources in a dynamically scaled and virtualized manner, agent-based cloud computing offers compelling advantages in cost, speed, and efficiency.

Along with the emergence of Service-Oriented Architecture (*SOA*), Software as a Service (*SaaS*) architecture has emerged as a new and evolving domain in cloud computing based on the request/reply design paradigm for Enterprise Software applications. Existing ESB-based systems cannot address the complexity of Enterprise Software applications due to the increase in number of clouds and their services. Therefore, service registration, discovery, scheduling, and composition of services are facing complexity and performances issues nowadays. To address such issues, our previous work focused mainly on the abstraction layer of Software as a service architecture, called Enterprise Cloud Bus (*ECB*) [1, 2]. It models the services, agents, and their interconnections for all the locations for satisfying the client needs. This approach is introduced by integrating agent technology in *ECB* framework.

Modeling and design methodologies for multi-agent-based cloud infrastructure have not taken a shape as yet. One of the most challenging domains is to model various agent-based architecture of *SOA* in distributed cloud computing environment to make the *SOA* system modeling more reliable and robust. Petri-net-based approach is a relevant choice for modeling and analyzing the dynamic behavior of such agent-based cloud architecture. However, those approaches are also less expressive for large systems like inter-cloud architecture comprising of multiple agents and components. Therefore, colored Petri-net (*CPN*) tool is an efficient tool that is used for constructing and analyzing such multi-cloud system. Many of the research works reveals about the behavioral analysis of multi-cloud architecture using colored Petri-net. But they are some shortcomings toward analysis of dynamics multi-cloud architecture. Therefore, high-level Petri-net-based approach is the most suitable one toward analysis of dynamics of such system.

With the aforementioned objectives, the chapter has been organized in six sections. In Sect. 6.2, previous researches related to modeling of multi-agent-based inter-cloud architecture have been summarized with major emphasis on the models based on cloud computing paradigm. In Sect. 6.3, the concept and importance of multi-agent-based inter-cloud architecture (*ECBS*) have been summarized with major emphasis on the conceptual definition followed by several issues that need to be handled related to multi-agent system (*MAS*) paradigm. This section also introduced the comprehensive summary of key benefits and challenges of *ECBS* in *MAS* environment. In Sect. 6.4, a novel approach on formal modeling and analysis of *ECBS* using high-level Petri-net has been summarized. Here, the colored Petri-net (*CPN*) tool is used for simulation of the model so that this chapter will serve as a valuable source of information for academia and industry related to multi-agent inter-cloud model-based testing especially for cloud-based enterprise applications in optimizing the performance, cost, elasticity, flexibility, high reliability, and availability of the computing resources. This section also includes the analysis of the behavioral features like, safeness, boundedness, liveliness etc., of the model in order to ensure the system dynamics such as high accuracy of system functionality, operational design of system flexibility that comprises of autonomous agents and system components, automation of cloud services and quantitative measurement of system processes, performance, and scalability. In Sect. 6.5, the future research directions of *ECBS* framework using high-level Petri-net have been summarized. Finally, the chapter has been concluded in Sect. 6.6 with identification of key areas of research in the domain of requirements engineering for service and multi-agent-based inter-cloud architecture.

6.2   Related Research

Nowadays, Enterprise Software applications are growing in complexity; therefore, there is a rapid increase in number of clouds and their web services. Thus, the demand for cloud computing technology toward organizations is growing exponentially. Lots of researchers discuss over the architectural design of cloud computing and its applications. Among them, [1–3] focus on the architectural driven environment for cloud applications that facilitates monitoring cloud services, composing, and adapting cloud applications. Putting a distributed cloud-based integration and deploying in Enterprise Service Bus with service-oriented architecture processes help enterprises to integrate their process over the cloud, and achieve scalable cloud enabled business applications with greater efficiency. In such cloud computing environment, the competition between service providers has led to a large number of cloud-based solutions that offered to consumers. Moreover, in the work proposed in [4] the author focuses on "vision, challenges and architectural elements of inter-cloud environments." The ability to run and manage the multi-cloud system [5, 6] is a challenge for preventing interoperability and increase scalability, elasticity, and autonomy of multi-cloud system.

The work in [7, 8] provides a "classification of the state-of-the-art of cloud solutions and discusses the dynamic provisioning, deployment and adaptation of dynamic multi-cloud behavior systems which aim at addressing the issues."

The author in [9] proposes a new approach for dynamic autonomous resource management in cloud computing. Several researches, in last decade, have devised conceptual model for multi-agent-oriented system [10, 11]. But, all these approaches have got certain limitations to exhibit the dynamism of internal behavior of the system which comprises of heterogeneous set of components.

In this context, analysis of such dynamics is a major challenge. For the purpose, proper mechanism is required to conceptualize and study the behavioral properties of multi-cloud architecture. Agent-based architecture is most acceptable paradigm to handle the dynamicity of such large-scale system like inter-cloud architecture. The works proposed in [12] have discussed about the structural definition of agent-based hybrid multi-cloud applications. In [13], the structural modeling of agent-based multi-cloud architecture called enterprise cloud bus (ECB) has been discussed followed by service discovery mechanism [14, 15] that helps to identify services during run time. The structural components of ECB system is modeled using UML 2.0 [16]. But, the UML modeling is not suitable for rigorous analysis of multi-cloud dynamics due to its semi-formal nature.

Petri-net [17]-based approach is an obvious choice for modeling and analyzing the dynamic behavior of agent-based inter-cloud architecture. In [18], the modeling and analysis of agent-oriented system has been stated by the author. However, those approaches are also less expressive for large systems like Inter-cloud architecture comprising of multiple agents and components. Moreover, in [19], the conceptual model of multi-cloud architecture called Enterprise Cloud Bus Petri-net (ECBP) has been proposed in MAS domain and modeled its dynamics using Petri-net-based tool called PIPE. For detail reference of modeling and analysis of multi-agent system refer [26–29] of additional reading section.

Therefore, colored Petri-net (CPN) Tools is an efficient tool [20] that is used for constructing and analyzing such multi-cloud system. The work in [21] reveals about the behavioral analysis of Multi-cloud architecture using colored Petri-net. But there are some shortcomings toward analysis of dynamics multi-cloud architecture. Therefore, high-level Petri-net-based approach [22, 23] is most suitable toward analysis of dynamics of such system and accepted as standard. In Sect. 6.3 of this chapter, the ECBS has been stated formally and modeled using high-level Petri-net-based approach, called high-level enterprise cloud bus Petri-net (HECBP) which further used to represent the behavioral analysis of ECBS using high-level Petri-net tool, called CPN.

Moreover, the concepts of HECBP have been implemented using a simulation tool called CPN for further validation of the architecture. The proposed approach is effective toward modeling interactions among the heterogeneous agent present within the cloud bus of ECBS. The model is also effective toward analysis of the key behavioral features of multi-cloud architecture. For detail reference on High-level Petri-net according to ISO/IEC [43] standard of additional reading section.

6.3 Multi-agent Based Inter-cloud Architecture (ECBS)

Enterprise Cloud Bus System (ECBS) [13, 14], describes a high-level abstraction layer of SaaS architecture in Inter-cloud environment, where different clouds interacts and collaborates through cloud agent from various locations in order to publish and/or subscribe their services. The detailed set of building blocks in the context of ECBS has been described as follows:

6.3.1 Building Blocks of ECBS

This subsection describes briefly the building blocks of the ECBS:

(a) **Client**: Client is the end-users/actor in multi-cloud environment; here, the *CLIENT* placed the service request through Provider Agent (*PA*).
(b) **Provider Agent (PA)**: *PA* invokes the request from the *CLIENT* and schedules the required services.
(c) **Cloud Universal Description Discovery and Integration (CUDDI)**: *CUDDI* is the extended meta-service registry where *PA* published the client request.
(d) **Enterprise Service Bus (ESB)**: *ESB* is the Bus where the services are published.
(e) **Cloud Enterprise Service Bus (CESB)**: *CESB* is extension of *ESB* that enhance the ESB's to register their services for single cloud environment.
(f) **Cloud Agent (CA)**: *CA* is deployed for collecting various services from different cloud service providers based on various locations, context, etc.
(g) **Hierarchical Universal Description Discovery and Integration (HUDDI)**: *HUDDI* is the extended meta-service registry of *CESB's* in *ECB* where *CA* published the services.
(h) **Scheduling Agent (SA)**: *SA* is deployed in ECB to configure, discover, and schedule the cloud services as per Quality of Service (QoS) parameters.
(i) **MAPPER**: *MAPPER* is the one of the Cloud Bus component where service mapping is done as per Client request.
(j) **LOGGER**: *LOGGER* holds the mapped services before dispatching.
(k) **RES**: *RES* are the resources shared by the cloud bus.

6.3.2 Formalization of ECBS

This chapter is the extensions of ESB's with formal approach toward analysis of dynamics of Inter-cloud architecture. The CloudBus *(CB)* is the set of agents and components (as refer in earlier section) of Enterprise Cloud Bus System. The structural representation of the CloudBus *(CB)* is defined as:

$$CB \rightarrow CLIENT \land PA \land CUDDI \land ESB \land CESB \land CA \land HUDDI \\ \land SA \land MAPPER \land LOGGER \land RES \tag{6.1}$$

A multi-cloud environment *Multi-CloudEnv* is that where components of *CB* will work using the following four tuples. It can be defined as

$$Multi - CloudEnv = \{Res, Actor, CB, Relation\} \tag{6.2}$$

In the given cloud environment, *Res* is the set of cloud resource, *Actors* are clients of the cloud environment, *CB* are the set of autonomous cloud bus entities with prespecified functions and *Relation* is the set of semantic association and interactions among the cloud bus entities.

In the context of multi-cloud environment, the cloud bus (*CB*) will comprehend the occurrences of events automatically and response toward the environment with a set of cloud services. Moreover, any agent or component of *CB* acts on the cloud resources Res and is able to function over the web services provided by various cloud service providers. Further, enterprise cloud bus system (*ECBS*) can be defined as

ECBS = *{CB, COL, I}*, where, *CB* is the set of Cloud Bus.

Thus, $\forall i$, $CB_i \in CB$. COL_{ij} identifies a set of Collaborations among CB_i and CB_j.

Thus, $\forall_{i, j}$, $COL_{ij} \in COL$, if $i \neq j$. The set I_{ij} determines the interaction path between any two Cloud Bus CB_i and CB_j in the *ECBS* system.

Thus, $\forall_{i, j}$, $I_{ij} \in I$, if $i \neq j$.

6.3.3 Conceptualization of ECBS in MAS Architecture

Conceptual architecture of *ECBS* defines a set of building blocks and their inter relationship to conceptualize the environmental elements, agents, related events, collaborations, and interactions among the *CESBs*. A conceptual architecture of *ECBS* deals with high-level representation of the agent and other component in inter-cloud architecture.

This section describes the conceptual definition of multi-agent-based enterprise cloud Bus system (*ECBS*). The concept of *MAS* definition in the proposed architecture is an extension of research works in [10, 11]. Agent-based system is the de facto paradigm to handle the dynamicity of multi-cloud architecture like *ECBS*.

The dynamicity of CB_i in the environment multi-CloudEnv are handled using three agents {*PA, SA, CA*} and other components relevant to single cloud architecture as described in Fig. 6.1.

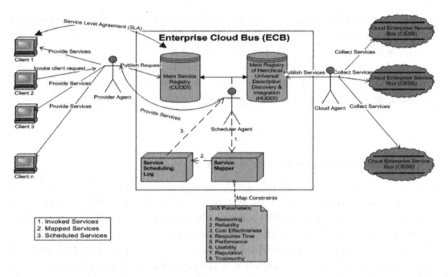

Fig. 6.1 Enterprise Cloud Bus System Framework (ECBS)

Formally, the dynamic model of any CloudBus *(CB_i)* can be defined as

$$CB_i = \{CA_i, PA_i, SA_i\} \qquad (6.3)$$

Each of the agents within the CloudBus *(CB_i)* will be invoked if the following conditions hold by different agents;

$ESB \wedge CESB \wedge HUDDI \wedge RES \rightarrow CA_i$

$CLIENT \wedge CUDDI \wedge RES \rightarrow PA_i$

$CUDDI \wedge HUDDI \wedge MAPPER \wedge LOGGER \wedge SCHEDULER \wedge RES \rightarrow SA_i$

Since, agents are the architectural basis of the *(CB_i)*. Therefore, the dynamic model of the *CB_i* is a multi-agent-based system and can be defined as a multi-agent definition as follows:

(a) *CB_i*. $A_i = [Role, E, C, R, PR, K, S, I]$ where, $A_i \in \{PA_i, SA_i, CA_i\}$.

(b) Each agent in the *CB_i* plays a specific set of Roles in the environment Multi-CloudEnv; *E* is the set of cloud events which occur during various states of the cloud service transitions.

(c) *C* is a set of environmental conditions in cloud to be checked in order to response on some event in Cloud Bus;

(d) *R* is a set of environmental cloud resources that are available and necessary for fulfillment of the goal of agents within the *CB_i*. Formally, *(R ⊂ Res)*;

(e) *PR* is the properties of agents within the *CB_i* which will hold the state of the cloud bus and also will maintain the state of the cloud resources *R* on which the agents is acting;

(f) K is the set of information that forms the main knowledge base. Initially, it comprises of the states of available cloud resources that the agents within the CB_i will use to response on some event. The K can be update dynamically.

(g) S is the set of cloud services that the agents within the CB_i can provide and conceptualize this will determine the capability of the cloud bus components;

(h) I is a set of interactions between the agents reside inside the CB_i.

6.3.4 Structural Analysis of ECBS

The structural analysis of the *ECBS* system can be studied using Eqs. (6.1), (6.2), and (6.3) as described in the earlier section. The analysis states that, CA_i exists if for all i, *ESB, CESB, HUDDI,* and *RES* components exist. This also implies that for any *CloudBus i*, any change in CA_i will affect the state of *ESB, CESB, HUDDI,* and *RES* only. Similarly, PA_i exists if for all *i, CLIENT, CUDDI,* and *RES* exist, which implies for any *CloudBus i*, any change in PA_i will affect the state of *CLIENT, CUDDI,* and *RES* only. Similarly, SA_i exists if for all *i, CUDDI, HUDDI, MAPPER, LOGGER, SCHEDULER,* and *RES* components exist. That implies, for any *CloudBus i*, change in SA_i will affect the state of *CUDDI, HUDDI, MAPPER, LOGGER, SCHEDULER,* and *RES* only.

6.3.5 ECBS Elements in MAS Architecture

The roles, events and related services along with the respective resources, properties, and knowledge base of each agents present within the CBi is summarized in Table 6.1.

Provider Agent (*PA*) starts working with the minimal set of knowledge of the environment to render the request, service, and resource token.

The set of Roles R as shown in Table 6.1 to be played by the *PA* will be

R = {*R0: Request Transmitter, R1: Service Provider, R2: Request Provider, R3: Resource Seeker}.

The set of Events E for the *PA* will be

E = {*E0: Request Transmitted, E1: Service Provided, E2: Request Registered, E3: Resource used & Released}.

These set of events will be performed after satisfying possible environmental constraints C.

The set of Resources RS = {*RS1: Web Service, RS2: Registries, RS3: Timestamp}.

Now the *PA* will use several properties to hold the state of the resources and the states of itself.

Table 6.1 Role collaboration templates of ECBS

Role	Event	Service	Cloud bus component
Agent: Provider Agent (PA)			
R0: Request Transmitter R1: Service Provider	E0: Request Transmitted E1: Service Provided	S0: SendRequest S1: ProvideService	CLIENT
R2: Request Provider	E2: Request Registered	S2: GetRequest	CUDDI
R3: Resource Seeker	E3: Resource used & Released	S3: GetResource S4: ReleseResource	RES
Agent: Cloud Agent (CA)			
R4: Service Invoker	E4: Service Invoked	S5: InvokeService	ESB
R5: Service Collector	E5: Service Collected	S6: CollectService	CESB
R6: Service Transmitter	E6: Service Registered	S7: PublishService	HUDDI
R7: Resource Seeker	E7: Resource used & Released	S8: GetResource S9: ReleseResource	RES
Agent: Scheduler Agent (SA)			
R8: Service Matcher	E8: Service Matched	S10: MatchService	CUDDI
R9: Service Seeker	E9: Service Discovered	S11:GetService	HUDDI
R10: Service Mapper	E10: Service Mapped	S12: MapService	MAPPER
R11: Service Scheduler	E11: Service Scheduled	S13: ScheduleService	SCHEDULER
R12: Service Logger	E12: Service Logged	S14: LogService	LOGGER
R13: Service Dispatcher	E13: Service Dispatched	S15: DispatchService	CLIENT
R14: Resource Seeker	E14: Resource used & Released	S16: GetResource S17: ReleseResource	RES

Hence, the set of Properties $PR = \{PR1:$ *status of Request type which can have various statuses, PR2: status of Service type which can have various statuses, PR3: status of Resource type which can have various statuses*$\}$.

PA starts working with the minimal set of knowledge of the environment to render the services. The knowledge base can be updated dynamically once the component of CloudBus starts working.

The set of knowledge

$K = \{K0:$ *Details of request, K1: Details of service, K2: Details of resource*$\}$.

With all these and with some defined set of Interactions I *PA* will be performing some services

$S = \{S0:$ *SendRequest, S1: ProvideService, S2: GetRequest, S3: GetResource, S4: ReleaseResource*$\}$.

Cloud Agent (*CA*) starts working with the minimal set of knowledge of the environment to render the request, service, and resource token.

The set of Roles R as shown in Table 6.2 to be played by the *CA* will be

$R = \{R4:$ *Service Invoker, R5: Service Collector, R6: Service Transmitter, R7: Resource Seeker*$\}$.

The set of events E for the CA will be

$E = \{E4:$ *Service Invoked, E5: Service Collected, E6: Service Registered, E7: Resource used & released}.*

These set of events will be performed after satisfying possible environmental constraints C.

The set of Resources $RS = \{RS1:$ *Web Service, RS2: Registries, RS3: Timestamp}.*

Now the CA will use several properties to hold the state of the resources and the states of itself.

Hence the set of Properties $PR = \{PR4:$ *status of Request type which can have various statuses, PR5: status of Service type which can have various statuses, PR6: status of Resource type which can have various statuses}.*

CA starts working with the minimal set of knowledge of the environment to render the services. The knowledge base can be updated dynamically once the component of CloudBus starts working.

The set of knowledge $K = \{K3:$ *Details of request, K4: Details of service, K5: Details of resource}.*

With all these and with some defined set of Interactions I, CA will be performing some services $S = \{S5:$ *InvokeService, S6: CollectService, S7: PublishService, S8: GetResource, S9: ReleaseResource}.*

Scheduling Agent (SA) starts working with the minimal set of knowledge of the environment to render the request, service, and resource token.

The set of Roles R as shown in Table 6.2 to be played by the SA will be $R = \{R8:$ *Service Matcher, R9: Service Seeker, R10: Service Mapper, R11: Service Scheduler, R12: Service Scheduler; R13: Service Logger; R14: Resource Seeker}.*

The set of Events E for the SA will be $E = \{E8:$ *Service Matched, E9: Service Discovered, E10: Service Mapped, E11: Service Scheduled, E12: Service Logged, E13: Service Dispatched E14: Resource used & Released}.*

Table 6.2 Mapping from ECBS Conceptual Architecture to HECBP

S. No.	Concepts in ECBS	Concept in HECBP
1	Properties, Knowledge, Cloud Services, Roles of (CLIENT, PA, CUDDI, ESB, CESB, CA, HUDDI, SA, MAPPER, LOGGER, RES)	Place, P
2	Events of (CLIENT, PA, CUDDI, ESB, CESB, CA, HUDDI, SA, MAPPER, LOGGER, RES)	Transitions, T
3	Collaborations among (PA, SA, CA)	Set of Arcs, N
4	Elements of (PA, SA, CA)	Color Function, C_f
5	Constraints of (PA, SA, CA)	Guard Function, G
6	Interactions among (PA, SA, CA)	Arc Expression, Exp
7	Users	Initialization Function, I

These set of events will be performed after satisfying possible environmental constraints *C*.

The set of Resources *RS* = *{RS1: Web Service, RS2: Registries, RS3: Timestamp}*.

Now the *SA* will use several properties to hold the state of the resources and the states of itself.

Hence the set of Properties *PR* = *{PR7: status of Request type which can have various statuses, PR8: status of Service type which can have various statuses, PR9: status of Resource type which can have various statuses}*.

SA starts working with the minimal set of knowledge of the environment to render the services. The knowledge base can be updated dynamically once the component of CloudBus starts working.

The set of knowledge *K* = *{K6: Details of request, K7: Details of service, K8: Details of resource}*. With all these and with some defined set of Interactions I *SA* will be performing some services *S* = *{S10: MatchService, S11: GetService, S12: MapService, S13: ScheduleService, S14: LogService, S15: DispatchService, S16: GetResource, S17: ReleaseResource}*.

6.4 High-Level Enterprise Cloud Bus Petri-Net (HECBP)

High-level enterprise cloud bus petri-nets *(HECBP)* is a graphical representation of *ECBS* system that allows visualization and analysis of the system dynamics and behavioral properties such as safeness, boundedness and liveliness, etc. Proposed *HECBP* is a colored petri-net *(CPN)*-based approach, which is capable to represent the interactions between agents and other cloud components within the cloud bus.

6.4.1 Definition: High-Level Enterprise Cloud Bus Petri-Net (HECBP)

A high-level Petri-net is defined as a directed bipartite graph that has two types of nodes namely places and transitions). The arcs are connector between these nodes that represents state of a transition of the given node. Hence in a formal manner, high-level enterprise cloud bus Petri-net, *HECBP*, is defined by the 8—tuples as follows:

(a) The various elements of the proposed *HECBP* is defined as
Σ = [*Color set for Request token, Color set for Service token, Color set for Resource token*]. C_f *is the color function where,* C_{re} = *{blue for request}*, C_s = *{red for service}*, C_r = *{black for resource token}*.

(b) Σ is a finite set of non-empty types, also called color sets. The set of types determines the data values of CloudBus components, resources, the operations, and functions that can be used in the net expressions (i.e., arc expressions, guards, and initialization expressions), Σ = . $C_s \cup C_{re} \cup C_r \cup G \cup E \cup I$;

(c) P is a non-empty finite set of places. It comprises of all the CloudBus and their environmental resources. Formally, $P = CB_i \cup Res$

(d) The *CloudBus* place contains all the agents, components, tokens, except events, of a *CloudBus*. T is a non-empty finite set of transitions include all events of any CloudBus, CB_i, and resource R_i, along with the interactions between the cloud bus present in environment,

(e) $T = CB_i \cup I \cup Ri*e_i$. N is the finite set of arcs that map into a pair where the first element is the source node and the second the destination node. The two nodes have to be of different kind. If we say that $T = e \cup I$, then it can be said that, $T \times P (CB_i) \cup (P \times T)$, because arc from T to P is not valid in case of resources. Hence,

(f) C_f is the color function. Formally, $C_f \rightarrow C_b$. The color function C_f maps each place P to a type C. C is the color function for CloudBus that contains various tokens of different colors. $C_b = C_s \cup C_{re} \cup C_r$, C_s is the color function for Service token, C_{re}, is the color function for Request token, and Cr is the color function for resources. Different tokens have different colors in the Net.

(g) The guard function G maps each transition, T into a Boolean expression where all variables have types that belongs to Σ. The arc expression function E maps each arc 'a' in the node function into an expression of type $C_f (p)$. This means that each arc expression must evaluate to multi-set over the type of the adjacent place, P. The initialization function I map each place, P, into a closed expression which must be of type $C_f (p)$.

An agent within the cloud bus of *ECBS* consists of various elements namely roles, events, constraints, resources, properties, knowledge, interactions, and services which together make *ECBS* successful to achieve the prespecified goal. Mapping of conceptual architectural to *HECBP* has been summarized in Table 6.2. A component will request for a resource. Once a resource is allocated to a component, it will hold the resource until the next transition is fired from that place.

Formally, $CB_i \rightarrow RES$. The graphical notation of place and transition are represented as usual notation of *CPN* and those are Circle and Bar, respectively.

6.4.2 HECBP Elements: Places and Transitions

The details of the places P, transitions T, and tokens t have been illustrated in Tables 6.3 and 6.4, respectively. In this Petri-net model, three types of tokens are considered. They are service, request, and resource token. In Table 6.4, the color set value of token is considered as $(P = 1; Q = 2; R = 3)$ to distinguish among themselves.

6.5 Analysis of ECBS Based on HECBP

High-level enterprise cloud bus Petri-net (*HECBP*) is a suitable tool to model the behavior of *ECBS* system. Moreover, several features of dynamic system like, occurrence of finite number of events, deadlock free operations, achievement of goals through firing of events, etc., can be analyzed through the analysis of *HECBP* properties like, safeness, boundedness, liveness, reachability, etc. Further, the *HECBP*-based analysis will give detail insight about the internal behavior of the system.

6.5.1 HECBP-Based Analysis of ECBS

Figure 6.2 shows the *HECBP* net of the *ECBS* system.

The process starts from a place *P0* which is the client and after a transition *T0* will reach a place *P10* from, which the scheduling agent of place *P7* will collect the service for delivering it to the client. The process continues further on and we finally arrive at the place *P7*. Serially as the transitions occur, the process moves on to each of the places as explained in the tables.

The place *P11* is the places for the resources *RS1*, *RS2*, and *RS3*, respectively. All the cloud bus components will request each of the resources as and when required and once the transition is fired will release it updating the knowledge base. In this system, a place have token such that $Token \rightarrow C \times K \times PR \times S \times R \times I$. From the *HECBP* net, the corresponding reachability graph is obtained and shown in Fig. 6.3.

Some of the crucial behavioral properties have been analyzed using the *HECBP* model. They are as follows:

Table 6.3 Places and transitions with its descriptions based on Table 6.1

Places	Component of places	Transitions	Events
P0	Client	T0	E0, E3
P1	PA	T1	E2, E3
P2	CUDDI	T2	E4, E7
P3	ESB	T3	E5, E7
P4	CESB	T4	E6, E7
P5	CA	T5	E8, E14
P6	HUDDI	T6	E9, E14
P7	SA	T7	E10, E14
P8	MAPPER	T8	E11, E14
P9	SCHEDULER	T9	E12, E14
P10	LOGGER	T10	E13, E14
P11	RESOURCE (RS1, RS2, RS3) RS1: Web Services; RS2: Registries; RS3: Timestamp	T11	E1, E14

Table 6.4 Token and its descriptions

Places	Token	Description of tokens	token parameters	Color set value of token
P0	t0	Request	Sent	1
P1	t0	Request	Provide	1
P2	t0	Request	Register	1
	t1	Service	Register	2
P3	t1	Service	Published	2
P4	t1	Service	Provide	2
P5	t1	Service	Collect	2
P6	t1	Service	Register	2
P7	t1	Service	Register	2
	t1	Service	Dispatch	2
P8	t1	Service	Discover	2
P9	t1	Service	Map	2
P10	t1	Service	Schedule	2
P11	t2	Resource	Request	3
	t2	Resource	Release	3

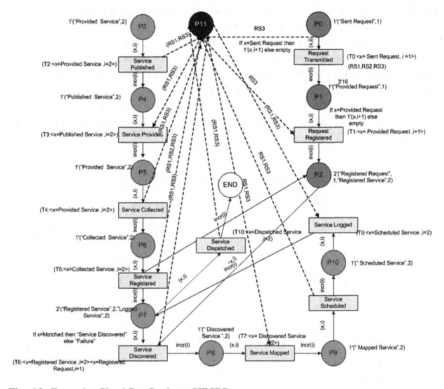

Fig. 6.2 Enterprise Cloud Bus Petri-net (HECBP)

(a) **Reachability**: Reachability property is a fundamental artifact for analyzing the dynamic properties of any *MAS*-based cloud architecture. However in this section, it has been established from Fig. 6.3 that all the markings in the *HECBP* net are reachable starting from any marking in the net, and hence reachability exists. This guarantee that the *HECBP* net modeled the *ECBS* that will meet the prespecified goal;

(b) **Home Properties**: A marking in the *HECBP* is said to be a home marking if it is a home space. It tells us about the markings to which it is possible to return. In the proposed *HECBP*, the initial marking *M0* is a Home marking and a marking $M0 \in M$ and a set of markings $Z \subseteq M$ be given as: *M0* is a home marking if: $\forall M' \in [M0] > : M \in [M']$; *and Z is a home space if:* $\forall M' \in [M0] > : Z \cap [M'] > \neq \varnothing$]. In this context, *M* is a home marking if $\{M\}$ is a home space.

(c) **Boundedness**: The boundedness property states that after considering all reachable markings, the number, and type of tokens a place may hold in the net. It can be concluded after analyzing the *HECBP* net that there is no unboundedness at any stage once the process starts and goes from place *P0* to *P7* via *P10*, and thus the boundedness of the *HECBP* net is guaranteed and safe;

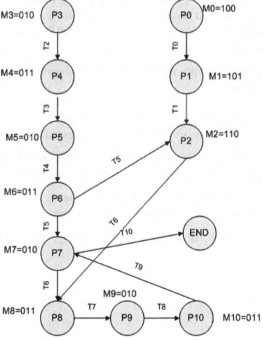

M (Weight)	P (Request)	Q (Service)	R (Resource)
M0	1	0	0
M1	1	0	1
M2	1	1	0
M3	0	1	0
M4	0	1	1
M5	0	1	0
M6	0	1	1
M7	0	1	0
M8	0	1	1
M9	0	1	0
M10	0	1	1

Fig. 6.3 Reachability graph corresponding to Fig. 6.2

(d) **Liveness**: The liveness properties of a *HECBP* model shows a continuous dynamic operation of the proposed net model and ensure that the system is live once transitions are fired. In the proposed *HECBP* net as the component of the cloud bus process starts from *P0* transitions *T0* through *T10* are fired and place *P7* is reached. The net is continuous and hence the liveness property is ensured. Thus the proposed net is live:

(e) **Fairness**: The net *HECBP* is said to be bounded-fairness because at a time single transition are fired. It can also be termed as unconditional fairness because every transition appears infinitely in a firing sequence. Here the net is *B-Fair*.

(f) **Safeness**: Any place in a *HECBP* is declared as safe, as the number of tokens at that place is either 0 or 1 and there is no deadlock present in the net. Also all the place in the concerned net is safe therefore the net as a whole is declared safe.

6.5.2 Simulation of HECBP

There are various tools to analyze Petri-net-based system behavior. In this section, *HECBP* Net is analyzed using *CPN* tools to study the behavioral aspects of multi-cloud architecture defined using proposed conceptual model of *ECBS*. Here, three colors sets namely red, blue, and black have been used to depict the three types of tokens namely request, service and resource token, respectively.

Thus few restrictions have been imposed for simulation of the *HECBP* Net using *CPN* simulation and are summarized as follows:

(a) Before and after Transitions the data types of Tokens have to be same or else transition will not be fired/enabled;

(b) During the simulation process, at any point of time, it cannot be clearly expressed which component is enabled after a Transition is fired;

(c) Multitoken pass can be done but only one single token is being passed at a time.

The advantage of using the concept of high-level Petri-net along with CPN simulator tool for analyzing dynamism of multi-cloud behavior is as follows:

(a) The dynamic component (*PA, CA, SA*) can be handled with ease.

(b) Validation of the agent-based multi-cloud architecture can be done.

The declarations for the generated *HECBP* net corresponding to Fig. 6.2 can be expressed as:

```
colset BOOL=bool;
colset INTINF = intinf;
colset TIME = time;
colset REAL = real;
colset UNIT = unit timed;
```

```
colset STR = with S timed;
var x: STR;
colset IN = with P | Q | R timed;
var i: IN;
colset PRO = product STR * IN timed;
var p: PRO;
```

6.5.3 HECBP Simulation Through CPN Tool

In this section, the *HECBP* net is simulated using *CPN* tool and the corresponding simulation results before and after transitions are shown. Figure 6.4 shows the simulation before resource is allocated to the place *P0*. Once the requested resources are allocated to the place *P0*, the relevant transition *T0* is fired and place *P1* is reached. The resources are held up by the place *P1*. They will be returned to the resource pool and only then the next transition will be enabled.

Figure 6.5 shows the simulation after resource is allocated to the required place. Once these resources are released, as shown in Fig. 6.6, next transition *T1* will be enabled and place *P2* will be reached. Hence, it can be seen that the resources are allocated and released dynamically. It is dynamicity of the cloud bus component properties that is very smoothly analyzed with the help of the proposed model.

This process of resource allocation and returning back after use will further continue and finally the place P10 is reached from which the token moves to the P7 from where the service are delivered. Once the simulation is executed, the place P0 will send a request signal for the resources RS3. The request signal is accepted. It can be seen that the net is waiting for transition T0 to be enabled.

Once the resources are allocated it can be seen in Fig. 6.4 that transition T0 is fired. Place P1 is reached and resources are now within place P1. The next transition T1 will be enabled only when the held up resources are freed or released. Further in Fig. 6.7 the service are discovered once the request token in *CUDDI* are matched with the service token by the *SA*. Thereafter, service is dispatched and resources are released.

6.5.4 State Space Analysis

Simulation conducts a finite number of executions of the model that is being analyzed. On conducting state-space analysis of the model, the simulation tool usually generates a state-space report that provides the details of the state space and standard behavioral properties of the proposed net. The report also gives a clear idea about the beat upper and lower bounds. After simulation of the HECBP net, the corresponding state-space reports are shown.

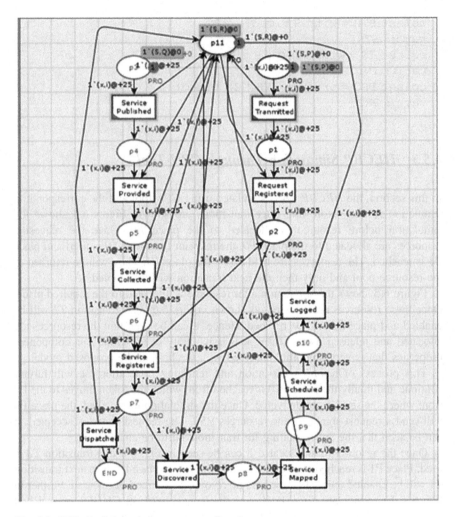

Fig. 6.4 CPN simulation—before resource allocation

The state-space report (Fig. 6.8) gives the state-space statistics. The boundedness properties are shown in Fig. 6.9 that tells the number of tokens a place may hold after considering all reachable markings. The best upper and lower bounds results are shown in Fig. 6.10. These reports exhibit that the proposed HECBP is bounded and safe.

The next part of the state-space report, Fig. 6.11, specifies the home properties, liveness properties, and fairness properties. In Home properties, the home marking is node *P12*. Even in liveness property node *P12* is regarded as dead because the execution of the process ends at that node namely *P12* from which scheduling agent (*P7*) takes the services and dispatch it to the end-users.

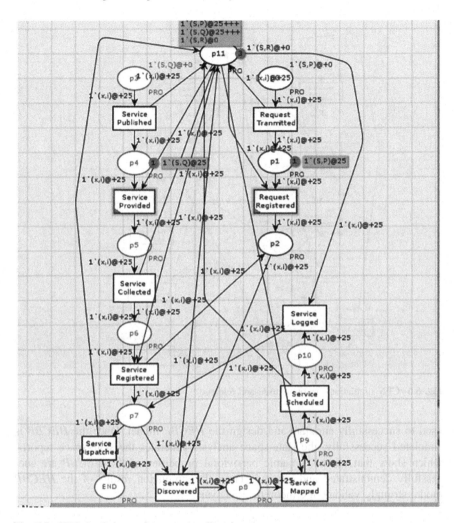

Fig. 6.5 CPN simulation—after resource allocation

It is observed that the *HECBP* net is live because there are no dead transitions. Similarly, we proved that the fairness property also is true since there is no infinite occurrence sequence in the net.

In the theoretical analysis, a discussion was made on *ECBS* and further using formalized and conceptual definition of the proposed ECBS a corresponding *HECBP* model and its reachability graph was obtained and through which basic dynamic behavioral properties like liveness, safeness, and boundedness were proved.

It was observed and established from the theoretical analysis that all the dynamic properties of *ECBS* were true for the *ECBS* considered as discussion. CPN tool was

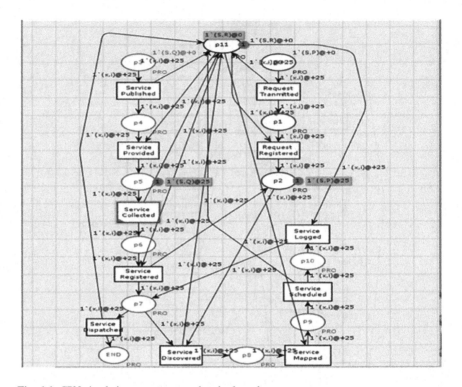

Fig. 6.6 CPN simulation—resource used and released

used to successfully simulate and design the *HECBP* model. Once the *HECBP* is simulated successfully, the state-space analysis generates the state-space reports, which show that all the dynamic behavioral properties of the *HECBP* are successfully demonstrated and verified. Thus, the simulation results of the *HECBP* model strongly validate the theoretical analysis.

6.6 Future Research Directions

With the advancement of requirements engineering for service and cloud computing technology, the enterprise software application has become a prevailing domain focusing on integration and automatic composition of web services over distributed cloud computing environment. Various potential research works still exist for the field of requirements engineering for service and cloud computing system design. In this context, several research proposals are there in literatures for meeting the increasing demands for distributed software as a service and making the software more accessible, scalable, configurable (over a distributed large-scale global network), and shareable. Several researchers have work on conceptual model

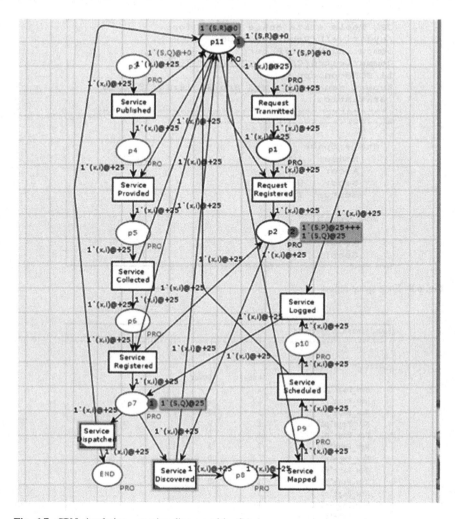

Fig. 6.7 CPN simulation—service discovered by SA

of multi-cloud architecture in order to address the problem of interoperability, dynamic provisioning, deployment, and adaptation of dynamic multi-cloud behavior systems.

Many of those approaches [24, 25] are also included with MAS based mechanism in inter-cloud architecture that exhibits the dynamism of internal behavior of the system. To handle the dynamicity of such large-scale computing system, Petri-net-based approach [26] are a most acceptable formal modeling tool nowadays. However, none of those proposals are still accepted as standard. Most of those proposals [27–29] are varied in the modeling and analyzing the dynamic behavior of the system. So, more researches are required toward the conceptual level

```
CPN Tools state space report for:
/cygdrive/D/Pendrivecloud
computing/Paper/Paper
Communicated/CPN/cp/CPNM@02-07-
14/ECB@cpn.cpn
Report generated: Wed Sep 30 14:15:38 2015
 Statistics
-----------------------------------------------
-----------------------------

    State Space
        Nodes:  12
        Arcs:   11
        Secs:   0
        Status: Full

    Scc Graph
        Nodes:  12
        Arcs:   11
        Secs:   0
```

Fig. 6.8 State space report

```
Boundedness Properties
------------------------------------------------------------------------

    Best Integer Bounds
                                Upper       Lower
        New_Page'END 1          1           0
        New_Page'P9 1           1           0
        New_Page'p0 1           1           0
        New_Page'p10 1          1           0
        New_Page'p1 1           1           0
        New_Page'p11 1          3           1
        New_Page'p2 1           2           0
        New_Page'p3 1           1           0
        New_Page'p4 1           1           0
        New_Page'p5 1           1           0
        New_Page'p6 1           1           0
        New_Page'p7 1           1           0
        New_Page'p8 1           1           0
```

Fig. 6.9 Boundedness properties

modeling using high-level Petri-net-based approach of MAS-based multi-cloud architecture with the aim of realizing the facets of such system more comprehensively.

Besides this, several other research directions are as follows:

(a) **Modeling and Analysis of Service Composition Pattern through HECBP Net**: Multi-agent system [24–27] based Inter-cloud architecture [33–36] requires formal modeling and analysis of service selection and composition

```
Best Upper Multi-set Bounds
        New_Page'END 1              1`(S,Q)
        New_Page'P9 1               1`(S,Q)
        New_Page'p0 1               1`(S,P)
        New_Page'p10 1              1`(S,Q)
        New_Page'p1 1               1`(S,P)
        New_Page'p11 1             1`(S,P)++
1`(S,Q)++
1`(S,R)
        New_Page'p2 1              1`(S,P)++
1`(S,Q)
        New_Page'p3 1               1`(S,Q)
        New_Page'p4 1               1`(S,Q)
        New_Page'p5 1               1`(S,Q)
        New_Page'p6 1               1`(S,Q)
        New_Page'p7 1               1`(S,Q)
        New_Page'p8 1               1`(S,Q)

    Best Lower Multi-set Bounds
        New_Page'END 1              empty
        New_Page'P9 1               empty
        New_Page'p0 1               empty
        New_Page'p10 1              empty
        New_Page'p1 1               empty
        New_Page'p11 1             1`(S,R)
        New_Page'p2 1               empty
        New_Page'p3 1               empty
        New_Page'p4 1               empty
        New_Page'p5 1               empty
        New_Page'p6 1               empty
        New_Page'p7 1               empty
        New_Page'p8 1               empty
```

Fig. 6.10 Upper and lower bounds

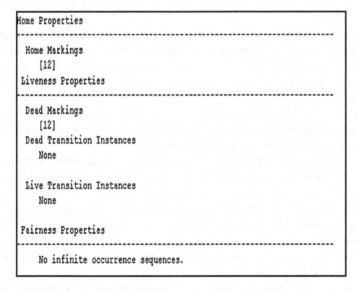

```
Home Properties
-----------------------------------------------------------

  Home Markings
     [12]
Liveness Properties
-----------------------------------------------------------

  Dead Markings
     [12]
  Dead Transition Instances
     None


  Live Transition Instances
     None


Fairness Properties
-----------------------------------------------------------
     No infinite occurrence sequences.
```

Fig. 6.11 State space report of other behavioral properties

pattern. Verification and validation of service composition in Inter-cloud architecture using high-level Petri-net is shown in [30–32]. The Petri-net-based approach of modeling and analysis of multi-agent system is addressed in [37–42]. But the proposed approach is less expressive when compared to the high-level Petri-net-based approach, which is applicable across majorly on large complex system. Moreover, many researchers have expressed the modeling and analysis using high-level Petri-net approach in [43–45]. Many of the research work are done using color Petri-net (CPN) tool that is further used for constructing and analyzing such multi-cloud system [46]. The work in [47, 48] reveals about the behavioral analysis of multi-cloud architecture using colored Petri-net. However, it does not have any formal background of service selection and composition design pattern. However, both of these proposals lack from the validation with the standard like high-level Petri-net. On the other hand, [49] is a formal methods of integrating high-level Petri-net with Z notation. Both [48, 49] are rigorously formal modeling techniques.

The *HECBP* model can be taken as a standard modeling, to select, compose, identify, and schedule the services during its run time. Service selection and composition modeling of such system is one of the challenging research issues. Compare to the existing methodologies of such modeling, very few methodologies are there based on high-level Petri-net-based approach. Using *HECBP* approach is one of the most prevailing modeling techniques to identify, define, visualize, and specify customer's requirements for formal modeling of service composition pattern. The approach will help to cater the state-of-the-art research and practice relating to requirements engineering for service and cloud computing.

More research directions are required toward the tools and techniques for customer's service requirement engineering and modeling and analysis of service composition pattern in the latest research field. The *HECBP* approach helps to cater the functional requirements of service composition for the needs of the industry. The analysis of the Service Composition Framework can be done based on the degree of heterogeneity of the cloud services. Further, the service composition analysis can be proposed under various categories like service choreography, orchestration, and hybrid.

(b) **Verification and Validation of the Service Composition Pattern using HECBP Net**: Few of the proposed models [50, 51] validate the composition pattern through high-level Petri-net-based approach using tools like CPN. The author in the papers [52, 53] has expressed the verification strategy for web services composition using enhanced stacked automata model. Thus for validation of the service composition pattern of any cloud-based system, the *HECBP* model can be used to validate properties like correctness and completeness of the system pattern.

Further, the verification and validation can be done by comparing the simulation result of *HECBP* model with the theoretical results. Large research initiative is required toward the validation of the composition pattern in cloud computing environment using high-level Petri-net.

(c) **Service Scheduling using HECBP Net based on QoS parameters**: Very few proposals like [54–56] supported the modeling of service scheduling on quality of service (*QoS*) parameters using high-level Petri-net based approach. Moreover, those proposals also are at cognitive levels. Further, researches are required toward the proposal of scheduling approach using high-level Petri-net model for further validation. The *HECBP* Net can be used for scheduling of cloud services as per user's requirement. This approach helps to identify the functional requirement and enhance the requirement engineering for service and cloud computing paradigm.

(d) **Quality Evaluations of HECBP model**: It is necessary to evaluate the quality metrics of the *HECBP* model of Inter-cloud Architecture. According to research work [57–59], the quality evaluation techniques along with metrics, such as operability, performance, scalability, reliability, etc., are measured based on customer's requirement toward service in cloud computing domain. These concepts are abstracts and cannot be measured directly, but the evaluation of quality metrics at early design phase is important to make the cloud bus system more robust and reliable in service requirements engineering field.

In view of this, there is a necessity of a set of objective quality measurements at the conceptual level design phase of such system to assess the quality metrics in terms of reusability. The scalability factor of the *HECBP* model is another issue that also influences the quality of early design of such system. Thus research effort is required to devise suitable framework for quality evaluation of *MAS*-based Inter-cloud architecture.

6.7 Conclusion

Multi-agent-based Inter-cloud Architecture represents dynamic and complex system that consists of heterogeneous autonomous entities (*CA, PA, SA*) and other components present inside the cloud bus. These autonomous entities play some specific roles in the system. Based on these roles, collaborations occur between the participating agents and components in *ECBS*. Participating agents in *ECBS* are proactive and thus interact with the multi-cloud environment or with some other components in the system.

Thus, collaborations and interactions among the participating agents and components are the key factors to design the dynamics of *ECBS* effectively. As a result of this dynamicity of *ECBS*, there are various behavioral properties exist in the *ECBS*. For the purpose, a high-level enterprise cloud bus Petri-net (*HECBP*) has been proposed to analyze and model the behavioral aspects of *ECBS* using a tool called *CPN* for service requirements engineering. The dynamicity of the proposed enterprise cloud bus system benefits the enterprise applications in optimizing the performance, cost, elasticity, flexibility, high reliability, and availability of the computing resource.

Further, a set of mapping rules have been described for representing the elements of the proposed conceptual framework of the *ECBS* into the *HECBP* net. The proposed requirements engineering methods capture the state-of-the-art research and practice relating to requirements engineering for service and cloud computing. The key benefits of using the proposed mechanism are the capability to represent study and analyze the interactions among the multiple agents present inside the Cloud Bus. Using *HECBP* concepts and corresponding reachability graph, the behavioral properties of an *ECBS* like reachability, safeness, Boundedness, liveness can be analyzed formally. Moreover, simulation of the proposed *HECBP* with *CPN* tool and generated results strongly validate the proposed claims. Interested readers may refer the Additional References for further concepts on cloud-based system and service-oriented system

Future work includes the quality analysis of *ECBS* dynamics from the proposed concepts of *HECBP*. Development of a dedicated simulation tool for the conceptual architecture of *ECBS* and *HECBP* is also a prime future objective. Simulation with *CPN* tool and generated state-space reports will strongly validate the said claims. We hope that this chapter will provide a comprehensive source of information regarding formalization of *MAS*-based inter-cloud architecture and study its behavioral properties.

References

1. Alexandros, K., Aggelos, G., Vassilis, S., Lampros K., Magdalinos P., Antoniou E., Politopoulou Z., 2014, A cloud-based Farm Management System: Architecture and implementation, In Journal Computers and Electronics in Agriculture, Vol no. 100, pp. 168–179.
2. Ardagna, D., Nitto, E.D., Casale, E., P, P., Mohagheghi, S., Mosser, P., Matthews, A., Gericke, C., Balligny, F. D., Nechifor, C.S, C, Sheridan., 2012. MODACLOUDS, A Model-Driven Approach for the Design and Execution of Applications on Multiple Clouds, International Workshop on Modelling in Software Engineering. pp. 50–56.
3. Brandtzæg, E., M. Parastoo, Mosser, E., 2012. Towards a Domain-Specific Language to Deploy Applications in the Clouds, 3rd International Conference on Cloud Computing, GRIDs, and Virtualization. IARIA, pp. 213–218.
4. Cavalcante, E., 2013. Architecture Driven Engineering of Cloud-Based Applications, IFIP/Springer-Verlag, Germany, Vol no. (22). pp. 175–180.
5. Divyakant, A., Abbadi, A., Das, S., Elmore, A.J., 2011. Database scalability, elasticity, and autonomy in the cloud, In Journal of Database Systems for Advanced Applications, Vol no. (2), pp. 2–15.
6. Buyya, R., Ranjan, R., Rodrigo, N., 2010. Intercloud: Utility-oriented federation of cloud computing environments for scaling of application services, In Algorithms and architectures for parallel processing, LNCS Springer Vol no. (6081). pp. 13–31.

7. Elmroth, E., Tordsson, J., Hernández, F., Ali-Eldin, A., Pette R, 2011. Self-management challenges for multi-cloud architectures, Lecture Notes in Computer Science Towards a Service-Based Internet, Vol no. 6994, pp. 38–49.

8. Ferry, N., Alessandro Rossini, Franck Chauvel, Brice Morin, and Arnor Solberg, 2013. Towards model-driven provisioning, deployment, monitoring, and adaptation of multi-cloud systems, In 2013 IEEE Sixth International Conference on cloud computing, pp. 887–894.

9. Saggar, R., Saggar, S., Khurana, N., 2014. Cloud Computing: Designing Different System Architecture Depending On Real-World Examples, International Journal of Computer Science and Information Technologies, Vol. 5 (4), pp. 5025–5029.

10. Sarkar, A., Debnath, N.C., 2012. Measuring Complexity of Multi- Agent System Architecture, 10th IEEE Conference on Industrial Informatics, pp. 998 – 1003.

11. Sarkar, A., 2013. Modeling Multi- agent system dynamics: Graph semantic based approach, 10th International Conference on Service Systems and Service Management. pp. 664–669.

12. Djamel, B., 2013. An agent-based approach for hybrid multi-cloud applications, In Journal of Scalable Computing: Practice and Experience 14, Vol no. 2.pp. 95– 109.

13. Khan, G., Sengupta, S., Sarkar, A., Debnath, N.C., 2014. Modeling of Inter-Cloud Architecture using UML 2.0: Multi- agent Abstraction based Approach, 23rd International Conference on Software Engineering and Data Engineering, pp 149–154.

14. Khan, G., Sengupta, S., Sarkar, A., 2014. WSRM: A Relational Model for Web Service Discovery in Enterprise Cloud Bus (ECB), 3rd International Conference on Eco-friendly Computing and Communication System, India, pp. 117–122.

15. Khan, G., Sengupta, S., Sarkar, A., 2015. Modelling of Services and their Collaboration in Enterprise Cloud Bus (ECB) using UML 2.0, 2015. International Conference on Advances in Computer Engineering and Applications, India, pp. 207–213.

16. Khan, G., Sengupta, S., Sarkar, A., Debnath, N.C., 2015. Web Service Discovery in Enterprise Cloud Bus Framework: T Vector Based Model, 13th IEEE International Conference on Industrial Informatics, pp. 1672–1677.

17. Sofiane, B., Bendoukha, H., Moldt, H., 2015. ICNETS: Towards Designing Inter-Cloud Workflow Management Systems by Petri-nets, In Enterprise and Organizational Modeling and Simulation, 198. Springer International Publishing. pp. 187– 198.

18. Chatterjee, A.K., Sarkar, A., Bhattacharya, S., 2011. Modeling and Analysis of Agent Oriented System: Petri-net Based Approach, 11th Intl. Conf. on Software Engineering Research and Practice (SERP 11), Vol. 1, PP 17 – 23.

19. Khan, G., Sengupta, S., Sarkar, A., 2015. Modeling and Analysis of Enterprise Cloud Bus using a Petri-net Based Approach, 3rd International Doctoral Symposium on Applied Computation and Security Systems (ACSS 2016), Kolkata, India.

20. Jensen, K., Kristensen, L.M., Wells, L.M., 2007. Coloured Petri-nets and CPN tools for modeling and validation of concurrent systems, International Journal on Software Tools for Technology Transfer, Vol no. 05. pp. 213 – 254.

21. Bhuvaneswari, A., Uma, S., Sakthitharan, S., Srinivasan, G., 2014. Assessment of Service Composition Plan using Colored Petri-nets, International Journal of Engineering And Computer Science, Vol no. 3(1), pp. 3736 – 3742.

22. Fitch, D., Xu, H., 2013. A Raid-Based Secure And Fault-Tolerant Model for Cloud Information Storage, International Journal of Software Engineering and Knowledge Engineering 23, Vol no. 05, pp. 627 – 654.

23. Chatterjee, R., Neha, Sarkar, A., 2015. Behavioral Modelling of Multi-agent System: High Level Petri-net Based Approach, International Journal of Agent Technologies and Systems, Vol no. 7(1), pp. 55 – 78.

Additional References

24. Zambonelli, F., Omicini, A., (2004). Challenges and Research Directions in Agent-Oriented Software Engineering, Journal of Autonomous Agents and Multi- agent Systems, Vol. 9, PP 253–283.
25. Bauer, B., Mulller, J. P., Odell, J., (2001). Agent UML: A Formalism for Specifying Multiagent Software Systems, International Journal of Software Engineering and Knowledge Engineering, Vol 11, No. 3, pp. 1– 24.
26. Far, B. H., Wanyama,T., (2003).Metrics for agent-based software development, Canadian Conference on Electrical and Computer Engineering (IEEE CCECE 2003), Volume 2, PP 1297–1300.
27. Wille, C., Brehmer, N., Dumke, R.R., (2004). Software measurement of agent based systems - an evaluation study of the agent academy, Technical Report Preprint No. 3, Faculty of Informatics, University of Magdeburg.
28. G′omes-Sanz, J. J., Pav′on, J., Garijo, F., (2005). Estimating cost for agent oriented software", In M¨uller, J. and Zambonelli, F., editors, Agent oriented software engineering V. 5th International Workshop, AOSE 2005, Utrecht, The Netherlands, July 2005, Revised Selected Papers, number 3950 in LNCS, pages 218–230, 2006.
29. Klügl, F., (2008). Measuring Complexity of Multi- agent Simulations – an Attempt using Metrics", Booktitle: Languages, Methodologies and Development Tools for Multi- agent Systems, Springer-Verlag Berlin, Heidelberg.
30. Dhavachelvan, P., Saravanan, S., Satheskumar, K., (2008).Validation of Complexity Metrics of Agent-Based Systems Using Weyuker's Axioms, International Conference on Information Technology (ICIT '08), PP 248– 251, 2008.
31. Mala, M., Cil, I., (2011). A taxonomy for measuring complexity in agent based systems, IEEE 2nd International Conference on Software Engineering and Service Science (ICSESS'11), pp. 851–854.
32. Cetnarowicz, K., Cetnarowicz, E., (2000). Multi-agent decentralized system of medical help, Management and control of production and logistics. AGH-University of Mining and Metallurgy, Krakow, Poland.
33. Tsai, W. T. (2005, October). Service-oriented system engineering: a new paradigm. In IEEE International Workshop on Service-Oriented System Engineering (SOSE'05) (pp. 3–6). IEEE.
34. Huhns, M. N., & Singh, M. P. (2005). Service-oriented computing: Key concepts and principles. IEEE Internet computing, 9(1), 75–81.
35. Arsanjani, A. (2004).Service oriented modeling and architecture. IBM developer works, 1–15. Zheng, Z., & Lyu, M. R. (2010, May). Collaborative reliability prediction of service-oriented systems. In Proceedings of the 32nd ACM/IEEE International Conference on Software Engineering-Volume 1 (pp. 35-44). ACM.
36. Papazoglou, M. P., Van Den Heuvel, W. J. (2003). Service-Oriented Computing: State-of-the-Art and Open Research Issues. IEEE Computer.
37. P. Gruer, V. Hilaire, A. Koukam and K. Cetnarowicz, "A Formal Framework for Multi- agent Systems Analysis and Design", Journal of Expert Systems with Applications, Vol. 23, No. 4, pp. 349–355, 2002.
38. B. Marzougui, K. Hassine, K. Barkaoui, "A New Formalism for Modeling a Multi-agent Systems: Agent Petri-nets", Journal of Software Engineering and Applications, Vol. 3, No. 12, pp 1118–1124, 2010.
39. Tadao Murata, "Petri-nets: Properties, Analysis and Applications", Proceedings of the IEEE, Vol. 77, No. 4, pp 541–580, April 1989.
40. J. R. Celaya, A. A. Desrochers, R. J. Graves, "Modeling and Analysis of Multi- agent Systems using Petri-nets", Jnl. of Comp., Academy Press, Vol. 4 (10), PP 981–996, 2009.
41. W. Chainbi, "Multi- agent Systems: A Petri-net with Objects Based Approach", IEEE/WIC/ACM International Conference on Intelligent Agent Technology, 2004.

42. S. Pujari, S. Mukhopadhyay, "Petri-net: A Tool for Modeling and Analyze Multi- agent Oriented Systems", Intl. Jnl. Intelligent Sys. and Appls., Vol. 10, 103–112, 2012.
43. ISO/IEC. (2002). High-level Petri-nets–Concepts, definitions, and graphical notation. Final Draft International Standard 15909, version 4.7.1.
44. Zhou, Y., Murata, T., and DeFanti, T. (2000). Modeling and performance analysis using extended fuzzy-timing Petri-nets for networked virtual environments. IEEE Transactions on Systems, Man, and Cybernetics 30(5), 737–756.
45. Zhou, Y., and Murata, T. (2001). Modeling and analysis of distributed multimedia synchronization by extended fuzzy-timing Petri-nets, Journal of Integrated Design and Process Science 4(4), 23–38.
46. Q. Bai, M. Zhang, K. T. Win, "A Colored Petri-net Based Approach for Multi- agent Interactions", 2nd Intl. Conf. on Autonomous Robots and Agents, PP 152–157, 2004.
47. Z. Jun, H. W. Ngan; L. Junfeng, W. Jie, Y Xiaoming, "Colored Petri-nets Modeling of Multi-agent System for Energy Management in Distributed Renewable Energy Generation System," Asia-Pacific Power and Energy Engineering Conference (APPEEC), pp. 1,5, 28–31, 2010.
48. Haas, P. (2002). Stochastic Petri-nets: Modeling, stability, simulation, Springer-Verlag.
49. He, X. (2001). PZ nets—A formal method integrating Petri-nets with Z. Information and Software Technology. 43, 1–18.
50. Dong, W. L., Yu, H., & Zhang, Y. B. (2006, October). Testing bpel-based web service composition using high-level Petri-nets. In 2006 10th IEEE International Enterprise Distributed Object Computing Conference (EDOC'06) (pp. 441–444). IEEE.
51. Chemaa, S., Bouarioua, M., & Chaoui, A. (2015). A high-level Petri-net based model for web services composition and verification. International Journal of Computer Applications in Technology, 51(4), 306–323.
52. Nagamouttou, D., Egambaram, I., Krishnan, M., & Narasingam, P. (2015). A verification strategy for web services composition using enhanced stacked automata model. Springer Plus, 4(1), 1.
53. Chen, C. S., Lin, C. H., & Tsai, H. Y. (2002). A rule-based expert system with colored Petri-net models for distribution system service restoration. IEEE Transactions on Power Systems, 17(4), 1073–1080.
54. Azgomi, M. A., & Entezari-Maleki, R. (2010). Task scheduling modelling and reliability evaluation of grid services using coloured Petri-nets. Future Generation Computer Systems, 26(8), 1141–1150.
55. Shen, W. (2002). Distributed manufacturing scheduling using intelligent agents. IEEE intelligent systems, 17(1), 88–94.
56. Yan, H. S., Wang, N. S., Zhang, J. G., & Cui, X. Y. (1998). Modelling, scheduling and simulation of flexible manufacturing systems using extended stochastic high-level evaluation Petri-nets. Robotics and Computer-Integrated Manufacturing, 14(2), 121–140.
57. Kim, H., Lee, H., Kim, W., & Kim, Y. (2010). A trust evaluation model for QoS guarantee in cloud systems. International Journal of Grid and Distributed Computing, 3(1), 1–10.
58. Ardagna, D., Di Nitto, E., Casale, G., Petcu, D., Mohagheghi, P., Mosser, S., ... & Nechifor, C. S. (2012, June). Modaclouds: A model-driven approach for the design and execution of applications on multiple clouds. In Proceedings of the 4th International Workshop on Modeling in Software Engineering (pp. 50–56). IEEE Press.
59. Gustafsson, J., Paakki, J., Nenonen, L., & Verkamo, A. I. (2002). Architecture-centric software evolution by software metrics and design patterns. In Software Maintenance and Reengineering, 2002. Proceedings. Sixth European Conference on (pp. 108–115). IEEE.

Chapter 7
Requirements to Services: A Model to Automate Service Discovery and Dynamic Choreography from Service Version Database

Swapan Bhattacharya, Ananya Kanjilal, Sabnam Sengupta, Jayeeta Chanda and Dipankar Majumdar

Abstract As the software industry is gradually moving toward the cloud computing in a fast pace, Service oriented architecture (SOA) is increasingly becoming more and more important, as far as the Software As a Service (SAAS) is concerned. As SOA applications are maturing, it becomes imperative to maintain the various versions of services published in the Enterprise Service Bus (ESB). However, for implementing a particular requirement, it may not always be cost-efficient, to use the latest version of the services. If a previous version matches the requirement, then that might be a cost-effective solution and enabling "reuse" to a larger extent can be a very useful method in cloud computing domain where pay per use is the accepted norm. In this chapter, we devise a comprehensive framework that models requirements in a formal manner and automatically extracts verbs to generate an activity model, which is then translated into BPMN notation based on a set of transformation rules. The BPMN nodes are mapped to services and an algorithm for dynamic discovery of appropriate service version is conceived. Thereafter we also verify the entire transformation process and ensure correctness by developing a traceability model and generate trace table to trace from requirements till services and apply it for a case study for substantiation of our approach.

S. Bhattacharya
Jadavpur University, Kolkata, India
e-mail: bswapan2000@yahoo.co.in

A. Kanjilal · S. Sengupta (✉) · J. Chanda
B. P. Poddar Institute of Management & Technology, Kolkata, India
e-mail: sabnam_sg@yahoo.com

A. Kanjilal
e-mail: ag_k@rediffmail.com

J. Chanda
e-mail: jayeeta.chanda@gmail.com

D. Majumdar
RCC Institute of Information Technology, Kolkata, India
e-mail: dipankar.majumdar@gmail.com

© Springer International Publishing AG 2017   151
M. Ramachandran and Z. Mahmood (eds.), *Requirements Engineering for Service and Cloud Computing*, DOI 10.1007/978-3-319-51310-2_7

Keywords Service-oriented architecture (SOA) · BPMN · Natural language · Systems modeling language (SysML) · Enterprise service bus · Requirements traceability

7.1   Introduction

As the software industry is making a paradigm shift toward cloud computing, developing a cost-efficient solution for requirement engineering is becoming more and more relevant. With the development of newer versions of software components with added functionality and features, designing software with appropriate and cost-effective version based on the requirement specified is becoming the need of the day. This approach enhances reusability of software components maintained in software engineering database and hence enhances the cost-effectiveness. Formal modeling of requirements and model-based testing play key roles in that context.

In this chapter, therefore, we focus on aspects of requirement engineering, formal modeling, model-based testing and reusability with an engineering database. We develop a framework that can automatically translate the requirements to business models. The requirements are based on a formal syntax named EARS [1], which consists of various constructs to represent many different types of requirements. A Requirements Parser and Analyzer analyzes the requirements and maps the verbs to form the processes/activities in the activity diagram. A set of transformation rules and two algorithms are defined to translate activity diagram into a BPMN model (Business Process Model Notation) by the generation of BPMN nodes and then flows between the nodes based on activity diagram.

Subsequently, the BPMN processes are realized/ implemented in services that are published enterprise service bus (ESB) (ESB). We envisage that an engineering database would be required to store all the service version information. In all realistic situations a BPMN process may be satisfied using multiple versions of a service but optimally the version that just suits the requirements should be chosen to promote reusability and reduce usage price on a cloud environment where services are hosted. We present new additions to the UDDI (Universal Description, Discovery and Integration) standard [2] for publishing services that caters to version details and differences in the services offered in each version. The UDDI registry format is enhanced to store the service version details as well map to a Service Version Database (SVD). The concept of SVD is based on the classical paper on software evolution by Luqi [3]. Our novel methodology helps in discovering correct service version matches based on the business functions extracted from the requirements and matching with the service version details stored in SVD. The version, which optimally satisfies the requirements, is chosen. Higher versions, with extra functionality are ignored. These service versions are then discovered in the ESB and an algorithm for choreography of the discovered services dynamically is presented.

Finally, the Requirements to Services framework can be tested and verified based on the concept of model based testing. We present a traceability framework that maps requirements to business processes to services to ensure verification of the overall software system. A graphical model that maps the various artifacts from requirements to verbs, verbs to processes, and processes to services is used for traceability. Algorithms to navigate the graph for forward and backward traceability of requirements to services complete the overall requirement engineering, service discovery and verification process.

The chapter is organized as follows—The next section discusses review of literature in the direction of requirement formalization, service versioning and dynamic service discovery followed by the Scope of work in Sect. 7.3. This work consists of three parts. Section 7.4 deals with the first part, which presents a requirement parser and analyzer, and using a formal specification it extracts functions from requirements and generate activity model. Section 7.5 translates the activity model into BPMN based on a set of transformation rules. The algorithms for node generation and flow generation between BPMN nodes are formulated. In Sect. 7.6 we focus on discovery of appropriate service versions from SVD based on the BPMN model. Section 7.7 presents a traceability model that establishes a rule-based trace table generation from requirements to services and vice versa, followed by conclusion in Sect. 7.8.

7.2 Review of Literature

The objective of our work is to provide a framework for unambiguous representation & interpretation of functional requirements and automated support for derivation of design models and selection of appropriate services so as to ensure verification of the entire process starting from requirements elicitation to implementation. This is only possible through the use of formal techniques. The review is done based on the three aspects of our work namely requirement formalization, service versioning & service discovery and finally traceability in software systems.

7.2.1 Requirement Formalization

Although there are several proposals to transform a more formal representation into use cases diagrams. Formalizations of Textual Requirements to UML Diagrams [4] is however scarce. Hence we here review the research works in the domain of formal specification of requirements.

Mavin et al. in [1, 5] put forward the three common forms of ambiguity in requirement specification: lexical, referential and syntactical. To overcome such problems that arise because of the association with Natural Language (NL), usage of other notations has been advocated for the specification of user requirements. Z [6], and graphical notations such as Unified Modeling Language (UML) [7] and Systems Modeling Language (SysML) [8] are worth mentioning in this domain of work.

There are also numerous scenario-based approaches [9], tabular approaches such as Table-Driven Requirements [10] and pseudocode. However, use of any of these nontextual notations often requires complex translation of the source requirements, which can introduce further errors. There are also many research works specifically about how to write better requirements like [11, 12] that focus on the characteristics of well-formed requirements and the attributes that should be included. Despite this large body of research works, there seems to be little simple, practical advice for the practitioner. A set of simple requirement structures would be an efficient and practical way to enhance the writing of high-level requirements. Previous work in the area of constrained natural language includes Simplified Technical English [13], Attempto Controlled English (ACE) [14], Easy Approach to Requirements Syntax (EARS) in [1] and Event Condition Action (ECA) [15]. In ECA, the event specifies the signal that triggers the rule and the condition is a logical test that (if satisfied) causes the specified system action.

We have applied the EARS framework conceived in [1] for specifying requirement syntax and defined a context-free grammar so as to automatically parse the EARS-based requirements to identify verbs that is used to generate the activity diagram.

7.2.2 Service Versioning and Dynamic Service Discovery

Web services are generally registered based on the UDDI which has become the de facto standard for registering services. UDDI stands for Universal Description, Discovery and Integration of web services, which is an XML (eXtended Markup Language) based registry to list services over the web. Generally, discovery of a service is done by searching based on the functional description in the UDDI registry.

As web services are used more frequently, their evolutionary changes pose a challenge in identifying changes and synchronizing those changes with the dependent services [2]. A service dependency model is presented in [10] for the synchronization of multiple service versions by relating the base service model with the dependent service versions to construct a service dependency graph and dependency matrices. However, these services are not evolved from or traced back to requirements, which forms the basis of our paper.

Authors in [16] present a new web services discovery model that takes into account functional and nonfunctional requirements like QoS (Quality of Service) for dynamically discovering services and extend the UDDI model to achieve the same. Taking cue from this, here we extend the UDDI to maintain information about various versions of services so that our framework can discover appropriate service versions while implementation.

Authors in [9] introduce model-aware services that work with models at runtime. These services are supported using a service environment, called Morse. Hiding the complexity of implicit versioning of models from users while respecting the principle of Universally Unique Identifiers (UUIDs), it realizes a novel transparent UUID-based model versioning technique. It uses the model-driven approach to automatically generate and deploy Morse services that are used by the model-aware services to access models in the correct version. We follow similar unique identifier-based service versioning scheme in our approach while discovering and choreographing services.

In [17] the authors describe a framework for dynamic service discovery that supports the identification of service during the execution time of service-based systems. In the framework, services are identified based on structural, behavioral, quality and contextual characteristics of a system represented in query languages. In our previous work [12], we have presented a context-aware dynamic service choreography framework that provides an optimized search in a subset of services retrieved based on contextual information. This paper also focuses on dynamic service discovery and choreography but for generic requirement scenarios by functionally mapping requirements and service version offerings.

The lack of standards-based guidance for service versioning is a major risk associated with the web service adoption. In [18] authors classify versioning services as message versioning and contract versioning. In this work, we typically focus on the versions of contracts. Contract versioning deals with addition of new operation, data structure and data types, new interface for an existing operation, etc.

In [19, 20] the authors discuss the issue of versioning of services in an SOA framework. They classify between different request types, operations, response types and present arguments as to how the version number should be managed to optimize the management of changes in services.

There has been some research work in the direction of dynamic service discovery. At the same time, very few research works are there to address the version-related considerations for web services. It is imperative to connect these two domains to provide an integrated methodology to enable dynamic service discovery of appropriate service versions.

We present a novel methodology to discover appropriate versions of services based on a requirement scenario and subsequently choreograph the services based on the order of requirements.

7.2.3 Traceability of Requirements

One of the biggest challenges in the software industry is to ensure that a software product meets all user specifications. Requirements traceability is one way to ensure confidence in the customer that all requirements have been correctly and consistently implemented.

Review of literature in this direction reveals that some of the works focus on recovering traceability information between two types of artifacts, e.g., design/code, code/documentation, requirements/design. Antoniol et al. discuss a technique for automatically recovering traceability links between object-oriented design models and code based on determining the similarity of paired elements from design and code in [21] and in [22] they propose an approach to recover trace information between code and documentation. In another work [23], Arlow et al. emphasize the need to establish and maintain traceability between requirements and UML design and present Literate Modeling as an approach to ease this task while Pohl et al. describe an approach based on scenarios and metamodels to bridge requirements and architectures in [24].

In contrast to many theoretical works on requirement traceability [25] follows an empirical approach and compares a wide range of traceability practices in industry and identifies four kinds of traceability link types. Grünbacher et al. discuss the CBSP approach that improves traceability between informal requirements and architectural models by developing an intermediate model based on architectural dimensions [26].

As discussed in this section, some of the existing works do provide solutions in various aspects like requirement formalization, service discovery and traceability separately but our work encompasses a larger scope in the sense that it consists of all of them. The next section discusses the scope of work in detail.

7.3   Scope of Work

We present a framework that can automatically translate the requirements to business models. It starts with formalization of requirements, identifying different categories and automatically identifying verbs that may qualify to be processes in an activity model. The activity model is then mapped to BPMN and the business processes are implemented through services that are stored in the service version database. We optimize and use the concept of reusability in selecting the correct service version that matches the functional needs. Finally, the entire process is verified through a traceability model.

The requirements are first parsed and activity model is generated from which a BPMN model is generated based on transformation rules. To achieve this we have developed a requirement parser that is based on the EARS syntax for requirement specification [1]. It is a formal model for requirements elicitation, which can be parsed for extracting verbs, which qualify as possible business process or functionality.

The BPMN processes are realized/implemented in services that are published in ESB. We present an engineering database that would be required to store all the service version information. In all realistic situations, a BPMN process may be satisfied using multiple versions of a service but optimally the version that just suits the requirements should be chosen to promote reusability and reduce usage price on a cloud environment where services are hosted. We present new additions to the

UDDI standard for publishing services that caters to version details and differences in the services offered in each version. The UDDI registry format is enhanced to store the service version details as well map to a service version database (SVD). The concept of SVD is based on the classical paper on software evolution by Luqi [13]. Our novel methodology helps in discovering correct service version matches based on the business functions extracted from the requirements and matching with the service version details stored in SVD.

Finally, we present a traceability framework that maps requirements to business processes to services ensuring verification of the overall software system. The Requirement to Services framework can be tested and verified based on the concept of model-based testing. A graphical model that maps the various artifacts from requirements to verbs, verbs to processes, processes to services is used for traceability. Algorithms to navigate the graph for forward and backward traceability of requirements to services complete the overall requirement engineering, service discovery and verification process.

Figure 7.1 gives a diagrammatic representation of our work.

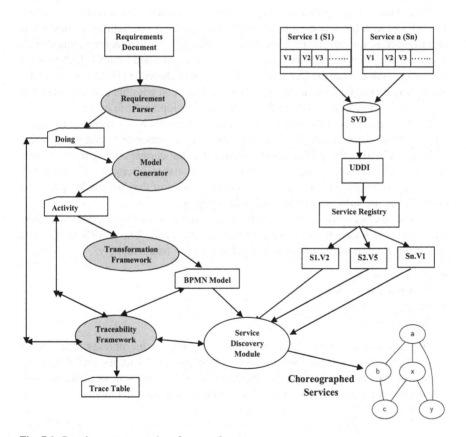

Fig. 7.1 Requirements to services framework

7.4 Requirement Parser and Analyzer

In this section, we describe a formal model based on EARS for elicitation and classification of functional requirements of the software system. We present a context-free grammar to validate the requirements structurally. Next, the validated requirements document is parsed to automatically extract functional verbs or "Doing verbs" as defined in [19]. These doing verbs may be thought of as business processes at a micro level that are implemented as operations in services. A requirement scenario comprises of a set of such "verbs" or functional processes at micro level operating in a particular sequence to realize a requirement at a macro level.

7.4.1 Requirement Classification

In order to move toward structured analysis and engineering of Functional Requirements available as text in Natural Language, the first step needs always to be the elimination of the problems like ambiguity, vagueness, complexity, omission, duplication, wordiness, inappropriate implementation and untestability as mentioned in [1], and consequently their approach toward the expression of requirements in such a way that they may be parsed by a requirements parser named EARS [1]. The Parser may be generated using the Context-Free Grammar as shown in [1]. The output of the parser may be used for the analysis of Requirements and possible automation of the requirements engineering phase of the software development life cycle.

Taking the cue from the above, we had made certain advancements in the same track with our work making the EARS Syntaxes more versatile so that it may work with varied kinds of requirements. Consequently, the corresponding parser generated can address a wider range and variety of functional requirements. The output of the parser so generated is processed for the generation of the Activity Diagrams as discussed in the subsequent sections of the chapter.

For the sake of automating the process of Requirements Engineering, we adopt the EARS [1] based Requirements Syntax as the basis. The EARS syntax has placed the Requirements under various classification heads namely:

- Ubiquitous
- Unwanted Behavior
- Event-Driven and
- State-Driven.

The principal objective of this paper is to decompose the phrases identified in EARS [1] further with an aim to identify the involved Entities and functional processes. We have made slight modifications by adding few sentence constructs so that it becomes better suited for use for formal requirement definition.

We use the following codes for the different types of requirements syntax, which are defined in Table 7.1. Few more additional constructs are defined to capture parallel flow of events and exclusive-OR events. These are highlighted in Table 7.1.

UB: Ubiquitous, EV: Event-driven, UW: Unwanted Behavior, ST: State driven, OP: Optional features, HY: Hybrid (Event-Driven and Conditional).

Table 7.1 Requirement types of EARS

Req. type	Definition in EARS (Additions are in bold)
UB	The <entity> shall <functionality> | The <entity> shall <functionality> the <entity> for <functionality>
EV	When <optional preconditions> the <entity> shall <functionality> | When <optional preconditions> the <entity> shall perform <functionality> | When <entity><functionality> the <entity> shall <functionality> | **When the <entity><functionality> the <entity> shall <functionality1> AND the <entity> shall <functionality2>** | *[This indicates a parallel execution of functionality1 and functionality2 simultaneously]* **When the <entity><functionality> the <entity> shall <functionality1> OR the <entity> shall <functionality2>** *[This indicates an either-or execution of functionality1 and functionality2, i.e., either functionality1 or functionality2 is executed]*
UW	IF <preconditions> THEN the <entity> shall <functionality> | **IF <preconditions> THEN the <entity> shall <functionality1> AND the <entity> shall <functionality2>** | *[This indicates a parallel execution of functionality1 and functionality2 simultaneously]* **IF <preconditions> THEN the <entity> shall <functionality1> OR the <entity> shall <functionality2>** *[This indicates an either-or execution of functionality1 and functionality2, i.e., either functionality1 or functionality2 is executed]* IF <preconditions> THEN the <functionality> of <functionality> shall <functionality> | IF <preconditions>THEN the <functionality> of <functionality> shall <functionality> to <functionality> |IF<preconditions> THEN the <functionality> of <functionality> shall <functionality> to <functionality> and <functionality>
ST	WHILE <in a specific state> the <entity> shall <functionality> | WHILE <in a specific state> the <functionality> shall <functionality>|
OP	WHERE <feature is included> the <entity> shall <functionality> | WHERE <preconditions> the <functionality> shall <functionality> | WHERE <preconditions> the <functionality> of <functionality> shall <functionality> to <functionality>
HY	<While-in-a-specific-state> if necessary the <functionality> shall <functionality> | <While-in-a-specific-state> if necessary the <entity> shall perform <functionality> | <While-in-a-specific-state> if <preconditions> the <functionality> shall <functionality>

7.4.2 Context-Free Grammar

We have defined a CFG (Context-Free Grammar) for the requirements formatted in EARS syntax [1]. Our CFG, as shown below, when implemented using "lex" and "yacc" programs available with Red Hat Enterprise Linux 5.0, generates a parse tree at its runtime. Such a parse tree unveils the potential functions/processes at a micro level of the system and their interrelationships. In this section, we extend the CFG further to handle the additional constructs, which are indicated in bold.

```
%token The shall as a an word When operation
% token trigger then While Where if necessary
%start translation_unit
%%
translation_unit: requirement_def
 | translation_unit requirement_def; requirement_def:
The <entity> shall <functionality>
| The <entity> shall <functionality> the <entity> for <functionality>
| When <preconditions> the <entity> shall <functionality>
|When <preconditions> the <entity> shall perform <functionality>
| When the <entity> <functionality> the <entity> shall <functionality1> AND the <entity> shall
  <functionality2>
| When the <entity> <functionality> the <entity> shall <functionality1> AND the <entity> shall
  <functionality2>
| When the <entity> shall <functionality>
|When <entity><functionality> the <entity> shall <functionality>
| IF <preconditions> THEN the <entity> shall <functionality>
|IF <preconditions> THEN the <entity> shall <functionality1> AND the <entity> shall
  <functionality2>
|IF <preconditions> THEN the <entity> shall <functionality1> OR the <entity> shall
  <functionality2>
|IF <preconditions> THEN the <functionality> of <functionality> shall <functionality>
| IF <preconditions> THEN the <functionality> of <functionality> shall <functionality> to
  <functionality>
| IF <preconditions> THEN the <functionality> of <functionality>shall <functionality> to
  <functionality> and <functionality>
| WHILE <in-a-specific-state> the <entity> shall <functionality>
| WHILE <in-a-specific-state> the <functionality> shall <functionality>
| WHERE <feature-is-included> the <entity>shall <functionality>
| WHERE <preconditions> the <functionality> shall <functionality>
| WHERE <preconditions> the <functionality> of <functionality> shall <functionality> to
  <functionality>
| WHILE <in-a-specific-state> if necessary the <functionality> shall <functionality>
| WHILE <in-a-specific-state> if <preconditions> the <functionality> shall <functionality>
text: word | text word;
entity: word;
system: text;
functionality: text;
remainder-text: text;
preconditions: text;
in-a-specific-state: text;
feature-is-included: text;
%%
```

7.4.3 Requirement Parser

Here we consider a case study of a "Order Processing" system. The requirements for this system are written in EARS format, and their corresponding types are shown in Table 7.2. The Requirement Parser module parses the verbs from the requirements. The <functionality> based on the EARS model qualify to be possible "doing verbs" which may correspond to possible business process functions [12]. The requirements are shown in Table 7.2.

Based on the order of elicitation in requirements document (in EARS format) [1], we can derive the verb dataset automatically. The preceding and succeeding verbs are also extracted to maintain the flow of information in requirements scenario.

The verb dataset that is generated is shown in Table 7.4 corresponding to the requirements in Table 7.3.

We also identify the parallel flow and exclusive-OR flow of events in the requirement scenario. The significance of the symbols "&" and "or" used are as follows:

- v1 & v2—This indicates that functions denoted by verbs v1 and v2 *is executed* in parallel
- v1 or v2—This indicates that either of the functions denoted by verbs v1 and v2 *is executed* but not both.

The Verbs extracted from requirements are stored in a table in a format shown in Table 7.5.

Table 7.2 List of requirements of "Place Order" system

Sl. No.	Requirements	Type
1	The *Customer* shall *Place Order*	UB
2	When *Customer* shall *Place Order* the *System* shall *Receive Order*	EV
3	When System *Receive Order* the *Accounts* shall *Send Invoice* AND *Inventory* shall *Fill Order*	EV
4	When *Send Invoice* is complete the *System* shall *Receive Payment*	EV
5	If the order is "Priority" then the *Shipment* shall *use overnight delivery*	UW
6	If the order is "Regular" then the *Shipment* shall *use regular delivery*	UW
7	When *Receive Payment* is complete and *Delivery Done* the *System* shall *Close Order*	EV

Table 7.3 Requirements table

Sl. No.	Attr_Name	Description
1.	req_id	Unique identifier for each requirement
2.	req_desc	Description of the requirement

Table 7.4 List of verbs for order processing system

Sl. No.	Verbs	Pre-verb	Post-verb
1	*Place Order*	–	1
2	*Receive Order*	1	3 & 5
3	*Send Invoice*	2	4
4	*Receive Payment*	3	8
5	*Fill order*	2	6 or 7
6	*Use overnight delivery*	5	8
8	*Close Order*	4, 6, 7	–

Table 7.5 Verb_Dataset table

Sl. No.	Attr_Name	Description
1.	req_id	Unique identifier for each requirement
2.	verb_id	Unique identifier for each verb extracted from the requirement. There can be many verbs corresponding to one requirement
3.	verb_desc	Description of the verb/function. This maps with the activity state of activity diagram

This verb dataset forms the basis of the Model generator module which automatically generates an activity model corresponding to the flow of events/activities for a requirement (Fig. 7.2).

The resulting graphical representation may be as shown in Fig: A.

Fig. 7.2 Verb dataset graph

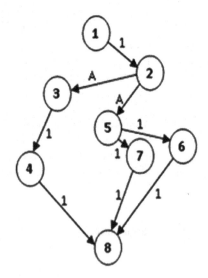

Few of the observations that comes up obviously from the diagrammatic representation is that the

- system is strongly connected
- starting node is node: 1
- terminating nodes is node: 8
- nodes 3 and 5 are succeeding node: 2 in Parallel Mode
- nodes 6 and 7 are succeeding node: 5 in EX-OR Mode.

This verb dataset forms the basis of the Model generator module, which automatically generates an activity model corresponding to the flow of events/activities for a requirement.

The corresponding adjacency matrix for VerbDataset_Graph is as follows:

	1	2	3	4	5	6	7	8
1		1						
2			A		A			
3				1				
4								1
5						1	1	
6								1
7								1
8								
Visited (Boolean)								

7.4.4 Model Generator: Generation of Activity Model for a Requirement Scenario

An Activity model is generated from the order of the verbs in the SRS document to model the flow of processes to implement the requirement. The different constructs of the Activity_Model is shown in Table 7.4. The activity_state is associated with an act_id (Table 7.6).

The Algorithm for Activity Model generation is given below.

Input : VerbDataSet_Graph(V, E)
Output : Activity_Model
Algorithm *ModelGeneration*
  Begin
    Insert the Start State of the Activity Model;
    Set FROM Node = Start State;
            Find v ∈ V | column(v) = Ø AND visited(v) = FALSE
            Insert the Activity-State for v
            Set TO Node = v
            Set the Visited Bit of v to TRUE
            Join (FROM Node, TO Node) with a Transition-Edge
            Lookup Row(v);
            if(row is empty)
            begin
                Join v with Terminating Node using a Transition State;
            end;
            else if(alphabetical character exists) then
            begin
                {$C_1, C_2, ... C_N$} = cluster the corresponding columns based on character.
                For All 1<=j<=N
                  For All i, Join v with c_{ij} | c_{ij} ∈ C_j such that separately using separate fork
                states;
            end;
            else if (only numeric character exist) then
            begin
                Join v with each non zero columns using Transition States.
            end;
  End;

Table 7.6 Activity_Model

Sl. No.	Construct	Symbol
1.	start_state	●
2.	activity_state*	▢
3.	fork_state	↓↓
4.	join_state	↓↓
5.	decision_state	◇
6.	end_state	◉
7.	transition	↓

*activity_state is associated with an act_id

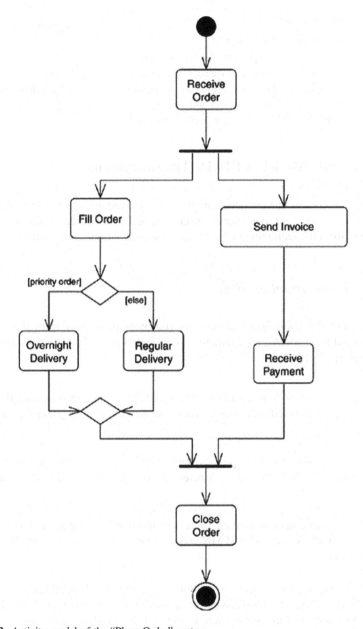

Fig. 7.3 Activity model of the "Place Order" system

The activity model of the "Order Processing" system is shown in Fig. 7.3. The generated activity model may be represented in a tabular format as given in Table 7.7.

Table 7.7 Activity model

Sl. No.	Attr_Name	Description
1.	act_id	Unique identifier for each activity
2.	act_node	Represents the activity state within the activity diagram
3.	act_desc	Description of the activity state/process. This maps with the "doing" verbs of requirements
4.	verb_id	Foreign key referencing the verb dataset

7.5 Activity Model to BPMN Transformation

After all the services that are necessary to satisfy the requirements of the consumer, are discovered, they are dynamically choreographed in accordance with the activity generated from the requirements based on the scenario modeled by activity models.

7.5.1 Transformation Rules

For deriving the choreographed services (business processes) from the activity models used for modeling requirements, we present a set of Transformation rules as given below:

Rule1
The activity whose node is marked as "start_state" is be assigned as Start Event of the BPMN node. The BPMN node is labeled as Activity ID (act_ID) of the activity node.

Rule 2
The activity whose node is marked as "end_state" is assigned as End Event of the BPMN node. The BPMN node is labeled as Activity ID (act_ID) of the activity node.

Rule 3
The activity whose node is marked as "action/decision" is assigned as Intermediate Event of the BPMN node. The BPMN node is labeled as Activity ID (act_ID) of the activity node.

Rule 4
The activity whose node is marked as "fork" is assigned as Parallel Gateway of the BPMN node if both the postElement of the activity node are of the type "basic". The BPMN node is 1 labeled as Activity ID (act_ID) of the activity node.

Rule 5
The activity whose node is marked as "fork" is assigned as Exclusive-OR Gateway of the BPMN node if one the postElement of the activity node is of the type "basic" and the other is of the type "alternate". The BPMN node is labeled as Activity ID (act_ID) of the activity node.

These rules are realized using two algorithms namely *NodeGeneration* and *FlowGeneration*.

7.5.2 Algorithm NodeGeneration to Generate BPMN Node

In this section, we present an algorithm to generate BPMN nodes from corresponding activity model depicting the sequence of operation of the "doing verbs". The following Table 7.8 lists the notations used and the mapping of the corresponding elements.

The algorithm *NodeGeneration* generates the BPMN nodes.

We define the transformation using the tuple relational calculus. The corresponding queries given below.

Query 1:

This is the realization of rule 1. It generates the Start of the BPMN node.

{t. BPMN_notation | BPMN_node (t) ^ t. ID = '1' ^
$ d (d.act_ID | ActivityState (d) ^ d.activity_node = t.activity_node ^   t.label = d.act_ID ^
d.activity_node = 'start')}

Query 2:

This is the realization of rule 2.It generates the End of the BPMN node.

{t. *BPMN* _notation | BPMN_node(t) ^ t.ID = '2' ^
$d(d.act_ID | ActivityState(d) ^ d.activity_node = t.activity_node ^ t.label = d.act_ID ^
d.activity_node = 'end')}

Table 7.8 Activity nodes and BPMN notation

ID	Name	Activity Node	BPMN notation
1	Start event	Start	◯
2	End event	End	◯
3	Intermediate event	Action, decision	◯
4	Parallel gateway	Fork, join	◈ ◈
5	Exclusive-OR gateway	Fork, join	◈ ◈

Query 3:

The following query is the realization of rule 3. It generates the #Intermediate of the BPMN node.
{t. *BPMN* _notation | BPMN_node(t) ^ t.ID = 3 ^
$d(d.act_ID | ActivityState(d) ^ d.activity_node = t.activity_node ^ t.label = d.act_ID ^
(d.activity_node = 'action'   d.activity_node = 'decision')) }

Query 4:

The following query is the realization of rule 4. It generates the graphical #notation for Parallel
Gateway.
{t. *BPMN* _notation | BPMN_node(t) ^ t.ID = 4 ^
$ q(q.act_ID | ActivityState(q) ^ q.activity_node = t.activity_node ^ t.label =   q.act_ID ^
q.activity_node = 'fork'$ r (r.postElement | ActivityState (t) ^ r.act_ID = q.act_ID ^ $ s(s.event_ID |
ActivityState(s) ^ s.act_ID = r.postElement ^$ p(p.event_ID | Usecase(p) ^ p.event_ID = s. event_ID
^ s.event_type = 'basic')))))}

Query 5:

The following query is the realization of rule 5. It generates the graphical #notation for Exclusive-OR
Gateway.
{t. *BPMN* _notation | BPMN_node(t) ^ t.ID = 5 ^
$ q(q.act_ID | ActivityState(q) ^ q.activity_node = t.activity_node ^ t.label = q.act_ID ^
q.activity_node = 'fork' ^ $ r (r.postElement | ActivityState (t) ^ r.act_ID = q.act_ID ^ $ s(s.event_ID |
ActivityState(s) ^ s.act_ID = r.postElement ^ $ p(p.event_ID | Usecase(p) ^ p.event_ID = s. event_ID
^ s.event_type = ' basic'   s.event_type =   'alternate')))))}

The outputs of this algorithm are different BPMN nodes. This output along with
the Array Activity _Flow is fed as input to the second algorithm named
FlowGeneration. The *FlowGeneration* algorithm generates the BPMN design
elements.

7.5.3 Algorithm FlowGeneration to Generate the Flow Between BPMN Nodes

We use an array representation Activity_flow to represent the flow between different activity nodes.

The array Activity_Flow is an [n, 3] array where n is the number of flows in the
formalized analysis model.

Activity _Flow[0][i] lists the source activity node of the flow for i = 0 to n
Activity _Flow [1] [i] lists the destination activity node of the flow i = 0 to n
Activity _Flow [2] [i] lists the types of flow between A[0][i] and A [1] [i] for i = 0
to n.

Entries in Activity _Flow [2] [i] are of the following types:

(1) S indicates Sequential flow
(2) D indicates Default flow
(3) C indicates Conditional flow
(4) I indicates Iterative flow.

The different types of Array flow are listed in Table 7.9 and BPMN flow are
listed in Table 7.10.

Table BPMN_Flow stores different graphical notations of BPMN flow and are
assigned with unique ID.

The BPMN model that depicts the choreography of the services is shown in
Fig. 7.4.

The algorithm *FlowGeneration* is presented as follows:

```
Input: Output of Nodegeneration algorithm, Activity _Flow[n,3] , Table BPMN_Flow
Output: BPMN model showing different flows between BPMN design elements.
Algorithm:
        for( m=0 ; m<=n-1;m++)
        {   flow. from = Activity _flow[m][0] ;
            flow. to = Activity _flow [m][1] ;
                If Activity _flow [m][2] = 'S'
            Flow.type = Select BPMN_Flow.Graphical_notation where BPMN_Flow.ID=1
                If Activity _flow [m][2] = 'D'
            Flow.type = Select BPMN_Flow.Graphical_notation where BPMN_Flow.ID=2
                If Activity _flow [m][2] = 'C'
                Flow.type = Select BPMN_Flow.Graphical_notation where BPMN_Flow.ID=3
            If Activity _flow [m][2] = 'I'
                Flow.type = Select BPMN_Flow.Graphical_notation where BPMN_Flow.ID=4
            }
```

Table 7.9 Array Activity_Flow

A[ ] [ ]	0	1	2	3	4	5	...	n−1
0(=ACi)	AC1	AC2	AC3	AC3	AC4	AC5		
1(=ACj)	AC2	AC3	AC4	AC5	AC6	AC2		
2(=value)	S	S	D	S	S	I		

Table 7.10 BPMN_Flow

ID	Name	Graphical_notation
1	Sequential flow	$\longrightarrow$
2	Default flow	$\longrightarrow$
3	Conditional flow	condition $\longrightarrow$
4	Iterative flow	$----\rightarrow$

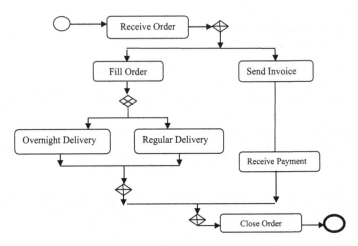

Fig. 7.4 BPMN model depicting choreography of services (appropriate versions) for the "Order Processing"

7.6 Service Version Discovery Based on BPMN Model

In order to satisfy the functionalities expressed in the Requirement document, the services are needed to be discovered from the Enterprise Service Bus (ESB). For each of the business processes of the BPMN model in Fig. 7.4, we need to discover the services that are available to be used. Additionally each service may have several versions with different sets of operations/functionalities to choose from. In this section, we present a methodology for automatic service version discovery.

7.6.1 Service Version Database (SVD)—ER Mapping

In this section, we design a Service Version Database (SVD) that stores the information of all the services available and published in the ESB. It is unique in the sense that it maintains a repository of all versions of services in a structured manner. This helps in efficient discovery of services based on the requirements.

Each service has a unique identifier, a list of business processes that are offered as service and a version number. Each version differs from its previous version due to new functional processes added to the newer version or older processes being deleted from the previous version.

Service = {**serv_id**, **BusinessProcess***, **version**, **versionDiff**}
where **serv_id** = unique service identifier
BusinessProcess = {process_id, process_desc}
process_id = unique process identifier
process_desc = process/function description
version = version number
versionDiff = {BusinessProcess*}

where, BusinessProcess refers to business processes or functionalities available in addition to the immediate previous version.

For a particular version, the list of process_id available within BusinessProcess are different. We model the structure of SVD using the ER model as shown in Fig. 7.5. Please note that the relationship "offers" between Version and BusinessProcess is true for the first version only. For subsequent versions, the other relationship "Differernce" is used to model the additional Business Processes present with respect to the previous version.

The corresponding table structures are shown in Tables 7.11, 7.12, and 7.13, respectively.

The table Service_Version models the Business_Process and the Version entity together. This holds the version number, service id and the business processes that are new to this version. So for the first version all the processes are new and hence present. For subsequent versions, only the additional business processes occur in this table.

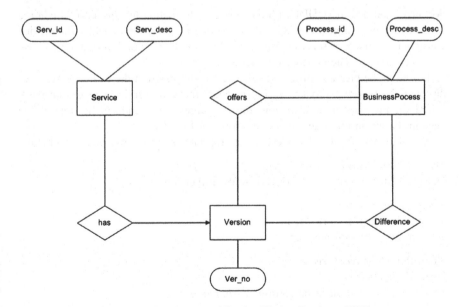

Fig. 7.5 ER model depicting the structure of Service Version Database (SVD)

Table 7.11 Service table

Sl. No.	Attr_Name	Description
1.	serv_id	Unique identifier for each service. This is same for all versions of a particular service
2.	serv_desc	Description or name of a service
3	Process_id	Foreign key referencing the **Business_Process** table

Table 7.12 Business_Process table

Sl. No.	Attr_Name	Description
1.	process_id	Unique identifier representing a business process
2.	process_desc	Description of the business function/ process. This maps with the activity node of activity diagram
3.	act_id	Foreign key referencing the **Activity** table

Table 7.13 Service_Version table

Sl. No.	Attr_Name	Description
1.	Serv_id	Foreign key referencing the **Service** table
2.	process_id	Foreign key referencing the **Business_Process** table
3.	ver_No	Unique number indicating version number for a particular service

7.6.2   Discovery of Services from ESB Based on SVD

We have modified the UDDI with the version information for the services that the version information gets available at the service registry. This enables the service consumers to discover services from the ESB with the version information and use relevant versions. The enhanced model is shown in Fig. 7.6.

Based on the business processes retrieved as discussed in the earlier section, we discover the possible service version matches from the service version database. Based on the version information, the consumers may choose the appropriate version, based on the requirement, as shown in Fig. 7.7.

The algorithm for this discovery of "appropriate" service version is given below:

Input: *"Verb" dataset* (Table 7.5)
Output: List of services of format **sv_id.pr_id.ver_no**

where sv_id = Service id
and pr_id = business process id
and ver_no = version number

Algorithm: *DiscoverService*
Open *Verb_Dataset*
String verb = Read an instance from *Verb_Dataset*

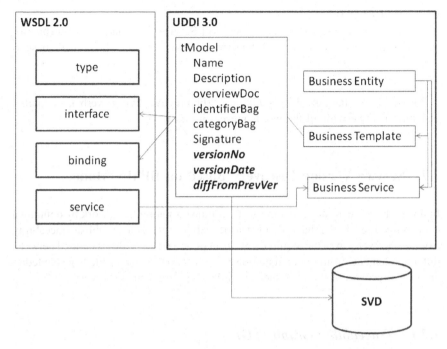

Fig. 7.6 UDDI model enhanced with the version information

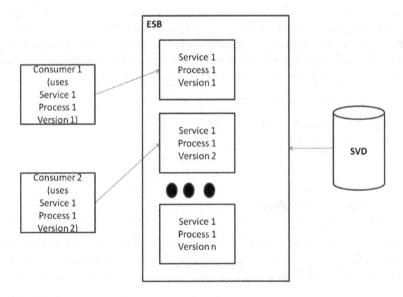

Fig. 7.7 Selection of appropriate service version

while (!end_of_file)
{T1 = {sv.serv_id, sv.process_id, sv.ver_no | Service_Version(sv) ^ $bp (bp.process_id | Business_Process(bp) ^ bp.serv_id = sv.serv_id ^ bp.process_desc = 'verb')}
}

Please note that in the condition—"(bp.process_desc = 'verb'), a partial matching is done with all the words present in the *verb*.

7.7 Service Version Discovery Based on BPMN Model

In this section, we ensure correctness of our transformation framework by defining a traceability model. We have defined a traceability graph to establish traceability from service version to the requirement. A set of traceability rules is defined between different elements from requirement to service version. A trace table is generated to ensure correctness of the implementation from requirements to services.

7.7.1 Traceability Graph (TG)

A traceability graph (TG) is defined that depicts the relationship between various artifacts that are involved in the implementation of requirements in the form of services. Requirements (R), verbs (V'), activity nodes (AC), business processes (BP), services (S), service version (SV) form the different types of nodes in the graph. Directed edges connect the nodes based on how the transformation process occurs from requirements till services (Fig. 7.8).

TG = (V, E), where TG is a traceability graph;

V is the set of nodes; $V \in \{R \mid AC \mid BP \mid S \mid SV\}$
E is the set of edges between V

7.7.2 Traceability Rules

In this section, we define a set of traceability rules based on the traceability graph defined in the previous section. These rules form the basis for the traceability model and a relational model-based query to generate a trace table in the next section.

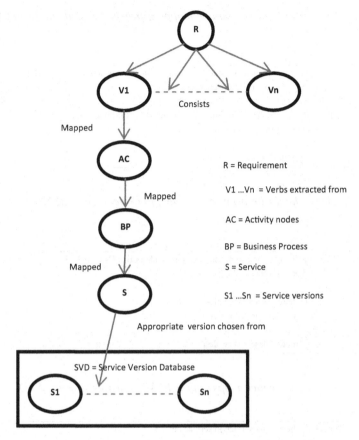

Fig. 7.8 Traceability graph

Rule 1: Each requirement of requirement document may consist of one or many verbs. Each verb has a unique identifier and description

R = {v* | v is a verb defined in the requirement}
           and v = (verb_id, verb_desc)

Rule 2: Each verb extracted from Requirements document should have a one-to-one mapping to an activity node.

v = (verb_id, verb_desc) and
AC = {ac_state* | where ac_state is an activity state in the activity model AC}
        and ac_state = (act_id, act_desc)
such that
          verb_desc = act_desc

Rule 3: There should be one-to-one mapping between Activity node and BPMN node.

AC = {ac_state* | where ac_state is an activity state in the activity model AC}
        and ac_state = (act_id, act_desc)
and
BP = {bp* | where bp is a business process node in BPMN model BP}
        and bp = (process_id, process_desc)
such that
        act_desc = process_desc

Rule 4: There should be a one-to-one mapping between a BPMN node and a service.

BP = {bp* | where bp is a business process node in BPMN model BP}
        and bp = (process_id, process_desc)
and
S = {s* | where s is a service in service table S}
        and s = (serv_id, serv_desc)
such that
        process_desc = serv_desc

Rule 5: The service which maps with a BPMN must exist in the SVD.

S = {s* | where s is a service in service table S}
        and s = (serv_id, serv_desc)
and
SV = {sv* | where sv is a specific service version in SVD)
        and sv = (serv_id, ver_no, sv_desc)
such that
        serv_desc = sv_desc

7.7.3 R2S: Traceability from Requirements to Services

In order to generate the Trace Table for traceability from Service Version to Requirement the following query is triggered:

{t.Req_id, t.Verb_id, t.Verb_desc, d.Act_id, p.Process_id, s.Serv_id, v.Ver_no | Service(s) (s.Serv_id AND v.Ver_no = Input ∧ ∃ p(p.Process_id | Business_Process (s) ∧ s.Process_id = p.Process_id ∃t(t t.Req_id, t.Verb_id, t.Verb_desc) | Verb_DataSet(t) ∧ t.Process_id = p.Process_id) }

Table 7.14 Trace table for "Place Order"

Req_id	Verb_id	Verb_desc	Act_id	Process_Id	Serv_id	Ver_no
R1	V1	Receive order	A1	P1	S1	V1
	V2		A2	P2	S2	V1
	V3		A3	P3	S3	V2
R2	V4	Fill order	A4	P4	S4	V3
	V5		A5	P5	S5	V2
	...	...	...	...	...	...
R3	V11	Send order	A11	P11	S11	V5

The schema of the trace table for tracing Requirements to version would be TRSV = {Req_id, Verb_id, Verb_desc, Act_id, Process_id, Serv_id, Ver_no} The partial trace table for the "Place Order" system is shown in Table 7.14.

Once the trace table is generated, it is easy to verify if all requirements have been correctly implemented based on service version descriptions.

7.8 Conclusion

Our approach helps in discovering correct service version matches based on the business functions extracted from the requirements automatically. A formal approach to categorize and document requirements helps in automatic generation of activity models. Moreover, the business process flows realized using activity models are used to dynamically choreograph the discovered services and generate corresponding BPMN model using a set of service versions. Our work helps in managing changes and maintain version repository for SOA. An automatic approach toward service discovery and choreography based on requirements helps in ensuring traceability of requirements.

References

1. Mavin, A., Wilkinson, P., Harwood, A., Novak, M., "Easy Approach to Requirements Syntax (EARS), 17th IEEE International Requirements Engineering Conference, RE '09, Aug. 31 2009–Sept. 4 2009.
2. Hogg, Jason, Don Smith, Fred Chong, Dwayne Taylor, Lonnie Wall, and Paul Slater. Web Service Security: Scenarios, Patterns, and Implementation Guidance for Web Services Enhancements (WSE) 3.0. Redmond, WA: Microsoft Press, 2005.
3. Luqi, "A Graph Model for Software Evolution", IEEE Transactions on Software Engineering, Vol. 16, Issue 8, pp. 917–927, August 1990.

4. Iam Graham, Requirements Modeling and Specification for Service Oriented Architecture, Wiley Publishers, ISBN: 978-0-470-77563-9, October 2008.
5. A. Mavin and P. Wilkinson, "Big Ears (The Return of "Easy Approach to Requirements Engineering")," *2010 18th IEEE International Requirements Engineering Conference*, Sydney, NSW, pp. 277–282, 2010.
6. Bernhard Beckert, "The Z Specification Language", http://formal.iti.kit.edu/~beckert/teaching/Spezifikation-SS04/11Z.pdf.
7. Grady Booch, The Unified Modeling Language User Guide, Pearson Education; 1 edition (2002).
8. Alan Moore, Rick Steiner, and Sanford Friedenthal, A Practical Guide to SysML: The Systems Modeling Language, Elsevier, 22-Nov-2011.
9. Holmes, T., Zdun, U., Dustdar, S., Automating the Management and Versioning of Service Models at Runtime to Support Service Monitoring, 16th IEEE International Enterprise Distributed Object Computing Conference, September 10–September 14, 2012.
10. Shuying Wang, Capretz, L. F., A service dependency model for multiple service version synchronization, 2009 11th IEEE International Symposium on Web Systems Evolution (WSE), 25–26 Sept. 2009.
11. Jayeeta Chanda, Sabnam Sengupta, Ananya Kanjilal and Swapan Bhattacharya, "FAM2BP: Transformation Framework of UML Behavioral Elements into BPMN Design Element", Proceedings of COSIT 2011, Bangalore, India, January 2–4, 2011.
12. Swapan Bhattacharya, Jayeeta Chanda, Sabnam Sengupta, Ananya Kanjilal, "Dynamic Service Choreography using Context Aware Enterprise Service Bus", proceedings of 23rd International Conference on Software Engineering and Knowledge Engineering (SEKE 2011), Miami, July 7–9, pp. 319–324, 2011.
13. Herbert Kaiser, A close look at Simplified Technical English, tcworld, magazine for the international information management, Sept 2013.
14. Norbert E. Fuchs, Uta Schwertel, Rolf Schwitter, "Attempto Controlled English (ACE) Language Manual Version 3.0", Technical Report 1999, University of Zurich ©1999.
15. G. Papamarkos, A. Poulovassilis, P. T. Wood, Event-condition-action rule languages for the semantic Web, in: Proceedings of the 1st International Workshop on Semantic Web and Databases, Berlin, Germany, 2003, pp. 309–327.
16. Shuping Ran, "A Model for Web Services discovery with QoS", ACM SIGecom Exchanges, Volume 4, Iss 1, pp 1–10, Spring 2003.
17. Zisman A., A Framework for Dynamic Service Discovery, 23rd IEEE/ACM International Conference on Automated Software Engineering, ASE 2008.
18. Evdemon, John. "Principles of Service Design: Service Versioning." Microsoft Developer Network, August 2005.
19. Brown, Kyle, and Michael Ellis. "Best Practices for Web Services Versioning." IBM Developer Works, January 2004.
20. Lhotka, Rocky. "A SOA Version Covenant." Enterprise.NET Community, April 2005.
21. Antoniol, G., Caprile, B., Potrich, A., Tonella, P., DesignCode Traceability Recovery: Selecting the Basic Linkage Properties, Science of Computer Programming, vol. 40, issue 2–3, pp. 213–234, July 2001.
22. Antoniol, G., Canfora, G., De Lucia, A., Casazza, G. Information Retrieval Models for Recovering Traceability Links between Code and Documentation Proceedings of the International Conference on Software Maintenance, 2000.
23. Arlow, J., Emmerich, W., Quinn, J., Literate Modelling—Capturing Business Knowledge with the UML, UML'98: Beyond the Notation 1998.
24. Gotel O. C. Z., Finkelstein A. C. W., An Analysis of the Requirements Traceability Problem. 1st International Conference on Rqts. Eng., pp. 94–101, 1994.

25. Balasubramaniam Ramesh, Matthias Jarke, "Toward Reference Models for Requirements Traceability", IEEE Transactions on Software Engineering, Vol 27, No. 1, pp 58–93, January 2001.
26. Grünbacher P., Egyed A., Medvidovic N., Reconciling Software Requirements and Architectures: The CBSP Approach, In: Proceedings 5th IEEE International Symposium on Requirements Engineering (RE01), Toronto, Canada, 2001.

Chapter 8
Architecturally Significant Requirements Identification, Classification and Change Management for Multi-tenant Cloud-Based Systems

Muhammad Aufeef Chauhan and Christian W. Probst

Abstract Involvement of numerous stakeholders in cloud-based systems' design and usage with varying degrees of nonfunctional requirements makes Architecturally Significant Requirements (ASRs) identification and management a challenge undertaking. The aim of the research presented in this chapter is to identify different types of design-time and run-time ASRs of the cloud-based systems, provide an ASRs classification scheme and present a framework to manage the requirements' variability during life cycle of the cloud-based systems. We have used a multifaceted research approach to address the ASRs identification, classification, and change management challenges. We have explored findings from systematic as well as structured reviews of the literature on quality requirements of the cloud-based systems including but not limited to security, availability, scalability, privacy, and multi-tenancy. We have presented a framework for requirements classification and change management focusing on distributed Platform as a Service (PaaS) and Software as a Service (SaaS) systems as well as complex software ecosystems that are built using PaaS and SaaS, such as Tools as a Service (TaaS). We have demonstrated applicability of the framework on a selected set of the requirements for the cloud-based systems. The results of the research presented in this chapter show that key quality requirements of the cloud-based systems, for example, multi-tenancy and security, have a significant impact on how other quality requirements (such as scalability, reliability, and interoperability) are handled in the overall architecture design of a cloud-based system. It is important to distinguish tenant-specific run-time architecturally significant quality requirements and corresponding cloud-based systems' components so that run-time status of the

M.A. Chauhan (✉) · C.W. Probst
Department of Applied Mathematics and Computer Science (DTU Compute),
Technical University of Denmark, Kongens Lyngby, Denmark
e-mail: muac@itu.dk

C.W. Probst
e-mail: cwpr@dtu.dk

M.A. Chauhan
Software and Systems Section, IT University of Copenhagen, Copenhagen, Denmark

© Springer International Publishing AG 2017
M. Ramachandran and Z. Mahmood (eds.), *Requirements Engineering for Service and Cloud Computing*, DOI 10.1007/978-3-319-51310-2_8

tenant-specific architecture quality requirements can be monitored and system configurations can be adjusted accordingly. For the systems that can be used by multiple tenants, the requirements change management framework should consider if the addition or modification (triggered by a specific tenant) of a quality requirement can impact quality requirements of other tenants, and whether or not a trade-off point should be introduced in the architecture (corresponding to the requirements). The trade-off point can also be referred as a variability point, that is, a compromise has to be made among the number of quality requirements and only some of the requirements can be satisfied. System analysts and software architects can use the proposed taxonomy and the management framework for identifying relevant quality requirements for multi-tenant cloud-based systems, for analyzing impact of changes in the requirements on the overall system architecture, and for managing variability of the architecturally significant requirements.

Keywords Cloud computing · Platform as a service (PaaS) · Software as a service (SaaS) · Architecturally significant requirements (ARSs) · Requirements classification · Requirements change management · Architecture quality

8.1 Introduction

Cloud computing's utility and service provisioning model offers on-demand scalability and flexible acquisition of computing and storage resources [6]. The cloud resources are offered as Infrastructure as a Service (IaaS), Platform as a Service (PaaS), and Software as a Service (SaaS) [18]. IaaS provides virtualization of underlying hardware infrastructure, whereas PaaS and SaaS utilize IaaS for providing platforms for cloud-enabled software development or on-demand software systems for end users. Cloud computing adoption can be broadly classified into three categories: (i) Utilizing Infrastructure as a Service (IaaS) [43] cloud environments (as a hosting platform) to deploy software applications. (ii) Migrating existing applications to the cloud to offer the applications as Software as a Service (SaaS) following pay-per-use model [7, 16, 17]. (iii) Developing new SaaS applications using IaaS and PaaS [43] cloud resources.

Development of the cloud-based systems for each of the above-mentioned purposes have associated challenges in terms of Architecturally Significant Requirements (ASRs) identification, analysis and management. Nonfunctional requirements that can have a significant impact on architecture of a software system are referred as ASRs [29]. Each cloud-based system can have a specific set of ASRs, which are more relevant to that system. In the cloud-based systems that use IaaS as a mean to acquire flexible and on-demand infrastructure resources, requirements such as scalability, elasticity, and security are important. For the systems that are to be migrated from old infrastructure to the cloud, the requirements such as interoperability, security, and privacy are more important [16]. The ability of the selected IaaS and PaaS clouds to support the future enhancements in the system are critical for developing new applications as well as migrating existing applications on the cloud [7, 17]. Some of the ASRs are equally important for different types of the cloud-based systems. For example, as cloud-based systems are aimed to serve many tenants, a characteristic that is referred as multi-tenancy [10] is critical for each of the IaaS, PaaS, and SaaS systems. Moreover, each tenant of the system can have its specific design-time and run-time architecturally significant requirements, including but not limited to security, privacy, availability, scalability, elasticity, and portability [18, 47]. Hence, managing different quality requirements for different tenants is also important. Specific types of cloud-based systems can have additional ASRs, for example, the systems that provision Tools as a Service (TaaS) need to support semantic and process-centric integration [19, 45]. Furthermore, as the data and services are hosted on geographically distributed locations, the cloud-based systems have to comply with additional constraints and regulatory requirements that can directly or indirectly impact architecture of the systems. Last, but not the least, the ASRs can change during life cycle of a cloud-based system. The changes can be either because of involvement of the new stakeholders or modifications in the requirements of the existing stakeholders.

To adequately address the above-mentioned challenges, there is a need to have a specialized approach for identification, classification, analysis, and management of the design-time and run-time architecturally significant requirements of the cloud-based systems and for variability management of the requirements. In particular, we aim to address the following objectives:

- Discuss important Architecturally Significant Requirements (ASRs) of the cloud-based systems, different dimensions of the requirements and the impact that the requirements can have on difference life cycle phases of the cloud-based systems (i.e., system design, system instantiation, system operation, and system evolution). The discussion on ASRs and their respective dimensions can facilitate analysis of the run-time and design-time architecture quality of a cloud-based system.
- Provide a classification scheme to group the ASRs into different categories based upon their impact on the life cycle phases of the cloud-based systems. The classification scheme can help to identify the requirements that should be focused during each phase (including the systems' deployment and operational phases with respect to the multi-tenancy configurations).
- Propose a quality requirements management approach so that the requirements corresponding to the specific tenants can be managed and their impact on each other can be analyzed when existing requirements are changed or modified, or the new requirements are added. The proposed management approach can facilitate to keep track of the changes in the requirements and to control the architecture quality of a cloud-based system in terms of inclusion of the desired ASRs in a specific cloud-based system.

This chapter is organized as follows. Section 8.2 provides an insight to the ASRs for the cloud-based systems. Section 8.3 explores the relation of the ASRs with multi-tenancy quality of the cloud-based systems. Section 8.4 describes a classification scheme that can be used for classifying the ASRs into different groups using the presented classification parameters. Section 8.5 presents a probabilistic analysis method to analyze the impact of the included ASRs on overall architecture quality of the systems. Section 8.6 describes the related work and Sect. 8.7 concludes this chapter.

8.2   Architecturally Significant Requirements of the Cloud-Based Systems

Architecturally Significant Requirements (ASRs) play a critical role in architecture design, development, and adoption of a software system [29]. The ASRs' impact on a software system raises the need to incorporate the ASRs at early stages of the software architecture design. If the ASRs are not analyzed and anticipated during initial phases of architecture design, a major architecture refactoring may be needed during later stages, which can result in multifold increase in development cost of a software system [29]. Hence, it is important to analyze different types of the ASRs (that can be important for the cloud-based systems) and their impact on different parts of the systems. A summarized view of the ASRs for the cloud-based systems is presented in Fig. 8.1. The details of the ASRs critical for the cloud-based systems are discussed in the following subsections.

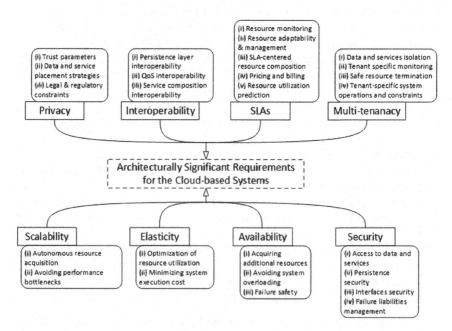

Fig. 8.1 An overview of Architecturally Significant Requirements (ASRs) for the cloud-based systems

8.2.1 Scalability

Scalability is one of the fundamental quality requirements of the cloud-based systems. Scalability supports on-demand provisioning of a cloud-based system by acquiring additional resources, as the number of users using the system grow [18]. Scalability needs for the cloud-based systems can be classified into two main groups. (i) Scalability requirements associated with identifying the system usage and bottlenecks so that a prediction (an estimation) can be made for the needed resources [35]. (ii) Autonomous resource acquisition requirements along with resource acquisition rules so that the resources from the public, private, or hybrid clouds can be acquired on-demand [5, 67].

The most commonly used system monitoring metrics are active profiling of CPU and identification of bottlenecks associated with response time using heuristics algorithms [35]. The cloud resources can be acquired from private, hybrid, or public clouds depending upon constraints on the data and the service. For more competitive and cost-effective resource acquisition approaches, different auction schemes such as Modified Vickery Auction (MVA) and Continuous Double Auction (CDA) can be adopted for sufficient resource availability and unsufficient resources availability, respectively [67]. Vertical scaling (when scalability patterns are adopted in multiple layers of a cloud-based system) and horizontal scaling (when scalability patterns are adopted in only one layer of a cloud-based system) can also be adopted in the cloud-based systems using private, hybrid, and public IaaS clouds [5]. Therefore, the scalability requirements for the cloud-based systems should consider all the above-mentioned factors.

8.2.2 Elasticity

While scalability handles acquisition of additional resources, elasticity deals with optimizing the resource acquisition process so that the extra IaaS resources can be disposed off when not needed [39, 41]. The elasticity requirements can be associated with different types of Quality of Service (QoS) parameters. Observing a time lapse between a request for a particular operation and response of the request is one of the frequently used QoS parameters [39]. Throughput of the layers and data retrieval time is another QoS parameter that is considered for elasticity [51]. Minimizing execution cost of a cloud-based system is also an important parameter to measure elasticity of the system [30]. Last but not the least, providing lowcost computing cycles is an important dimension to consider for achieving elasticity in a PaaS system [52].

8.2.3 Availability

Availability quality requirements guarantee that a cloud-based system and its constituting services are available for utilization as specified in a Service Level Agreement (SLA) [18]. Availability quality characteristics in the cloud-based systems can be achieved in the following ways: (i) Acquiring additional infrastructure resources for hosting the system's services and data for redundant deployment to avoid complete system failures [26]. (ii) Avoiding overloading of the system's resources by replicating the components and services to distribute load among the replicated resources [66]. (iii) Achieving increased application performance by replicating the computing resources to distribute computing intensive tasks and workflows [4, 37].

There are a number of additional constraints that need to be examined corresponding to the availability requirements. The specific location constraints on the IaaS cloud resources that can be used for hosting the system's components (e.g., computing and storage resources available on the IaaS cloud nodes or geographical regions where the physical infrastructure is available) should be examined [26]. The nature of the required availability approaches, i.e., active or passive approaches should be considered [4]. Moreover, the requirements associated with the questions such as whether to make the cloud monitoring mechanism an integral part of the system or to carry out the monitoring via external monitoring agents should also be considered [37].

8.2.4 Security

As the cloud-based systems are accessible via Internet, security becomes an essential quality requirement of the cloud-based systems [18]. The security quality characteristics of the cloud-based systems can be classified into four categories: (i) Access to the cloud-hosted data and services. (ii) Security of the persisted data on the cloud. (iii) Security of the APIs through which the cloud services are exposed to the external world. (iv) Security liabilities of the cloud providers and cloud-hosted Virtual Machines (VMs).

Each of the security quality requirements categories can be further broken down into a number of sub-quality requirements with respect to the nature and types of security attacks that can target a cloud-based system. To restrict the users so that they can have access to the system only according to the desired privileges, different types of the authorization requirements can be incorporated, such as authorization based upon users' roles (e.g., if a specific user is authorized to perform certain operations in the system or can have access to a specific type of data) or users' hierarchy in the users access tree structure (e.g., administrators and super users have more privileges than normal users) [18]. Quality requirements associated with data persistence on the cloud deal with data confidentiality and integrity [55].

The confidentiality requirements for the persisted data deal with threats to the stored data, undesired use of the stored data and availability of the stored data. There can also be data encryption requirements for using different types of encryption algorithms [25, 32], e.g., using ElGamal public key cryptosystems [23]. The requirements for protection against undesired or illegal use of data can require embedding certain types of auditing schemes for data usage history [21, 63]. The requirements concerning the security of the Application Programable Interfaces (APIs) encompass protection from code-centric or SQL injection attacks, hijacking of user sessions, and XML/SOAP wrapping or flooding attacks (the attacks in which huge volume of XML data are sent to APIs to fail the access control and authentication mechanisms) [1]. The requirements for cloud providers security liabilities include handling of plausible service deniability, anonymizing data, and service indexes, introducing intermediate security services to protect direct access to the cloud-hosted data and catering oblivious routing of the data [14]. Protecting the internal application services and providing standards-based end point abstractions for secured communication among the services are also important security considerations [59]. The integrity requirements encompass inclusion of Byzantine Fault Tolerance approaches in the persistence services of the cloud-based systems [3].

8.2.5 Privacy

Privacy requirements of the cloud-based systems are closely related to the security requirements. Privacy on the cloud means that the data is stored and processed on the cloud as defined in privacy specifications. The privacy quality requirements can be classified into three categories: (i) The requirements for specifying trusted cloud parameters and identifiers (that can be used to capture stakeholders' privacy constraints and to select the cloud resources according to the specified constraints). (ii) The requirements for data storage and service placement strategies corresponding to the privacy constraints. (iii) The privacy requirements to comply with legal and regulatory constraints.

The requirements for identification of parameters that can characterize trusted cloud services (and when the services should be opened to remote users) and trusted external services are derived from further refinements of the privacy requirements [8]. Similarly, the privacy specific location parameters that specify where the data and services can be hosted (and which can be driven by legal or regulatory constraints) are a critical part of the privacy requirements [8]. The requirements for services matching process (to facilitate service composition) are a core factor that can influence the design of a cloud-based system. For example, if the end users are allowed to specify their privacy parameters and select the services that are to process the data, a market-oriented cloud-broker infrastructure can be helpful. The cloud-broker can facilitate the users to interact with a cloud market in which the users can specify their privacy constraints and the cloud-broker selects the services with optimal match to the privacy constraints [11]. Hence, in order to incorporate the security in a cloud-based system, the requirements for the brokerage infrastructure should be considered.

8.2.6 Interoperability

Cloud interoperability enables multiple cloud-enabled systems to collaborate with each other [15]. Cloud interoperability can be classified into multiple dimensions as follows: (i) Interoperability of the data persistence layer so that the data can be stored on the cloud resources satisfying location, security, and privacy constraints on the data. (ii) Interoperability among different layers of the cloud service model (i.e., IaaS, PaaS, and SaaS) so that the underlying cloud infrastructure satisfying location, security, and privacy constraints can be selected. (iii) Interoperability of the cloud-hosted services so that the services can be composed at runtime according to the desired Quality of Service (QoS) parameters.

The requirements for the above-mentioned interoperability dimensions can be broken down further into multiple sub-requirements. Cloud services and persistence interoperability requirements deal with how to handle multiple collaborative cloud services, how to select the appropriate persistence store of the data, details on the mechanisms of storing and retrieving the data from the data persistence units, and on-the-fly migrating of the data and services among heterogeneous clouds [31, 57]. The requirements for the brokerage process among the clouds deal with defining and executing the mechanisms for selection of the desired cloud resources via cloud brokerage [64]. Defining interlayer mappings among the cloud resources to categorize the resources that can be replaces with one another is vital for interoperability [15]. The requirements of defining, identifying, and selecting interoperable cloud services can facilitate not only service selection process but also run-time composition of the services [56]. Decentralized deployment of the cloud infrastructure can facilitate satisfaction of the security and privacy constraints on the data and the services, hence the cloud-based systems' requirements for the decentralized deployment should be matched with the infrastructure support of the underlying cloud [50]. The requirements for autonomous selection and composition of the underlying cloud resources and the hosted cloud-based systems' services explore different parameters needed for resources or services identification and the attributes for which the search queries can be run [48]. The selection and composition requirements can also facilitate the resources and services matching and portability of the services among the clouds [49]. These requirements can also be used for discovering and composing heterogeneous cloud services on the fly [68].

8.2.7   Service Level Agreement (SLA) Compliance

The compliance of the cloud-hosted data and services with Service Level Agreements (SLA) between the cloud-resource providers and the cloud-resource consumers is vital; especially when a large number of tenants with varying service quality needs are being served [40]. Hence, the requirements related to SLAs compliance focus on the following dimension: (i) Monitoring requirements for the cloud resources and cloud-hosted services to monitor the quality attributes of interest. (ii) Resources' adaptability and management requirements corresponding to the monitoring parameters. (iii) Service composition requirements for satisfying SLAs. (iv) Billing requirements for managing pricing variability with respect to the SLAs. (v) Requirements for predicting the system's behavior with respect to the run-time quality requirements in order to enable the SLA compliance for unforeseen scenarios.

For the cloud-resource providers to comply with SLAs, the providers have to monitor the resources for quality attributes of interest such as scalability [38]. The monitoring requirements need to be focused on key performance indicators of the system (e.g., elasticity, scalability, and performance) and the monitoring should be nonintrusive so that the monitoring mechanism do not affect normal operations of the system [34]. Adaptability requirements should be focused on quality of service parameters for services transmission and communication environments, and should focus on key performance indicators [34]. SLA requirements should also include requirements associated with availability of the qualified candidate services [53], optimal service composition approaches to be adopted for QoS specific services' composition [46] and requirements for license management of the virtualized cloud resources [12].

For services and data management in the cloud-based systems, the focus of the requirements engineering and management effort should be on characterizing SLA compliance and regulatory requirements for data retention, intercloud migration of the services and data, and confidentiality constraints on the data and the services [42, 60]. The requirements for run-time management of the SLAs (including enforcement of fine-grained SLA compliance policies for managing data and handling run-time services operations, enforcement of data retention policies on data persistence objects, and management of billing corresponding to the run-time quality requirements) are also critical [11]. Moreover, the requirements for resource discovery and monitoring in accordance with SLAs are also important. To conclude, the SLA compliance requirements need to focus on consistency, scalability [20], workload management driven by applications and users behavior [40], monitoring of the resources deployed on different platforms [70], anticipation of the system behavior for desired QoS parameters [27], customization of the monitoring parameters for different types of the systems following users' specifications [13], and optimization of profit margins while satisfying SLAs [9].

8.3 Relationship of the Architecturally Significant Requirements with Multi-tenancy Quality Characteristics

Multi-tenancy quality characteristic (requirement) of the cloud-based systems facilitates secured sharing of the resources among multiple tenants and adoption of the systems with respect to tenant-specific configurations [62]. Multi-tenancy characteristic affects the design of the cloud-based systems from two-different perspectives. First, multi-tenancy determines security to provide isolation among different services belonging to different tenants in a cloud-based system. Services' isolation is also referred as security dimension of multi-tenancy. Second, multi-tenancy determines a specific configuration of a cloud-based system for a specific tenant with respect to the quality requirements discussed in Sect. 8.2. The security requirements of the multi-tenancy can be classified into three broad categories: (i) Isolation among the data and services belonging to different tenants. (ii) Monitoring of the resources for their compliance with QoS parameters and their usage (so that the tenants can be billed accordingly). (iii) Safe termination of the resources once tenant-specific operations are completed so that run-time state of tenant-specific configuration of the system cannot be exploited via a cross tenant attack. Specification and management of the run-time quality requirements for different tenants are determined by the nature of the run-time system's operations and constraints on the data processing services and need for exposure of the data to external systems.

Security requirements of the multi-tenancy focus on the following dimensions. To control access to the multi-tenant systems, the requirements focus on hierarchical Role-Based Access Control (hRBAC) mechanisms or conditional Role-Based Access Control (cRBAC) mechanisms [10]. For hRBAC mechanisms, different users and external systems are grouped into hierarchical clusters of users, and access rights are determined based upon the position of a user or an external system in the hierarchy. For cRBAC mechanisms, the users and systems are granted access to the system to perform a specific operation if all the preconditions are satisfied. The preconditions include not only authentication and authorization but also if the prerequisite operations have been completed and the data needed for the current operations (to be performed) is available. To have a centralized security control mechanism for all the system provided by a particular cloud platform, an aspect-oriented security mechanism can be adopted [2]. The requirements for the aspect-based security control mechanism focus on database requirements to maintain architecture description of the hosted systems and security constraints desired by different tenants, management system requirements to define and integrate security in the hosted systems, and interface requirements through which the security aspects can be integrated in the hosted systems.

The focus of handling generic quality requirements for multi-tenant cloud-based systems is on feature-based resource management, cost-based resource optimization, tenant distribution over the resources, and monitoring of the services and hosted platforms for their compliance with SLAs. The requirements associated with feature-based resource management focus on models that can be used to share instances of the services among the tenants with similar quality requirements [44]. These requirements also focus on resource allocation model to analyze failure cost of wrong service placement strategy and cost of successful service placement strategy in terms of energy footprint and price of the used resources. For distributing tenant-specific resources on hybrid clouds to satisfy the privacy and security constraints, the scheduling and routing algorithms should focus on context of the operations and data requests [24]. For monitoring the deployed resources on the hybrid clouds, observers on all layers of the cloud service and deployment model can be needed [28]. Moreover, to satisfy the run-time performance parameters for SLA compliance, the multi-tenancy requirements should focus on monitoring, scheduling, load balancing and provisioning of the components, and services and data according to available computing resources for each specific tenant [61].

8.4 A Classification Scheme for Management of Architecturally Significant Requirements

Traditionally, architecturally significant quality requirements are classified into two broad categories: (i) design-time quality requirements and (ii) run-time quality requirements [29]. However, in order to organize the requirements for complex software systems, such as cloud-enabled systems, the requirements need to be further classified into sub-groups. The sub-groups facilitate to establish the relationship among different types of the requirements' classes and analyze the impact of changes in the requirements across the sub-groups. In this section, we identify different attributes that can be used to classify the architecturally significant quality requirements of the cloud-based systems into different groups and discuss a selected set of the requirements to explain the classification approach. An overview of the requirements classes and the classification parameters is shown Fig. 8.2 and the details of the sub-classes along with description of the classification parameters are summarized in Table 8.1.

8.4.1 System Management Requirements for Hosted Services and Data

The requirements that can be classified into this group are associated with provisioning of the cloud-hosted services following the desired run-time quality parameters, providing communication among the hosted services, and handling the security and privacy constraints. In the following subsections, we describe the details on classification parameters for different dimensions of the system management requirements.

Fig. 8.2 Architecturally
Significant Requirements
classes and key classification
parameters for the
cloud-based systems

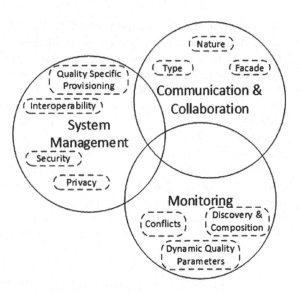

8.4.1.1 Quality Specific Provisioning

The requirements of the cloud-enabled systems can be classified into *Quality Specific Provisioning* group if the requirements satisfy to the following conditions:

- The requirements defining the parameters for initialization and deployment of the services, data, or a combination of these on the cloud.
- The requirements that can have an impact on run-time behavior of a cloud-based system.
- The requirements that either specify the parameters for SLAs management or deal with the system compliance with the SLAs.
- The requirements classifying the nature and types of the client systems or services that are to interact with a cloud-based system.
- The requirements specifying the nature and type of the end user devices that are to interact with the system.

8.4.1.2 Interoperability and Integration Requirements

The *Interoperability and Integration Requirements* group encapsulates the requirements satisfying the following conditions:

- The requirements that deal with specifying system interfaces. For example, REST-based interfaces, SOAP-based interfaces, or translucent callback interfaces.

Table 8.1 Requirements classes and parameters used for classification

Requirement classes	Classification parameters
Quality specific provisioning	Controlling initialization and deployment
	Effecting run-time system behavior
	Facilitating SLAs achievement
	Dealing with nature and type of client systems and services
	Dealing with end-user devices
Interoperability and integration	Enabling translucent system interfaces
	Governing cloud federation
	Specifying interoperability of the hosted services
Security and privacy	Accessing data and services
	Dealing with multi-tenancy
	Specifying data encryption requirements
	Trusting cloud and the hosted services
	Complying with legal and regulatory requirements
	Handling data and service placement strategies
	Managing liabilities of the cloud-hosted services
Communication and collaboration	Enabling communication and interaction with heterogeneous cloud environments and externally services
	Securing inter service communication
	Providing services interface facades
	Abstracting service end points
Monitoring	Checking compliance with respect to dynamically changeing quality characteristics
	Adapting run-time quality parameters
	Monitoring quality parameters
	Managing run-time quality conflicts
	Optimizing system configuration with respect to quality characteristics
	Enabling autonomous services selection and composition
	Managing services distribution and scheduling mechanisms
	Enabling dynamic cloud resource discovery
	Handling redundant service deployments

- The requirements that handle specification, management, and governance of the federated cloud. That is, what kind of cloud resources should be combined to form a federated cloud, when the cloud federation should take place, and under which conditions specific services from a federated cloud should be selected.
- The requirements which deal with nature and type of the data that should be exchanged among the services. For example, whether XML-based data structures or a language-specific data structures are to be used for interoperability and integration among the services.

8.4.1.3 Security and Privacy Requirements

The *Security and Privacy* group includes the requirements dealing with one or more of the following specifications.

- The requirements dealing with access to the cloud-hosted data and services. These requirements include both authentication and authorization requirements.
- The requirements handling different aspects of the multi-tenancy characteristic of a cloud-based system. For example, whether the tenant-specific service instances should be isolated from each other or not, what quality of service parameters are desired by each tenant, and how multiple services can be composed to meet QoS constraints of a specific tenant.
- The requirements associated with security of the data. For example, whether the data should be encrypted or not, what kind of encryption algorithm should be applied on the data, and how the data should be persisted.
- The requirements specifying constrains on the trusted execution of the services on the cloud. These requirements can include the characteristics of the trusted cloud environments and the parameters to be used for the selection of a trusted cloud environment.
- The requirements specifying legal and regulatory constrains on the systems. For example, for how long the data history of a system should be maintained before permanently deleting the data.
- The requirements specifying the strategies for hosting the services and persisting the data on different cloud environments. For example, a constraint specifying that sensitive data should always be stored on a private cloud in an encrypted format.
- The requirements specifying system liabilities and penalties for cases in which a cloud-based system fails to comply with desired operational conditions. These requirements can also include how to handle the exceptional cases in which desired security and privacy constraints could not be satisfied.

8.4.2 Communication and Collaboration Requirements

Communication and collaboration among the services and hosting cloud environments, when a cloud-based system is operational, are a critical run-time property of the cloud-based systems. The requirements associated with *communication and collaboration* group can be classified based upon the following properties.

- The requirements that specify the parameters for communication and interaction among heterogeneous cloud environments as well as interaction among the services hosted on the heterogeneous cloud environments.
- The requirements defining nature and type of the communication. For example, whether the communication is to be encrypted or not, or whether a specific

communication protocol (e.g., publisher subscriber pattern) should be followed to exchange the notifications and data.

- The requirements defining services' facade.
- The requirements defining types of interfaces and signatures of interfaces for services' end points.

8.4.3 Monitoring Requirements

Services monitoring requirements handle observation of the run-time system behavior and adaptation based on the analysis of the monitoring parameters. The requirements can be classified into this category based upon the following properties.

- The requirements monitoring system compliance with respect to the dynamically changing architecture quality attributes. For example, security and privacy requirements of the data can be different for different types of tenants and can vary according to the nature and type of the data.
- The requirements dealing with monitoring of specific run-time quality attributes of a cloud-based system.
- The requirements specifying mechanisms to handle conflicting run-time quality requirements.
- The requirements associated with optimization methods based upon the systems' monitoring metrics.
- The requirements specifying concrete methods to achieve the quality attributes. For example, services distribution and scheduling mechanisms.
- The requirements specifying details of resource discovery and composition.

8.5 A Probabilistic Analysis Method to Analyze Impact of Changes in Architecturally Significant Requirements

The different types of the architecturally significant requirements discussed in Sects. 8.2 and 8.3 can be classified into different groups as discussed in Sect. 8.4. A change in one of the requirements can impact one or more of the related or dependant requirements. As a result, to manage and track changes in the requirements, a systematic approach is required that can be used to analyze the impact of the changes with reference to the nature and type of relationships that exist among different requirements and the degree of impact that the requirements can have on each other. In this section, we describe a probabilistic analysis method to analyze impact of the changes in architecturally significant requirements.

The requirements can be related to each other with different types of relations to represent dependency, composition, complementation, contradiction, and proportionality relationships. These relationships are explained as follows:

- *Dependency relation* represents a relationship among the architecturally significant requirements such that a requirement B is dependent upon a requirement. In other words, in order to satisfy the requirement B, the system first has to satisfy the requirement A.
- *Composition relation* represents a relationship among the architecturally significant requirements such that the composition of a number of sub-requirements is needed in order to satisfy a higher order requirement.
- *Complementation relation* represents a relationship among the architecturally significant requirements such that incorporation of a requirement A in the system can complement a requirement B, i.e., incorporating the requirement A in the system can make it easy to incorporate the requirement B.
- *Contradiction relation* represents a relationship among the architecturally significant requirements such that a requirement A is contradictory to a requirement B, i.e., it is not possible to completely satisfy both the requirements (A and B) in the system at the same time. In other words, either the requirements A and B are mutually exclusive or a trade-off has to be made for degree of satisfaction of each requirement in the system.
- *Inverse proportionality relation* represents a relationship among the architecturally significant requirements such that the degree of achieving a requirement A can have an inverse impact on the degree of achieving a requirement B. For example, if a cloud-based system satisfies a requirement A 90% of the time, the requirement B can only be satisfied 10% of the time, and vice versa.

Each of the defined relationships has a probabilistic value, which represents the degree of strength of the relationship between two requirements. For example, a probabilistic value of 50% with *dependency relation* between the requirements A and B shows that the requirement B is at least 50% dependent on the requirement A. Figure 8.3 shows the symbolic representation of the relationships that can exist among the requirements and describes an example scenario. The relationships can be used for not only to establish a link among the requirements of the cloud-based systems but also to analyze impact of changes in one of the requirements on the other system requirements.

Figure 8.3 shows the details of the proposed approach for the analysis of two types of high-level Architecturally Significant Requirements (ASRs), i.e., high response time and security of a cloud-based system. The probability score associated with the different relations in the diagram is based upon the expert opinion of the authors of this chapter. An alternative approach to the expert opinion can be to seek input from the stakeholders of the system and calculate the probability score using weighted averages (e.g., for cases in which some of the stakeholders have more control on the requirements engineering and management than others). The relations to achieve the change management shown in Fig. 8.3 are linked to each

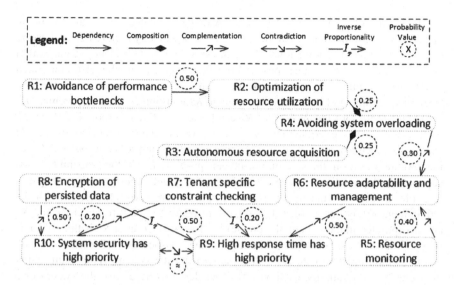

Fig. 8.3 Relationships of the probabilistic analysis method and an example application scenario

other in the following manner. The requirement *R2* for optimization of the resource utilization is dependant on the requirement *R1*, which deals with avoidance of the performance bottlenecks of the systems. A probability value score of 0.50 is assigned, indicating that *R2* is 50% dependent upon *R1*. To avoid system overloading, the requirement *R4* is composed of R2 (for optimization of the resource utilization) and *R3* (for autonomous resource acquisition). Each of the requirements *R2* and *R3* complement 25% to the achievement of *R4*, whereas remaining 50% is handled by the requirement *R4* itself. The requirement *R6* is associated with resource adaptability and management. *R6* can be complemented by *R4* by delegating system overloading avoidance capability to *R4*. The probability score of 0.30 is assigned, which indicate that 30% of the *R6* responsibility can be handled by *R4*. Similarly, the requirement *R5* handling resource monitoring contributes 40% to *R6* and subsequently *R6* contributes 50% to the requirement *R9*. *R9* describes that high response time is of higher priority for the system than security. The requirements *R7* and *R8* deal with security in terms of tenants specific security constraints checking and encryption of persisted data, respectively. *R7* and *R8* are inversely proportional to *R9* because incorporating more security measures in the system decreases response time. The probability values associated with inverse proportionality relationships have negative contributions, i.e., *R7* decreases response time by 20% and *R8* decreases response time by 50%. The requirement *R10* described that higher system security is desired. *R7* and *R8* have positive contribution to *R10* and can facilitate to incorporate *R10* in the system by the factor of 20% and 50%, respectively. As shown in Fig. 8.3, *R9* and *R10* are contradictory requirements and both cannot be fully satisfied at the same time, hence a trade-off has to be made to decide to which extend each of *R9* and *R10* should be incorporated in the system.

The quality of architecture in terms of ASR can be calculated in the following manner. A maximum score 1 can be assigned to each quality requirement indicating that it can be completely incorporated in the system. For dependency, composition and complementation relations, probability value assigned with the relation is added to the target requirement's score (for the requirements incorporation into the system). For example, in Fig. 8.3 the requirement R1 contributes to the requirement R2 with value 0.50. This means 50% of R2 can be achieved by incorporating R1 in the system. Similarly, the requirements R4 is composed of the requirements R2 and R3 each with a factor of 0.25. This means that each of R2 and R3 contributes 25% for incorporation of R4 in the system. For inverse proportionality, the probability value score with the relation is subtracted from the target requirement's score. For example, in Fig. 8.3, the requirements R7 and R8 are inversely related with the requirement R9 by factors of 0.20 and 0.50, respectively. As a result, if R7 and R8 are incorporated in the system, the probability for satisfaction of R9 is the system is only 0.30 (1–0.20–0.50). Only of the requirements associated with each other with a contradiction relation cannot be fully satisfied by the system. As a result, either only one of the requirements should be considered to be part of the system or a trade-off has to be made among the requirements for their respective degree of incorporation in the system. Table 8.2 lists the relations that can exist between the requirements versus their contributions to a system's architecture quality.

The probability value scores associated with the relations (as shown in Fig. 8.3) can be calculated in the following manner: (i) If there is a consensus among the stakeholders on the probability score of a relation, the agreed probability score can be assigned directly. (ii) If the stakeholders cannot reach a consensus, then the weighted averages for a relation k can be taken according to the following formula, in which k corresponds to identifier of each relation and N corresponds to the total number of stakeholders involved in the decision making process of the relation k.

$$Probability\,Score(k) = \frac{\sum_{i=1}^{N} Weight(k)_i \times Score(k)_i}{N}$$

The values of each of the $Weight(k)_i$ and $Score(k)_i$ can range between 0 and 1, depending upon the value of a specific stakeholder's weight for a specific relation and the probability score assigned by the stakeholder to the relation. The weighted average of a relation k specifies probability score value of the relation k between two requirements. For example, let us assume that there are two stakeholders of the

Table 8.2 Contribution of the relations between ASRs to overall system quality

Relation	Relation's contribution
Dependency	Positive
Composition	Positive
Complementation	Positive
Contradiction	Mutually exclusive (trade-off required)
Inverse proportionality	Negative

requirements *R1* and *R2* and they cannot reach a consensus on the probability score of the dependency relation between *R1* and *R2*. If first stakeholder has 0.75 weight (stakes on the requirements) and choose a probability value score of 0.80 for the relation, and second stakeholders has 0.50 weight and choose a probability value score of 0.25. The probability score of the dependency relation between the requirements *R1* and *R2* can be calculated as follows:

$$\frac{0.75(Weight_1) \times 0.80(Score_1) + 0.50(Weight_2) \times 0.25(Score_2)}{2(N)} = 0.36$$

The weighted averages for all the relations among the requirements in case of disagreements can be calculated in the similar manner.

The relations and probabilities assigned with the relations (as shown in Fig. 8.3) can also be used to analyze impact of the changes in the requirements on overall architecture quality of a cloud-based system. Addition of new requirements or removal of existing requirements from the probabilistic analysis model can result in addition or removal of the relations and changes in the respective probabilities of the relations. Modification in the requirements can require reanalysis of the probabilities assigned to the relations. Addition, removal or modification in some of the requirements can require recalculation of the whole probabilistic analysis model. Hence, the probabilistic analysis method presented in this section provides not only the traces among different types of the requirements but also the types of the traces (in terms of the relations) and strength of the traces (in terms of the probability values), which in turn provides a mechanism to evaluate overall requirements quality of a cloud-based system.

8.6 Related Work

A number of studies have focused on requirements for cloud-based system and variability management of the requirements. Ramachandran [54] has proposed a business-oriented requirements engineering approach for the cloud-based systems. The proposed approach takes market requirements as a baseline for requirements engineering and cloud business strategy. In subsequent stages, the requirements are elicited, and cloud services are designed and tested. The business analysis is consisted of tasks, knowledge, and techniques that can be used to identify business needs and solution to the business needs. Dey and Lee [22] have proposed a requirements elicitation and variability management approach. The presented approach proposed that the requirements elicitation should focus on the social, environmental, and economic context. The proposed variability management approach focused on recording and analyzing identified conflicts, identifying key changes for the system redesign, identifying users expected behavior for different states of the system and identifying most feasible set of requirements for the cloud-based systems. Iankoulova and Daneva [33] have presented a systematic review of the studies discussing cloud computing security requirements. The review has identified access control, integrity, auditing, privacy, and nonrepudiation as commonly reported security requirements. Kalloniatis et al. [36] have analyzed the cloud deployment scenarios with respect to security and privacy requirements. The authors have argued that the security analysis should be performed with respect to organizational needs and cloud-deployment models.

Rimal et al. [58] have described the architecture requirements for the cloud-based systems in terms of provider requirements, enterprise requirements, and user requirements. The requirements describe cloud-service models, cloud deployment models, cloud quality characteristics, and billing requirements. Wind and Schrodl [65] have provided a comparison framework of the requirements engineering models for the cloud-based systems. Four well-known software development models including V Model, Rational Unified Process, Extreme Programming, and Volere are explored in terms of their suitability for requirements engineering to analyze cloud offerings with respect to suppliers and customers viewpoints, orchestration, and application components. Zardari and Bahsoon [69] have presented a goal oriented requirements engineering approach to support cloud adoption. The presented approach focuses on matching-desired goals with features of the cloud service providers. After features selection, matches are analyzed for risks and finally cloud services with least risks are selected for utilization.

The related work discussed in this section focus on higher level enterprise and business requirements for the cloud-based systems, and describe approaches to match the requirements with available cloud services. On the contrary, the research presented in this chapter focuses on multiple dimensions of the architecturally significant requirements for the cloud-based systems, relations among the requirements and an approach to manage changes in the requirements.

8.7 Conclusions

A clear understanding of the Architecturally Significant Requirements (ASRs) and relation among different dimensions of the ASRs is critical to achieve quality in architecture of the cloud-based systems. The biggest challenge for architecting quality in the cloud-based systems is to have an understanding of the details to which the ASRs should be explored and how the changes in one type of the ASRs can impact the other ASRs. In this chapter, we have presented a set of core ASRs of the cloud-based systems and have explored the requirements' relationships with the multi-tenancy quality characteristic of the cloud-based systems. The ASRs are classified into three classes including system management requirements, communication and collaboration requirements, and monitoring requirements. We have identified key classification attributes for each of the requirements classes. For example, monitoring requirements handle dynamic monitoring of the quality parameters, identification of the run-time quality conflicts, and dynamic discovery and composition of the system services (or components) to maintain the run-time quality of a cloud-based system. We have also presented a probabilistic analysis method to analyze the impact of the ASRs on each other as well as to analyze impact of change in one of the requirements on other related and dependant requirements. The presented analysis method utilizes five different types of the relations (i.e., dependency, composition, complementation, contradiction, and inverse proportionality) to evaluate impact of the changes.

We foresee that the presented research can be used by the researchers and practitioners to identify core quality characteristics of the cloud-based systems and to use the identified dimensions of the ASRs to elicit the requirements' details. The presented probabilistic analysis method can be used to control run-time system configuration to achieve desired quality in a cloud-based system. In future, we tend to explore the presented research for its suitability for managing SaaS product lines. We also plan to extend the presented research to provide the traces among the live components of the cloud-based systems so that the quality of on-the-fly system composition for multi-tenant cloud-based systems can be determined.

Acknowledgements Part of the research leading to these results has received funding from the European Union Seventh Framework Program (FP7/2007-2013) under grant agreement no. 318003 (TRE$_S$PASS). This publication reflects only the authors' views and the Union is not liable for any use that may be made of the information contained herein.

References

1. Al-Aqrabi, H., Liu, L., Xu, J., Hill, R., Antonopoulos, N., Zhan, Y.: Investigation of it security and compliance challenges in security-as-a-service for cloud computing. In: Object/Component/Service-Oriented Real-Time Distributed Computing Workshops (ISORCW), 2012 15th IEEE International Symposium on. pp. 124–129. IEEE (2012).
2. Almorsy, M., Grundy, J., Ibrahim, A.S.: Tossma: A tenant-oriented saas security management architecture. In: Cloud computing (cloud), 2012 ieee 5th international conference on. pp. 981–988. IEEE (2012).
3. AlZain, M.A., Soh, B., Pardede, E.: A byzantine fault tolerance model for a multi-cloud computing. In: Computational Science and Engineering (CSE), 2013 IEEE 16th International Conference on. pp. 130–137. IEEE (2013).
4. An, K., Shekhar, S., Caglar, F., Gokhale, A., Sastry, S.: A cloud middleware for assuring performance and high availability of soft real-time applications. Journal of Systems Architecture 60(9), 757–769 (2014).
5. Ardagna, C.A., Damiani, E., Frati, F., Rebeccani, D., Ughetti, M.: Scalability patterns for platform-as-a-service. In: Cloud Computing (CLOUD), 2012 IEEE 5th International Conference on. pp. 718–725. IEEE (2012).
6. Armbrust, M., Fox, A., Griffith, R., Joseph, A.D., Katz, R., Konwinski, A., Lee, G., Patterson, D., Rabkin, A., Stoica, I., et al.: A view of cloud computing. Communications of the ACM 53 (4), 50–58 (2010).
7. Babar, M.A., Chauhan, M.A.: A tale of migration to cloud computing for sharing experiences and observations. In: Proceedings of the 2nd international workshop on software engineering for cloud computing. pp. 50–56. ACM (2011).
8. Belimpasakis, P., Moloney, S.: A platform for proving family oriented restful services hosted at home. Consumer Electronics, IEEE Transactions on 55(2), 690–698 (2009).

9. Beloglazov, A., Abawajy, J., Buyya, R.: Energy-aware resource allocation heuristics for efficient management of data centers for cloud computing. Future generation computer systems 28(5), 755–768 (2012).
10. Bernabe, J.B., Perez, J.M.M., Calero, J.M.A., Clemente, F.J.G., Perez, G.M., Skarmeta, A.F. G.: Semantic-aware multi-tenancy authorization system for cloud architectures. Future Generation Computer Systems 32, 154–167 (2014).
11. Buyya, R., Pandey, S., Vecchiola, C.: Cloudbus toolkit for market-oriented cloud computing. In: Cloud Computing, pp. 24–44. Springer (2009).
12. Cacciari, C., Mallmann, D., Zsigri, C., D'Andria, F., Hagemeier, B., Rumpl, A., Ziegler, W., Martrat, J.: Sla-based management of software licenses as web service resources in distributed computing infrastructures. Future Generation Computer Systems 28(8), 1340–1349 (2012).
13. Calero, J.M.A., Aguado, J.G.: Monpaas: an adaptive monitoring platformas a service for cloud computing infrastructures and services. IEEE Transactions on Services Computing 8(1), 65–78 (2015).
14. Vera-del Campo, J., Pegueroles, J., Herna´ndez-Serrano, J., Soriano, M.: Doccloud: A document recommender system on cloud computing with plausible deniability. Information Sciences 258, 387–402 (2014).
15. Celesti, A., Tusa, F., Villari, M., Puliafito, A.: How to enhance cloud architectures to enable cross-federation. In: Cloud Computing (CLOUD), 2010 IEEE 3rd International Conference on. pp. 337–345. IEEE (2010).
16. Chauhan, M.A., Babar, M.A.: Migrating service-oriented system to cloud computing: An experience report. In: Cloud Computing (CLOUD), 2011 IEEE International Conference on. pp. 404–411. IEEE (2011).
17. Chauhan, M.A., Babar, M.A.: Towards process support for migrating applications to cloud computing. In: Cloud and Service Computing (CSC), 2012 International Conference on. pp. 80–87. IEEE (2012).
18. Chauhan, M.A., Babar, M.A., Benatallah, B.: Architecting cloud-enabled systems: a systematic survey of challenges and solutions. Software: Practice and Experience (2016).
19. Chauhan, M.A., Babar, M.A., Sheng, Q.Z.: A reference architecture for a cloud-based tools as a service workspace. In: Services Computing (SCC), 2015 IEEE International Conference on. pp. 475–482. IEEE (2015).
20. Chen, T., Bahsoon, R., Tawil, A.R.H.: Scalable service-oriented replication with flexible consistency guarantee in the cloud. Information Sciences 264, 349–370 (2014).
21. Daniel, W.: Challenges on privacy and reliability in cloud computing security. In: Information Science, Electronics and Electrical Engineering (ISEEE), 2014 International Conference on. vol. 2, pp. 1181–1187. IEEE (2014).
22. Dey, S., Lee, S.W.: From requirements elicitation to variability analysis using repertory grid: A cognitive approach. In: 2015 IEEE 23rd International Requirements Engineering Conference (RE). pp. 46–55. IEEE (2015).
23. ElGamal, T.: A public key cryptosystem and a signature scheme based on discrete logarithms. In: Advances in cryptology. pp. 10–18. Springer (1984).
24. Fehling, C., Leymann, F., Mietzner, R.: A framework for optimized distribution of tenants in cloud applications. In: Cloud Computing (CLOUD), 2010 IEEE 3rd International Conference on. pp. 252–259. IEEE (2010).
25. Fernandes, D.A., Soares, L.F., Gomes, J.V., Freire, M.M., Ina´cio, P.R.: Security issues in cloud environments: a survey. International Journal of Information Security 13(2), 113–170 (2014).
26. Fr^incu, M.E.: Scheduling highly available applications on cloud environments. Future Generation Computer Systems 32, 138–153 (2014).
27. Garc´ıa, A.G., Espert, I.B., Garc´ıa, V.H.: Sla-driven dynamic cloud resource management. Future Generation Computer Systems 31, 1–11 (2014).
28. Goldschmidt, T., Murugaiah, M.K., Sonntag, C., Schlich, B., Biallas, S., Weber, P.: Cloud-based control: A multi-tenant, horizontally scalable soft-plc. In: Cloud Computing (CLOUD), 2015 IEEE 8th International Conference on. pp. 909–916. IEEE (2015).

29. Gorton, I.: Essential software architecture. Springer Science & Business Media (2006).
30. Han, R., Ghanem, M.M., Guo, L., Guo, Y., Osmond, M.: Enabling cost-aware and adaptive elasticity of multi-tier cloud applications. Future Generation Computer Systems 32, 82–98 (2014).
31. Hassan, M.M., Song, B., Huh, E.N.: A market-oriented dynamic collaborative cloud services platform. Annals of telecommunications-annales des te'le'communications 65(11–12), 669–688 (2010).
32. Huang, W., Ganjali, A., Kim, B.H., Oh, S., Lie, D.: The state of public infrastructure-as-a-service cloud security. ACM Computing Surveys (CSUR) 47(4), 68 (2015).
33. Iankoulova, I., Daneva, M.: Cloud computing security requirements: A systematic review. In: 2012 Sixth International Conference on Research Challenges in Information Science (RCIS). pp. 1–7. IEEE (2012).
34. Inzinger, C., Hummer, W., Satzger, B., Leitner, P., Dustdar, S.: Generic event-based monitoring and adaptation methodology for heterogeneous distributed systems. Software: Practice and Experience 44(7), 805–822 (2014).
35. Iqbal, W., Dailey, M.N., Carrera, D., Janecek, P.: Adaptive resource provisioning for read intensive multi-tier applications in the cloud. Future Generation Computer Systems 27(6), 871–879 (2011).
36. Kalloniatis, C., Mouratidis, H., Islam, S.: Evaluating cloud deployment scenarios based on security and privacy requirements. Requirements Engineering 18(4), 299–319 (2013).
37. Kanso, A., Lemieux, Y.: Achieving high availability at the application level in the cloud. In: Cloud Computing (CLOUD), 2013 IEEE Sixth International Conference on. pp. 778–785. IEEE (2013).
38. Katsaros, G., Kousiouris, G., Gogouvitis, S.V., Kyriazis, D., Menychtas, A., Varvarigou, T.: A self-adaptive hierarchical monitoring mechanism for clouds. Journal of Systems and Software 85(5), 1029–1041 (2012).
39. Kaur, P.D., Chana, I.: A resource elasticity framework for qos-aware execution of cloud applications. Future Generation Computer Systems 37, 14–25 (2014).
40. Kerte'sz, A., Kecskemeti, G., Brandic, I.: An interoperable and self-adaptive approach for sla-based service virtualization in heterogeneous cloud environments. Future Generation Computer Systems 32, 54–68 (2014).
41. Kirschnick, J., Alcaraz Calero, J.M., Goldsack, P., Farrell, A., Guijarro, J., Loughran, S., Edwards, N., Wilcock, L.: Towards an architecture for deploying elastic services in the cloud. Software: Practice and Experience 42(4), 395–408 (2012).
42. Li, J., Stephenson, B., Motahari-Nezhad, H.R., Singhal, S.: Geodac: A data assurance policy specification and enforcement framework for outsourced services. Services Computing, IEEE Transactions on 4(4), 340–354 (2011).
43. Louridas, P.: Up in the air: Moving your applications to the cloud. IEEE software 27(4), 6 (2010).
44. Moens, H., Truyen, E., Walraven, S., Joosen, W., Dhoedt, B., De Turck, F.: Cost-effective feature placement of customizable multi-tenant applications in the cloud. Journal of Network and Systems Management 22(4), 517–558 (2014).
45. Moser, T., Biffl, S.: Semantic integration of software and systems engineering environments. Systems, Man, and Cybernetics, Part C: Applications and Reviews, IEEE Transactions on 42(1), 38–50 (2012).
46. Nae, V., Prodan, R., Iosup, A.: Sla-based operations of massively multiplayer online games in clouds. Multimedia Systems 20(5), 521–544 (2014).
47. Nidd, M., Ivanova, M.G., Probst, C.W., Tanner, A., Ko, R., Choo, R.: Tool-based risk assessment of cloud infrastructures as socio-technical systems. The cloud security ecosystem. Syngress (2015).
48. Paik, I., Chen, W., Huhns, M.N.: A scalable architecture for automatic service composition. IEEE Transactions on Services Computing 7(1), 82–95 (2014).

49. Paraiso, F., Merle, P., Seinturier, L.: socloud: A service-oriented component-based paas for managing portability, provisioning, elasticity, and high availability across multiple clouds. Computing 98(5), 539–565 (2016).

50. Peifeng, S., Chuan, S., Xiang, Z.: Intelligent server management framework over extensible messaging and presence protocol. Communications, China 10(5), 128–136 (2013).

51. Perez-Sorrosal, F., Patin~o-Martinez, M., Jimenez-Peris, R., Kemme, B.: Elastic si-cache: consistent and scalable caching in multi-tier architectures. The VLDB Journal—The International Journal on Very Large Data Bases 20(6), 841–865 (2011).

52. Prodan, R., Sperk, M.: Scientific computing with google app engine. Future Generation Computer Systems 29(7), 1851–1859 (2013).

53. Qi, L., Dou, W., Zhang, X., Chen, J.: A qos-aware composition method supporting cross-platform service invocation in cloud environment. Journal of Computer and System Sciences 78(5), 1316–1329 (2012).

54. Ramachandran, M.: Business requirements engineering for developing cloud computing services. In: Software Engineering Frameworks for the Cloud Computing Paradigm, pp. 123–Springer (2013).

55. Ren, K., Wang, C., Wang, Q.: Security challenges for the public cloud. IEEE Internet Computing (1), 69–73 (2012).

56. Rezaei, R., Chiew, T.K., Lee, S.P., Aliee, Z.S.: A semantic interoperability framework for software as a service systems in cloud computing environments. Expert Systems with Applications 41(13), 5751–5770 (2014).

57. Ribeiro, L.S., Viana-Ferreira, C., Oliveira, J.L., Costa, C.: Xds-i outsourcing proxy: ensuring confidentiality while preserving interoperability. IEEE journal of biomedical and health informatics 18(4), 1404–1412 (2014).

58. Rimal, B.P., Jukan, A., Katsaros, D., Goeleven, Y.: Architectural requirements for cloud computing systems: an enterprise cloud approach. Journal of Grid Computing 9(1), 3–26 (2011).

59. Ryan, J.: Rethinking the esb: building a secure bus with an soa gateway. Network Security 2012(1), 14–17 (2012).

60. Serrano, D., Bouchenak, S., Kouki, Y., Ledoux, T., Lejeune, J., Sopena, J., Arantes, L., Sens, P.: Towards qos-oriented sla guarantees for online cloud services. In: Cluster, Cloud and Grid Computing (CCGrid), 2013 13th IEEE/ACM International Symposium on. pp. 50–57. IEEE (2013).

61. Sousa, F.R., Machado, J.C.: Towards elastic multi-tenant database replication with quality of service. In: Proceedings of the 2012 IEEE/ACM Fifth International Conference on Utility and Cloud Computing. pp. 168–175. IEEE Computer Society (2012).

62. Takabi, H., Joshi, J.B., Ahn, G.J.: Security and privacy challenges in cloud computing environments. IEEE Security & Privacy (6), 24–31 (2010).

63. Tari, Z., Yi, X., Premarathne, U.S., Bertok, P., Khalil, I.: Security and privacy in cloud computing: Vision, trends, and challenges. Cloud Computing, IEEE 2(2), 30–38 (2015).

64. Villegas, D., Bobroff, N., Rodero, I., Delgado, J., Liu, Y., Devarakonda, A., Fong, L., Sadjadi, S.M., Parashar, M.: Cloud federation in a layered service model. Journal of Computer and System Sciences 78(5), 1330–1344 (2012).

65. Wind, S., Schro¨dl, H.: Requirements engineering for cloud computing: a comparison framework. In: International Conference on Web Information Systems Engineering. pp. 404–415. Springer (2010).

66. Wu, L., Garg, S.K., Buyya, R.: Sla-based admission control for a software-as-a-service provider in cloud computing environments. Journal of Computer and System Sciences 78(5), 1280–1299 (2012).

67. Wu, X., Liu, M., Dou, W., Gao, L., Yu, S.: A scalable and automatic mechanism for resource allocation in self-organizing cloud. Peer-to-Peer Networking and Applications 9(1), 28–41 (2016).

68. Xu, Z., Mei, L., Liu, Y., Hu, C., Chen, L.: Semantic enhanced cloud environment for surveillance data management using video structural description. Computing 98(1–2), 35–54 (2016).

69. Zardari, S., Bahsoon, R.: Cloud adoption: a goal-oriented requirements engineering approach. In: Proceedings of the 2nd International Workshop on Software Engineering for Cloud Computing. pp. 29–35. ACM (2011).

70. Zhang, Y., Zhou, Y.: Transparent computing: spatio-temporal extension on von neumann architecture for cloud services. Tsinghua Science and Technology 18(1), 10–21 (2013).

Part III
Requirements Validation, Evaluation, and QoS for Service and Cloud Computing

Chapter 9
Cyber Security Requirements Engineering

Christof Ebert

Abstract Virtually every connected system will be attacked sooner or later. This holds specifically for cloud-based services and systems. A 100% secure solution is not feasible. Therefore, advanced risk assessment and mitigation is the order of the day. Risk-oriented security engineering helps in both designing for robust systems as well as effective mitigation upon attacks or exploits of vulnerabilities. Security must be integrated early in the design phase to understand the threats and risks to expected functionality. The security analysis provides requirements and respective test vectors so that adequate measures can be derived for balancing security costs and efforts. This book chapter provides experience and guidance concerning how information security can be successfully achieved with a security requirements engineering perspective. Our experiences from embedded security in critical IT systems show that security is only successful with a systematic understanding and handling of security requirements and their interaction with functional requirements. Four requirements engineering-related levers for achieving security are addressed: security requirements elicitation, security analysis, security design, and security validation. We will show for each of these levers how security is analyzed and implemented. A case study from automotive systems will highlight concrete best practices. Only systematic and disciplined security requirements engineering will ensure that security needs are met end to end from concept to architecture to verification and test and—most relevant—operations, service, and maintenance.

Keywords Cloud-based systems · Cyber security · Embedded systems · Quality requirements · Validation · Systems engineering

C. Ebert (✉)
Vector Consulting Services, Stuttgart, Germany
e-mail: christof.ebert@vector.com

© Springer International Publishing AG 2017
M. Ramachandran and Z. Mahmood (eds.), *Requirements Engineering for Service and Cloud Computing*, DOI 10.1007/978-3-319-51310-2_9

209

9.1 Introduction

IT evolution is driven by five forces: Collaboration, Comprehension, Connectivity, Cloud, and Convergence (Fig. 9.1):

- Collaboration, i.e., consumer Internet, social network interaction, single customer segmentation, configurators for products and services, digital money, computer-assisted collaboration tools, crowdsourcing;
- Comprehension, i.e., augmented reality, semantic search, big data handling, smart data, data analytics, data economy, online data validation, data quality;
- Connectivity, i.e., ubiquitous mobile computing, mobile services, cyber-physical systems, industry 4.0, machine-to-machine (m2m) communication, sensor networks, multisensor fusion;
- Cloud, i.e., applications and services in the cloud, location-based networks, new license models for software and application, sustainability, energy efficiency;
- Convergence, i.e., mobile enterprise, bioinformatics, Internet of things, pervasive sensing, autonomous systems.

The five forces all relate to cyber security and will not work adequately without end-to-end cyber security engineering. Coupled with the underlying complexity and scale these drivers demand new solutions for cyber security. Examples include new IT architectures that facilitate seamless connectivity, robust infrastructures for cyber-physical systems in safety-critical environments, or data analytics to predict choices and behaviors to improve overall customer experience. Such software-driven solutions can create nontraditional market entry points and

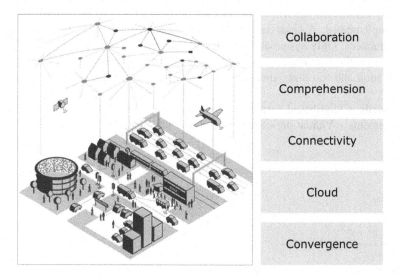

Fig. 9.1 Cyber security is impacted by five forces: collaboration, comprehension, connectivity, cloud, and convergence

consequently entirely new mechanisms to address a single customer with time-specific and location-specific services.

New technologies not only create numerous opportunities but also introduce complexity. Thereby, these solutions introduce new challenges, for instance, with respect to information security, robustness, and usability.

Security and robustness have tremendous impact on business decisions. The more we share and network, the more we are exposed to attacks of all kinds. The exploding need for secure software and protection schemes for our business processes, end to end, indicate this impact. Imagine automotive suppliers working on multisensor fusion connected to GPS and vehicle-to-vehicle communication to predict critical situations and foresee appropriate measures at situations where even the driver might not even be aware of what will happen. Another example is service companies who leverage their sales channels to flexibly provide related services such as door-to-door transportation, or firms that offer a single service card for identification, payment, and access to services of various providers both physical and in the cloud.

Complexity and scale demand focus on usability. We already face situations where users without adequate training are forced to operate systems which they do not understand sufficiently to meaningfully assess risks and stay in control across normal day-to-day scenarios. Insufficient usability today is a major source of critical failures caused by humans in health care, transportation, and production plants.

For embedded software–hardware systems complexity and technology will grow fast. The resulting competence gap will lead to even stronger fight for skills. From the survey and interviews, we can see that companies will continue to invest in growth through innovation by developing new products and solutions, because this determines their market position. They are aware of the volatile market situation and want their development teams across the world to be as lean and innovative as possible.

The IT industry deals already since years with strategies for data protection and to provide secured networks to prevent them against unauthorized access. Wide experiences are available here that, with special considerations, can be adapted and are useful for different industries. This allows, for instance, taking over the proven software architecture of Ethernet, so that a number of approved protocols are available as well for a secured data transmission. Essentially, they are based on cryptography, software algorithms based on more or less complex mathematics. The algorithms itself are not the secret and are available to the public, but keys provide the secret and they must be created, distributed, and maintained carefully. A popular key management system used by the IT industry is the PKI (Public Key Infrastructure). It contains a hierarchical certificate management with associated keys and builds the basis for an authenticated communication between partners.

We will look in this book chapter to key elements of security requirements engineering, namely requirements elicitation and security requirements analysis.

Our examples mostly come from automotive systems, because unlike any other industry, automotive connects three relevant drivers of modern IT systems, namely the following:

- Systems Engineering with a combination and integration of mechanics, hardware, and software;
- Embedded real-time systems with safety-critical requirements;
- IT systems with huge computing power and distributed cloud services.

On this basis technology transfer to other industries is easily feasible.

9.2 Cyber Security Requirements

Security is a quality attribute which heavily interacts with other such attributes, such as availability, safety, or robustness. It is the sum of all attributes of an information system or product which contributes toward ensuring that processing, storing, and communicating of information sufficiently protects confidentiality, integrity, and authenticity. Cyber security implies that it is not possible to do anything with the processed or managed information which is not explicitly intended by the specification of the embedded system [1, 2].

Based on the specific challenges of cyber security, system, and service suppliers have to realize an effective protection against manipulations of IT and embedded electronic and electric systems. Key points in the development of protected systems are the proper identification of security requirements, the systematic realization of security functions, and a security validation to demonstrate that security requirements have been met. The following items need to be considered to achieve security in the development process:

- Standardized process models for a systematic approach which is anchored in the complete development process. This starts in the requirements analysis through the design and development to the test and integration of components and the network.
- Quick software updates to close vulnerabilities in installed operational software, be it in the cloud or embedded in systems.
- Reliable governance that is state of the art and meets long-term security demands, such as key management and updates of crypto algorithms.
- Robust networks and system architecture that provides flexibility and scalability and are designed under consideration of security aspects.

Based on our experiences in many cyber security projects, we show which security engineering activities are necessary to create secure systems and how these activities can be performed efficiently. In the following discussion, we want to examine each of these topics, the current activities, and provide suggestions concerning how to mitigate the security risks.

Traditionally systems and electronics requirements are function driven. But, by defining functionalities alone, there is nothing said about the correlation of features which is where security risks typically show up (see our introductory example). We will start with explicit security requirements, as they have emerged in IT systems over time [1–5]:

- Confidentiality demands for information being unavailable for unauthorized entities. Note that data may be gathered by unauthorized entities without losing confidentiality, as long as the information contained in the data is not revealed.
- Integrity requires information remaining unchanged by unauthorized entities.
- Authenticity necessitates that the origin of information or the identity of a communication partner can be satisfactorily proven.
- Availability hardens that the system to be protected by making it highly reliable, including all necessary cyber security mechanisms.
- Governance ensures that agreed policies and protection mechanisms both hard and soft, specifically those being people oriented, are used and part of the culture, independent of time pressure or budget impacts.

Security requirements encountered in IT, cloud services, and embedded systems development typically target its dependability. Such systems are embedded into a technical process, thus dependability is imperative to prevent failures of the technical process itself or its environment. Dependability demands that system functionality, determined by its functional requirements, is delivered correctly—considering feature correlations and disturbances from the outside. Besides accurate realization of the functionality, information needs to be correctly processed during operations of the embedded system, i.e., without being distorted during transmission or storage. Additionally to the need for correct information processing, embedded systems interact with real-world objects, which means they are subject to real-time requirements of these real-world objects. Information must not only be processed correctly, but also within determined time limits.

Both cyber security requirements and embedded systems' reliability requirements have one thing in common: They aim to deflect unauthorized manipulation of information inside of computer systems—be it interferences with the system environment or intentional manipulations of unauthorized entities (i.e., attacks).

9.3 Risk-Oriented Security

Over the past decade trends like IoT, connected service workflows and driver assistance systems among others have led to software and connectivity playing an increasingly important part in developing critical systems and also for business models of OEMs and suppliers likewise.

Devastating impact of security issues is already known from industrial sectors like IT-infrastructure, aviation, information technology and telecommunications, industrial control systems, and energy and financial payments. Virtually every connected system will be attacked sooner or later. A 100% secure solution is not feasible. Therefore, advanced risk assessment and mitigation is necessary to protect assets. Consequently, the typical solution to security in these industries relies on suitable risk assessment that projects threats on assets of interests. Thereby cost of implementing specific security measures can be compared with the probability of a particular threat that they counter.

Security in a complex system cannot be achieved by applying countermeasures on single items. It requires an analysis of the complete functionality or system as a whole and to apply countermeasures as an integral part. First, you need to identify what are the assets I want to protect. Besides financial aspects also confidentiality and safety functions must be considered carefully. The next step would be a threat analysis: who has access to my assets, what are potential attackers, and where are my access points. A typical approach to this is the construction of a data flow diagram in which the assets are identified. It provides an overview of all connections and access points, where attacks and manipulations can be achieved. From the material above a risk assessment can be done to obtain the measurements and results in a classification of the risk. An example of such a risk assessment can be found in the picture below. Here, as an example, the classification was defined in three categories: Low, medium, and high (Fig. 9.2).

This process provides systematic means to deal with the subject and results in a balanced trade-off for cost and efforts. Depending on the determined security level, countermeasures can be defined on system level and further derived as security input requirements. The analysis phase provides now also requirements for hardware extensions, e.g., if hardware acceleration is needed for authentication or if a specific key management is required for higher security measures. The requirements are also an input to define test vectors on functional (e.g., for an ECU) and system level (e.g., for the vehicle). These tests, together with standard penetration tests, then will help to provide evidence for successful application of the security to the function and system.

Asset-based risk assessment is a suitable tool for companies to steer efforts for security engineering in a systematic and comprehensive way and thereby involve all relevant stakeholders in the organization. For example, a CEO may not find it very helpful to have a long exhaustive list with every attack vector or potential threat— they need to be provided with a ranked listing and useful decision-support tools which clearly shows alternatives and consequences. From the view of a system

Fig. 9.2 Definition of security level derived from threat analysis and risk assessment

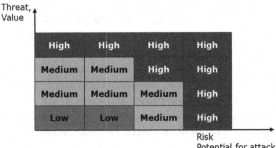

developer, a flat listing of potential threats might not help to improve the system. To really help, they need to be able to map security threats, countermeasures and requirements to system/architecture elements in their scope of the project.

The systematic management of security threats and associated security goals is essential to actually providing safe and competitive products, and to protect valuable assets and business models.

But what makes security engineering so complex?

Developers face the challenge of securing a system against attackers whose capabilities and intentions are at best partially known. Some attacks might today appear infeasible, but today's impossible attacks might become more likely in the near future. An example of this is attacking a vehicle simply by exploiting wireless interfaces, 20 years ago would have been extremely unlikely; however, today a cheap software-defined radio accomplishes these types of attacks with little effort. On the other hand, an attacker might invest more effort into launching an attack the more valuable a successful attack is to him. Some attacks represent more effort to the attacker than others given the specific potential of the attacker. It is this risk/reward payoff that is analyzed in security engineering.

Likewise during testing and verification, suitable methods to verify that the vehicle has the required security level and process goals like test strategy and coverage need to be chosen.

Furthermore, the assets to be protected from attacks are decided by stakeholders involved, e.g., drivers would indicate different assets of their vehicle to be protected compared with what a developer considers an asset. However, customers/drivers need to be satisfied with their vehicle in order to buy another one from the same company. Consequently, security engineering must seek trade-offs between cost of security measures and benefit to assets in order to make sustainable decisions.

Security concepts must balance the cost of not having enough security and thus being successful attacked with all damaging consequences and the cost spent to implement appropriate security mechanisms and keep them updated along the life cycle—covering service workflows as well (Fig. 9.3).

To summarize, the relationship between assets, attackers and threatsis complex and dynamic (e.g., attacks are more probable the less effort is required and the more

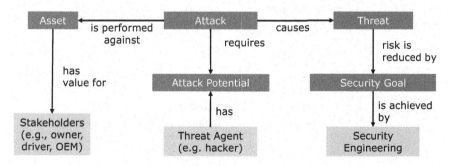

Fig. 9.3 Overview of cyber security analysis process

value successful attacks represent; attack vectors and effort change over time). Furthermore, common understanding of assets among all stakeholders of security engineering is mandatory in order to provide information for steering the security engineering.

Choosing the right set of security engineering methods for analysis, concept, and testing is challenging but required in order to enable goal-oriented and manageable security engineering.

Risk-based Security Engineering combines state-of-the-art methods for cyber security risk assessment in a practical framework and supports all involved stakeholders to develop "secure-enough" products. The method and our approach for proposing a concrete technical security concept is based upon security best practices such as the following:

- ISO 15408 (Evaluation criteria for IT security) with its focus on IT systems, specifically the seven evaluation assurance levels (EAL) for security requirements and guidance on common criteria.
- ISO 27001 (Information security management systems) with its governance requirements for security engineering across the entire value chain.
- IEC 62443 (Industrial communication network security) with its strong view on distributed systems and necessary security technologies and governance.

The Vector Security Check and our security engineering method adopt the state of the art not only from standards mentioned above but also from significant research work. For example, several research projects like "E-safety vehicle intrusion protected applications" (EVITA) funded by European Union and HEAVENS, proposed solutions for security risk assessment (Fig. 9.4).

We will further on show by examples how to use the risk-oriented security concept covering the entire security life cycle with focus on the upper left activities, namely

HSM	EVITA full	EVITA medium	EVITA light
Internal NVM	Yes	Yes	Optional
Internal CPU	Programmable	Programmable	None
HW crypto algorithms (incl. key generation)	ECDSA, ECDH, AES/MAC, WHIRLPOOL/HMAC	AES/MAC, Key storage, Microcontroller.	AES/MAC
HW crypto acceleration	ECC, AES, WHIRLPOOL	AES	AES
RNG	TRNG	TRNG	PRNG w/ ext. seed
Counter	16x64bit	16x64bit	None
Intended use-case	C2x,...	Gateway, engine control, head unit,...	Sensors, actuators, ...

Fig. 9.4 EVITA classification for the hardware security module (HSM)

- Asset Definition and Threat and Risk analysis
- Security Goals
- Security Concept.

9.4   Industry Case Study

To better illustrate evolving cyber security needs we will look to modern automotive systems. Figure 9.1 shows the interaction of functions in their distributed
networks being an essential part for our today's modern infrastructures with their
needs for safety and comfort. Besides the further development of innovative sensors
like radar and camera systems and the analysis of the signals in highly complex
systems, the connected cars will be a driving factor for tomorrow's innovation.
Internet connections will not only provide the need for information to the
passenger.

Cloud-based functions like eCall or communication between cars or car to
infrastructure (vehicle2x) shows high potential to revolutionizing the individual
traffic. This includes the improvement of the traffic flow controlled by intelligent
traffic lights, warnings from roadside stations, or brake indication of adjacent cars.
This builds the basis for enhanced driver assistant systems and automated driving.
But the connection to the outer world also bears also the risk for attacks to the car.

Figure 9.5 shows interworking for vehicle2x and external communication that
are already available today or will become available in the near future. Each connection to the car has a potential risk for an attack, regardless whether it is wireless

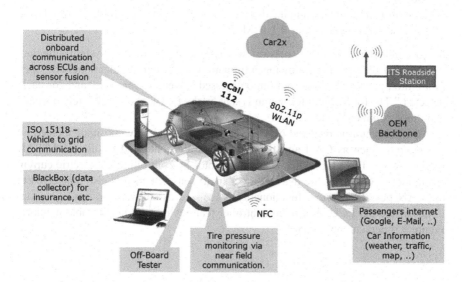

Fig. 9.5 Car with remote connections

or wired. Just the threat is different. The access through a connector is only possible for a limited amount of cars, whereas a far field connection can be accessed from anywhere in the world. But also near field connections play an important role, such as tire pressure monitoring system, Bluetooth, and wireless LAN. Security and reliability of these connections will be essential for the acceptance and success of these systems. With the introduction of this technology precautions must be taken to increase the reliability and to reduce the vulnerability to the system.

We will show security engineering with the example of a connected car. The car is connected to an external cloud from which it receives secured updates and diagnosis support. The car itself has numerous controllers (so-called ECU, electronic control units) which are connected by secured bus systems (see also Fig. 9.1).

As an example, we utilize the simplified functionality of an Automotive embedded control unit (ECU) that controls the automatic opening and closing of the roof of a convertible. Security impacts are manifold with this example, from getting access to the car and its contents to inserting a safety hazard to the driver if the roof opens during driving. The top level functional requirements are presumed to be (the abbreviation FR denominates functional requirements and SR security requirements):

- The roof is to be opened, if the open roof button is pressed (FR 1).
- The roof is to be closed, if the close roof button is pressed (FR 2).
- When the roof is completely opened or closed, feedback is given to the driver (FR 3).
- Additionally, two-top level safety requirements are supposed:
- The roof is not allowed to move, if the speed of the car is greater than 10 km/h (SR 1).
- If an obstacle is detected in the direction of movement of the roof, the roof has to stop the movement within 0.1 s (SR 2).

To conduct the security analysis, we assume the following system situation. A controller receives the following information to execute its functionality: "open roof button pressed," "close roof button pressed," "vehicle velocity," and "obstacle detected." The following information is sent by the ECU: "roof completely opened" and "roof completely closed."

All information is received or sent via the embedded network, implemented by bus systems such as CAN and Flexray, which are controlled by the AUTOSAR base software. The ECU actuates the roof motor by controlling the electric current to the motor. Obstacles are detected by a smart sensor, which is also connected to the CAN bus. The system functionality is realized as software on one microcontroller inside the ECU. The microcontroller features internal nonerasable memory. Figure 9.6 depicts the system.

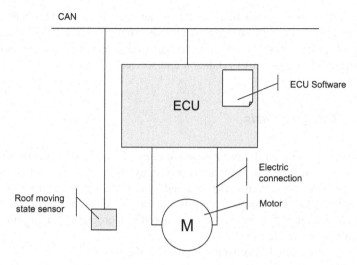

Fig. 9.6 Assumed system layout

9.5 Security Requirements Elicitation

A first step is setting the security objectives. When considering above requirements, it becomes clear that the detail level of such information is not sufficient for security analysis. Possible security threats emerge from unauthorized information gathering and manipulation. To judge these possible attack vectors, more detailed knowledge of the embedded system in question is required. To discuss security threats, the communication transactions of the system must be known as well as the effect of these transactions.

Knowledge of the communication technology to be employed is equally important, because different communication standards imply different vulnerabilities, where an attacker can mount an attack. The same holds true for determination of security threats against device software. The distribution of functions on different devices is to be known as well as underlying hardware details. The device hardware constitutes, which (hardware) interfaces can be used by attackers and if stored information can be deleted or modified.

9.6 Security Analysis

To understand vulnerabilities and determine security risks we apply misuse cases. Similar to use cases, misuse cases show a specific way to use a system. Misuse cases describe sequences of events that, taken together, lead to a system doing something that is not intended or even unwanted. Misuse cases that imply an unacceptable risk are taken to deduce concrete security requirements which are subsequently translated into functional requirements. Here is additional concrete guidance: Each identified security requirement must be linked to at least one functional requirement that is linked to design artifacts and test cases and monitored until closure—from design to validation and service.

9.6.1 Threat Analysis

In the first step, we will discuss the possibilities of an attack on the convertible's roof. First, the information that are received by the roof ECU and used to act accordingly are to be considered. Second, the ECU software program, which implements the ECU functionality, needs to be regarded. Both information entities, transmitted via communication systems or stored as a program, can, in principle, be tampered with by an attacker.

Different transmitted information is used by the roof ECU:

- Information that the roof is to be opened or closed (from FR 1, FR 2)
- Information on vehicle velocity (from SR 1)
- Information if an obstacle is detected (from SR 2).

As depicted in Sect. 9.3, there are different ways to attack communication. The network, which is used to transmit information concerning the roof ECU, shows vulnerabilities against all these ways of attack. Thus, the following functionalities need to be considered to protect such distributed communication:

- Protection of confidentiality to prevent acquisition of information by attackers
- Protection of content integrity to detect manipulation of messages by attackers
- Protection of authenticity to detect broadcasting of messages by attackers
- Protection of temporal integrity to detect delay or replay of messages by attackers.

The program controlling the ECU is verified by means of checksums, making it difficult for an attacker to change it. Attack paths thus need to consider software updates starting from the code creation and its validation up to its delivery in a repair shop anywhere in the world. Determining attacker motivation is difficult in the given case. Generally, it seems unlikely in the example that someone would manipulate functionality as the one depicted above. However, we will look into possible impacts of manipulations to determine which protection functionalities need to be realized and which can be disregarded.

9.6.2 Risk Assessment

Possible hacker motivations may include curiosity or sabotage. Thus, we quantify attacker motivation with "3," meaning a medium motivation to attack.

Because of the high degree of publicity of bus specifications, its vulnerabilities to attacks, and the availability of hardware/software tools for manipulation, attacker capabilities need to be judged at least to be "4," meaning the attacker possesses advanced capabilities to manipulate the bus.

Effects of attacks depend on the information to be manipulated. Misuse cases related to the functional requirements presented result in malfunctions that may be inconvenient but are essentially harmless. A forged request to open or close the roof would result in the opening or closing of the roof, without the driver requesting this operation. Here we have a security requirement with clear safety impacts. If the messages containing information about vehicle velocity or obstacle detection are manipulated, the roof could be opened at high speed or the closing roof would not be interrupted despite an obstacle in the path of the roof. Both incidents can result in the mentioned effects, so the cost effect is assigned to be "5," resulting in a risk priority number of 60.

Assuming an acceptable residual risk of 50, one would define the following security requirements:

- Vehicle velocity data communication must be protected
- Obstacle detection data communication must be protected.

We see that dependability requirements are a good starting point to identify relevant security requirements and to guide elicitation of further functional requirements that will mitigate security risks. The same technique as outlined here can be applied for other scenarios—always starting with attacker motivation or functional risks due to the system architecture. Our guidance: Do not limit exposure to known incidents and defects as some textbooks suggest. Security analysis is not a checklist approach. It has to consider attack motivations of persons thinking different than the usual engineer. However with an engineering mind, we can easier identify vulnerabilities in our architectures.

9.7 Security Design

Although one might argue that design is not much related to security requirements engineering, we will elaborate some of the techniques to show how traceability from security requirements to their implementation is achieved. Without such traceability not only the validation is impossible but also there would be no way to prove—after an incident—that the necessary cautions had been taken.

9.7.1 Security Functionality with Minimal Resource Impact

Different mechanisms exist to realize protection of communication: encryption for protection of confidentiality, message authentication codes for protection of content integrity, digital signatures for protection of authentication, and time stamps as well as sequence numbers for temporal integrity protection. Since these mechanisms need to be deployed to embedded systems at field level, the realization of the mechanisms must strive for minimal resource (especially memory) consumption. Therefore, the notion is to avoid the use of monolithic protective mechanisms, such as digital signatures, but to identify more fine-grained mechanisms instead, which provide protection functionalities by combination of one or more of such smaller mechanisms. Ideally, these protective mechanisms can be used to provide different protection functionalities, while being implemented only once.

To provide confidentiality, encryption is the mechanism of choice. For content integrity, cryptographic hash functions exist, but an attacker, who is able to change the content of a message, will also be able to compute the hash value and change it, pretending the integrity being intact. Therefore, keyed hash functions exist, which secure message integrity against purposeful manipulation by incorporating encryption into the hash value. If encryption already has been selected to realize confidentiality, it can be reused in conjunction with hashing to provide content integrity consequently saving resources.

Likewise, authenticity can be provided by digital signatures, which can also be constructed using an ID and keyed hash functions. It is then realized with a non-ambiguous identifier of a device and the reuse of hash and encryption functions. Finally, temporal integrity can be verified with time stamps and sequence numbers, but for these mechanisms to work, it is required that an attacker is not able to manipulate time stamps/sequence numbers or pretend to be the origin of the message. This requires the aforementioned mechanisms. The delineated dependencies yield a layered structure where major implementations are linked with security requirements thus facilitating semi-automatic consistency checks (Fig. 9.7).

To manipulate functionality, attackers with physical access to devices can flash the device memory with new programs, which fulfill the attackers' requirements. Examples for this kind of attack are manipulations of mileage indicators or unlocking of programmed limitations (e.g., maximum speed) of motorized vehicles. Modern microcontrollers can usually be flashed using defined interfaces, such as

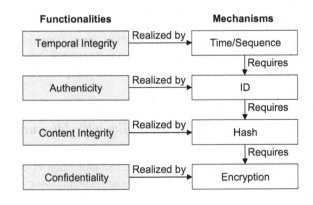

Fig. 9.7 Protection functionalities and mechanisms for communication

Fig. 9.8 Protection of functional integrity and communications security

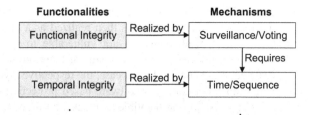

JTAG or SPI. In consequence, surveillance functionality is required to monitor the integrity of device functionality, i.e., the program code. A complete deletion of the device memory would also eradicate the surveillance functionality. Therefore, surveillance functionality must be distributed to different devices, which then monitor the functional integrity of other devices.

In case of detection of irregularities, e.g., manipulated code or unreachable devices, the monitoring devices can vote for counter measures (assumed, there is more than one device monitoring the manipulated one) and react in an appropriate way, for instance, by ignoring messages of the manipulated device or by transferring the technical process into a safe state.

For distributed surveillance and voting, communication is required. This communication must be protected against manipulation. Otherwise, an attacker might exploit this functionality to simulate manipulated devices. Thus, the layered structure can be extended with a fifth layer (Fig. 9.8).

9.7.2 Composition of the Layers

The layers, i.e., the mechanisms to realize the desired functionalities, each provide a service. Every service specifies what activities are to be realized on a certain layer, but not how the activities are realized. To satisfy real-time requirements, the realization, i.e., the selected algorithms must be deterministic. This is the case for most cryptographic algorithms, making it possible to calculate an execution time for the algorithms. To meet the demands of timing constraints, efficient algorithms ought to be selected.

This composition offers a high degree of adaptability and flexibility. It is possible to adapt to three different conditions, which need to be determined during the risk analysis phase of security engineering:

- Parts of the system are secured by physical protection. Thus, only unprotected parts need to be protected by software-based mechanisms. If, e.g., a field device is physically protected, it is not necessary to implement functional integrity checks. Thus, the lower four layers need to be realized with software-based mechanisms, the fifth layer is then realized as a physical mechanism.

- Certain system elements are not vulnerable to specific attacks, because they already include security mechanisms or there are intrinsic features that prevent or detect these attacks. In that case, the respective layer can be a "dummy" layer, which does not contain a software-based protective mechanism.
- Even if a system is susceptible to attacks, it might be the case that there are only minimal resources available in a controller. It is then possible to select mechanisms that consume few resources (which might result in reduced protection strength). Another possibility is to realize only a "base" protection, using only lower layers.

While these adaptations can be made during development time, it is also possible that ambient conditions change during run time. During the long life span of field level system elements, it is probable that specific protective mechanisms are compromised, which has been the case with several cryptographic algorithms during the last years. Thus, it is necessary to be able to exchange protective mechanisms, even when cars are already on the road. The ability to flexibly exchange protective mechanisms during run time depends on the implementation of the mechanisms, which is depicted in the next section.

9.7.3 Implementing Security Functionality

When implementing protective mechanisms, the limited resources of embedded systems need to be considered. Additionally, implementations of these mechanisms should be tested and well proven. Otherwise, vulnerabilities due to faulty code could be inserted into the system. On this account, reuse of existing software components is a promising approach. Therefore, a software component technology has been selected, which allows for implementation in structured programming languages. Such structured components for embedded systems are implemented in "structured C."

Figure 9.9 shows the assembly of one layer. The layer component ("SecurityLayerX") can access different interfaces ("ISecurityMechanismA," "-B," "-C") of protective mechanisms ("SecurityMechanismA," "-B," "-C"). So, multiple mechanisms can be used on every layer, e.g., to provide different kinds of encryption. The interface "ISecurityLayerX" is used to make the service of layer X available to the upper layer X + 1 in a uniform way. Likewise, the layer component uses the interface "ISecurityLayerX − 1" to access the service of the lower layer X − 1 (Fig. 9.9).

To realize protection, the required protection functionalities need to be selected. All layers, which provide required services, are to be set in. Furthermore, the concrete mechanisms are to be chosen, which fulfill the given requirements (e.g., integration into an existing system that requires asymmetric encryption). The

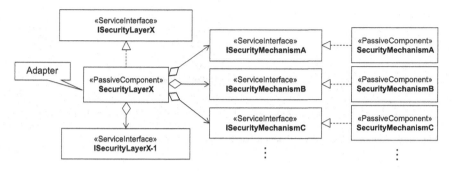

Fig. 9.9 Assembly of a layer

chosen layer components ("SecurityLayerX," "-X-1," ...) need to be connected to each other in order to be able to access the lower layer services and to the selected mechanism components, which implement the services of the layer. With the ability to dynamically exchange components during run time (given the underlying hardware platform supports modification of software at run time, e.g., by flashing), there is a high degree of flexibility of the concept. With this flexibility, it is possible to update implementation failures as well as compromised algorithms. Modern security modeling tools allows tracing security requirements (and their functional counterparts) down to the code-level as requested when security certification should be done before release.

9.8 Security Validation

Security validation is conducted on two different tiers. To ensure the quality of the software components, every component is subject to a rigid review process looking for typical design errors and manually checking adherence to security requirements. Additionally, comprehensive unit and system tests are made. Like all other software components, the test cases themselves may contain errors as well and should be checked before use. Such quality ensuring procedures are imperative for security functionality, because these are often targeted by attackers to manipulate the protected system.

Automatic regression testing of security requirements is absolutely mandatory due to the many changes to the code during the product life cycle. To automate testing of security requirements, an automatic penetration test tool for embedded systems has been created and used in real-world embedded systems. This penetration test tool makes it possible to define attacks against embedded systems based on the identified security requirements. The prototype allows for automatic execution of these attacks and detection of attack results, i.e., if an attack was successful or has been neutralized by the security functionality.

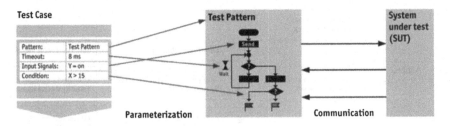

Fig. 9.10 Automated security validation based on specific security test patterns

Abstraction is a commonly used and important method for handling complexity in software development and system design. Abstraction on the signal level is a common way to test ECU functionality. In a common distributed network system, for example, an interaction layer in the ECU provides the signal abstraction. Abstraction layers in ECU and test environment must utilize the same abstractions to allow same reference signals, authentication checks, and even sandboxing of unknown signal patterns. Simultaneously, signal abstraction also represents—at least on the protocol level—the remaining bus simulation. For example, it ensures that periodic signals are actually transmitted periodically. This allows using security test pattern also for real-signal load and overload or DOS-attacks. When a change is made to the system's communication matrix, such test patterns and associated test cases are reused thus ensuring consistency during the life of a component.

Figure 9.10 shows security validation on the basis of security test patterns. Tools such as PREEvision are used to model the system, its embedded components, the network (both sensors and actuators) to the level, where the control algorithm is detailed in a controller model.

9.9 Relevance and Outlook

Security is thus of growing relevance to all industry areas. Both advanced IT systems as well as embedded systems increasingly utilize cloud-based networked software components based upon standardized open architectures. Due to their long lifetime within changing environments, different versions and configurations are combined in different variants over time with software or hardware upgrades.

Currently used concepts, such as proprietary subsystems, the protection of components, firewalls between components and the validation of specific features are insufficient to ensure security on a systems level [5]. Intelligent attack scenarios evolve from different directions, such as attacks on unprotected networks, introduction of dangerous code segments through open interfaces, changes to configurations, and prove that security has to become a topic throughout the entire organization and with high management attention.

Systematically ensuring security from requirements to service of systems

- protects against manipulations,
- increases the safety and reliability of users, and
- facilitates even more software-driven services, applications and business models.

Security demands an end-to-end requirements engineering perspective. The article with its many practical examples underlines that security of IT and embedded systems can be achieved with clear and systematic focus and limited extra effort on the basis of disciplined requirements engineering. Security engineering in embedded systems has to start with a clear focus on security requirements and related critical quality requirements, such as safety, footprint, or performance and how they map to functional requirements.

Software suppliers and integrators first define the key functional requirements. These requirements are then analyzed on their security risks and impacts. Security requirements are expanded into further functional requirements or additional security guidelines and validation steps. Requirements engineering security concepts are subsequently and consistently (i.e., traceable) implemented throughout the development process. Finally, security is validated on the basis of previously defined security requirements and test cases.

We practically showed how security requirements engineering is mastered along the entire system life cycle. Many security attacks are the result of poorly managed software updates and uncontrolled complexity growth. Architectures, systems, and protocols have to be developed with security in mind (i.e., design for security). Competences have to be developed around security engineering, and employees have to be trained how to design, verify, and sustain security throughout the product's life cycle. Most important it is that before-mentioned methods and processes are implemented consistently, systematically, and rigorously with traceable effects. Only with continuous measurements on their effectiveness the value of security measures improves.

Traditional embedded software engineering ignored security for various reasons, such as having isolated components, dealing with heavily constrained resources, and being unable to handle the computational overheads. Today however, embedded security is in the foreground due to safety, legislative, and intellectual property concerns [5].

With our described product life cycle-oriented security requirements engineering, the good news is that different from Internet security securing embedded systems is likely to succeed in the next 5 years. By doing so, embedded system suppliers and integrators are increasingly in a position that allows marketing and selling security as part of an overall quality concept. It will help to master liability risks and to ultimately increase revenues.

References

1 Cyber Security and Functional Safety white papers and practice guides: www.vector. com/security, www.vector.com/safety
2. Ebert, C.: Systematic Requirements Engineering. Dpunkt, Heidelberg, Germany, 5. edition, 2014.
3. Firesmith, D. G.: Engineering Security Requirements. Journal of Object Technology, Vol. 2, pp. 53–68, 2003.
4. Giorgini, P., F. Massacci, and N. Zannone: Security and Trust Requirements Engineering. In Foundations of Security Analysis and Design III—Tutorial Lectures, LNCS 3655, pages 237–272. Springer, 2005.
5. Haley, C.B., J.D. Moffett, R. Laney, B. Nuseibeh: A framework for security requirements engineering. Proc. SESS 2006, 2006.
6. ISO/IEC 15446:2004. Information technology—security techniques—Guide for the production of protection profiles and security targets. 2004.
7. ISO/IEC 15408:2005. Information technology—Security techniques—Evaluation criteria for IT security (Common Criteria v3.0), 2005.
8. ISO 27001:2006, Information Security Management—Specification With Guidance for Use. International Or-ganization for Standardization, 2006.
9. Mead, N.R.: How to compare the security quality requirements engineering (SQUARE) method with other methods. Software Eng. Inst., CMU/SEI-2007-TN-021, Aug. 2007.
10. Poulsen, K.: Slammer worm crashed Ohio nuke plant network. SecurityFocus, http://www. securityfocus.com /news/ 6767, 19.08.2003.
11. Ramachandran, M: Software Security Engineering: Design and Applications. Nova Science Publishers, New York, USA. ISBN: 978-1-61470-128-6, https://www.novapublishers. com/catalog/product_info.php?products_id=26331, 2012.
12. Ramachandran, M : Software Security Requirements Engineering and Management as an Emerging Cloud Service, International Journal of Information Management, Vol. 36, No. 4, pp 580–590, 2016. doi:10.1016/j.ijinfomgt.2016.03.008.
13. S. Myagmar, A. J. Lee W. Yurcik: Threat Modeling as a Basis for Security Requirements, National Center for Supercomputing Applications (NCSA), University of Illinois
14. Sindre, G. and A. L. Opdahl: Eliciting security requirements with misuse cases. Requirements Engineering, No. 10, pp. 34–44, 2005.
15. Wired: Hackers remotely killed a Jeep—with me in it. www.wired.com/2015/07/hackers-remotely-kill-jeep-highway, July 2015
16. Whitman, M., Mattord, H., Principles of Information Security, Course Technology, Boston, 2007.
17. Yoshioka, N., S.Honiden, A.Finkelstein: Security Patterns: A Method for Constructing Secure and Efficient Inter-Company Coordination Systems. IEEE Int. Conf. on Enterprise Distributed Object Computing, 2004.

Chapter 10
Appraisal and Analysis of Various Self-Adaptive Web Service Composition Approaches

Doaa H. Elsayed, Eman S. Nasr, Alaa El Din M. El Ghazali
and Mervat H. Gheith

Abstract Service-Oriented Requirements Engineering (SORE) plays a significant role in eliciting, specifying, and validating service requirements that will be developed by Web service technology. With the increasing complexity of users' requirements, Web services need to be combined together to fulfill them. The process of building new value-added services by integrating sets of existing Web services to satisfy users' requirements is called Web Service Composition (WSC). The main objective of WSC is to develop composite services to satisfy users' requirements, which does not only include Functional Requirements (FR), but also Non-Functional Requirements (NFR). One of the main challenges of WSC is how it deals with dynamic environments. Since the Web service properties and composition requirements are frequently changeable, this demands that SORE activities must be equipped with a self-adaptation mechanism to provide the most appropriate composite services and satisfy users' requirements emerged. Self-adaptation occurs in either a proactive or reactive manner. In this chapter, we appraise and analyze existing reactive adaptation research that deals with the problem of WSC in a dynamic environment in order to identify the research gaps in this field. These approaches are classified into three categories: used of variability models, context-awareness, and multi-agent approaches. Most of these approaches are not able to deal with continuous and unanticipated changes in complex uncertain contexts because they need to define the contexts in design time. It is usually

D.H. Elsayed (✉) · M.H. Gheith
Institute of Statistical Studies and Research, Cairo University, Cairo, Egypt
e-mail: doaa.hani@hotmail.com

M.H. Gheith
e-mail: mervat_gheith@yahoo.com

E.S. Nasr
Independent Researcher, Cairo, Egypt
e-mail: nasr.eman.s@gmail.com

A.E.D.M. El Ghazali
Sadat Academy for Management Sciences, Cairo, Egypt
e-mail: a.elghazali@gmail.com

© Springer International Publishing AG 2017
M. Ramachandran and Z. Mahmood (eds.), *Requirements Engineering
for Service and Cloud Computing*, DOI 10.1007/978-3-319-51310-2_10

difficult to predict all of the possible situations that might arise in an uncertain environment.

Keywords Web service composition · Reactive adaptation · User requirement

10.1 Introduction

Service-Oriented Architecture (SOA) is an architectural approach to design and develop distributed systems in the form of interoperable services. Interoperability is the ability of two or more systems to work together to achieve a common goal [1, 2]. A Web service is a technology that implements SOA [3]. Web services achieve interoperability between applications using three major Web technologies to provide an industrial standard for deploying, publishing, discovering, and invoking enterprises' services. The standard technologies for implementing Web services are Web Services Description Language (WSDL), Universal Description, Discovery and Integration (UDDI), and Simple Object Access Protocol (SOAP) [4]. With the increasing complexity of users' requirements, Web services need to be combined together to fulfill them [5]. The process of developing a composite service that satisfies users' requirements is called Web Service Composition (WSC). The ultimate objective of WSC is to develop composite services to satisfy users' requirements, and hence Requirements Engineering (RE) could be considered the most critical phase of WSC [6]. RE establishes the goals and objectives of the system in consultation with all relevant stakeholders. RE could be divided into Functional Requirements (FR) and Non-Functional Requirements (NFR) [7]. FR represent functionality in a system or component (i.e., what the system does). NFR are treated as requirements on quality of the system, such as Quality of Services (QoS), cost, scalability, usability, maintainability, etc. FR are represented by task/function, while NFR are operationalized by quality constraints. If FR and NFR are not defined correctly in the beginning, the resulting WSC will not fully satisfy a user's request.

RE has evolved from classical methods to object-oriented methods and finally to Service-Oriented Requirements Engineering (SORE) [8]. SORE defines methodologies to elicit, specify, and validate the services' requirements from two different standpoints: the service consumer and the service provider [8]. The service provider needs to understand the functional and non-functional parts of the service being offered. For the service consumers, the challenge is to find the best-matched service for the requirements while making a tradeoff among cost, FR, and NFR. One of the key research challenges of WSC is how WSC deals with dynamic environments. In dynamic composition environments, the change occurs during design and runtime, such as the availability of Web services, a composition of requirements, and changes in QoS (e.g., price, reputation, etc.) [9]. Therefore, WSC should be equipped with self-adaptation mechanisms to ensure the ability to adapt to meet changing requirements, and seek to minimize user interventions in order to provide the most appropriate composite services and satisfy user's requirements [9]. SORE activities need to be performed at design time with more explicit constructs to specify requirements for Self-Adaptation Software (SAS), and are also needed for runtime adaptation for adaptable WSC approaches to deal with contextual changes in a dynamic environment [9]. SAS supports adaptation in either a proactive or reactive manner [10]. Proactive adaptation is able to predict the need for adaptation before the problem occurs [10]. Moustafa and Zhang [7] propose a proactive adaptation approach in WSC, which uses Markov Decision Process (MDP) to model WSC process and uses Q-learning for Reinforcement Learning (RL) technique to adapt to dynamic change in the WSC environments proactively. This approach monitors the WSC to determine proactive adaptation via analyzing the historical data in the Web service execution log. Aschoff and Zisman [11] also propose a ProAdapt framework for proactive adaptation in WSC. This framework triggers proactive adaptation in case of changes in response times of service operation or unavailability of operations in services and providers. It uses Exponentially Weighted Moving Average (EWMA) technique to predict response times of operations. The adaptation process occurs during the execution of WSC. Moustafa and Zhang [7] and Aschoff and Zisman [11] need to extend to support adaptive WSC in other types of QoS aspects and other circumstances, for example, the availability of new (better) service operations in comparison to the ones used in a composition, and changes in the structure of the WSC's workflow. Contrary to proactive adaptation, reactive adaptation is able to react to change; this means that adaptation occurs after an event which causes the need for adaptation [12].

This chapter presents various reactive adaptation WSC approaches to deal with the changes that might occur within and outside the dynamic composition environment; approaches are analyzed and compared. These approaches are classified into three categories: variability model, context-aware WSC, and multi-agent approaches. To the best of our knowledge, no survey on reactive adaptation WSC in the dynamic environment has been published yet. The rest of this chapter is organized as follows. Section 10.2 presents adaptation aspect and self-adaptation properties in WSC. Section 10.3 presents levels and challenges for RE for self-adaptive systems; Sect. 10.4 presents requirement specification models in WSC. Various self-adaptive WSC approaches are classified in Sect. 10.5; the comparison and limitation of approaches are presented in Sect. 10.6. Finally, Sect. 10.7 gives the conclusion and future work.

10.2   Self-Adaptive WSC

WSC needs to provide adaptive capabilities in order to respond to evolving demands and changes without compromising operational and financial efficiencies [13]. Avila [14] presents five of the main aspects that are considered parts of adaptation in WSC as shown in Fig. 10.1. The first aspect is the adaptation goal, which defines the adaptation purpose based on FR and/or QoS needs. Some

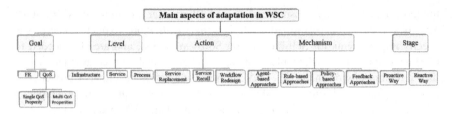

Fig. 10.1 The main aspects of adaptation in WSC

approaches such as Deng et al. [15] deal with single QoS optimization, while Liu et al. [16], Shanshan et al. [17], and Qiqing et al. [18] deal with multi QoS criteria. The second aspect is the adaptation level. These levels are identified differently in the literature. Raik [19] classifies them into three levels: infrastructure, service, and process. Various approaches concerned with process level are focused on in this chapter. The third aspect is adaptation action, which is used to solve an adaptation problem. This action can involve service replacement, workflow redesign, and service recall. The fourth aspect is the adaptation mechanism, which means the approaches that could be applied to execute an adaptation action such as agent-based, rule-based, policy-based, or feedback approaches. We focus on three adaptation mechanisms, namely variability model, context-aware, and multi-agent. The fifth aspect is the stage of adaptation, which means the time when the adaptation occurs. An adaptation could be triggered in a proactive or reactive way as explained before. Reactive approaches are focused on in this chapter.

Self-adaptation (self-*) properties are important in adaptive WSC too. Self-* properties enable WSC to deal with dynamic WSC execution environment. Figure 10.2 shows self-* properties applied to WSC. These self-* properties are self-healing, self-optimizing, self-configuring, and self-aware [14]. Self-healing is automatic discovery and correction of the failure of WSC by itself due to changes in QoS and/or FR without any human intervention and without stopping the WSC [20]. As WSC is done dynamically, they need to balance themselves with the changing environment. If the Web service cannot balance itself, then it leads to several faults such as incorrect order, misunderstood behavior, QoS service failure such as poor response and service unavailability, etc. [21]. Incorrect order occurs due to message flow through SOAP [22]. When the packets arrive in an order different on receiver side from sender side, this leads to incorrect order [22]. Misunderstood behavior occurs when the requester receives a service different from what he expects [22]. For example, if the requester requests a service for stock exchange quotes, and the provider returns a service supplying exchange rate quotes. This type of fault occurs if the description of a service is incorrect, or if the service provider misinterpreted the request from the requester [22]. QoS service failures occur during runtime [21].

Self-optimizing aims to select services at runtime, in order to maintain the expected QoS of the entire WSC [23]. The main objective of self-optimization WSC is to find the best Web service for each abstract service to achieve the FR as well as optimize QoS requirements. An abstract service is a set of Web service

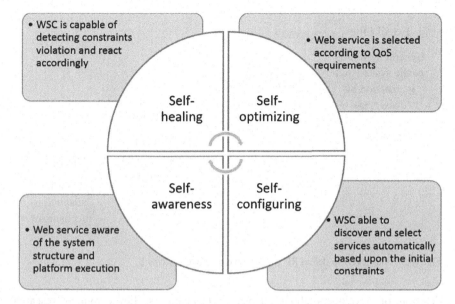

Fig. 10.2 Self -* properties in adaptive WSC

instance nodes in the WSC model that describes the functionality of the corresponding service [3]. Service selection for each abstract service is based on local or global QoS requirements. In the local optimization approach, service selection for each abstract service is based on the QoS of individual service. These approaches are useful in decentralized and dynamic environments. Local optimization approaches are the best in case there is no requirement to identify global constraints. This approach is suitable when the global QoS constraints are decomposed into local QoS constraints. The global optimization approach considers QoS constraints and preferences as a whole, e.g., when the whole response time is constrained.

Self-configuring aims to search for an optimal configuration of WSC components based upon the initial constraints [23]. Self-configuring WSC indicates that the WSC is able to discover and select services automatically. Self-awareness enables services to be aware of the system structure and platform execution. Self-awareness also enables the service to predict the impact of changes in their behavior and the effects of adaptation actions [14]. Self-awareness is aimed to ensure that the proactive adaptation of QoS requirements is satisfied [14].

10.3 RE for Self-Adaptive Systems

RE for dynamic adaptive systems is defined in the fourth level [10] as shown in Fig. 10.3. Level one is a general definition of the system and its reaction by developers. Level two is RE at runtime for achieving adaptation. Level three is

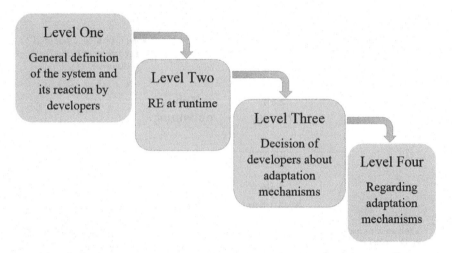

Fig. 10.3 Four levels to define RE for dynamic adaptive systems

decision of developers about adaptation mechanisms. Level four is research regarding adaptation mechanisms. RE for self-adaptive systems must deal with uncertainty because the execution environment information is unknown, and therefore the requirements for system behavior may need to change at run time in response to changes in the environment [24]. Requirement for self-adaptive system is specified as "incomplete" [24]. Chang [24] highlights research challenges for RE for self-adaptive systems. These challenges are new requirements language, mapping requirements language to architecture, managing uncertainty, requirements reflection, and traceability from requirements to implementation.

The traditional RE models such as i* and KAOS are not supported adaptivity or uncertainty. Various approaches are proposed to include runtime capabilities for RE. Baresi et al. [25] propose FLAGS, a goal model-based approach that generalizes the KAOS model, for modeling requirements at runtime. Pasquale et al. [26] present a FLAGS infrastructure to support requirements at runtime. Tropos 4AS is an agent-based methodology to model SAS requirement based on Tropos [27]. CARE is also modeling SAS requirement based on Tropos but it focuses on service-based applications for modeling [27].

The basic characteristics of the system become self-awareness and context-awareness to achieve adaptive behavior. Self-awareness describes the ability of a system to be aware of itself [10]. Context-awareness means that the system adapts its behavior based on the context of the application and the user [28]. Context is defined as "any information that can be used to characterize the situation of an entity. An entity is a person, place, or object that is considered relevant to the interaction between a user and an application, including the user and applications themselves" [10]. Bucchiarone et al. [29] propose a framework for adaptively of service-based applications according to context changing. This framework utilizes the concept of process fragments as a way to model processes. Business processes and fragments are modeled as Adaptable Pervasive Flows (APFs). APFs add annotating activities with preconditions and effects besides classical workflow language. This makes business processes and fragments suitable for adaptation and execution in dynamic environments. At design time, abstract activities are specified for each fragment in terms of the goal it needs to achieve. Different adaptation mechanisms and strategies are used to handle dynamicity of context-aware pervasive systems. Adaptation mechanisms are refinement mechanism, local adaptation mechanism, and compensation mechanism. The adaptation strategies are one-shot adaptation, re-refinement strategy, and backward adaptation strategy; other context-aware approaches are founded in Sect. 10.5.2.

10.4   Requirements Specification Models in WSC

Li [6] classifies requirement models in WSC into three categories: WSC based on workflow, WSC based on Artificial Intelligent (AI) planning technique, and model-driven WSC as shown in Fig. 10.4. In WSC based on workflow, the logic of WSC can be captured using workflow pattern of Web service. In this approach, users' requirements are modeled in terms of workflow which refers to the logical execution order of action [6]. When implementing a WSC, atomic Web services are selected and invoked according to each action defined in the workflow, after that, the WSC is executed according to the predefined execution orders [6]. Workflow is generated in either a static or dynamic manner [30]. Static WSC workflow means that users are required to describe all the necessary actions and all possible execution orders among these actions. The selection of Web service is done automatically. In dynamic WSC workflow, creating business workflow or model and selecting Web service is done automatically.

WSC based on AI planning requires an algorithm to translate WSC problem to AI planning technique problem such as Planning Domain Definition Language (PDDL) [31], Hierarchical Task Network (HTN) [32], and graph plan [33]. This approach requires users to specify their composition requirements in different technical languages, which includes the descriptions of initial state, goal state,

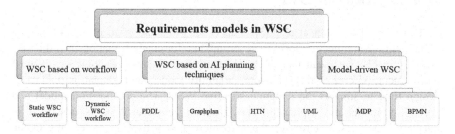

Fig. 10.4 Requirements models for WSC

possible domain states, and different actions that can be performed. For further information about WSC based on AI planning, it can be found in [34].

Model-driven approach for WSC uses models to describe user requirement (FR and NFR), business processes, abstract Web services, and dependence between Web services. The models are separated from executable WSC specifications. WSC can be modeled using Unified Modeling Language (UML) [35–37], MDP [38, 39], and Business Process Model and Notation (BPMN) [40, 41].

10.5   Classification of Self-Adaptive WSC Approaches

SAS modifies its own behavior in response to changes in the WSC environment. These environments are classified into the dynamic environment or static environment. In the dynamic environment, new WSC behavior and adaptation plans can be introduced during runtime. Contrary to the dynamic environment, the static environment is self-contained and not able to support the addition of new behaviors. In this section, approaches for reactive adaptation are classified into three categories: used of variability models, context-awareness, and multi-agent approaches.

10.5.1   Used of Variability Models

Variability is the ability of a service to change its behavior efficiently in the dynamic configurations [42]. The two important concepts concerning variability are variation points and variants. Variation points are located in a software system in which variation will occur, and variants are the alternatives that can be selected at those variation points [42]. Modeling and managing variability in a process can be classified into an architectural level and an implementation level. In an architectural level, variants are modeling inside software architecture such as BPMN and UML. In an implementation level, variants are modeling inside WSC language.

10.5.1.1   Architecture Level

Alférez et al. [41], Sun et al. [43], Yua et al. [40], and Xiao et al. [44] model variants in the architecture level to accommodate for changes that occur in FR. By changes in FR, we mean that the changes occur in a business logic or business requirement. Alférez et al. [41] create variability models and adaptation policies at design time to support the dynamic adaptive WSC. The composition model and variability model are separated. The dynamic adaptive WSC is described in adaptation policies in terms of the activation or deactivation of features in the variability model. The activation and deactivation of features in the variability model result in changes that occur in the WSC by adding or removing fragments of

Business Process Execution Language (WS-BPEL) code, that are deployed at runtime. The variability model and its possible configurations are verified at design time using Constraint Programming (CP). Sun et al. [43] extended ConIPF Variability Modeling Framework (COVAMOF) to allow it to configure the variability in a WSC. COVAMOF is a variability management framework that is used with software product families. COVAMOF variability concepts are modeled using UML diagrams and Variation point Interaction Diagram (VID). COVAMOF-VS tool suite is used to automated variability management in WSC at runtime.

Yua et al. [40] and Xiao et al. [44] propose model-driven based approaches for WSC. Yua et al. [40] propose an approach called the Model-Driven Development of Dynamically Adaptive Service-Oriented Systems with Aspects and Rules (MoDAR) to support the development of dynamically adaptive WS-BPEL-based systems. MoDAR includes the base model, the variable model, and the weave model. The base model follows the flow logic of the system. Variable model is used to take the decision aspect of a business requirement, which is changeable at runtime. Variable model is specified by business rule. Weave model is the aspect-oriented approach used to integrate the base model and the variable model. Xiao et al. [44] present model-driven variability-based WSC approach. Variability is defined within VxUML that is a UML extension. Class diagram, activity diagram, sequence diagram, and deployment diagram are extending to specify the variation points and variants. Variation point Interaction Diagram (VID) defines the dependencies between variation points and variants. Rule-based transformation language is used to transform VxUML to VxBPEL. VxBPEL is a BPEL extension to support variability at the implementation level.

Yua et al. [40], Alférez et al. [41], and Sun et al. [43] approaches are modeled to adapt the changes in the business process but these changes are fully known at design time to model the variability model. Furthermore, these approaches are not suitable for use in the dynamic environment because they are not able to deal with continuous and unanticipated changes in complex uncertain contexts.

10.5.1.2 Implementation Level

Imed et al. [45] solve the variability of QoS (vQoS) by introducing three variability operators: replicate, delete, and replace. Replicate and delete operators are used to adding and removing service instance in WSC, while the replace operator is used to change some faulty Web services. These operators are used to reconfigure automatic WSC when the SLA contract is violated. WSC reconfiguration (variability model) is modeling and verifying using Event-B. ProB model checker is used to trace possible design errors. Variability model is not required to define all at design time but variability operators that are used to adapt WSC are not enough to solve correctly vQoS problem. Koning et al. [46] propose VXBPEL language which is an extension of the standard BPEL language to adapt the changes in the business process. VXBPEL adds XML extension elements that store variability information inside the process definition BPEL which result in their being time-consuming, tedious, difficult to manage, and error-prone. This approach is very complex in the case of having a large number of variation points. Furthermore, this approach is not working in the dynamic environment like those approaches at the architecture level. Sun et al. [47] also adapt the changes in the business process by executing VXBPEL WSC using VxBPEL ODE engine. The performance of VxBPEL_ODE is compared with VxBPEL_ActiveBPEL. From the experimental result, VxBPEL_ODE shows a comparable performance of VxBPEL_ActiveBPEL.

10.5.2   Context-Awareness

Alférez and Pelechano [48] present a runtime model to guide the dynamic evolution of context-aware WSC to deal with unforeseen QoS events in the dynamic environment. Tactics are used to preserve the requirements that can be negatively affected by unknown context events. These tactics are known at design time, but they are used to tackle unknown context events. The negative effect of selected tactics to other expected goals is not taken into consideration. Bucchiarone et al. [49] and Cubo et al. [50] focus on changes that occur in FR. Bucchiarone et al. [49] define a formal framework that uses a planning technique to adapt the execution of the WSC at runtime in case of context changes. At design time, the context properties and their evolution are modeled by defined context property diagrams. Context property diagrams present the possible values of the property as the diagram states and the changes of the property values as transitions. The changes of the service are annotated with the effects on the context properties. The business policy over the service is annotated with preconditions on the context property values to determine in which context setting the service may be executed. Adaptation activities are not explicitly represented inside context change. They are dynamically derived from the currently observed context, the state of a business process, and business goals. This framework is implemented and validated using a scenario from the logistics domain. Cubo et al. [50] extend Discovery, Adaptation and Monitoring of Context-Aware Services and Components (DAMASCo) framework with feature models to represent the variability and self-adaptive WSC according to context change situations. This approach is implemented in the Intelligent Transportation Systems (ITS) domain. This approach is not supported self-adaptive of the service to context change at runtime. This means that DAMASCo execution plan does not support the switching from one running configuration to another.

Li et al. [51], Cao et al. [52], and Wang and Tang [53] propose approaches that deal with changes that occur in FR and QoS. Li et al. [51] present case-based reasoning for self-healing ability in WSC. Previous failure instances as cases are stored in a case base. When a new fault occurs, the closest cases in the case base are retrieved. Cao et al. [52] present context-aware adaptive WSC framework that contains five main function modules. The first module is the design of BPEL process. The second module is the parse and execution of the BPEL document. The third module is the search agent. The fourth module is a context-aware agent. The fifth module is an update agent. All of these modules are implemented using WSIG technology and Java language. The first three modules are used to execute BPEL process. The context-aware WSC is classified into service contexts and service composition contexts. Service context is responsible for gathering and checking context information before service establishment. Service composition contexts work while a composite service is performed. When perceiving the changes of contexts value, service composition may need to make some adjustment such as adding, deleting, or replacing a service, or fundamentally changing the whole combination process. When receiving a message about a variation of context value from a context-aware agent, update agent will search the most suitable policy from a policy library and send it to BPEL execution engine which will change the composition process according to chosen policy. Wang and Tang [53] present an architecture for self-adaption WSC. This architecture contains a context module that is responsible for adapting WSC to the changing at QoS and satisfies the service consumer's requirements. The context is categorized into service context, user context, and device context. Service context describes the properties of the service and the required execution environment of a service. These properties and preferences for services are written by a service provider and updated by user ratings. User context describes requirements and the environment that the service consumer can provide. Device context describes the real execution environment, including hardware and software environment. Changing contexts are handled according to user-defined personalized policies. Recomposition in Web services is made in a case where input and output changed only. Otherwise, changing contexts are handled according to user-defined personalized policies. This approach is not suitable for the dynamic environment because the contexts are predefined and other undefined contexts are not supported. It is difficult to predict all the possible situations arising in an uncertain environment.

10.5.3   Multi-Agent Approaches

Wang et al. [54] present self-adaptive WSC framework based on RL. MDP is used in this framework to model WSC. Workflows and alternative services are integrated into a single WSC. At runtime, the concrete workflows and services selection are specified based on the environment and the status of services. Q-Learning is used to find an optimal policy to follow up the dynamic environment. Wang et al. [55] extend the RL framework that was introduced in Wang et al. [54]. This study presents a Multi-Agent Reinforcement Learning (MARL) mechanism to enable adaptive WSC. The WSC process is modeled as MDP to adapt dynamic evolution of user requirements. The Q-learning algorithm is used to find an optimal policy to follow up the dynamic environment. This mechanism introduces a sharing strategy in the composition process to share information with an agent that make agent use the policies explored by the others. The MDP model needs complete knowledge and observation about the environment, which may be difficult to achieve in practical application. WSC may contain some failure services that can reach to a complete disability of this WSC workflow. This case is not taken into consideration. Wang et al. [56] also proposed a new model for large-scale and adaptive WSC based on MARL. This model integrates State-Action-Reward-State-Action (SARSA) learning algorithm and same theory. Multi SARSA algorithm which is extended from single-agent SARSA is utilized to find the optimal solution. Team Markov Games (TMG) is used to model multi-agent WSC. This algorithm does not take into consideration the case of some failure service that can reach complete disability of this WSC workflow. Wang et al. [57] also use TMG to model multi-agent WSC like in Wang et al. [56] but it used Q-learning instead of multi SARSA algorithm.

Moustafa and Zhang [58] design two algorithms to fulfill data efficiency by saving experience data and using it to make updates to the learned policy. The first algorithm introduces an offline learning scheme for WSC. Offline learning scheme avoids the limitation of online reinforcement learning algorithms. This limitation is the time which is taken to achieve convergence which may exceed the limits imposed by service consumers. The second algorithm presents a coordination mechanism in order to enable MARL to learn the WSC task cooperatively. A collaborative learning algorithm is a group of independent agents who learn to organize their action selection strategies and each agent notifies other agents with its action selections to make WSC collaboratively. Q-table is used to connect and communicate with each agent directly. This shared Q-table records the most recent QoS information of Web services and the rate with which these services have been chosen by other agents. Hsieh and Lin [1] use Holonic Multi-agent System (HMS) architecture to design SAS systems. A Workflow Adaptation Problem (WAP) is formulated and an interaction mechanism between agents is proposed based on Contract Net Protocol (CNP) to find a WAP solutions. Self-* scheme is proposed to respond to the structural and non-structural change workflow. Structural changes refer to changes in FR, which means changes in a business process. Non-structural changes refer to changes in NFR such as changes in processing time, the number of available resources, and available time slots of resources. When the change occurs, an affected agent will apply CNP to determine the best services provided by the existing downstream agents.

10.6 Comparison and Limitations of Self-Adaptive WSC Approaches

In this section, we compare between the approaches we presented in Sect. 10.5 and present the limitations of some of these approaches. The comparison between these approaches is given in Table 10.1. We compare between these approaches according to

- Category of these approaches according to classification in Sect. 10.5;
- RE classification according to changes in FR, changes in QoS, and changes in both FR and QoS;

Table 10.1 Analysis and comparison between self-adaptive WSC approaches

Approaches	Category	RE classification	Adaptation mechanism	Composition model
Alferez et al. [41]	Used of variability models	FR	Feature model	BPMN
Sun et al. [43]	Used of variability models	FR	COVAMOF, UML and VID	BPEL
Yua et al. [40]	Used of variability models	FR	Business rule	BPMN
Xiao el al. [44]	Used of variability models	FR	VxUML	Not defined
Imed et al. [45]	Used of variability models	QoS	VxBPEL	Not defined
Koning et al. [46]	Used of variability models	FR	Event-B	Not defined
Sun et al. [47]	Used of variability models	FR	VxBPE	Not defined
Alferez and Pelechauo [48]	Context-awareness	QoS	Tactics strategies	BPMN
Bucchiarone et al. [49]	Context-awareness	FR	Planning techniques	Not defined
Cubo et al. [50]	Context-awareness	FR	Extend DAMASCo framework with feature models	BPEL and windows workflow foundation(WF)
Li et al. [51]	Context-awareness	FR and QoS	Case-based reasoning	WS-BPEL
Cao et al. [52]	Context-awareness	FR and QoS	Not defined	BPEL
Wang and Tang [53]	Context-awareness	FR and QoS	Personalized policies	SHOP2 as Al planning technique
Wang et al. [54]	Multi-agent approach	QoS	MARL	MDP
Wang et al. [55]	Multi-agent approach	QoS	MARL	TMG-WSC
Wang et al. [56]	Multi-agent approach	QoS	MARL	TMG-WSC
Wang et al. [57]	Multi-agent approach	QoS	RL	MDP
Moustafa and Zhang [58]	Multi-agent approach	QoS	RL MARL	MDP

- Adaptation mechanism which described in Sect. 10.2;
- Composition model which described in Sect. 10.4.

The limitations are summarized in Table 10.2. Most of the approaches, e.g., Alférez et al. [41], Sun et al. [47], Yua et al. [40], Xiao et al. [44], Imed et al. [45], Koning et al. [46], Wang and Tang [53], Wang et al. [54, [55], and Wang et al. [57], are not suitable for use in dynamic environments because they are not able to deal with continuous and unanticipated changes in complex uncertain contexts. A study by Imed et al. [45] is suitable for use in a dynamic environment through the use of variability operators, but they are not enough to solve correctly vQoS problem. Imed et al. [45], Koning et al. [46], and Sun et al. [47] store variability information

Table 10.2 Some WSC adaptation approach limitations

Approaches	Limitations
Alférez et al. [41], Sun et al. [43], Yua et al. [40] and Xiao et al. [44]	These approaches are not able to deal with continuous and unanticipated changes in complex uncertain contexts. This means that they are not suitable for use in dynamic environments
Imed et al. [45], Koning et al. [46] and Sun et al. [47]	These approaches store variability information inside languages which result in their being time-consuming, tedious, difficult to manage, and error-prone. They are very complex in the case of a large number of variation points. In addition, they do not work in dynamic environments
Alférez and pelechano [48]	The selected tactics strategies that are used to adapt the changes may be negative effective to other expected goals
Cubo et al. [50]	This approach is not supported self-adaptation of the service to context change at runtime. This means that DAMASCo execution plan does not support the switching from one running configuration to another
Imed et al. [45]	Variability operators that are used to adapt WSC are not enough to solve correctly the vQoS problem
Wang and Tang [53]	This approach is not suitable for the dynamic environment because the contexts are predefined and other undefined contexts are not supported. It is difficult to predict all the possible situations arising in an uncertain environment
Wang et al. [54, [57]	WSC process is modeled as a MDP model. This model needs complete knowledge and observation about environment, which may be difficult to achieve it in practical application
Wang et al. [54], [56, 57]	These algorithms are not taken into consideration the case of some failure service that can reach to a complete disability of this WSC workflow

inside language which result in their being time-consuming, tedious, difficult to manage, and error-prone. Therefore, their approaches are very complex in the case of a large number of variation points.

Alférez and Pelechano [48] use tactics to tackle unknown context events. The selected tactics strategies may be negative effective to other expected goals. Cubo et al. [50] approach does not support the switching from one running configuration to another at runtime. Wang et al. [54] and [55] model WSC process as a MDP model. WSC process is modeled as a MDP model. This model needs complete knowledge and observation about environment, which may be difficult to achieve in practical application. Wang et al. [54], [55], and Wang et al. [57] do not take into consideration the case of some failure service that can reach complete disability of this WSC workflow.

10.7   Conclusion and Future Work

WSC is a key issue in SOA. The objective of this chapter is to analyze and compare various self-adaptive WSC approaches to deal with the changes that may occur within and outside the dynamic composition environment. These approaches are classified into three categories: used of variability models, context-awareness, and multi-agent approaches. These approaches have some limitations. One of the limitations is that the approaches, which deal with changes that occur in QoS, adapt the WSC process based on changes in local and single QoS criteria. Another limitation is that most of these approaches are not able to deal with continuous and unanticipated changes in complex uncertain contexts because they need to define the contexts in design time and other undefined contexts are not supported. It is usually difficult to predict all of the possible situations that might arise in an uncertain environment. In future work, we intend to overcome these limitations by combining QoS-aware WSC approaches such as ant colony optimization or genetic algorithm with multi-agent approaches to obtain an optimal policy in case of multi QoS criteria. Partially Observable Markov Decision Process (POMDP) is used to model composition requirement instead of MDP because POMDP does not need the full knowledge observation of environment.

References

1. F.-S. Hsieh and J.-B. Lin, "A Self-adaptation Scheme for Workflow Management in Multi-agent Systems," *Journal of Intelligent Manufacturing,* vol. 27, no. 1, p. 131–148, 2016.
2. N. Ide and J. Pustejovsky, "What Does Interoperability Mean, Anyway? Toward an Operational Definition of Interoperability for Language Technology," in *Proceedings of the 2nd International Conference on Global Interoperability for Language Resources (ICGL),* 2010.
3. B. Rohallah, M. Ramdane and S. Zaidi, "Agents and Owl-s based Semantic Web Service Discovery with User Preference Support," *International Journal of Web & Semantic Technology (IJWesT),* vol. 4, no. 2, pp. 57–75, April 2013.
4. I. sommerville, Software Engineering (9th Edition), 2011, p. 509.
5. L. Wang and J. Shen, "A Systematic Review of Bio-Inspired Service Concretization," *IEEE Transactions on Services Computing,* vol. PP, no. 99, p. 3, 2014.
6. W. Li, "Towards a Resilient Service Oriented Computing based on Ad-hoc Web Service Compositions in Dynamic Environments(Doctoral Dissertation)," *Institut d'Optique Graduate School,* 2014.
7. A. Moustafa and M. Zhang, "Towards Proactive Web Service Adaptation," in *Proceedings of the 24th International Conference Advanced Information Systems Engineering (CAiSE),* 2012.
8. P. v. Eck and R. Wieringa, "Requirements Engineering for Service-Oriented Computing: A Position Paper," in *Proceedings of the 1st International Workshop on e-Services at ICEC,* 2003.
9. N. B. Mabrouk, S. Beauche, E. Kuznetsova, N. Georgantas and V. Issarny, "QoS-aware Service Composition in Dynamic Service Oriented Environments," in *Proceedings of the 10th International Middleware Conference,* 2009.

10. C. Krupitzer, F. M. Roth, S. VanSyckel, G. Schiele and C. Becker, "A Survey on Engineering Approaches for Self-adaptive Systems," *Pervasive and Mobile Computing*, vol. 17, pp. 186, Part B, February 2015.
11. R. Aschoff and A. Zisman, "QoS-driven Proactive Adaptation of Service Composition," in *Proceedings of the 9th International Conference on Service Oriented Computing (ICSOC)*, 2011.
12. S. Vansyckel, D. Schäfer, G. Schiele and C. Becker, "Configuration Management for Proactive Adaptation in Pervasive Environments," in *Proceedings of the IEEE 7th International Conference on Self-Adaptive and Self-Organizing Systems*, 2013.
13. C. Pahl, "Dynamic Adaptive Service Architecture—Towards Coordinated Service Composition," in *Proceedings of the 4th European Conference Software Architecture (ECSA)*, 2010.
14. S. D. G. Avila, "QoS Awareness and Adaptation in Service Composition(Doctoral Dissertation)," *The University of Leeds*, pp. 34–38, 2014.
15. D. Shuiguang, L. Huang, W. Tan and Z. Wu, "Top- Automatic Service Composition: A Parallel Method for Large-Scale Service Sets," *IEEE Transactions on Automation Science and Engineering*, vol. 11, no. 3, pp. 891–905, 2014.
16. J. Liu, J. Li, K. Liu and W. Wei, "A Hybrid Genetic and Particle Swarm Algorithm for Service Composition," in *Proceedings of the 6th International Conference on Advanced Language Processing and Web Information Technology (ALPIT)*, 2007.
17. Z. Shanshan, W. Lei, M. Lin and W. Zepeng, "An Improved Ant Colony Optimization Algorithm for QoS-aware Dynamic Web Service Composition," in *Proceedings of the International Conference on Industrial Control and Electronics Engineering*, 2012.
18. F. Qiqing, P. Xiaoming, L. Qinghua and H. Yahui, "A Global QoS Optimizing Web Services Selection Algorithm based on MOACO for Dynamic Web Service Composition," in *Proceedings of the 2009 International Forum on Information Technology and Applications*, 2009.
19. H. Raik, "Service Composition in Dynamic Environments: From Theory to Practice (Doctoral Dissertation)," *University of Trento*, p. 40, 2012.
20. S. Poonguzhali, R. Sunitha and G. Aghila, "Self-Healing in Dynamic Web Service Composition," *International Journal on Computer Science and Engineering (IJCSE)*, vol. 3, no. 5, p. 2055, 2011.
21. S. Poonguzhali, L. JerlinRubini and S. Divya, "A Self-Healing Approach for Service Unavailability in Dynamic Web Service Composition," *International Journal of Computer Science and Information Technologies*, vol. 53, p. 4381, 2014.
22. K. May Chan, J. Bishop, J. Steyn, L. Baresi and S. Guinea, "A Fault Taxonomy for Web Service Composition," in *Proceedings of the International Conference on Service-Oriented Computing (ICSOC)*, 363–375.
23. S. D. G. Avila and K. Djemame, "A QoS Optimization Model for Service Composition," in *Proceedings of the 4th International Conference on Adaptive and Self-Adaptive Systems and Applications*, 2012.
24. B. H. Cheng, R. d. Lemos, H. Giese, P. Inverardi and J. Magee, "Software Engineering for Self-Adaptive Systems: A Research Roadmap," in *Software Engineering for Self-Adaptive Systems*, 2009, pp. 1–26.
25. L. Baresi, L. Pasquale and P. Spoletini, "Fuzzy Goals for Requirements-driven Adaptation," in *Proceedings of the 18th IEEE International Requirements Engineering Conference*, 2010.
26. L. Pasquale, L. Baresi and B. Nuseibeh, "Towards Adaptive Systems through Requirements@Runtime," in *Proceedings of the 6th International Workshop on MODELS@Runtime*, 2011.
27. K. Angelopoulos, V. E. S. Souza and J. Pimentel, "Requirements and Architectural Approaches to Adaptive Software Systems: A Comparative Study," in *Proceedings of the 8th International Symposium on Software Engineering for Adaptive and Self-Managing Systems (SEAMS)*, 2013.

28. G. D. Abowd, A. K. Dey, P. J. Brown, N. Davies, M. Smith and P. Steggles, "Towards a Better Understanding of Context and Context-Awareness," in *Proceedings of the 1st International Symposium Handheld and Ubiquitous Computing (HUC)*, 1999.

29. A. Bucchiarone, A. Marconi, M. Pistore and H. Raik, "Dynamic Adaptation of Fragment-based and Context-aware Business Processes," in *Proceedings of the IEEE 19th International Conference on Web Services*, 2012.

30. S. G. H. Tabatabaei, W. M. N. W. Kadir and S. Ibrahim, "A Review of Web Service Composition Approaches," in *Proceedings of the 1st International Conference on Computer Science and Information Technology (CCSIT)*, 2011.

31. O. Hatzi, D. Vrakas, M. Nikolaidou, N. Bassiliades, D. Anagnostopoulos and I. Vlahavas, "An Integrated Approach to Automated Semantic Web Service Composition through Planning," *IEEE Transactions on Services Computing*, vol. 5, no. 3, pp. 319–332, 2011.

32. X. Yihong, Z. Xianzhong and H. Xiaopeng, "Automated Semantic Web Service Composition Based on Enhanced HTN," in *Proceedings of the 5th IEEE International Symposium on Service Oriented System Engineering*, 2010.

33. Y. Bo and Q. Zheng, "Semantic Web Service Composition using Graphplan," in *Proceedings of the 4th IEEE Conference on Industrial Electronics and Applications*, 2009.

34. J. Rao and X. Su, "A Survey of Automated Web Service Composition Methods," in *Proceedings of the 1st International Conference on Semantic Web Services and Web Process Composition (SWSWPC)*, 2005.

35. B. Orriens, J. Yang and M. P. Papazoglou, "Model Driven Service Composition," in *Proceedings of the 1st International Conference Service-Oriented Computing (ICSOC)*, 2003.

36. Q. Z. Sheng and B. Benatallah, "ContextUML: A UML-Based Modeling Language for Model-driven Development of Context-aware Web Services," in *Proceedings of the International Conference on Mobile Business (ICMB)*, 2005.

37. C. C. Dumez, A. Nait-sidi-moh, J. Gaber and M. Wack, "Modeling and Specification of Web Services Composition using UML-S," in *Proceedings of the 4th International Conference on Next Generation Web Services Practices*, 15–20.

38. V. Uc-Cetina, F. Moo-Mena and R. Hernandez-Ucan, "Composition of Web Services using Markov Decision Processes and Dynamic Programming," *The Scientific World Journal*, vol. 2015, 2015.

39. A. Gao, D. Yangx, S. Tang and M. Zhang, "Web Service Composition using Markov Decision Processes," in *Proceedings of the 6th International Conference Advances in Web-Age Information Management (WAIM)*, 2005.

40. J. Yua, Q. Z. Shengb, J. K. Sweeb, J. Hanc, C. Liuc and T. H. Noorb, "Model-driven Development of Adaptive Web Service Processes with Aspects and Rules," *Journal of Computer and System Sciences*, vol. 81, no. 3, p. 533–552, May 2015.

41. G. Alférez, V. Pelechano, R. Mazo, C. Salinesi and D. Diazca, "Dynamic Adaptation of Service Compositions with Variability Models," *The Journal of Systems and Software*, vol. 91, pp. 24–47, 2014.

42. M. Svahnberg, J. v. Gurp and J. Bosch, "A Taxonomy of Variability Realization Techniques: Research Articles," *Journal of Software:Practice & Experience*, vol. 35, no. 8, pp. 705–754, 2005.

43. C.-A. Sun, R. Rossing and M. Sinnema, "Modeling and Managing the Variability of Web Service-based Systems," *The Journal of Systems and Software*, vol. 83, no. 3, p. 502–516, 2010.

44. H. Xiao, F. Yanmei, S. Chang-Ai, M. Zhiyi and S. Weizhong, "Towards Model-driven Variability-based Flexible Service Compositions," in *Proceedings of the IEEE 39th Annual International Computers, Software & Applications Conference (COMPSAC)*, 2015.

45. A. Imed, M. Graiet, S. Boubaker and N. B. Hadj-Alouane, "A Formal Approach for Verifying QoS Variability in Web Services Composition using EVENT-B," in *Proceedings of the 2015 IEEE International Conference on Web Services.*, New York, 2015.

46. M. Koning, C.-a. Sun and M. Sinnema, "VxBPEL: Supporting Variability for Web Services in BPEL," *Information and Software Technology*, vol. 51, no. 2, p. 258–269, 2009.

47. C.-A. Sun, P. Wang, X. Zhang and M. Aiello, "VxBPEL_ODE: A Variability Enhanced Service Composition Engine," in *Web Technologies and Applications*, 2014, pp. 69–81.

48. G. H. Alférez and V. Pelechano, "Facing Uncertianty in Web Service Compositions," in *Proceedings of the IEEE 20th Internatinal Conference on Web Services (ICWS)*, 2013.

49. A. Bucchiarone, R. Kazhamiakin, M. Pistore and H. Raik, "Adaptation of Service-based Business Processes by Context-aware Replanning," in *Proceedings of the IEEE International Conference on Service-Oriented Computing and Applications (SOCA)*, 2011.

50. J. Cubo, N. Gamez, L. Fuentes and E. Pimentel, "Composition and Self-Adaptation of Service-based Systems with Feature Models," in *Proceedings of the 13th International Conference on Software Reuse (ICSR)*, 2013.

51. G. Li, L. Liao, D. Song, J. Wang, F. Sun and G. Liang, "A Self-healing Framework for QoS-aware Web Service Composition via Case-Based Reasoning," in *Proceedings of the 15th Asia-Pacific Web Conference (APWeb)*, 2013.

52. Z. Cao, X. Zhang, W. Zhang, X. Xie, J. Shi and H. Xu, "A Context-aware Adaptive Web Service Composition Framework," in *Proceedings of the 2015 IEEE International Conference on Computational Intelligence & Communication Technology*, 2015.

53. B. Wang and X. Tang, "Designing a Self-adaptive and Context-aware Service Composition System," in *Proceedings of the IEEE Computers, Communications and IT Applications Conference (ComComAp)*, 2014.

54. H. Wang, Q. Wu, X. Chen, Q. Yu, Z. Zheng and A. Bougu, "Adaptive and Dynamic Service Composition Using Q-Learning," in *Proceedings of the 22nd International Conference on Tools with Artificial Intelligence*, 2010.

55. H. Wang, X. Wang, X. Hu, X. Zhang and M. Gu, "A Multi-Agent Reinforcement Learning Approach to Dynamic Service Composition," *Journal of Information Sciences*, vol. 363, pp. 96–119, 2016.

56. H. Wang, Q. Wu, X. Chen, Q. Yu, Z. Zheng and A. Bougu, "Integrating On-policy Reinforcement Learning with Multi-agent Techniques for Adaptive Service Composition," in *Proceedings of the 12th International Conference Service Oriented Computing (ICSOC)*, 2014.

57. H. Wang, Q. Wu, X. Chen, Q. Yu, Z. Zheng and A. Bougu, "Adaptive and Dynamic Service Composition via Multi-agent Reinforcement Learning," in *Proceedings of the IEEE International Conference on Web Services*, 2014.

58. A. Moustafa and M. Zhang, "Learning Efficient Compositions for QoS-aware Service Provisioning," in *Proceedings of the IEEE International Conference on Web Services*, 2014.

Chapter 11
Transition from Information Systems to Service-Oriented Logical Architectures: Formalizing Steps and Rules with QVT

Nuno Santos, Nuno Ferreira and Ricardo J. Machado

Abstract Specifying functional requirements brings many difficulties namely when regarding the cloud services. During the analysis phase, the alignment between the process-level requirements (information systems) with the product-level requirements (service-based software) may not be properly achieved or even understood. In this chapter, we describe an approach that supports the creation of the intended requirements, beginning in a process-level and evolving to a product-level perspective, to elicit requirements for specifying services that execute in a cloud computing environment. The transition between perspectives are supported by UML model transformations, encompassing a set of transition rules using QVT, from one perspective to the other, in order to assure that process- and product-level requirements are aligned.

Keywords Information systems design · Logical architectures · Requirement analysis · Model transformation · Service-oriented logical architecture · UML use cases · Transition rules

N. Santos (✉) · R.J. Machado
CCG/ZGDV Institute, University of Minho, Guimarães, Portugal
e-mail: nuno.santos@ccg.pt

R.J. Machado
e-mail: rmac@dsi.uminho.pt

N. Santos · R.J. Machado
ALGORITMI Research Centre, University of Minho, Guimarães, Portugal

N. Ferreira
I2S – Insurance Software Systems, Porto, SA, Portugal
e-mail: nuno.ferreira@i2s.pt

11.1 Introduction

The "generalized" adoption of cloud computing paradigm in software industry, together with the industry's high competitiveness, results in a highly demand for new releases that make use of cloud computing platforms with quality but developed in lesser time. It is a common problem in software projects that the final product is misaligned with the stakeholders' needs. The stakeholders are responsible for the business model development, and the development team is responsible for implementing it in software. However, in many cases, there is no stable context for eliciting requirements in Cloud Computing projects, and requirements engineering (RE) for Software-as-a-Service (SaaS) [1] and Service-Oriented Architecture (SOA) [2] are major challenging. A proper alignment is not always easy and bad requirements are one of the main reasons of projects' failure [3]. The elicitation of product-level (service-based software) requirements is achievable by using a process-level perspective to elicit process or (business process) needs and then use the resulting artifacts, like an information system logical architecture, as inputs for modeling of software functional needs. The first effort should be to specify the requirements of the overall system in the physical world; then to determine necessary assumptions about components of that physical world; and only then to derive a specification of the computational part of the control system [4]. There are similar approaches that tackle the problem of aligning domain-specific needs with software solutions. For instance, goal-oriented approaches are a way of doing so, but they do not encompass methods for deriving a logical representation of the intended system processes with the purpose of creating context for eliciting product-level requirements.

Our main problem, and the main topic this chapter addresses, is assuring that product-level (IT-related, in the software engineering domain) requirements are perfectly aligned with process-level requirements (in the information systems domain), and hence, are aligned with the organization's business requirements. The process-level requirements express the need for fulfilling the organization's business needs, and we detail how they are characterized within our approach further in Sect. 11.2. These requirements may be supported by analysis models, that are implementation agnostic [5]. According to [5], the existing approaches for transforming requirements into an analysis model (i) do not require acceptable user effort to document requirements, (ii) are efficient enough (e.g., one or two transformation steps), (iii) are able to (semi-)automatically generate a complete (i.e., static and dynamic aspects) consistent analysis model, which is expected to model both the structure and behavior of the system at a logical level of abstraction. For that, requirements are modeled by successive derivation (for more details, please refer to our approach of a V-Model [6, 7]) using UML models, first in process-level perspective, and then in product-level perspective.

Our proposal is to provide context for RE for cloud computing projects, by using a process-level approach for the initial eliciting of business needs, in order to give context to the product-level functionalities elicitation. Our product-level approach includes the use of models to define functional and nonfunctional requirements for SaaS and SOA solutions, initially in form of UML use cases, and in deriving a service-oriented logical architecture by executing the Four-Step-Rule-Set (4SRS) method [6–8]. This paper intends to detail the steps and rules required to perform the transition between the process- and product-level perspectives within the V+V Model (presented in [9]) using Query/View/Transformation (QVT) [10] in order to achieve that transition between UML models. This way, we formalize the transition between perspectives that is required in order to align the requirements of both V-Models. In comparison with [9], besides the use of QVT transformations, we include additional contributes to support of the rules, like a formalization of a UML metamodel extension. In addition, we strengthen the state-of-the-art section. The result is an integrated approach, beginning in information system architecture and ending in a service-oriented logical architecture.

This chapter will be structured as follows: Sect. 11.2 briefly presents the macro-process for information systems development based on both process- and product-level V-Model approaches; Sect. 11.3 describes the transition steps and detail the model transformations required for applying the transition rules between both perspectives; in Sect. 11.4 we present a real industrial cloud-based demonstration case on the adoption of transition steps between process- and product-level perspectives; in Sect. 11.5 we compare our approach with other related work; and in Sect. 11.6 we present the conclusions.

11.2 The V+V Model

The V+V Model [11] is an approach for information systems development. The entire V+V Model is not presented in this paper, since it is already detailed in [11] and its composing artifacts presented in [6, 7]. Rather, in Fig. 11.1 is depicted the main artifacts, and those artifacts are the ones involved in the transition process. The transition process is presented in [9]. The main difference from our proposed approach to other information system development approaches is that it is applicable for eliciting product-level requirements in cases where there is no clearly defined context for eliciting product requirements within a given specific domain, by first eliciting process-level requirements and then evolving to the product-level requirements, using a transition approach that assures an alignment between both perspectives. Other approaches (described further in Sect. 11.5) typically apply to a single perspective.

The first V-Model (in which the most important artifacts are depicted in the left side of Fig. 11.1, the remaining models are out of the scope of this paper) is executed at a process-level perspective performing the identification of business needs and then, by successive artifact derivation, transiting from business-level artifacts (i.e., process-level use case diagrams) to an IT-level artifact (i.e., information system logical architecture) that is assured by the execution of the Four-Step Rule-Set (4SRS) method. For the scope definition of our work, we characterize our

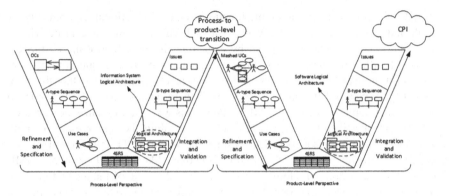

Fig. 11.1 V+V process framed in the development macro-process (from [11])

process-level perspective by: (i) being related to real-world activities (including business); (ii) when related to software, those activities encompass the typical software development lifecycle.

Our process-level approach is characterized by using refinement (as one kind of functional decomposition) and integration of system models. Activities and their interface in a process can be structured or arranged in a process architecture [12]. The process-level 4SRS method execution (see [6–8] for details about the process-level 4SRS method) assures the transition from the problem to the solution domain by transforming process-level use cases into process-level logical architectural elements, and results in the creation of a validated architectural model which allows creating context for the product-level requirements elicitation and in the uncovering of hidden requirements for the intended product design. Use cases are mandatory to execute the 4SRS method.

The second V-Model (in which the most important artifacts are depicted in the right side of Fig. 11.1) is executed at a product-level perspective. By product-level, we refer as the typical software requirements. The second execution of the V-Model is performed by gathering information from the process-level V-Model in order to create a new model referred as *Mashed UCs* (preliminary product-level use case models). The creation of this model is detailed in the next section of this paper as transition steps and rules. *Mashed UC* model is then used as input for successive artifact derivation until requirements are modeled in product-level use case diagrams that gather typical software user requirements. The remaining models from Fig. 11.1 are out of the scope of this paper. Like in the first V-Model, use cases are input for the 4SRS method (but in its product-level perspective, detailed in [13–15]), which then outputs a service-oriented logical architecture that depict system requirements derived from the original user requirements. The resulting architecture is then considered a design artifact that contributes for the creation of context for product implementation (*CPI*) as information required by implementation teams. Note that the design itself is not restricted to that artifact, since in our approach it also encompasses behavioral aspects and nonfunctional requirements representation.

As depicted in Fig. 11.1, the result of the first V-Model (process-level) execution is the information system logical architecture. The architectural elements that compose this architecture are derived (by performing transition steps) into product-level use cases (*Mashed UC* models). The result of the second V-Model (product-level) execution is the service-oriented logical architecture. The *Mashed UC* model is the output of the model transformations presented in the next section.

11.3 Steps and QVT Rules for Transition Between V-Models

The V+V process is useful for both stakeholders, organizations and technicians, but it is necessary to assure that they properly reflect the same system. This section begins by presenting a set of transition steps whose execution is required to create the initial context for product-level requirements elicitation, referred to as Mashed UC model. The purpose of the transition steps is to assure an aligned transition between the process- and product-level perspectives in the V+V process, that is, the passage from the first V-Model to the second one. By defining these transition steps, we assure that product-level use cases (UCpt's) are aligned with the architectural elements (AEpc's) from the information system logical architecture diagram; i.e., software use case diagrams are reflecting the needs of the information system logical architecture. The application of these transition rules to all the partitions of an information system logical architecture gives origin to a set of *Mashed UC* models. To allow the recursive execution of the 4SRS method [13, 15–17], the transition from the first V-Model to the second V-Model must be performed by a set of steps. The output of the first V-Model must be used as input for the second V-Model; i.e., we need to transform the information system logical architecture into product-level use case models. The transition steps to guide this mapping must be able to support a business to technology changing. These transition steps (TS), presented in [9], are depicted in Fig. 11.2 and are structured as follows:

TS1—Architecture Partitioning: By applying collapsing and filtering techniques as detailed in [13], it is possible to identify major groups of elements in the information system logical architecture that must be computationally supported by software. In this transition step, the AEpc's under analysis are classified by their computation execution context with the purpose of defining software boundaries to be transformed into UCpt's. The final software boundary is represented after the execution of filtering and collapsing techniques in the AEpc's. Each of the identified major groups of elements is subject to a separate execution in the following transition steps.

TS2—Use Case Transformation: This transition step is applied to each partition defined in the previous transition step (i.e., to each major groups of elements) with

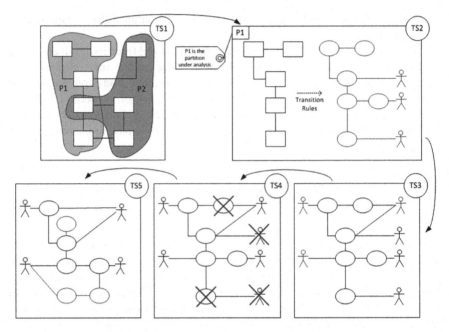

Fig. 11.2 Process- to product-level transition

the purpose of transforming elements of the information system logical architecture (AEpc's) into software use cases and actors. In this transition step, AEpc's are transformed into software use cases and actors that represent the system under analysis. This is the most critical transition step of the transition process and, as such, we have devised a set of transition patterns that must be applied as rules that are later described in this section.

TS3—Original Actors Inclusion: For each defined partition, the original actors that were related to the use cases from which the architectural elements of the process-level perspective are derived (in the first V-Model execution) must be included in the representation. The purpose of this transition step is to introduce into the product-level perspective the necessary information regarding the skills and stakeholders of the originally defined processes. The traceability between the process-level use cases and the AEpc's is assured by the process-level 4SRS execution [6–8].

TS4—Redundancy Elimination: In the previous transition steps there is a possibility of including redundancy in the model in the form of actors and use cases generated by the transition rules. For each partition defined in the first transition step, it is important to remove such redundancy by explicitly removing the unnecessary actors and use cases from the model.

TS5—Gap Filling: This final transition step intents to create, in the form of use cases to be added to the model, the necessary information of any requirement that is intended to be part of the design and that is not yet present. Typical missing use cases are connections between existing use cases that were automatically created by the transition rules.

During the execution of these transition steps, a specific stereotype of use cases, called transition use cases (UCtr's), bridge the AEpc's and serve as basis to elicit UCpt's. UCtr's also provide traceability between process- and product-level perspectives using tags and annotations associated with each representation. The identification of each partition is first made using the information that results from the packaging and aggregation efforts of the previous 4SRS execution (step 3 of the 4SRS method execution as described in [6, 7]). Nevertheless, this information is not enough to properly identify the partitions. Information gathered in scenarios that were elicited in early models in the first V-Model must also be accounted. A partition is created by identifying all the relevant architectural elements that belong to a given organizational configuration scenario. The rules to support the execution of the TS2 are applied in the form of transition rules and must be applied in accordance to the stereotype of the envisaged architectural element. There are three stereotyped architectural elements: *d-type*, which refer to generic decision repositories (data), representing decisions not supported computationally by the system under design; *c-type*, which encompass all the processes focusing on decision-making that must be supported computationally by the system (control); and *i-type*, which refer to process' interfaces with users, software, or other processes. The full descriptions and specifications of the three stereotypes are available in [6].

The proposed process not only includes activities for perspective transition (as it is performed by the application of transition rules in TS2) but it also concerns to obtain a stable model (by performing TS3-5). By analyzing the perspectives on which the steps from the transition process are performed, the steps are easily classified.

The transition process naturally starts in the process-level perspective with AEpc's. In Table 11.1 it is possible to realize that after TS1 the transition is still dealing with AEpc's as input; the execution of TS2 results in the perspective transition, since it is in this TS that UCtr's are introduced and they relate to product-level; in the remaining transition steps, naturally they relate to product-level perspective. The purpose of the remaining transition steps is to promote completeness and reliability in the model. The model is complete after adding the associations that initially connected actors (the ones who trigger the AEpc's) and the AEpc's, and then by mapping those associations to the UCtr's. The model is reliable since the enforcement of the rules eliminates redundancy and assures that there are no gaps in the UCtr's associations and related actors. Only after the execution of all the TS we consider the resulting model as containing product-level (software) use cases (UCpt's), which will compose the *Mashed UC* model. In summary, in TS1 the artifact regards AEpc's, in TS2-5 the focus is in UCtr's and only when the Mashed UC model is finished UCtr's become UCpt's.

Table 11.1 Transition steps overview

Transition step	Description	Perspective
TS1	The AEpc's under analysis are classified by their computation execution context	Process-level
TS2	AEpc's are transformed into software use cases and actors that represent the system under analysis through a set of transition patterns that must be applied as rules	Product-level
TS3	The original actors that were related to the use cases from which the architectural elements of the process-level perspective are derived (in the first V execution) must be included in the representation	Product-level
TS4	The model is analyzed for redundancies	Product-level
TS5	The necessary information of any requirement that is intended to be part of the design and that is not yet present is added, in the form of use cases	Product-level

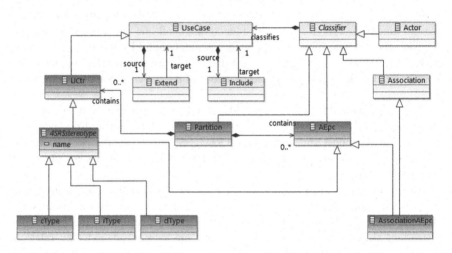

Fig. 11.3 Excerpt of AEpc and UCtr extension

For the sake of understandability we present in Fig. 11.3 an excerpt of the UML extension that supports the creation of AEpc's, UCtr's and partitions (please note that UCpt's regard the traditional use cases). We consider that a partition is a container of AEpc's or UCtr's and acts as a border delimiter for the combinations of possible systems candidates to be analyzed.

After delimiting all the partitions, it is necessary to focus on a particular one (called inbound partition) and execute the required transformations considering all the remaining neighbor partitions (outbound partitions).

A proper way of defining the transformations between models is by means of using OMG's QVT [10]. QVT is a set of languages (QVT-Operational, QVT-Relations, and QVT-Core) that enables models transformations. QVT-Operational enables unidirectional transformations of a given model into another. QVT-Relations allow bi-directional transformations. QVT-Core can be considered a subset of QVT-Relations. All the QVT set of languages are associated with model-driven approaches. These model-driven approaches are usually associated with design and implementation models and lack support to requirements and analysis models. The requirements specification (in any perspective) is a crucial task in any software development process. As such, models that support requirements specification should be integrated into model-driven methods.

In our proposed approach we have chosen QVT as a mean to transform AEpc's models into UCtr's models, or being more specific, transforming information system logical architectural models into *Mashed UC* models. This relates to integrating models that support requirements specifications into a model-driven approach. In [9], the steps and rules were already described, but without technological formalization. Associated with the transition rules, we present a subset of the QVT-Operational (-like) code that supports the transformation intended by a given rule. The defined transition rules, from the logical architectural diagram to the *Mashed UC* diagram, are presented in [9] and are as follows:

TR1—an inbound *c-type* or *i-type* AEpc is transformed into an UCtr of the same type (see Fig. 11.4). By inbound we mean that the element belongs to the partition under analysis.

The QVT-like specification that supported the transformation for TR1 is as follows:

```
if (AEpc.Partition=inbound) and
(AEpc.4SRSstereotype=cType or
AEpc.4SRSstereotype=iType) then { UCtr.name:=Aepc.name;
UCtr.4SRSstereotype:=AEpc.4SRSstereotype}
endif;
```

TR2—an inbound d-type AEpc is transformed into an UCtr and an associated actor (see Fig. 11.5). This is due to the fact that d-type AEpc's correspond to decisions not computationally supported by the system under design and, as such, it requires an actor to activate the depicted process.

Fig. 11.4 TR1—transition rule 1 (from [9])

Fig. 11.5 TR2—transition
rule 2 (from [9])

TR2 is supported by the following:

```
if (AEpc.Partition=inbound) AND
(AEpc.4SRSstereotype=dType) then {
UCtr.name:=AEpc.name;
UCtr.4SRSstereotype:=AEpc.4SRSstereotype;
Actor.name:=self.name;
Actor.association:=UCtr}
endif;
```

Rules TR1 and TR2 are the most basic ones and the patterns they express are the most used in the transition step 2. The remaining rules regard more specific situations, however require equal attention from the analyst. The remaining rules are as follows:

TR3—an inbound AEpc, with a given name x, which also belongs to an outbound partition, is transformed into an UCtr of name x, and an associated actor, of name y, being responsible for outbound actions associated with *UCtrx* (Fig. 11.6).

The specification for TR3 is:

```
if (AEpc.Partition=multiple) and
(AEpc.4SRSstereotype=cType) then {
UCtr.name:=AEpc.name;
UCtr.4SRSstereotype:=AEpc.4SRSstereotype;
Actor.name:=self.name;
Actor.association:=UCtr }
endif;
```

The connections between the use cases and actors produced by the previous rules must be consistent with the existing associations between the AEpc's. The focus of this analysis is UCtr's and is addressed by the following two transition rules.

Fig. 11.6 TR3—transition
rule 3 (from [9])

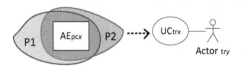

Fig. 11.7 TR4—transition
rule 4 (from [9])

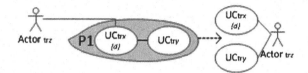

TR4—an inbound d-type UCtr of name x with connections to an (any type) UCtr of name y and to an actor z, gives place to two UCtr's, x and y, maintaining the original types (see Fig. 11.7). Both are connected to the actor z. This means that all existing connections on the original d-type AEpc that were maintained during execution of TR2 or TR3 are transferred to the created actor must be consistent with the existing associations between the AEpc's. The focus of this analysis is UCtr's and is addressed by the following two transition rules.

The previous rule is executed after TR1, TR2, or TR3, so it only needs to set the required association between the UCtr's and the actors, that is to say, after all transformations are executed (TR1, TR2, and TR3), a set of rules are executed to establish the correct associations to the UCtr's.

Regarding TR4, the necessary specification is

```
if (UCtr.Partition=inbound) and
(UCtr.4SRSstereotype=dType) and
(Actor.associations().FilterByPartition(UCtr).Count >
1) then {
   Actor.Association:= Ac-
   tor.associations().FilterByPartition(UCtr).GetUCtr())
   }
   endif;
```

TR5—an inbound UCtr of name *x* with a connection to an outbound AEpc of name *y* (note that this is still an AEpc, since it was not transformed into any other concept in the previous transition rules) gives place to both an UCtr named *x* and to an actor named *y* (see Fig. 11.8). AEpc's that were not previously transformed are now transformed by the application of this TR5; this means that all AEpc's which exist outside the partition under analysis having connections with inbound UCtr's will be transformed into actors. These actors will support the representation of

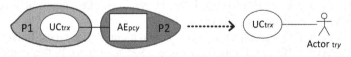

Fig. 11.8 TR5—transition rule 5 (from [9])

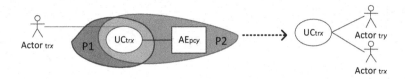

Fig. 11.9 TR5.1—transition rule 5.1 (from [9])

required external inputs to the inbounds UCtr's created during application of TR1, TR2, or TR3.

For TR5, the supporting specification is

```
if (AEpc.Partition=outbound) then {
Actor.name:=Aepc.name
Actor.Association:= Ac-
tor.associations().FilterByPartition(UCtr).GetUCtr()) }
endif;
```

A special application of TR5 (described as TR5.1) can be found in Fig. 11.9 where we can see an UCtr with a connection to an outbound AEpc and another connection to an actor. In this case, TR5 is applied and the resulting UCtr is also connected to the original actor. Note that an UCtr belonging to multiple partitions is first and foremost, an inbound UCtr due to being under analysis.

The application of these transition steps and rules to all the partitions of the information system logical architecture gives origin to a set of Mashed UC models. In the next section, we present a demonstration case study an information system logical architecture is transformed into a product-level *Mashed UC* model by executing the transition steps.

11.4 Demonstration Case on the Transition Process

The applicability of the proposed approach was assessed with a real project that is analyzed in this manuscript as a case study: the ISOFIN project (Interoperability in Financial Software) [18]. This project aimed to deliver a set of coordinating services in a centralized infrastructure, enacting the coordination of independent services relying on separate infrastructures. The resulting ISOFIN platform allows for the semantic and application interoperability between enrolled financial institutions, e.g., Banks, Insurances, and others.

The global ISOFIN architecture relies on two main service types: Interconnected Business Service (IBS) and Supplier Business Service (SBS). In this context, there are two external business domain entities with access to the ISOFIN Platform:

ISOFIN Customers and ISOFIN Suppliers. An ISOFIN Customer is an entity whose domain of interactions resides in the scope of consuming, for economic reasons, the functionalities exposed by IBSs. An ISOFIN Supplier is a company that interacts with the ISOFIN SaaS Platform by supplying the platform with functionalities (SBSs) that reside in their private clouds. IBS's concern a set of functionalities that are exposed from the ISOFIN core platform to ISOFIN Customers. An IBS interconnects one or more SBS's and/or IBS's exposing functionalities that relate directly to business needs. SBS's are a set of function-alities that are exposed from the ISOFIN Suppliers production infrastructure. SBSs are made available in the ISOFIN Supplier private cloud by the use of generators and are composed, in the public cloud where the ISOFIN SaaS Platform resides implement an IBS. Composition of basic SBSs into IBSs give origin to more powerful functionalities that are exposed by the platform.

The requirements elicitation of activities in the ISOFIN project resulted in a model composed by 39 use cases (i.e., the process-level use cases from Fig. 11.1). From the demonstration case, we first present a subset of the information system logical architecture in Fig. 11.10, that resulted from the execution of the 4SRS method at a process-level perspective [6–8]; i.e., the execution of the first (process-level) V-Model. The information system logical architecture is composed by architectural elements that represent processes executed within the ISOFIN platform. The first V-Model execution ended with 74 documented architectural elements (not counting associations). This means that we added more details to the problem description. All of these architecture elements from the logical architecture were input for the transition process.

The logical process-level architecture of the ISOFIN project has embedded design decisions that are initially injected in the processes descriptions. The design decisions concern the deployment of the system in a public cloud environment and

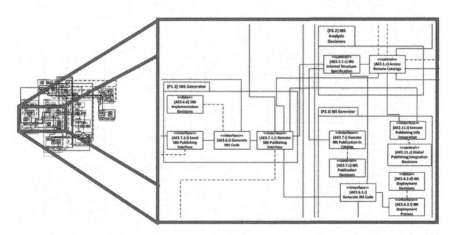

Fig. 11.10 Subset of the ISOFIN information system logical architecture (from [9])

its interoperability with several other private clouds as defined in the project objectives.

The resulting logical model of the system architecture, based on the processes that are intended to be executed, shows a software solution able to be deployed in IaaS layer. That layer will support the execution of a set of services that will allow suppliers to specify the behavior of the services they intend on supplying, in a PaaS layer. This will allow customers, or third-parties, to use the platform's services, in a SaaS layer and be billed accordingly. Additionally, processes regarding the provider perspective (e.g., infrastructure management) were also considered.

In Fig. 11.11, we depict the execution of TS1 to a subset of the entire information system logical architecture, i.e., the partitioning of the information system logical architecture, by marking its architectural elements in partition areas, each concerning the context where services are executed, which resulted in two partitions: (i) the ISOFIN platform execution functionalities (in the area marked as P1); (ii) the ISOFIN supplier execution functionalities (in the area marked as P2).

The identification of the partitions will enable the application of the transition steps to allow the application of the second V-Model to advance the macro-process execution into the product implementation. Presenting the information that supported the decisions regarding the partitions in the case of the ISOFIN project is out of the scope of this paper.

TS1 ends with the collapsing of AEpc's from outside the boundaries and without any associations to inbound AEpc's. In the subset of Fig. 11.11, such only applied to *{AE3.7.2.i} Local SBS Publishing Interface*. Thus, this AEpc is immediately excluded from the remaining steps.

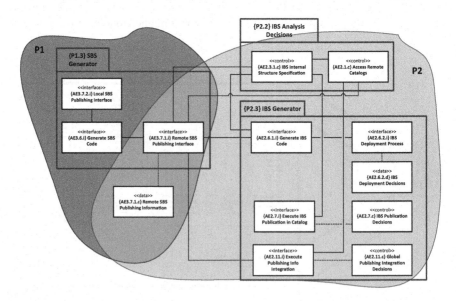

Fig. 11.11 Partitioning of the information system logical architecture (TS1) (from [9])

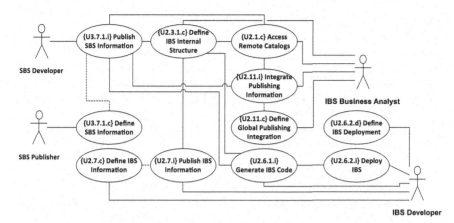

Fig. 11.12 *Mashed UC* model resulting from the transition from process- to product-level (from [9])

In Fig. 11.12, we depict the final *Mashed UC* model (the first product-level artifact in the second V-Model), resulting from the execution of TS2-5. Due to space restrictions, we only show the result of the execution of these four transition steps altogether. The resulting mashed use cases are the result of the application of the transition rules in TS2.

Table 11.2 summarizes the application of QVT transformations to the AEp'cs from Fig. 11.11. It is possible to objectively recognize the effect of the application of some transition rules previously described. TR1 was the most applied transition rule and one example is the transformation of the AEpc named *{AE2.1.c} Access Remote Catalogs* into one UCtr named *{U2.1.c} Access Remote Catalogs*. One example of the application of TR2 is the transformation of the AEpc named *{AE2.6.2.d} IBS Deployment Decisions* into the UCtr named *{U2.6.2.d} Define IBS Deployment* and the actor named *IBS Developer*. TR3 was applied, for instance, in the transformation of the AEpc named *{AE3.7.1.c} Define SBS Information* into the UCtr named *{U3.7.1.c} Define SBS Information* and the actor named *SBS Publisher*. Finally, we can recognize the application of TR5.1 in the transformation of the AEpc named *{AE3.6.i} Generate SBS Code* into the actor named *SBS Developer*. All the other actors result from the execution of TS3. We must refer, for instance, that the actor *SBS Developer* results from the execution of TS4, since the original actor and the actor resulting from an application of TR2 and TR5.1 and also the inclusion of the original actor in TS3, result in the same actor which brings the need to eliminate the generated redundancy. The resulting model allows to identify potential gaps in use cases or actors (in the execution of TS5), but in this case such wasn't required.

After the execution of the transition steps, the resulting *Mashed UC* model is the first artifact that composes the product-level V-Model and that is then used as starting point for the rest of the V-Model execution. Thus, after performing the

Table 11.2 Executed QVT transformations to the model

QVT rule	Process-level (transformation source)	Output	Product-level (transformation target)
TR1	AEpc {AE2.1.c} Access Remote Catalogs	UCtr	{U2.1.c} Access Remote Catalogs
	AEpc {AE2.3.1.c} IBS Internal Structure Specification	UCtr	{U2.3.1.c} Define IBS Internal Structure
	AEpc {AE2.6.1.i} Generate IBS Code	UCtr	{U2.6.1.i} Generate IBS Code
	AEpc {AE2.6.2.i} IBS Deployment Process	UCtr	{U2.6.2.i} Deploy IBS
	AEpc {AE2.7.i} Execute IBS Publication in Catalog	UCtr	{U2.7.i} Publish IBS Information
	AEpc {AE2.7.c} IBS Publication Decisions	UCtr	{U2.7.c} Define IBS Information
	AEpc {AE2.11.i} Execute Publishing Info Integration	UCtr	{U2.11.i} Integrate Publishing Information
	AEpc {AE2.11.c} Global Publishing Integration Decisions	UCtr	{U2.11.c} Define Global Publishing Information
TR2	AEpc {AE2.6.2.d} IBS Deployment Decisions	UCtr	{U2.6.2.d} Define IBS Deployment
		Actor	IBS Developer
TR3	AEpc {AE3.7.1.i} Remote SBS Publishing Interface	UCtr	{U3.7.1.i} Publish SBS Information
		Actor	SBS Developer
TR3	AEpc {AE3.7.1.c} Remote SBS Publishing Information	UCtr	{U3.7.1.c} Define SBS Information
		Actor	SBS Publisher
TR5.1	AEpc {AE3.6.i} Generate SBS Code	Actor	SBS Developer

transition process, the *Mashed UC* model was used for deriving a new set of artifacts, this time regarding a product-level perspective, in a new V-Model execution. Like in the process-level perspective, the process ends with the 4SRS method execution, where a service-oriented logical architecture was derived.

The derivation of this architecture is out of the scope of this paper, so this demonstration case skips directly from the *Mashed UC* model to the software system logical architecture. We depict in the second architecture of Fig. 11.13 the entire software system logical architecture obtained after the execution of the V+V process, derived by transforming product use cases in architectural elements using product-level 4SRS method, having as input the information system logical architecture (the first architecture of Fig. 11.13) previously presented.

The software system logical architecture is composed by architectural elements (depicted in the zoomed area) that represent services that are executed in the platform. The alignment between the architecture elements in both perspectives is supported by the transition steps. It would be impossible to elicit requirements for a service-oriented logical architecture as complex as the ISOFIN platform (the overall

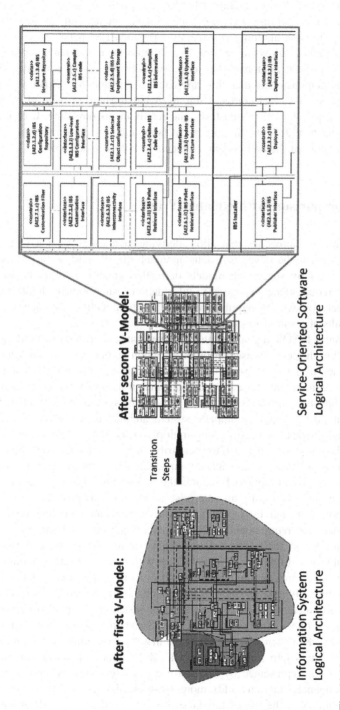

Fig. 11.13 Subset of the ISOFIN service-oriented logical architecture based on the information system logical architecture (from [9])

information system logical architecture was composed by near 80 architectural elements, and the resulting service-oriented logical architecture by near 100) by adopting an approach that only considers the product-level perspective.

Our V+V process allows to perform RE activities in an integrated approach, and the ISOFIN project demonstration case (namely the service-oriented logical architecture) demonstrated that this approach is suitable for Cloud Computing projects. The services that compose this SOA-based platform were identified, by performing sequential RE-related tasks and requirements modeling. It is also possible to depict in Fig. 11.13 the alignment (supported by the transition steps and QVT rules) between the architecture elements in both perspectives.

11.5 Comparison with Related Work

There are many approaches that allow deriving at a given level a view of the intended system to be developed. Our approach clearly starts at a process-level perspective, and by successive models derivation creates the context for transforming the requirements expressed in information system logical architecture into product-level context for requirements specification. Other approaches provide similar results at a subset of our specification.

For instance, KAOS, a goal-oriented requirement specification method, provides a specification that can be used in order to obtain architecture requirements [19]. This approach uses two step-based methods, which output a formalization of the architecture requirements for each method. Since it uses two methods, each of the derived architectures provides a different view of the system. It is acknowledged in software engineering that a complete system architecture cannot be represented using a single perspective [20]. Using multiple viewpoints, like logical diagrams, sequence diagrams, or other artifacts, contributes to a better representation of the system and, as a consequence, to a better understanding of the system. An important view considered in our approach regards the architecture. The organization's processes can be represented by an enterprise architecture, as proposed in [21], and representation extended by including in the architecture modeling concerns as business goals and requirements [22]. However, such proposals do not intend to provide information for implementation teams during the software development process, but instead to provide to stakeholders with business strategic requirements. Most agree that an architecture concerns both structure and behavior, with a level of abstraction that only regards significant decisions, is influenced by its stakeholders and the environment where it is intended to be instantiated and also encompasses decisions based on some rationale or method. Some architecture views can be seen in [20, 23–25]. Krutchen's work [20] refers that the description of the architecture can be represented into four views: logical, development, process, and physical. The fifth view is represented by selected use cases or scenarios. Our stereotyped usage of sequence diagrams adds more representativeness value to the specific model. Additionally, the use of this kind of stereotyped sequence diagrams at the first stage of analysis phase (user requirements modeling and validation) provides a friendlier perspective to most stakeholders, easing them to establish a direct correspondence between what they initially stated as functional requirements and what the model describes. Ullah and Lai [26] models business goals and derives system requirements, but it outputs a UML state chart. Our approach outputs system requirements in an architectural diagram and stereotyped sequence diagrams.

The relation between what the stakeholders want and what implementation teams need requires an alignment approach to assure that there are no missing specifications on the transition between phases. Tarafdar and Qrunfleh [27] argues that an alignment between business and IT can be "strategic" and "tactical," and [28] presents an alignment approach also based on architectural models. An approach that enacts the alignment between domain-specific needs and software solutions, is the GQM + Strategies (Goal/Question/Metric+Strategies) [29]. This approach uses measurement to explicitly link goals and strategies from business objectives to project operations. Another goal-oriented approach is the Balanced Scorecard (BSC) [30]. BSC links strategic objectives and measures through a scorecard in four perspectives: financial, customer, internal business processes, and learning and growth. It is a tool for defining strategic goals from multiple perspectives beyond a purely financial focus, and can be properly aligned with four key elements of IT-business alignment (integrated planning, effective communication, active relationship management, and institutionalized culture of alignment) [31], as well as for information security management [32]. Another approach, COBIT [33], is a framework for governing and managing enterprise IT. It provides a comprehensive framework that assists enterprises in achieving their objectives for the governance and management of enterprise IT. It is based on five key principles: (1) meeting stakeholder needs; (2) covering the enterprise end-to-end; (3) applying a single, integrated framework; (4) enabling a holistic approach; and (5) separating governance from management. As far as the authors of this paper are concerned, none of the previous approaches encompasses processes for deriving a logical representation of the intended system processes with the purpose of creating context for eliciting product-level requirements. Those approaches have a broader specification concerning risk analysis, auditing, measurement, or best practices in the overall alignment strategy.

The 4SRS method is used for transforming functional user requirements into logical architectural models representing system requirements. It can be executed either in a process-level [7–9] and in a product-level perspective [13–15] but the method executed alone does not allow to transit between perspectives. Tan et al. [34] presents an approach to transform a functional analysis model (in a data flow diagram) into object-oriented design and implementation. This approach is executed in a product-level perspective and, like 4SRS, the transformation only regards a single perspective. In a product-level perspective, there are several approaches that support model transformations to software architectures based on requirements, like the work in [34], the Component-Oriented Platform Architecting Method for product family engineering (COPA) [35], the Reuse-driven Software Engineering Business (RSEB) [36], the Family-Oriented Abstraction, Specification and Translation (FAST) [37], the Feature-Oriented Reuse Method (FORM) [38], the

Komponentenbasierte Anwendungsentwicklung (german for component-based product line engineering—KobrA) [39], or the Quality-driven Architecture Design and Analysis (QADA) [40]. In a process-level perspective, Tropos [41] is a methodology that uses notions of actor, goal, and (actor) dependency as a foundation to model early and late requirements, architectural and detailed design; afterwards, the SIRA approach describes a software requirements and architectural models from the perspective of an organization in the context of Tropos, using i* models (a goal-oriented approach to describe both the system and its environment in terms of strategic actors and social dependencies among them) [42], in [43] is presented a process to generate Acme ADL [44] architectural models from i* models; and in [45] is described a method for obtaining architectural models based in KAOS requirements models. None of these presented approaches support process- to product-level transition.

There are many approaches that allow deriving at a given level a view of the intended system to be developed. Our approach clearly starts at a process-level perspective, and by successive models derivation creates the context for transforming the requirements expressed in an information system logical architecture into product-level context for requirements specification. Other approaches provide similar results at a subset of our specification.

In [46] it is specified a mapping technique and an algorithm for mapping business process models, using UML activity diagrams, and use cases, so functional requirements specifications support the enterprise's business process. In our approach, we use information system logical architecture diagram instead of an activity diagram, since an information system logical architecture provides a fundamental organization of the development, creation, and distribution of processes in the relevant enterprise context [47].

In literature, model transformations are often related to the Model-Driven Architecture (MDA) [48] initiative from OMG. An MDA-based approach uses model transformations in order to transform a high-level model (Platform-Independent Model—PIM) to a lower level model (Platform-Specific Model—PSM). MDA-based model transformations are widely used but, as far as the authors know, the supported transformations do not regard perspective transition, i.e., are perspective agnostic since they concern model transformations within a single perspective (typically the product-level one). Model-driven transformation approaches were already used for developing information systems in [49]. In [50] business process models are derived from object-oriented models.

The existing approaches for model transformation attempt to provide an automated or automatic execution. Yue et al. [5] provides a systematic review and evaluation of existing work on automating of transforming requirements into an analysis model and, according to the authors, none of the compared approaches provide a practical automated solution. The transition steps and rules presented in this work intent to provide a certain level of automation into our approach and improve the efficiency, validation, and traceability of the overall V+V process. The transitions depicted in the present work are able to be fully implemented in development tools that support QVT transformations, like the well-known Eclipse IDE.

11.6 Conclusions

We have described the transition steps and rules for assuring an alignment between process- and product-level requirements within the execution of the V+V process. This approach is adopted to create context for software implementation teams in Cloud Computing projects where requirements cannot be properly elicited. The V +V process is based on successive models construction and recursive derivation of logical architectures (first an information system one and then for a service-oriented one), and makes use of model derivation for creating use cases, based on high-level representations of desired system interactions.

We presented a real industry demonstration case in order to elicit requirements for developing a platform that provides interoperability between financial institutions by providing services in a cloud environment. Our approach is supported on a set of transition steps and QVT-based transition rules in order to execute the transition from process- to product-level perspective. These transition steps use as basis an information system logical architecture to output a product-level use case model. The product-level requirements are specified in a software system logical architecture, having as basis the information system logical architecture.

It is a common fact that domain-specific needs, namely business needs, are fast changing. Information system architectures must be in a way that potentially changing domain-specific needs are local in the architecture representation. Our approach enables requirements traceability within three stages of its process, namely within the derivation of both process- (information system) and product-level (service-oriented) logical architectures and during the transition between perspectives. Each V-Model uses software engineering techniques, such as operational model transformations to assure the execution of a process that begins with business needs and ends with a logical architectural representation of a system. Each V-Model from our proposed V+V process encompasses the derivation of a logical architecture representation that is aligned with domain-specific needs by executing the 4SRS method and any change made to those domain-specific needs is reflected in the logical architectural model, and the transformation and traceability is properly assured by the 4SRS method. Since the *Mashed UC* model (and, consequently, the perspective transition) is derived from a model transformation based on QVT mappings (from AEpc's to UCtr's), traceability between AEpc's and UCpt's is guaranteed, thus any necessary change on product-level requirements due to a change on a given business needs is easily identified and propagated alongside the models that comprise the V+V process.

Since we are designing SOA and Cloud Computing solutions, using SOA Modeling Language (SoaML) diagrams, an instantiation of UML models for SOA contexts, instead of UML diagrams, may be more adequate. Within SoaML diagrams, 4SRS was already used to derive participants, requests, services, and properties by using UML use cases as input. As future work, we intend to include in our approach the derivation of other SoaML diagrams, like Service Contracts, Service Architectures, Interfaces, Service Choreographies, amongst others, in order to improve our process, since we believe that using additional diagrams will improve the specification of the SOA and cloud services. However, SoaML notation should be used throughout the entire V-Model, in order to obtain information regarding services at the end of the requirements elicitation phase. We intend to develop this V-Model in future work, as we believe that the rationale regarding the RE-tasks present in the V-Model as described in this paper will be similar for developing a SoaML variation of the V-Model.

References

1. Mell, P., Grance, T.: The NIST Definition of Cloud Computing. (2009).
2. Bianco, P., Kotermanski, R., Merson, P.: Evaluating a service-oriented architecture. (2007).
3. Standish Group: CHAOS Report 2014. (2014).
4. Maibaum, T.: On specifying systems that connect to the physical world. New Trends Softw. Methodol. Tools Tech. (2006).
5. Yue, T., Briand, L.C., Labiche, Y.: A Systematic Review of Transformation Approaches between User Requirements and Analysis Models. Requir. Eng. Vol. 16, (2011).
6. Ferreira, N., Santos, N., Machado, R., Fernandes, J.E., Gasević, D.: A V-Model Approach for Business Process Requirements Elicitation in Cloud Design. In: Bouguettaya, A., Sheng, Q. Z., and Daniel, F. (eds.) Advanced Web Services. pp. 551–578. Springer New York (2014).
7. Santos, N., Teixeira, J., Pereira, A., Ferreira, N., Lima, A., Simões, R., Machado, R.J.: A demonstration case on the derivation of process-level logical architectures for ambient assisted living ecosystems. In: Garcia, N.M. and Rodrigues, J.J.P.C. (eds.) Ambient Assisted Living Book. pp. 103–139. CRC Press (2015).
8. Salgado, C., Teixeira, J., Santos, N.: A SoaML Approach for Derivation of a Process-Oriented Logical Architecture from Use Cases. Explor. Serv. .... (2015).
9. Ferreira, N., Santos, N., Soares, P., Machado, R., Gašević, D.: A Demonstration Case on Steps and Rules for the Transition from Process-Level to Software Logical Architectures in Enterprise Models. In: Grabis, J., Kirikova, M., Zdravkovic, J., and Stirna, J. (eds.) The Practice of Enterprise Modeling. pp. 277–291. Springer Berlin Heidelberg (2013).
10. OMG: Meta Object Facility (MOF) 2.0 Query/View/Transformation (QVT), http://www.omg. org/spec/QVT/1.1.
11. Ferreira, N., Santos, N., Soares, P., Machado, R.J., Gasevic, D.: Transition from Process- to Product-level Perspective for Business Software, (2012).
12. Browning, T.R., Eppinger, S.D.: Modeling impacts of process architecture on cost and schedule risk in product development. IEEE Trans Eng. Manag. 49, 428–442 (2002).
13. Machado, R.J., Fernandes, J., Monteiro, P., Rodrigues, H.: Refinement of Software Architectures by Recursive Model Transformations, http://dx.doi.org/10.1007/11767718_38, (2006).
14. Machado, R.J., Fernandes, J.M., Monteiro, P., Rodrigues, H.: Transformation of UML Models for Service-Oriented Software Architectures, (2005).
15. Fernandes, J., Machado, R., Monteiro, P., Rodrigues, H.: A Demonstration Case on the Transformation of Software Architectures for Service Specification. In: Kleinjohann, B., Kleinjohann, L., Machado, R., Pereira, C., and Thiagarajan, P.S. (eds.) From Model-Driven Design to Resource Management for Distributed Embedded Systems. pp. 235–244. Springer US (2006).
16. Azevedo, S., Machado, R.J., Muthig, D., Ribeiro, H.: Refinement of Software Product Line Architectures through Recursive Modeling Techniques, http://dx.doi.org/10.1007/978-3-642-05290-3_53, (2009).

17. Azevedo, S., Machado, R., Maciel, R.: On the Use of Model Transformations for the Automation of the 4SRS Transition Method. In: Bajec, M. and Eder, J. (eds.) Advanced Information Systems Engineering Workshops. pp. 249–264. Springer Berlin Heidelberg (2012).
18. ISOFIN: ISOFIN Research Project. http://isofincloud.i2s.pt/, (2010).
19. Jani, D., Vanderveken, D., Perry, D.: Experience Report: Deriving architecture specifications from KAOS specifications. (2003).
20. Kruchten, P.: The 4+1 View Model of Architecture. IEEE Softw. 12, 42–50 (1995).
21. The Open Group: TOGAF—The Open Group Architecture Framework, http://www.opengroup.org/togaf/.
22. Engelsman, W., Quartel, D., Jonkers, H., van Sinderen, M.: Extending enterprise architecture modelling with business goals and requirements. Enterp. Inf. Syst. 5, 9–36 (2010).
23. Clements, P., Garlan, D., Little, R., Nord, R., Stafford, J.: Documenting software architectures: views and beyond, (2003).
24. Hofmeister, C., Nord, R., Soni, D.: Applied software architecture. Addison-Wesley Professional (2000).
25. Chen, D., Doumeingts, G., Vernadat, F.: Architectures for enterprise integration and interoperability: Past, present and future. Comput. Ind. 59, 647–659 (2008).
26. Ullah, A., Lai, R.: Modeling business goal for business/it alignment using requirements engineering. J. Comput. Inf. Syst. 51, 21 (2011).
27. Tarafdar, M., Qrunfleh, S.: IT-Business Alignment: A Two-Level Analysis. Inf. Syst. Manag. 26, 338–349 (2009).
28. Strnadl, C.F.: Aligning Business and It: The Process-Driven Architecture Model. Inf. Syst. Manag. 23, 67–77 (2006).
29. Basili, V.R., Lindvall, M., Regardie, M., Seaman, C., Heidrich, J., Munch, J., Rombach, D., Trendowicz, A.: Linking Software Development and Business Strategy Through Measurement. Computer (Long. Beach. Calif). 43, 57–65 (2010).
30. Kaplan, R.S., Norton, D.P.: The balanced scorecard–measures that drive performance. Harv. Bus. Rev. 70, 71–79 (1992).
31. Huang, C.D., Hu, Q.: Achieving IT-business strategic alignment via enterprise-wide implementation of balanced scorecards. Inf. Syst. Manag. 24, 173–184 (2007).
32. Herath, T., Herath, H., Bremser, W.G.: Balanced Scorecard Implementation of Security Strategies: A Framework for IT Security Performance Management. Inf. Syst. Manag. 27, 72–81 (2010).
33. Information Technology Governance Institute (ITGI): COBIT v5—A Business Framework for the Governance and Management of Enterprise IT. ISACA (2012).
34. Tan, H.B.K., Yang, Y., Bian, L.: Systematic Transformation of Functional Analysis Model into OO Design and Implementation. IEEE Trans. Softw. Eng. Vol. 32, (2006).
35. Obbink, H., Müller, J., America, P., van Ommering, R., Muller, G., van der Sterren, W., Wijnstra, J.G.: COPA: A component-oriented platform architecting method for families of software-intensive electronic products. In: Tutorial for the First Software Product Line Conference., Denver, Colorado. (2000).
36. Jacobson, I., Griss, M., Jonsson, P.: Software Reuse: Architecture, Process and Organization for Business Success. Addison Wesley Longman (1997).
37. Weiss, D.M.: Software Product-Line Engineering: A Family-Based Software Development Process. Addison-Wesley Professional (1999).
38. Kang, K.C., Kim, S., Lee, J., Kim, K., Shin, E., Huh, M.: FORM: A feature-oriented reuse method with domain-specific reference architectures. Ann. Sw Eng. (1998).
39. Bayer, J., Muthig, D., Göpfert, B.: The library system product line. A KobrA case study. Fraunhofer IESE. (2001).
40. Matinlassi, M., Niemelä, E., Dobrica, L.: Quality-driven architecture design and quality analysis method, A revolutionary initiation approach to a product line architecture. VTT Technical Research Centre of Finland (2002).

41. Castro, J., Kolp, M., Mylopoulos, J.: Towards requirements-driven information systems engineering: the Tropos project. Inf. Syst. (2002).
42. Yu, E.: Modelling strategic relationships for process reengineering. In: Yu, E., Giorgini, P., Maiden, N., and Mylopoulos, J. (eds.) Social Modeling for Requirements Engineering. pp. 11–152. The MIT Press (2011).
43. Lucena, M., Castro, J., Silva, C., Alencar, F., Santos, E., Pimentel, J.: A model transformation approach to derive architectural models from goal-oriented requirements models. In: OTM Confederated International Conferences" On the Move to Meaningful Internet Systems." pp. 370–380. Springer Berlin Heidelberg. (2009).
44. Garlan, D., Monroe, R., Wile, D.: Acme: an architecture description interchange language. CASCON First Decad. High Impact Pap. (2010).
45. Lamsweerde, A. Van: From system goals to software architecture. Form. Methods Softw. Archit. (2003).
46. Dijkman, R.M.: Deriving use case diagrams from business process models. Tech. report, CTIT Tecnhical Rep. (2002).
47. Winter, R., Fischer, R.: Essential Layers, Artifacts, and Dependencies of Enterprise Architecture, (2006).
48. OMG: MDA Guide Version 1.0.1, (2003).
49. Iribarne, L., Padilla, N., Criado, J., Asensio, J.-A., Ayala, R.: A Model Transformation Approach for Automatic Composition of COTS User Interfaces in Web-Based Information Systems. Inf. Syst. Manag. 27, 207–216 (2010).
50. Redding, G., Dumas, M., Hofstede, A.H.M. ter, Iordachescu, A.: Generating Business Process Models from Object Behavior Models. Inf. Syst. Manag. 25, 319–331 (2008).

Chapter 12
Improving the QoS of a Composite Web Service by Pruning its Weak Partners

**Kuljit Kaur Chahal, Navinderjit Kaur Kahlon
and Sukhleen Bindra Narang**

Abstract Quality of Service (QoS)-aware web service composition is based on nonfunctional properties of component (or partner) web services. In a dynamic environment, these properties of partner web services change on the fly. There exist several research proposals that take into account QoS degradation of partner web services at run-time, and propose solutions to maintain the optimality of the service composition in such circumstances. In this paper, we focus on the problem from a different perspective. We take into account the situation when quality (QoS values) of some of the partner web services improves, but for some others it remains the same. With the passage of time, if the quality of these web services does not improve, they act as bottlenecks or the weakest links in an otherwise efficient process. We simulate a framework which identifies such web services, and expands the search domain by sending a selective query to remote/premium service registries/brokers for finding better alternatives of such services. The proposed approach is effective, efficient, and scalable as well.

Keywords Service computing · SOA · Service composition · Web services · Supply-Chain network · Quality of Service · Weakest link

12.1 Introduction

In the Service-Oriented Architecture, a Composite Web Service (CWS) is created to serve functionality which the existing web services are not able to provide. In addition to the functionality, a CWS is also supposed to fulfill the expected non-functional requirements of its end users. QoS attributes of a web service describe its

K.K. Chahal (✉) · N.K. Kahlon
Department of Computer Science, Guru Nanak Dev University, Amritsar, India
e-mail: kuljitchahal@yahoo.com

S.B. Narang
Department of Electronics Technology, Guru Nanak Dev University, Amritsar, India

© Springer International Publishing AG 2017
M. Ramachandran and Z. Mahmood (eds.), *Requirements Engineering
for Service and Cloud Computing*, DOI 10.1007/978-3-319-51310-2_12

nonfunctional properties. It encompasses a number of performance metrics of a web service such as availability, reputation, price, execution time, response time, etc. A CWS depends upon its partner web services to fulfill functional as well as nonfunctional requirements of its end users. Successful execution of partner web services contributes to meet user's expected QoS of the CWS. Inability to do so may lead to loss of current as well as future business of the CWS, though the cause of the deficient service lies outside the ambit of the CWS provider.

Several methods have been proposed in the research literature to accurately estimate aggregate QoS value of a CWS given the QoS values of its partner (component) web services [4]. A web composition can be static in which partner web services are decided at design-time [8]. However, such a composition is not suitable for a dynamic environment in which partner web services are controlled by third parties and may become unavailable or their QoS values degrade during run-time [1]. We need solutions which are dynamic as well as proactive to manage QoS degradation of partner web services in such a way that aggregate quality level of the CWS can be maintained.

We conjecture that a suboptimal (QoS aware) solution may not always be due to QoS degradation of some of the partner web services of a CWS. A solution may also become suboptimal when quality of most of the services improves barring a few. In such a situation, there is need to look into the web services whose QoS value is worst and stable (i.e., neither degrades nor improves).

Performance (in terms of QoS) of a CWS is dependent on the performance of its partner web services (in combination). We define weakest link of a CWS as a partner web service that limits the web service in attaining higher efficiency beyond a certain threshold. Therefore, identification and penalization (i.e., substitution) of weakest links becomes imperative to improve performance of the CWS. The idea of identifying a weakest link in a CWS (when comprehended as a value chain) is akin to identification of bottlenecks in a supply-chain network.

We propose to use log analysis of the previous CWS execution traces to identify a weakest link in its execution. A weakest link, in a CWS execution process, is a web service whose QoS value contributes the maximum (or minimum) to the global (aggregate) QoS value of the process to deviate it from attaining a better value. For example, a set of partner web services of a CWS has the following values for the Execution Time (ET) QoS attribute (in ms): $\{w_1 = 0.3, w_2 = 0.4, w_3 = 0.6, w_4 = 0.7, w_5 = 2.5\}$. If ET for the CWS is calculated using the aggregation formula for a serial workflow (i.e., sum of all the values), it is 4.5 ms. In this aggregate value, maximum contribution is of the web service W_5. It has the maximum value for the ET, and the value is significantly different from the corresponding values of the other web services. Now W_5's ET value may be high due to the nature of the task it performs. For a complex task, ET will be high. If nature of the task is not complex, then high ET indicates low quality level of the web service in comparison to other web services in the value chain. Then, such a web service is identified as the weakest link.

We suggest that search space can be expanded on demand. When all other services in a web service composition improve, we should be able to identify a web service which proves to be a weakest link in the configuration. Such web services can be replaced with alternative web services by exploring remote and/or premium repositories to look for alternatives.

The remainder of the paper is organized as follows: Next section defines the problem with the help of a motivating example. Section 12.3 presents the related work. Section 12.4 explains the research methodology. Section 12.5 shows evaluation of the proposed framework. Section 12.6 mentions limitations of the study. Last section concludes the paper followed by the references.

12.2 Problem Definition

Consider a situation in which execution time of some of the partner web services of a CWS improves over a period of time. There is a partner web service, for example, whose ET neither improves nor degrades. Had its ET degraded, it would have got substituted with a better alternative. Therefore, it continues to be a part of the configuration. With the passage of time, its ET is significantly different from the execution times of other web services in the CWS. As no degradation happens in its execution time over the period of time, it cannot be identified by a framework that may have been used to manage QoS degradation of partner web services [16]. There is need to identify this bottleneck service and find alternatives of this service (may be from global/premium service repositories). However, to the best of our knowledge, there does not exist any proposal that tackles the issues in a dynamic environment of a service oriented solution from this point of view

In an ideal situation, the best web service for a task, wherever it exists on the planet should be searched and included in the composition. But reality is very different from this. A number of service registries exist. It is not possible for a service discovery module to look into all the possible service registries in real time to get the best services in a time-efficient manner when a composite web service is configured from scratch. There is a tradeoff between finding the best services and time complexity of a service discovery process [2, 7]. Moreover, some registries are public, and some are private and available at a premium. Therefore, for time and cost efficiency, a service discovery module should expand the search to premium registries only in exigent cases. Previous work in the service discovery domain [6] acknowledges the need for creating registry federations to carry out the discovery process in multiple registries [3]. Such an approach gives more useful results than a centralized repository. Among the numerous efforts to improve the efficiency of the service discovery module in SOA, Sivashanmugam et al. [17] propose a crawler engine that searches the web services information from multiple registries and other heterogeneous resources and creates a centralized large database called Web Service Storage (WSS). The large data set needs to be updated regularly by the crawler as changes occur in the services in their base locations. Changes in the web services are very frequent in the dynamic Internet based environment. Hence, such solutions are inefficient. As they not only require high maintenance to reflect latest updates, but also suffer from single point of failure syndrome, and are not scalable as well. In distributed or decentralized approaches of web service registry management, a locally maintained registry is searched first. If the search request is not satisfied by the local registry, then it is sent to global registries. We also propose to involve global registries selectively as retrieval of web service information from global repositories is not cost effective for routine searching in the beginning of the web service composition process [2]. It takes time in tens of seconds [19]. We suggest that search space can be expanded on demand during the web service life cycle. When all other services in a web service composition improve, we should be able to identify a web service which proves to be a weakest link in the configuration. Then explore remote and/or premium repositories to look for an alternative.

We propose, in this paper, to start with a CWS (may be created with local optimization approach criteria alone or along with a global optimization approach) and then improve the solution in the dynamic environment. It is not (economically) feasible to create a CWS with global optimization criteria for every user request especially when the CWS is a long-term solution, and is invoked frequently. Once a CWS is created, it should be self-optimizing after that. We propose a framework which can identify partner web services, not in sync with other web services in the execution plan of the CWS. Such web services can be replaced with alternative web services. The premise of our proposal is that a discovery algorithm is able to search a subset of service repositories for web services required for a CWS. Searching in all the possible (under the sky) service repositories is not cost effective. A CWS may be created with whatever is available at the first instance in a local repository. It can be later improved by expanding the search scope to find alternatives for a few web services which are not in sync with others in the combination. This expanded search scope may encompass service repositories which are remote or are available at a premium.

Next, we analyze the weakest link approach for managing QoS of a CWS with a long life span. There exist a few web service composition approaches that consider life span of a CWS as well to decide the composition process to follow [12, 15]. A CWS with a short life span responds to a few requests for a short period of time. As soon as the business goal is fulfilled, the CWS ceases to exit. For every request, the CWS is created from scratch. In case of a CWS with long life span, configuration of the CWS is created once and then used many times. Jiang et al. [12] distinguish between two composition approaches as one time query, and continuous query. One time query corresponds to a CWS with short span, and is created from scratch for a new request. In continuous query, an old instance of a CWS is (re)used with some adaptation (if required) for the new requests. Liu et al. [15] define a long-term composed service (LCS) as a web service with long-term business goal (or an open-ended life time). It has a stable relationship with its partner web services to serve a continuous stream of requests. In such a situation, creating a CWS from scratch for every request is not right from efficiency point of view.

Table 12.1 Example of a typical scenario

Trace	Service bindings	Remarks
1	WS = {WS$_{11}$, WS$_{21}$, WS$_{34}$, WS$_{42}$, WS$_{53}$, WS$_{61}$} ET = {1000, 1200, 1300, 2000, 1300, 1400}	WS$_{42}$ has the maximum execution time in the set
2	WS = {WS$_{11}$, WS$_{21}$, WS$_{34}$, WS$_{42}$, WS$_{53}$, WS$_{63}$} ET = {1000, 1200, 1300, 2000, 1300, 1200}	WS$_{63}$ replaces WS$_{61}$ as WS$_{61}$'s ET increases
3	WS = {WS$_{11}$, WS$_{21}$, WS$_{34}$, WS$_{42}$, WS$_{53}$, WS$_{63}$} ET = {1000, 1200, 1300, 2000, 1300, 1200}	=no change=
4	WS = {WS$_{11}$, WS$_{25}$, WS$_{34}$, WS$_{42}$, WS$_{53}$, WS$_{61}$} ET = {1000, 1100, 1300, 2000, 1300, 1200}	WS$_{25}$ replaces WS$_{21}$ as WS$_{21}$'s ET increases

12.2.1 Motivating Example

An analysis of previous traces of the CWS on client side (see Table 12.1), shows that web service WS$_{42}$ is spending maximum time in execution (measured in ms), and thus delays the overall process. This service is also not being replaced (in the following traces) as its ET remains the same (i.e., does not degrade). We assume that a better alternative of the web service is not available in the primary set of registries that the service discovery module explores while searching for new services. So there is need to extend the search boundary to include a distant repository (may be of a premium category).

Our proposed work contributes in the following ways:

- We define a strategy to identify those web services in a value chain which contribute in making the CWS sluggish. A web service is defined as a weakest link if its QoS values are worst and stable for a long period of time.
- We make a case for the service discovery module to look for candidate web services in premium/remote service repositories only in exigent cases. The search space should expand as per demand, only if a better alternative is not available in the local repository.
- The proposed framework is applied on two types of CWS—one with short term use, and second with long term use.

12.3 Related Work

Major issue in the web service composition process has been to find a QoS-aware optimal solution for the service composition problem. Researchers proposed several methods to search for an optimal solution such as exact algorithms [5], heuristic algorithms (e.g., [14], and meta-Heuristic algorithms [20] using local optimization or global optimization as the criteria. These solutions look for an optimal or near optimal solution by focusing on two perspectives: reducing time complexity of the algorithm, and limiting the search space. Most of the solutions are applicable in static environments only. However, web services-based solutions are realized using the Internet. The Internet being a dynamic entity, a web service composition configuration should remain optimal in the dynamic environment otherwise the optimal solution is limited to a few instances only. As soon as the environment changes, the solution goes below the optimum level.

Keeping the dynamism of the operating environment in mind, researchers in the past have focused on handling QoS degradation of web services to maintain the optimality of the solution in a dynamic environment. Research in this area has handled QoS degradation of partner web services, and proposed solutions to adapt the configuration of a CWS by replacing the degraded partner web service with a better alternative [16].

We also work toward realizing an optimal solution for the web service composition problem. But we look at this problem from a different point of view. We monitor not only degradation of the (partner) web services, but also the web services which do not degrade themselves but become bottlenecks when all other services in a configuration improve in their QoS values. The questions that we aspire to answer are: what if (rather than degrading) some of the partner web services improve in their quality except a few of them? Would not it lead to the web services (whose quality does not improve) acting as bottlenecks or weakest links in the value chain? As better alternatives for these services are not available in the registries explored by the service-oriented application in routine, solution lies in expanding the search space to include more repositories. We observe that this improves the solution quality in a time-efficient manner as search in this case is for selective web services (a subset of the total set of services) only.

In a dynamic environment, managing QoS degradation of the partner web services requires querying the service resources for latest information about their QoS values. Keeping in mind the running time overhead that is incurred for collecting this information, Harney and Doshi [9] propose to use a selective query approach. In this, full information is not requested from the resource providers for all the services at one time. Only those services whose QoS values may have changed are queried for the information. We also use selective querying, but in a different context. They use selective querying, from monitoring point of view, to collect latest information at the execution time. We too use this approach during execution phase of the CWS but from discovery point of view. Their target of the query is a service registry/broker that is already supporting the application. We target the query at a service registry/broker which has not been yet explored by the application for the service discovery task.

Finding the weakest link in a supply-chain network is of interest for every business. But we could not find any solution from this domain that can be adopted for finding the weakest link in a service network in the context of SOA for managing the solution in an automated way. We chose a statistical approach to identify the web service which contributes maximum to the aggregate QoS value of the CWS. For the sake of simplicity, we have assumed only one dimension of the QoS value, e.g., execution time. Execution time is a QoS attribute with a negative dimension, i.e., lower is the value, better is the quality. Multiple attributes can also be incorporated easily in this approach by using approaches like Simple Additive Weighting to find a utility score for a web service.

During exploration of the related research literature, we could find only one other research paper which focuses on the same issue of finding a weakest link in a CWS configuration. Research work in [10] focuses on the weak points in a QoS composition to improve it. The approach to identify weak point is similar to ours— a service with biggest impact on the composition with respect to a QoS attribute. Unlike our statistical approach, the authors suggest two approaches for doing so— in brute force method all the services are tried one by one to identify the web service with the biggest impact, and in branch and bound method a branch (in a parallel workflow pattern) with the highest execution time is followed to identify the weak point web service. Unlike our framework, they assume that a better alternative of the weak point web service does not exist in the service repository. Therefore, the solution to replace the weak web service with a set of alternatives is limited to the available web services in the local repository. The solution is then another combination of existing web services realized after analyzing various arrangements for different workflow composition patterns.

We premise that such a solution is more relevant for a CWS with an open-ended life time. A few solutions already exist which focus on managing partner web services of a CWS created for long-term use [12, 15].

Jiang et al. [12] perceive the requirement of a mechanism to support execution of a CWS which responds to a continuous stream of requests. For a one time composition request, a CWS is created from scratch, and it ceases to exist as soon as the response is generated. However, when there is continuous flow of requests for a CWS on the service network, an old CWS instance can be (re)used to respond to the requests. In case of dynamic changes in the partner services of the CWS, only affected services are replaced and not the whole web service space. The continuous query-based approach has good scalability, and is more efficient than creating a CWS from scratch for every request.

Liu et al. [15] propose a solution to manage changes that pertain to top level view of a LCS (Long Composed composite web Service). For example, owners of the LCS may have different functionality (due to business changes) or QoS (due to new competitors in the market) requirements. Therefore, changes are introduced from the top. As requirements change, web services may be added to or removed from the LCS configuration. Unlike them, we manage changes in a LCS from bottom to top. We detect web services whose QoS values are stable but worst in the configuration, then change the LCS configuration by pruning such web services, and replace them with better alternatives.

12.4   Research Methodology

We propose to analyze execution trace of a CWS periodically. Duration of periodicity can be determined by the service owner on the basis of cost/benefit tradeoff of executing the analysis. The execution trace records every partner web service's QoS value (e.g. Execution Time). Web services advertise their processing time or provide methods to inquire about it. Kahlon et al. [13] propose publish-subscribe mechanism based solution to provide web service QoS values to its clients.

12.4.1   The Statistics

This study explores analysis of the extreme values in an execution trace using Interquartile Ranges and Tukey Fences [18] as the statistics. Interquartile range is the statistic to measure variability in a data set. It is the difference between the first Quartile, Q_1, and the third Quartile, Q_3. It gives the range of the middle 50% values in a data set. The formula to calculate is

$$\text{InterQuartile Range (IQR)} = Q_3 - Q_1 \tag{12.1}$$

The Quartiles Q_1, and Q_3 represent respectively the least 25%, and the largest 25% of the values of a data set.

Tukey Fences is a popular method of identifying extreme values in a data set. After calculating the first and third Quartiles for a data set, the Tukey Fences are calculated as follows:

$$\text{Lower limit} = Q_1 - 1.5\,(\text{IQR}) \tag{12.2}$$

$$\text{Upper limit} = Q_3 + 1.5\,(\text{IQR}) \tag{12.3}$$

12.4.2   Identifying the Outlier(s)

In the present case, the data set consists of QoS values of partner web services of a composite web service. A QoS attribute can have a positive or a negative dimension.

For identifying an outlier in the case of a negative QoS attribute, first find the maximum value in the data set. If the maximum value is greater than the upper limit (defined in Eq. 12.3), then the corresponding data item is an extreme value in the data set. Similarly for finding an outlier in the case of a positive attribute, if the minimum value is lower than the lower limit (Eq. 12.2), then that is the extreme value in the data set. For a given data set regarding ET of 7 partner web services that constitute a CWS, let us examine the statistics in Table 12.2.

Table 12.2 Statistics for an example data set

Data set	Median	Q_1	Q_3	IQR	Upper limit
{70, 200, 400, 560, 756, 832, 2200}	560	300	794	494	1301

As per the given values, the maximum value in the data set (i.e., 2200) is greater than the upper limit of the Tukey Fences (i.e., 1301). Therefore, it is an extreme value. We know that a better web service is not available in the service repositories being explored by the service discovery module in the normal routine (otherwise this web service would have got replaced already). There is need to expand the search boundary to find a better web service.

12.4.3 Analyze the Influence of the Outlier

A workflow in a service composition may follow serial, cyclic, or parallel, or a combination of the three execution patterns of partner web services. Aggregate value of a QoS attribute for a CWS is calculated using different formulae for the different workflow patterns [11]. In this paper, we consider that service composition follows a serial workflow pattern. In a serial pattern, the partner web services execute one after another. Output of one web service becomes input of another in a serial order. Aggregate value of the Execution Time QoS for a CWS is the sum of Execution Times of all its partner web services. In our context, the model is an aggregate function Sum, it takes ET values of various web services and gives ET of the CWS as output. We assume the workflow pattern as a simple sequence of service executions. Here, the aggregate (global) value for the QoS attribute ET is sum of the ET value of each partner service.

The influence of a data point on the aggregate is calculated by first finding the difference between the original aggregate (which included the said data point) and the modified aggregate (excluding the said data point). The influence is defined as a ratio between this difference and the number of data points contributing to this change. When there is more than 1 outlier, influence values can be used to order the pruning actions. An outlier with maximum influence is pruned first.

12.5 Results and Analysis

The weakest link analysis approach is analyzed for a CWS with short span of life (in Experiment 1), as well as for a CWS with long span of life (in Experiment 2). A CWS, with short life, is created from scratch for every new request. Whereas a CWS, with long life, is (re)used to respond to forthcoming requests. We use a synthetic data set in the experiment. Values for the QoS attribute ET are generated using a uniform random process. The solution is implemented in C++ using

CodeBlocks 11.0 IDE with gcc as the compiler on an Intel machine with Core 2 Duo CPU, 2 GB RAM, and Windows XP as the operating system.

12.5.1 Experiment 1

Here, we consider a simple situation in which a CWS is created from scratch for every request. A new configuration for the CWS is created by searching the local/global repositories and then executed. Our proposed solution is to analyze execution trace of a CWS to identify the partner web services that contributed the maximum in QoS (parameters with negative dimension such as Execution Time) of that instance of the CWS.

This section presents the evaluation of the framework by comparing it with other two naïve approaches. We use local optimization as the criteria for selecting web services from the candidate set of services.

We create three different cases to analyze the results of the proposed approach. First two cases model two different base (benchmark) situations. In the first case, service discovery is limited to a local repository. By using an exhaustive strategy, best service for each task is selected from the candidate web services in the local repository. In the second case, service discovery is expanded to a global repository, and selection strategy is exhaustive again. In the third case (the proposed approach), service composition is created using candidate web services from the local repository, and then service discovery is expanded to global repository only when the need is felt to manage web services with worst QoS value in the configuration.

In order to compare the cases, we measure

- Efficiency, i.e., the time taken to generate the CWS configuration,
- Quality of the solution in terms of aggregate QoS value of the resultant CWS.

Before we compare the proposed approach with the two basic approaches, we discuss the effectiveness (i.e., the usefulness) of the proposed approach in the next paragraph.

12.6 Effectiveness

Figure 12.1 shows results of the simulation in which ET of all the partner web services improves except one service. ET is increased at different rates at 10% in the second run, at 25% in the third run. Then the web service which does not see any improvement in its ET QoS attribute in the first two runs is identified by the framework as the weakest link. When it is substituted with an alternate web service (with 25% better ET) from a distant repository in the fourth run, aggregate ET of the CWS improves by 33%. It improves only by 5 and 8% in the earlier two runs. It shows that the proposed approach is promising.

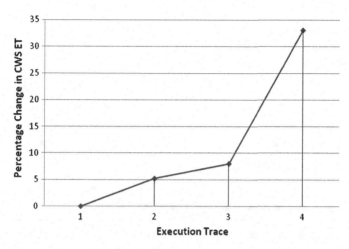

Fig. 12.1 Improvement in CWS ET after pruning and substituting its weakest link WS

12.7 Efficiency

We simulated one service repository at the local machine, and one global repository on a different machine. Network latency value of 101 ms between the two sites was taken on the basis of the monitoring information available on the Dotcom-Monitor cloud network (https://www.dotcom-tools.com/internet-backbone-latency.aspx) on June 10, 2016. The Dotcom-monitor provides standard baseline network latency between different locations that it monitors across the globe. We selected Mumbai (India), and Hongkong (China) as the two locations for simulating the process. Mumbai has the least network latency with Hongkong.

Both the repositories were populated with web services with similar functionalities. A few web services with better QoS values (than the local repositories) were made available in the distant repository only.

For the first case, only the local repository was used in the discovery process. Local optimization was used to create the initial composition configuration. Here, the running time increases at a polynomial rate of growth when number of tasks is five (Fig. 12.2). The best fit equation in this case is $y = 13.45x^2 - 133.8x + 345.6$ with $R^2 = 0.833$ for five tasks. However, as the situation becomes more complex with a higher number of tasks, running time starts following an exponential growth rate (Fig. 12.3). Here, the best fit equation is found to be $y = 41.10e^{0.251x}$ with $R^2 = 0.740$.

In the second case, the local as well the global repository was searched during the service discovery process. This approach is very poor in scalability as the running time curve follows an exponential rise as the number of candidate web services in the registry increases. The best fit equation is $y = 0.347e^{0.596x}$ for 5 tasks with coefficient of determination $R^2 = 0.975$. Similarly, $y = 0.289e^{0.685x}$ for 10 tasks

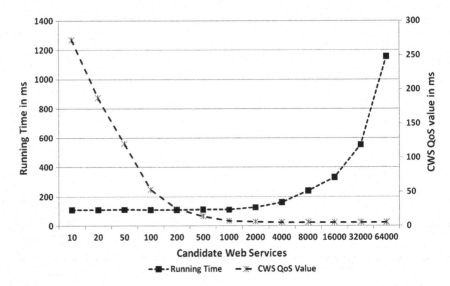

Fig. 12.2 Using local repository with local optimization for number of tasks = 5

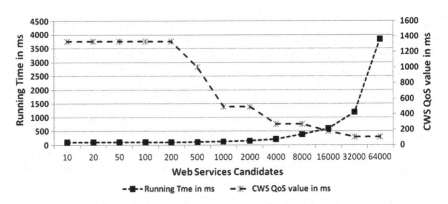

Fig. 12.3 Using local repository with local optimization for number of tasks = 10

with $R^2 = 0.985$. It happens in both the cases: when number of tasks is five (see Fig. 12.4), or is increased to ten (see Fig. 12.5).

The third case corresponds to the proposed work in this paper. A configuration was analyzed to identify the weakest link in the service sequence, and the global repository was searched only when there was a weakest link to find an alternative web service for the weakest link web service only. In this case, running time follows a polynomial rate of growth represented by the equation $y = 12.71x^2 - 126.7x + 333.1$ with $R^2 = 0.852$ for 5 tasks (Fig. 12.6). When number of tasks was increased to ten, even then the running time followed a polynomial growth rate (Fig. 12.7) with the best fit equation as $y = 31.42x^2 - 315.4x + 673.1$, and coefficient of

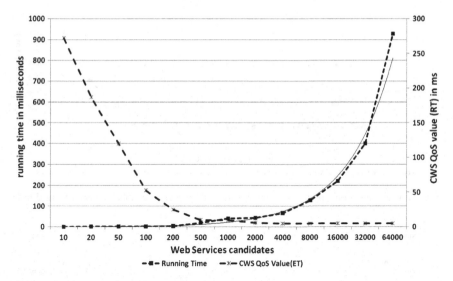

Fig. 12.4 Using local as well as global repository with 5 tasks

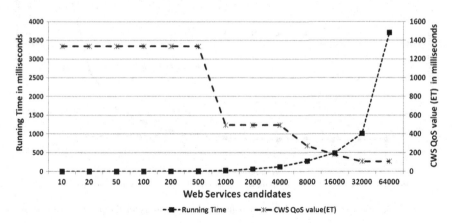

Fig. 12.5 Using local as well as global repository with 10 tasks

determination $R^2 = 0.801$. We analyzed the results for increasing the number of tasks to 20 (Fig. 12.8). The running time is still with polynomial growth rate represented by $y = 54.11x^2 - 533.9x + 1049$ with $R^2 = 0.867$ as the best fit equation.

12.8   Quality of the Solution

We measure quality of solution in terms of the aggregate QoS value for the Execution Time of the CWS. It can be observed (see CWS QoS value in Figs. 12.2, 12.3, 12.4, 12.5, 12.6, 12.7 and 12.8) that quality of the solution improves as the

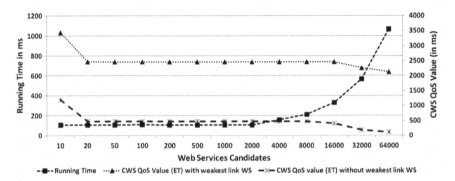

Fig. 12.6 Results for the proposed solution using local as well as a global repository with 5 tasks

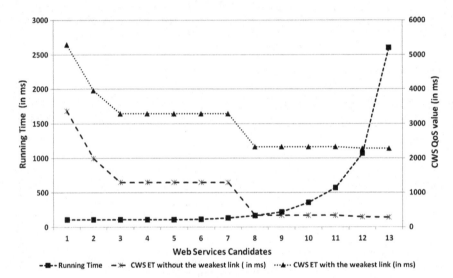

Fig. 12.7 Results for the proposed solution using local as well as a global repository with 10 tasks

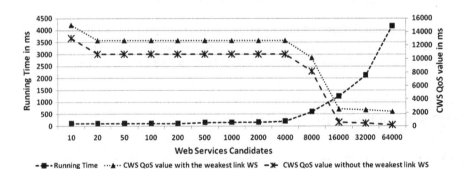

Fig. 12.8 Results for the proposed solution using local as well as a global repository with 20 tasks

search space is expanded in all the cases. Aggregate value of the Execution Time of a CWS decreases as more and more number of services are added to the search domain. As the number of tasks in a CWS increases, the aggregate ET values also increases, and intuition also implies the same. However, the cost of improvement is the least in case of the proposed solution.

12.8.1 Experiment 2

Analysis of the proposed framework for a CWS with long span of life is presented in this section. This section presents the evaluation of the framework by comparing it with a solution that does not use any policy to analyze a CWS execution plan to identify partner web services posing as weakest links in the value chain. In the first case, service discovery is limited to a local repository. By using an exhaustive strategy, best service for each task is selected from the candidate web services in the local repository. In the second case (or for the proposed approach), service composition is created using candidate web services from the local repository, and then service discovery is expanded to global repository only when the need is felt to manage web services with worst QoS value in the configuration.

In order to compare the approaches, we measure

- Quality of the solution in terms of aggregate QoS value of the CWS.
- Efficiency, i.e., the time taken to generate the CWS configuration
- Scalability, i.e., the response of the proposed approach as the problem size scales up.

We use a synthetic data set in the experiment. Values for the QoS attribute ET are generated using a uniform random process. The solution is implemented in C++ using CodeBlocks 11.0 IDE with gcc as the compiler on an Intel machine with Core 2 Duo CPU, 2 GB RAM, and Windows XP as the operating system.

12.9 Quality of the Solution

We measure quality of solution in terms of the aggregate QoS value for the Execution Time of the CWS. In the first case, only the local repository was used in the discovery process. Local optimization was used to create the initial composition configuration. In a static environment, a CWS is created only once, and responds to all the requests that it gets after that. Figure 12.9a shows the CWS QoS value for first and the subsequent requests in case of static composition. It stays almost the same for the 20 requests the CWS was run for. When the proposed framework is used to analyze the CWS execution process for weakest link web services in a static environment, CWS QoS value improves (for request number 2 in the Fig. 12.9).

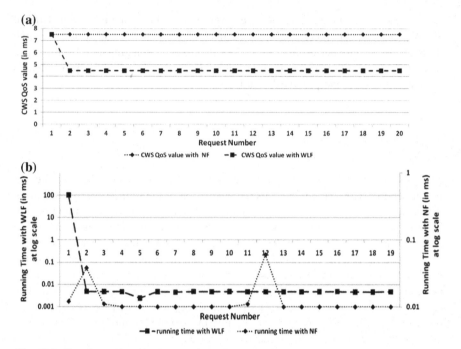

Fig. 12.9 Experimental results for a static environment

We use NF for No Framework, and WLF for the Weakest Link Framework proposed in this paper.

For the proposed solution, we simulated one service repository at the local machine, and one global repository on a different machine. Network latency value of 101 ms between the two sites was taken on the basis of the monitoring information available on the Dotcom-Monitor cloud network (https://www.dotcomtools.com/internet-backbone-latency.aspx) on June 10, 2016.

In the second case, we considered a dynamic environment in which QoS values of the partner web services change (improve) randomly. The experiment results (in Fig. 12.10a) show that CWS QoS values improve consistently in both the cases (without as well as with the framework). However, improvement in case of the Weakest Link Framework (WLF) is far better than the case when no framework is used.

12.10 Efficiency

Figures 12.9b and 12.10b present the running time of composing a CWS in static and dynamic environments respectively. The running time of the naïve approach (no framework) is better than the proposed approach in the static environment. With

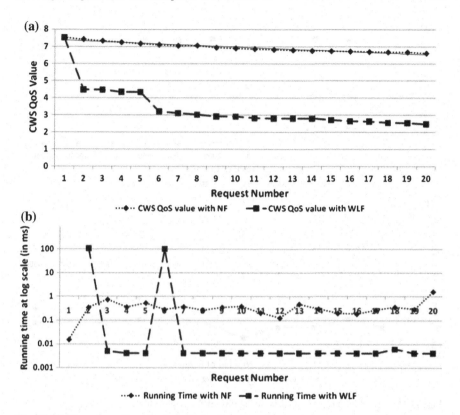

Fig. 12.10 Experimental results for a dynamic environment

the framework, running time is considerably high for the first request. But with support for the weakest link analysis and replacement with a better alternative, the running time decreases significantly for the subsequent requests.

In the dynamic environment, as QoS of the partner web services improve a few web services become weakest links. We can see spikes in the running time for the proposed framework. Otherwise, the running time for the proposed framework is better than the naïve approach.

12.11   Scalability

Figure 12.11a, b gives a comparison of the average CWS QoS value, and average running time for both the approaches. When we scale up the number of requests that invoke the CWS, the average CWS QoS value improves in case the proposed framework is employed. However, it remains almost at the same level throughout for the naïve approach. The average running time is also better (than the naïve

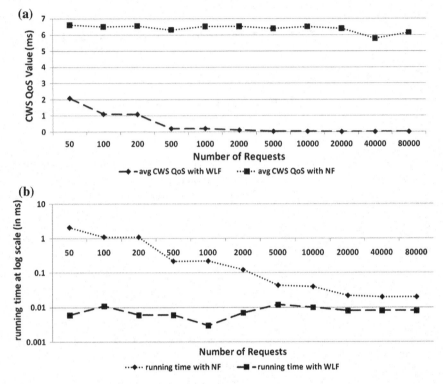

Fig. 12.11 Experiment results to show scalability of the approach

approach) for the proposed framework as the number of requests scale up from 50 to 80,000. In this case running time is almost constant. Actually, extra overhead to deal with the weakest link web services gets distributed in multiple requests.

12.12   Limitations of the Study

Three factors determine optimization of a web service composition problem: number of tasks of the CWS, number of candidate web services for the tasks, and number of QoS factors to watch for optimization. This study focuses on only the first two. For the third one, we assumed a simple QoS model with only one dimension.

The proposed approach follows local optimization as the evaluation criteria for service selection. It does not consider global constraints on the solution. Though improvements in global QoS value are appreciated and given preference.

12.13 Conclusions

This paper proposes an approach to improve QoS of a composite web service when some of its partner web services become weakest links in the workflow. The weakest links are identified, and then pruned from the configuration of the composite web service. Alternatives of such web services do not exist in the service registry that the service discovery module explores in routine. Therefore, the search space is expanded to bring some distant/premium service repositories/brokers in the ambit of the service discovery module. Simulation results show that the proposed approach is effective and efficient as well. In the present case, a web service composition configuration is created from scratch for every request. Such an approach is not efficient when requests for the same CWS are pouring at a continuous rate (called a long term composed service). In the second experiment, CWS QoS analysis in static as well as dynamic environments shows that the proposed framework gives better quality of the solution. At the same time, running time (computation cost) of the proposed solution is better. Scalability of the proposed framework is tested for running it for 50 requests to 80,000 requests. Its running time is stable as the number of requests scales up. At present, we are working on a prototype to implement the proposed solution in a real-world application.

References

1. Alamri, A. et al. (2006). Classification of the State-of-the-Art Dynamic Web Services Composition Techniques, International Journal of Web and Grid Services, vol. 2, pp. 148–166, Sept. 2006.
2. Al-Masri, E., Mahmoud, Q. (2007). Crawling Multiple UDDI Business Registries, WWW 2007(poster paper), May 8–12, 2007, Banff, Alberta, Canada, pp. 1255–1256.
3. Baresi, L., Miraz, M. (2006). A Distributed Approach for the Federation of Heterogeneous Registries, (Eds.) A. Dan, W. Lamersdorf Proceedings 4th International Conference Service-Oriented Computing ICSOC 2006:, Chicago, IL, USA, December 4–7, 2006. Springer Berlin Heidelberg, Berlin, Heidelberg, pp. 240-251.
4. Cardoso, J. et al. (2004). Quality of Service for Workflows and Web Service Processes, Journal of Web Semantics, vol. 1, pp. 281–308.
5. Chen, M., Yan, Y. (2014). QoS-aware service composition over graphplan through graph reachability, in Proceedings of the 2014 IEEE International Conference on Services Computing, pp. 544–551.
6. Crasso, M., Zunino, A., Campo, M. (2011). A Survey of Approaches to Web Service Discovery in Service-Oriented Architectures, J. Database Management. Vol 22, issue 1, pp. 102–132.
7. Deng, S., Wu, Z., Wu, J. (2012). An Efficient Service Discovery Method and its Application in (Eds.) Zhang, L. Innovations, Standards, and Practices of Web Services: Emerging Research Topics. Information Science Reference, IGI Global.
8. Dustdar, S., Schreiner, W. (2005). A Survey on Web Services Composition, International Journal on Web and Grid Services, vol. 1, pp. 1–30, Aug 2005.

9. Harney, J., Doshi, P. (2008). Selective querying for adapting web service compositions using the value of changed information, IEEE Transactions on Services Computing, 1 (3), pp. 169–185.

10. Jaeger, M., Ladner, H. (2006). A Model for the Aggregation of QoS in WS Compositions Involving Redundant Services, Journal of Digital Information Management, 2006, Digital Information Research Foundation.

11. Jaeger, M., Rojec-Goldmann, G., Muehl, G. (2004). QoS Aggregation for Web Service Composition using Workflow Patterns, Proceedings of the 8th International Enterprise Distributed Object Computing Conference (EDOC 2004), Monterey, California, USA, IEEE CS Press, pp. 149–159.

12. Jiang, W., Hu, S., Lee, D., Gong, S., Liu, Z. (2012). Continuous Query for QoS-Aware Automatic Service Composition. IEEE International Conference Web Services (ICWS), 2012.

13. Kahlon, N.K., Chahal, K. K., Kapoor, S.V., Narang, S.B. (2015). Managing Availability of Web Services in Service Oriented Systems, Proceedings of 2015 Asia-Pacific Software Engineering Conference (APSEC), New Delhi, pp. 316–321.

14. Li, J., Zhang, X., Chen, S., Song, W., Chen, D. (2014). An Efficient and Reliable Approach for QoS aware service composition, Information Sciences, vol. 269, pp. 238–254, June 2014.

15. Liu, X., Bouguettaya, A., Wu, X. and Zhou, Li. (2013). Ev-LCS: A System for the Evolution of Long-Term Composed Services. IEEE Trans. Serv. Comput. 6, 1 (January 2013), 102–115.

16. Ma, H., Bastani, F., Yen, I., Mei H. (2013). QoS-Driven Service Composition with Reconfigurable Services, IEEE Transactions on Services Computing, 6(1):20–34.

17. Sivashanmugam, K., Verma, K., Sheth, A. (2012). Discovery of Web Services in a Federated Registry Environment, Proceedings of the Second International Conference on Computer Science, Engineering and Applications (ICCSEA 2012), May 25–27, 2012, New Delhi, India, Volume 1.

18. Tukey, J. (1977). Exploratory Data Analysis, Addison-Wesley, 1977, pp. 43–44.

19. Zeng, L., Benatallah, B., Ngu, A., Dumas, M., Kalagnanam, J. and Chang, H. (2004). QoS-Aware Middleware for Web Services Composition, IEEE Transactions on Software Enggineering. 30(5): 311–327, 2004.

20. Zhou, X., Shen, J., Li, Y. (2013). Immune based chaotic artificial bee colony multiobjective optimization algorithm, in Proceedings of the 4th International conference on Swarm Intelligence, vol. 7928, pp. 387–395.

Chapter 13
Using Distributed Agile Patterns for Supporting the Requirements Engineering Process

Maryam Kausar and Adil Al-Yasiri

Abstract This chapter discusses the challenges practitioners face while choosing to develop their projects at offshore locations. As offshore development introduces new challenges in the software development process such as trust, socio-cultural, communication and coordination and knowledge transfer issues, it has been observed that these challenges affect how requirements are defined and managed while using agile practices in offshore software development. Using the notions of Distributed Agile Patterns we discuss how they can facilitate the requirements engineering process in offshore software development. We present a catalogue of the complete set of patterns, but only gave details of selective patterns from the catalogue that are related to the requirements engineering process. The whole catalogue is available online for anyone interested in it. At the end we developed a process flow showing the distributed agile patterns mapped onto the traditional requirements engineering process to show how these patterns address and improve the requirements engineering process for agile offshore projects.

Keywords Distributed agile patterns · Global software engineering · Requirements engineering

13.1 Introduction

The process of requirements elicitation is one of the most challenging tasks in software development. In traditional software development methodologies, the client would predefine all their requirements to the development team before the start of subsequent phases. The team would then analyse the requirements and finalise a software requirements specification (SRS) document. Once the client has approved the document, they would start the development phase. This process of requirements elicitation has problems such as; a long time is spent in preparing this

M. Kausar · A. Al-Yasiri (✉)
School of CSE, University of Salford, M5 4WT Salford, Greater Manchester, UK
e-mail: a.al-yasiri@salford.ac.uk

© Springer International Publishing AG 2017
M. Ramachandran and Z. Mahmood (eds.), *Requirements Engineering for Service and Cloud Computing*, DOI 10.1007/978-3-319-51310-2_13

documentation, which causes issues in dealing with future requirements change requests from the client once the actual development phase starts. Over decades of software development we have learnt that requirements change is inevitable during the development stage, because neither the client nor the developers are 100% sure of all the requirements of the system at the start of the project.

In agile software development, this problem is solved with the use of story cards, which is a lighter process for the definition of very high-level requirements and is an artefact of methods such as SCRUM and XP. They contain just enough information for the developer to be able to estimate how much effort and time will be required to develop them and can handle change requests with little effort. There is also an agile requirements change management process to control changing requirements throughout the software development lifecycle. Based on this process, new requirements can be added and reprioritized based on the client's request [1]. Figure 13.1 illustrates the agile requirements change management process:

However, in distributed agile software development, as the team is distributed over different time zones, the process of gathering and documenting requirements becomes more complex. As any change in the requirements need to be communicated over different locations and due to cultural and language differences, requirements can be misunderstood.

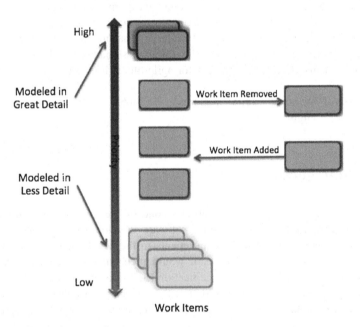

Fig. 13.1 Agile requirements change management process

In this chapter we will discuss how agile methods are used in offshore software development, what are the challenges facing the requirements elicitation process in agile offshore software development and how we can use distributed agile patterns to overcome these challenges.

13.2 Agile Offshore Software Development

Since the creation of the agile manifesto it has brought unprecedented changes to how software is being developed [2]. The manifesto focuses on four points, which are:

   i. Individuals and interaction over processes and tools
  ii. Working software over comprehensive documentation
 iii. Customer collaboration over contract negotiation and
 iv. Responding to change over following a plan.

Nowadays many companies are using agile for developing their offshore projects [3]. However, the use of agile methods on offshore projects is not a straightforward process. Taylor et al. [4] claim that projects that use agile for offshore development go through many problems because of the differences in the development practices and the complex development environments. Table 13.1 shows a characteristic comparison of agile and offshore development, done by Šmite et al. [5], showing the differences in the development styles.

Table 13.1 shows that the application of agile methods is not a straightforward process in offshore development. Based on extensive literature review on offshore software development four key challenges have been identified that affect the adoption of agile practices. Table 13.2 shows the results of how these challenges affect agile practices.

Table 13.2 summarises the agile practices that cannot be used as they are in offshore software development and that the requirements engineering process is affected in offshore development. In the next section we have identified how these challenges affect the requirements engineering process in agile offshore development.

Table 13.1 Comparison of agile development versus offshore development [5]

Characteristics	Agile development	Offshore development
Communication	Informal Face-to-face Synchronous Many-to-many	Formal Computer-mediated Often synchronous Tunnelled
Coordination	Change-driven Mutual adjustment, Self management	Plan-driven Standardisation
Control	Lightweight Cross-functional team	Command-and-control Clear separation of roles

Table 13.2 Agile practices affected by offshore challenges

No.	Offshore challenge	Agile practice	Affect of challenge on agile practice
1.	Trust	Collective ownership	Dispute over code ownership among the onshore and offshore team members
		Sustainable pace	Difficulties in maintaining a sustainable pace of project development
2.	Socio-cultural	Iterative and incremental development	Delays in frequent delivery of code
		Self-organising teams	Problems in understanding each other's cultural and social values can cause a barrier in the formation of self-organising teams
3.	Communication and coordination	Sprint planning	As the team is distributed, due to lack of sufficient communication, it can cause problems is designing a correct sprint
		Continuous integration	Multiple versions of code developed at different location can cause any build to break due to errors being integrated in the code
4.	Knowledge transfer	Product backlog	Any change in the product backlog not documented correctly can cause a project to fail
		Sprint review	As the sprint is being developed at multiple locations it causes problems in determining the progress of the work done

13.3 Challenges in Requirements Engineering Process in Agile Offshore Development

This section discusses the challenges and effect of agile offshore development on the process of gathering and documenting requirements. Table 13.3 shows the effect of agile offshore development challenges on the requirements elicitation process. As the table demonstrates the four challenges identified in our study have direct impact on the gathering, analysis and change management of requirements.

13.4 Distributed Agile Patterns

Based on the previous section we can see that applying agile on offshore project is not a straightforward process. We studied over 200 cases from the literature and interviewed practicing professionals involved in distributed teams, which resulted in observing a number of solutions addressing common agile issues in offshore software development settings, which we presented as Distributed Agile Patterns.

Table 13.3 Requirements engineering process affected by challenges of agile offshore development

No.	Challenges in agile offshore development	Affect on requirements engineering process in agile offshore development
1.	Trust	Establishing correct user story estimates as onshore team does not have clear understanding of the skills of the offshore team
		Getting the main objective and core functional requirements of the project clear to all the team members located at different sites
2.	Socio-cultural	Differences in cultural values and language can cause misunderstanding of requirements
		As at the beginning of the project the client is not sure of all the requirements, which can result in vague requirements, which need to be later clarified to the teams who are not on-site
3.	Communication and coordination	Changes in the requirements, needs to be communicated to all the distributed teams. Any mistake in recording the change can cause problems in the development of the system
4.	Knowledge transfer	As the project is being developed at different locations, there can be inconsistencies in the work done and documented user stories
		Maintaining bidirectional traceability of requirements across different sites is difficult as each site is working on different use stories
		Managing requirements, on-site customer and daily meetings become difficult with distributed teams

The term "pattern" is commonly referred to as a reusable solution for a recurring problem within a given context [6]. Based on this definition, we defined **Distributed Agile Patterns** as, adaptation of an agile practice that is being repeatedly applied in order to solve a recurring challenge in a distributed project scenario.

Generally a pattern has four essential elements [6]:

- The **pattern name**: to give a high level of abstract to the pattern. It gives us the idea of what problem the pattern is providing a solution for in a word or two. Giving a name to a pattern makes it easy for us to talk about it with people and for documentation.
- The **problem**: helps in describing when the pattern can be applied. It provides details of the problem and its context. It may include lists of conditions or scenarios, which must be met in order to apply the pattern.
- The **solution**: describes the elements that make up the agile patterns, their relationships and responsibilities. The solution does not describe a particular concrete agile practice or implementation, because a pattern is like a template that can be applied in many different scenarios. A pattern does provide an

abstract description of an agile practice problem and how a general arrangement of elements/practices can solve it.

- The **consequence**: describes the outcome of applying the pattern. They are critical for evaluating a pattern and for understanding the benefit of applying a pattern to see if it helped in solving the problem and if yes, up to what extent. For software the consequence often refer to space and time trade-offs. In distributed agile patterns, the consequence includes flexibility, extensibility and team coordination and collaboration.

The Distributed Agile Pattern's catalogue is developed based on literature and interviews and adopted Gamma's pattern template in order to preserve familiarity, as they are perceived as the first pattern catalogue documented by the software community. A customised template was then developed to capture the specific findings related to distribute agile practices. The distributed agile patterns template contains the following sections:

- **Pattern Name**: As patterns represent generic knowledge it is vital to give a good name that would make it recognisable and reusable. A good name also helps in facilitating communication among practitioners about the pattern.
- **Intent**: A short statement that highlights the issues and problems that are required to be solved by applying the pattern.
- **Also known As**: The pattern's other well-known names, if any are mentioned in this section.
- **Category**: Based on the similarities of the patterns we grouped them into different categories to be able to provide an abstract view of all the patterns.
- **Motivation**: It consists of the description of the problem and why the pattern should be used in order to avoid the problem from recurring. It provides scenarios that help understand the abstract description of the pattern.
- **Applicability**: Under what conditions the pattern can be applied.
- **Participants**: The participants are those people that are required in applying the pattern.
- **Collaboration**: How participants will coordinate with each other in order to fulfil their responsibilities that are required to complete the projects.
- **Consequences**: Discuss the trade-offs of applying the patterns such as advantages and difficulties faced when applying it.
- **Known uses**: Examples of real scenarios found that follow the pattern in order to provide clarity of how the pattern can be used.
- **Related Pattern**: List of similar patterns in order to identify which patterns can be used together to improve a particular situation.

Following is the summary of list of the identified distributed agile patterns [7]:

1. **Distributed Scrum of Scrum Pattern**: To apply scrum, sub-teams are formed based on location. Each team has its own scrum. Scrum of scrum meetings are arranged to discuss the progress of the project, which is attended by key people.

2. **Local Standup Meetings Pattern**: To discuss daily updates on work done, each local team will conduct their own stand-up meetings.
3. **Follow the Sun Pattern**: Onshore and offshore teams will work 9 a.m–5 p.m according to their own time zones.
4. **Onshore Review Meeting**: The onshore team will present the demo as they are located where the client is.
5. **Collective Project Planning**: Both the onshore team and the offshore team will collectively work in the project planning phase.
6. **Project Charter Pattern**: Before starting the project planning activity, agile teams use project charter in order to have a central document between the onshore and offshore team that defines the project.
7. **Collaborative Planning Poker**: Only Key people will hold this activity from onshore and offshore team.
8. **Global Scrum Board**: There will be an online-shared Scrum board, which, both onshore and offshore team can use to view product backlog, storyboard, task board, burn down charts and other agile artefacts using online tools such as wikis.
9. **Local Sprint Planning**: Each team will have their own sprint planning meetings.
10. **Local Pair Programming**: Make pair programming teams from the same location.
11. **Central Code Repository**: The whole team will maintain a central code repository so that both team can see each other's code and see the progress of the work done.
12. **Asynchronous Retrospective Meetings**: Teams conduct separate retrospective meetings based on location and share the key information via email. The Scrum Masters discuss possible improvements with the team based on the feedback from the client.
13. **Asynchronous Information Transfer**: Due to the time difference between the onshore and offshore team use online tools to exchange information with each other. Each team should response to queries within 12 h.
14. **Synchronous Communication**: In order to discuss issues the teams used synchronous tools for voice, video conferencing, document sharing, application sharing, etc.
15. **Visit onshore–offshore Teams**: Both onshore and offshore teams should quarterly/annually visit each other in order to build trust, exchange cultural values and improve team coordination.

Fifteen distributed agile patterns were identified and organised into four categories based on the type of problem they solve, which are **management, communication, collaboration** and **verification patterns**. Table 13.4 shows the 15 distributed agile patterns according to their categories.

Table 13.4 Categories of distributed agile pattern

	Category			
	Management patterns	Communication patterns	Collaboration patterns	Verification patterns
Pattern names	Distributed scrum of scrum	Global scrum board	Collaborative planning poker	Project charter
	Local stand-up meeting	Central code repository	Follow-the-sun	Onshore review meeting
	Local sprint planning	Asynchronous information transfer	Collective project planning	
	Local pair programming	Synchronous communication	Visit onshore–offshore	
	Asynchronous retrospective			

- **Management patterns** help in managing the onshore and offshore team members and their activities to effectively apply agile in a distributed environment.
- **Communication patterns** focus on providing solutions to how distributed team members can maintain an effective communication channel in an agile setting using different online tools which provide both synchronous and asynchronous method for communication.
- **Collaboration patterns** provide solutions regarding which activities the onshore and offshore team members should conduct together to improve team coordination and project progress.

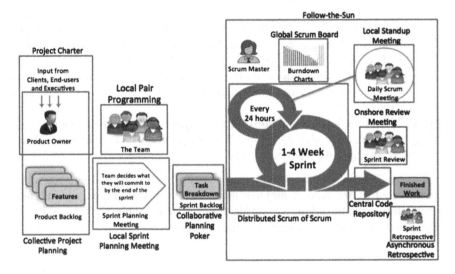

Fig. 13.2 Distributed agile patterns application of software development lifecycle

- **Verification patterns** focuses on how efficiently the clients can get a distributed project developed according to their requirements and monitor the progress of what has been developed.

The identified distributed agile patterns are spread across the Scrum software development lifecycle as shown in Fig. 13.2. In this chapter we have only presented the patterns that map to the requirements engineering process, however, the full catalogue is available online [8].

13.5 Distributed Agile Patterns Used for Requirements Engineering Process

In this section we present the selective Distributed Agile Patterns that are used in the Requirements engineering process, which are further explained in the following section showing how they are used to gather and document requirements.

13.5.1 Project Charter Pattern

In project management, a project charter is a statement that defines the scope, objectives and participants of a project. It is used to explain the roles and responsibilities, outline of the project objectives and identify main stakeholders. It has been observed that while starting a distributed project using agile many organisation use project charter to clarify the goals and objectives of the project to both onshore and offshore team [8] (Table 13.5).

13.5.2 Collective Project Planning Pattern

Agile focuses on individuals and interactions over processes and tools. While planning for the project the whole team is present. Unlike the traditional development where a project manager hands a project plan to the team, in agile the whole team takes part in the planning activity in order to determine when and how the project will be developed. It has been observed that even if the project is of a distributed nature it is better to co-locate the onshore and offshore teams for the project planning activity. The motivation of this pattern is to address the trust, socio-cultural, communication and coordination and knowledge transfer challenges. For example, consider a team that is divided into sub-teams that are located on

Table 13.5 Project charter pattern

No.	Pattern element	Detail
1.	Pattern name	Project charter pattern
2.	Intent	Before starting the project planning activity, agile teams use project charter in order to have a central document between the onshore and offshore team that defines the project
3.	Also known as	Project definition or project statement
4.	Category	Verification category, as this pattern helps the onshore and offshore team to have a central document clarifying the project goals and objectives, which is written by the product owner/client
5.	Motivation	The motivation of this pattern is to address the trust, communication and coordination and knowledge transfer challenges. For example when a project is distributed to a team that is divided over different time zones, a central document is written known as the project charter, which clarifies the onshore and offshore goals and objectives of the project. It also identifies the roles and responsibilities of the onshore and offshore team. The purpose of this activity is to have a document that helps the team in the project planning task
6.	Applicability	Use project charter pattern when: • Team is distributed over different time zones
7.	Participants	• Distributed onshore and offshore agile team • Client
8.	Collaboration	The client gives the project charter to the onshore team and offshore team to clarify the goals of the project
9.	Consequences	The project charter pattern has the following benefits: 1. It allows the onshore and offshore teams to understand the project. This helps overcome communication and coordination, and knowledge transfer challenges 2. Since it is a single document stating the goals and objectives of the project it helps establish trust between the onshore and offshore team members 3. It is intended to clearly set the stage for the project by aligning the team and settings goals and expectations
10.	Known uses	IONA technologies used project charter for their distributed projects in order to have a central document that clarifies the goals of the project to both onshore and offshore team members [17]. Similarly in a case study conducted by Brown [18] on Agile-at-Scale Delivery it was observed that organisations use project charter
11.	Related patterns	Project charter pattern is often used with visit onshore–offshore team pattern

different time zones and both the teams at the beginning of the project come to one location to do the project planning activity; this helps the team members to understand each other and establish working standards for the project. The detail table for this pattern can be found in Appendix 1.

13.5.3 Local Sprint Planning Meeting Pattern

In agile, a scrum consists of many sprints. The duration of a sprint varies from 1 to 4 weeks depending on the size of the project. At the start of every sprint the team has a sprint planning meeting in which the team defines the goal of the sprint and prepare the sprint backlog. When the team is divided and is working on different modules of the project it has been observed that the onshore team members and offshore team members conduct their own separate sprint planning meetings. The motivation of this pattern is to address the communication and coordination and knowledge transfer challenges. For example when a project is distributed to a team that is divided over different time zones, it is better that each location has their own sprint planning as it helps each team to decided their own tasks without having to wait for the other teams to be present. The detail table for this pattern can be found in Appendix 2.

13.5.4 Collaborative Planning Poker Pattern

An agile team plays a planning poker to put point estimation on each story card. The product owner also takes part in this activity. He/She tells the team the intent and value of a story card based upon which development team assigns estimation on the card. Based on the points assigned, the team members who assigned the lowest and highest estimation will justify their reasons. The team will have a brief discussion on each story and assign a fresh estimation upon which the whole team agrees on.

It has been observed that even when the team is distributed the planning poker activity is conducted when both teams are co-located for the project planning activity. The motivation of this pattern is to address the trust, socio-cultural, communication and coordination and knowledge transfer challenges. For example when a project is distributed over different locations, team members located at different locations, do not know each other's skill set so with the help of collaborative planning poker, each member can assign estimation points according to their skills. The detail table for this pattern can be found in Appendix 3.

13.5.5 Global Scrum Board Pattern

Agile has many artefacts such as product backlog, sprint backlog, storyboard, task board, team velocity and burndown charts which help the team in managing the project. It has been observed that when the team is divided to different locations they maintain an online record of all these artefacts so that they can share them with each other using online tools such as Wiki's, Rally and Jira [9–11]. The motivation of this pattern is to address the trust, socio-cultural, communication and coordination and knowledge transfer challenges. As the team is distributed over different time zones, any change in the requirements and sprint can be viewed in real time with the help of the global scrum board. The detail table for this pattern can be found in Appendix 4.

13.5.6 Central Code Repository Pattern

In agile, when a team is using Scrum and XP, the team members are divided in pairs of two and are working on different tasks during a sprint. When a task is completed the team members commit their code to a share repository for continuous integration of the code. It is observed that even when the team members are geographically apart they still use a share code repository where they commit their code so that all the team members can see the code as well as determine the progress of the project. The motivation of this pattern is to address the communication and coordination and knowledge transfer challenges. As the team members are distributed over different locations, with the help of the central code repository, all the team members can see the progress of the project. The detail table for this pattern can be found in Appendix 5.

13.5.7 Asynchronous Information Transfer Pattern

Agile emphases on close face-to-face communication between the team members rather than detailed documentation. When a team is distributed on different time zones it has been observed that the teams adopted asynchronous tools for sharing information with each other such as emails, Wikis, SharePoint. The motivation of this pattern is to address the communication and coordination and knowledge transfer challenges. Due to different time zones, the team members can use asynchronous communication methods to share information with each other. The detail table for this pattern can be found in Appendix 6.

13.5.8 Synchronous Communication Pattern

Agile emphases on close face-to-face communication between the team members rather than detailed documentation. When a team is distributed on different time zones it has been observed that the teams adopted asynchronous tools for sharing information with each other such as emails, Wikis, SharePoint. The motivation of this pattern is to address the trust, socio-cultural, communication and coordination and knowledge transfer challenges. For example, in case of any confusion, team members can communicate with each other using real time synchronous tools for communication. The detail table for this pattern can be found in Appendix 7.

13.5.9 Visit Onshore–Offshore Team Pattern

As agile emphases on close face-to-face communication between the team members it has been observed that when the team is divided on different time zones, the team members travel quarterly or annually to visit each other. This activity helps build trust among the team members and helps them understand each other's cultural differences [12–15]. The motivation of this pattern is to address the trust, socio-cultural, communication and coordination and knowledge transfer challenges. For example, in order to establish trust and understand each other's culture, team members should quarterly/annually travel and do team activities. The detail table for this pattern can be found in Appendix 8.

13.6 Use of Distributed Agile Patterns in Requirements Engineering Process in Agile Offshore Development

In order to verify and validate the identified distributed agile patterns, we conducted a reflection workshop based on Norm Kerth [16], **'The keep/try reflection workshop'**. Based on the workshop we designed Table 13.6, which shows how Distributed Agile Patterns address requirements engineering challenges in offshore development, which were mentioned in Table 13.3, to the relevant distributed agile pattern addressing them.

13.7 Mapping Distributed Agile Patterns on the Requirements Engineering Lifecycle

In this section we map the distributed agile patterns onto the traditional requirements engineering lifecycle, to show how these patterns facilitate the requirements engineering process. As shown in Fig. 13.3, the four key features of this process are as following:

- **Feasibility Study**: In this process, we decide whether or not the proposed system is worthwhile. By writing down the Project Charter document in the beginning of the project, we can achieve this. As stated in the Project Charter we define the aim, objectives and core functional requirements of the proposed system.

Table 13.6 Using distributed agile patterns to address requirements engineering challenges in agile offshore development

No.	Requirements challenge in agile offshore development	Distributed agile pattern	Solution
1.	User story estimation	Collective planning poker	By doing the planning poker activity together all team members will get a better understanding of each other's skills
2.	Objective and core functional requirements	Project charter	Having a project charter document written at the start of the project, will give all the team members a clear understanding of the project's objective and core functional requirements
3.	Misunderstanding of requirements	Collective project planning	Since the whole team will be part of the planning activity, the chances of misunderstanding a requirement will be reduced
		Asynchronous information transfer	In case of any misunderstanding, the team members can communicate with each other using asynchronous tools
		Synchronous communication	For a real time response to any misunderstanding, the team members can use synchronous methods for communication
4.	Vague requirements	Visit onshore–offshore	To clarify vague requirements, onshore team members should visit offshore team members and vice versa to discuss the requirements in order to avoid defects
5.	Changes in the requirements	Global scrum board	Any change in the requirements will be updated on the global scrum board, which is accessible by all team members in real time.
6.	Inconsistencies	Central code repository	To avoid any inconsistency between the work done and the user stories, all the team members use a central code repository, which is accessible by the whole team. All the code is committed in that repository, enabling the whole team to see what work is done and what is remaining
7.	Bidirectional traceability of requirements	Central code repository	With the help of a central code repository, we can map each requirement with its code, allowing traceability of all the requirements being developed at different locations
		Global scrum board	Status of all requirements being developed can be recorded using a global scrum board, which helps in maintaining traceability of requirements
8.	Managing requirements	Local sprint planning	Each site can manage their requirements and daily meetings using local sprint planning

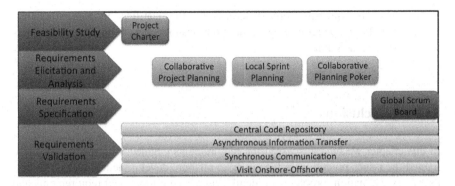

Fig. 13.3 Mapping distributed agile patterns on traditional requirements engineering process

- **Requirements Elicitation and Analysis**: The purpose of this process is to identify the application domain; the services it will provide and what are the limitations. Three distributed agile patterns are applied in these phases. Collaborative project planning helps the team to find out what the requirements of the application to be developed. Local sprint planning helps team members in their respective locations to discuss in detail the user stories allocated to them and determine the constrains associated with them. Collaborative Planning Poker, allows the team members to discuss the services that the system will provide and estimate how much effort is required to develop them.
- **Requirements Specification**: Once the requirements have been identified, we document them in the SRS document. As in agile software development, requirements are documented using user stories, in distributed agile software development; we use a Global Scrum Board, where all the story cards are placed. Hence any change or modification in the requirements will be updated on the Global Scrum Board, which is accessible by all the team in real time.
- **Requirements Validation**: In this process, the requirements are validated by reviewing them to make sure that the identified requirements are in accordance with what the client wants. Four distributed agile patterns make sure that the correct requirements are identified. Central Code Repository helps the client verify that the code being developed is according to requirements. Asynchronous Information Transfer provides a platform to the team members and the clients to communicate and coordinate the progress of the system being developed and in case of any confusion, the team can either use asynchronous or synchronous tools for communication, according to the communication standards defined using

Synchronous Communication Pattern. For further clarification of requirements, distributed agile patterns suggest that both onshore and offshore team members should visit each other.

13.8 Conclusions

In this chapter we have discussed the requirements engineering process and highlighted the issues practitioners face in agile offshore development such as incorrect user story estimation, problems in identifying the core functional requirements and vague requirements. Based on our observation and literature, we found that these challenges affect the whole requirements engineering process. Using distributed agile patterns, practitioners can avoid these challenges. They can use them at the beginning of their offshore projects and make informed decisions about how to adopt agile approaches to gather and document requirements, as generalised patterns make it easier for other companies to reflect on and to apply the results to their own cases.

Appendix 1: Collective Project Planning Pattern

See Table 13.7.

Table 13.7 Detail of collective project planning pattern

No.	Pattern element	Detail
1.	Pattern name	Collective project planning pattern
2.	Intent	Both the onshore team and the offshore team will collectively work in the project planning phase. Once both teams have engaged in the project planning activity, the team will prepare the project backlog
3.	Also known as	Project planning or agile project planning
4.	Category	Coordination category, as this pattern helps the onshore and offshore team to work together and come up with a project plan
5.	Motivation	The motivation of this pattern is to address the trust, socio-cultural, communication and coordination and knowledge transfer challenges. For example consider a team that is divided into sub-teams that are located on different time zones and both the teams come to one location to do the project planning activity. In the beginning of any distributed project, the offshore team is invited to the onshore location so that they may work together and understand each other's requirements.

(continued)

Table 13.7 (continued)

No.	Pattern element	Detail
		While the teams are co-located they worked on preparing the product backlog and they spend at least one or two sprints together before the offshore team leaves and starts working on the project [9, 15]. This helps the onshore team by making the offshore team understand their working style and work standard
6.	Applicability	Use collective project planning pattern when: • Team is distributed over different time zones
7.	Participants	Distributed onshore and offshore agile team
8.	Collaboration	Onshore team and offshore team work together to make a product backlog
9.	Consequences	The collective project planning pattern has the following benefits and liabilities: 1. It allows the onshore and offshore teams to work together and understand each other. This helps build trust among the team members and overcome communication and coordination challenges 2. Onshore team works with the offshore team and makes them understand what type of work they want. This helps overcome the socio-cultural and knowledge transfer challenges 3. It adds additional cost of travel and stay of the offshore team at the onshore location
10.	Known uses	FAST, a search company with headquarters in Norway while building a search application on top of their core search platform used collective project planning to co-locate the team and make them work together in project planning activities [10]. Siemens also used collaborative planning for their distributed projects [19, 20] in which team members from multiple sites got involved in the early stages of the project in order to create an open communication channel and high level of trust among the distributed team members [21]
11.	Related patterns	Collective project planning pattern is often used with Project charter pattern as it provides a central document that consists of the goal and objectives of the project written by the client

Appendix 2: Local Sprint Planning Meeting Pattern

See Table 13.8.

Table 13.8 Detail of local sprint planning meeting pattern

No.	Pattern element	Detail
1.	Pattern name	Local sprint planning meeting pattern
2.	Intent	Each team will have their own sprint planning meetings
3.	Also known as	Sprint planning meeting or iteration meeting
4.	Category	Management category, as this pattern helps the onshore and offshore teams work on their separate modules and conduct independent scrum and sprint planning meetings

(continued)

Table 13.8 (continued)

No.	Pattern element	Detail
5.	Motivation	The motivation of this pattern is to address the communication and coordination and knowledge transfer challenges. For example when a project is distributed to a team that is divided over different time zones, and are working on different modules of the project and are conducting their own scrums. As the onshore and offshore teams conduct their separate scrums, they also conduct separate sprint planning meetings to decide what they will develop during a sprint. Both teams prepare their sprint backlogs, which are shared using online tools
6.	Applicability	Use local sprint planning meeting pattern when: • Team is distributed over different time zones and is working on different modules/subsystems of the project
7.	Participants	Distributed onshore and offshore agile team
8.	Collaboration	The onshore team and offshore team share sprint backlog with each other to show the work they will be doing over the next sprint
9.	Consequences	The local sprint planning meeting pattern has the following benefits: 1. It allows both teams to work independently without having to wait for the onshore team to be available to conduct the meeting, which helps overcome the communication and coordination challenges 2. It provides control to both onshore and offshore team to work on their scrum and conduct their own sprint planning meetings, which avoids the offshore team from having to adjust working hours based on the onshore team availability. This helps overcome the communication and coordination challenges 3. Both teams can share their sprint backlog with each other, which provides visibility of the project progress and helps overcome the knowledge sharing challenges 4. As both the teams are working independently, it can cause the teams to feel, as they are not part of one team, rather create an effect that they are two separate teams
10.	Known uses	When CheckFree decided to move their work to an Indian offshore consulting firm they used local sprint planning meetings to plan their sprint activities [9]
11.	Related patterns	Local sprint planning pattern is often used with global scrum board pattern as the meetings minutes of the planning meeting are shared with both onshore and offshore team members

Appendix 3: Collaborative Planning Poker Pattern

See Table 13.9.

Table 13.9 Detail of collaborative planning poker pattern

No.	Pattern element	Detail
1.	Pattern name	Collaborative planning poker pattern
2.	Intent	Only key people will hold this activity from onshore and offshore teams
3.	Also known as	Planning poker or scrum poker

(continued)

Table 13.9 (continued)

No.	Pattern element	Detail
4.	Category	Collaborative category, as this pattern helps the onshore and offshore teams to discuss the duration of a story card
5.	Motivation	The motivation of this pattern is to address the trust, socio-cultural, communication and coordination, and knowledge transfer challenges. For example when a project is distributed to a team that is divided over different time zones, it is important that all the team members agree on the time duration of a feature before they start developing the project. This helps estimate the duration of the project completion as well as it provides visibility of project progress. For this purpose the onshore and offshore team members play planning poker in order to collectively agree on the estimation of a story card. Once the estimation is decided they write it down and approved by the product owner/client and move on to the next story card, till all the story cards are estimated
6.	Applicability	Use planning poker pattern when: • Team is distributed over different time zones and will be working on different story cards in a sprint
7.	Participants	• Distributed onshore and offshore agile team • Product owner/Client
8.	Collaboration	The client approves the estimation made by the team members
9.	Consequences	The planning poker pattern has the following benefits: 1. It allows the onshore and offshore teams to agree on a story card estimation, which helps the team establish their team velocity. Since members from both locations are present during this activity, this helps overcome trust and socio-cultural challenges 2. It provides the product owner/client with estimation of project completion, which helps overcome the communication and coordination, and knowledge transfer challenges 3. If all team members do not agree on estimation on a story card it can lead to a long discussion, resulting the planning poker to prolong
10.	Known uses	US hardware has development centres across North America, South America and Asia. When transitioning to distributed agile environment they used planning poker for estimating their story cards [22]
11.	Related patterns	Planning poker pattern is often used with Collective Project Planning as its better to conduct this pattern when the whole team is co-located. The estimated story cards are then shared on the Global Scrum board so that whole team can view them during the project

Appendix 4: Global Scrum Board Pattern

See Table 13.10.

Table 13.10 Detail of global scrum board pattern

No.	Pattern element	Detail
1.	Pattern name	Global scrum board pattern
2.	Intent	An online-shared Scrum board, will be used by, both onshore and offshore teams to view the product backlog, storyboard, task board, burn down charts and other agile artefacts using online tools

(continued)

Table 13.10 (continued)

No.	Pattern element	Detail
3.	Also known as	Scrum Board or Agile Story Board
4.	Category	Communication category, as this pattern helps the onshore and offshore team communicate with each other using an online tool to view each other's work and understand the progress of the overall project
5.	Motivation	The motivation of this pattern is to address the trust, socio-cultural, communication and coordination, and knowledge transfer challenges. For example when a project is distributed to a team that is divided over different time zones, and are working on different modules of the project, to share their work they use an online tool to display agile artefacts. Based on the work done by both teams it is easier to see the progress of the project and it helps understand if there is a problem with a team
6.	Applicability	Use global scrum board pattern when: • Team is distributed over different time zones
7.	Participants	Distributed onshore and offshore agile team
8.	Collaboration	The onshore team and offshore team share agile artefacts with each other to show their progress
9.	Consequences	The Global Scrum board pattern has the following benefits: 1. It allows the whole team to discover the requirements, which creates visibility of the project and helps in overcoming trust challenges. The scrum board is designed keeping the socio-cultural differences in mind 2. It allows the onshore and offshore teams to understand the progress of the project, which helps overcome the communication and coordination challenges 3. It increases the visualisation of the work done by each team, which helps overcome knowledge transfer challenges
10.	Known uses	FAST, a search company with headquarters in Norway while building a search application on top of their core search platform experimented with a couple of online tools to keep both teams updated with the progress of the project. They tired XPlanner and Jira and settled for Jira, which is a web-based tool that allowed the remote team members to view the backlog and update tasks whenever they wanted [10]. Similarly in a study done by Cristal et al. [33] on an organisation that has development centres across North America, South America and Asia concluded with that the use of a global scrum board can help improve the productivity of global agile teams. Similarly companies like Valtech [11], Telco [12], BNP Paribas [23], Aginity LLC [24] and SirsiDynix [25] used online tools to share agile artefacts with their offshore team members
11.	Related patterns	Global scrum board pattern is often used with central code repository pattern as the team shares all the agile artefacts and code using an online tool

Appendix 5: Central Code Repository Pattern

See Table 13.11.

Table 13.11 Detail of central code repository pattern

No.	Pattern element	Detail
1.	Pattern name	Central code repository
2.	Intent	The whole team will maintain a central code repository so that both teams can see each other's code and view the progress of the work done
3.	Also known as	Source code repository or global build repository

Table 13.11 (continued)

No.	Pattern element	Detail
4.	Category	Communication category, as this pattern helps the onshore and offshore team members to write code and share it on a central code repository where all team members can review the code and edit it if required
5.	Motivation	The motivation of this pattern is to address the communication and coordination, and knowledge transfer challenges. For example when a team is divided over different time zones and are working on different modules/subsystems of a project they use a central code repository to share their work with all team members. They can use online tools such as GitHub for committing their code and maintain versions of the project [26]. This helps the whole team to see the code and provides visibility of the project progress
6.	Applicability	Use central code repository when: • Team is distributed over different time zones and is working on different modules/subsystem of the project
7.	Participants	Distributed onshore and offshore agile team members
8.	Collaboration	The onshore team and offshore team members share a keyboard with a fellow team member from their respective location and once they have finished a task they commit their code to a central code repository
9.	Consequences	The central code repository pattern has the following benefits: 1. It allows the onshore and offshore team members to review each other's code, which helps overcome communication and coordination challenges 2. It helps in determining the progress of the project, which helps overcome knowledge transfer challenges 3. As all the team is committing to a central repository, if a team commits code with errors it can affect the whole build of the project
10.	Known uses	WDS global is a leading global provider of knowledge-based services to mobile operators, manufacturers and application and sales channels. In 2004 they combined their developments, which were located in UK, USA and Singapore. They shared their code on a central code repository to minimise duplications and reduce cost of maintenance [27]. Many companies use central code repository for their distributed projects such as Valtech [11], Manco [12]. Aginity LLC [24], SirsiDynix [25], Extol International [28], CE Informant [29] and ABC Bank [30]
11.	Related patterns	Central code repository pattern is often used with Global Scrum Board Pattern

Appendix 6: Asynchronous Information Transfer Pattern

See Table 13.12.

Table 13.12 Detail of asynchronous information transfer pattern

No.	Pattern element	Detail
1.	Pattern name	Asynchronous information transfer
2.	Intent	Due to the time difference between the onshore and offshore teams, they use online tools to exchange information with each other. Each team should respond to queries within 12 h
3.	Also known as	Information transfer or knowledge sharing

(continued)

Table 13.12 (continued)

No.	Pattern element	Detail
4.	Category	Communication category as this pattern helps the onshore and offshore team members to answer each other's queries within 12 h
5.	Motivation	The motivation of this pattern is to address the communication and coordination, and knowledge transfer challenges. For example when a team is divided over different time zones they may have queries about work but due to the time difference they cannot get a direct reply at that time so they use emails to communicate queries, which are then answered within 12 h max. Organisations have set standards for response time in order to avoid delays in work [31]
6.	Applicability	Use asynchronous information transfer when: • Team is distributed over different time zone
7.	Participants	Distributed onshore and offshore agile team members
8.	Collaboration	The onshore and offshore team members share information and ask queries using asynchronous tools
9.	Consequences	The asynchronous information transfer pattern has the following benefits: 1. It allows the onshore and offshore team members to exchange information when synchronous communication cannot be conducted due to working hour's time difference. This helps overcome the knowledge transfer challenges 2. It frees team members from waiting for an onshore team member availability to ask a query. This helps overcome the communication and coordination challenges 3. If the team members do not respond timely it can cause delays in the project
10.	Known uses	VTT Technical Research Centre of Finland and National University of Ireland conducted a research on two organisations that were developing a system together. One organisation was a customer organisation in U.S and the other organisation was a development organisation located in Ireland. Based on their findings the companies used asynchronous tools for communication. They used Wikis for storing documents and meeting minutes and used Emails for decisions and queries [32]. Similarly Valtech used Twiki for asynchronous communication [11]
11.	Related patterns	Asynchronous information transfer pattern is often used with global scrum board and synchronous communication pattern

Appendix 7: Synchronous Communication Pattern

See Table 13.13.

Table 13.13 Detail of asynchronous information transfer pattern

No.	Pattern element	Detail
1.	Pattern name	Synchronous communication pattern
2.	Intent	In order to discuss issues the teams use synchronous tools for voice, video conferencing, document sharing, application sharing, etc.
3.	Also known as	Synchronous knowledge transfer

(continued)

Table 13.13 (continued)

No.	Pattern element	Detail
4.	Category	Communication category, as this pattern helps the onshore and offshore team members to answer each other's queries within 12 h
5.	Motivation	The motivation of this pattern is to address the trust, socio-cultural, communication and coordination and knowledge transfer challenges. For example, when a team is divided over different time zones they may have queries about work but due to the time difference they cannot get a direct reply at that time so they use emails to communicate queries, which are then answered within 12 h max. Organisations have set standards for response time in order to avoid delays in work [31]
6.	Applicability	Use synchronous communication pattern when: • Team is distributed over different time zones
7.	Participants	Distributed onshore and offshore agile team members
8.	Collaboration	The onshore team and offshore team members share information and ask queries using asynchronous tools
9.	Consequences	The synchronous communication pattern has the following benefits: 1. It allows onshore and offshore team members to exchange information when synchronous communication cannot be conducted due to working hour time difference. This helps overcome knowledge transfer, communication and coordination challenges 2. Team members can ask each other questions which build trust and help understand each other's socio-cultural differences, which helps overcome trust and socio-cultural challenges 3. It frees team members from waiting for an onshore team member availability to ask a query. This helps overcome the communication and coordination challenges 4. If the team members do not respond timely it can cause delays in the project
10.	Known uses	CampusSoft is a UK based company that used synchronous communication when they moved to agile with their offshore suppliers in India and Romania. They used video conferencing facilities for planning sessions and later shifted to WebEx sessions and Go To Meeting so that they could share desktops with the remote team members. For daily Scrum meetings they preferred to use Skype call and made everyone wear headsets to make the meeting easier. For sprint review meetings they used sharing desktop tools as well as conference phones so that members from both end could talk with each other [13]
11.	Related patterns	Synchronous communication pattern is often used with global scrum board and asynchronous information transfer pattern

Appendix 8: Visit Onshore–Offshore Team Pattern

See Table 13.14.

Table 13.14 Detail of visit onshore–offshore pattern

No.	Pattern element	Detail
1.	Pattern name	Visit onshore–offshore team pattern
2.	Intent	Both onshore and offshore teams should quarterly/annually visit each other in order to build trust, exchange cultural values and improve team coordination

(continued)

Table 13.14 (continued)

No.	Pattern element	Detail
3.	Also known as	Travel onshore–offshore
4.	Category	Collaboration category, as this pattern helps the onshore and offshore team members to co-locate and understand each other and build a relationship, which improves team coordination
5.	Motivation	The motivation of this pattern is to address the trust, socio-cultural, communication and coordination, and knowledge transfer challenges. For example when a team is divided on different time zones they do not feel that they are both part of one team and they do not trust each other. They do not understand each other's cultural values and work ethics. In order to solve these issues the onshore and offshore teams visit each other to develop the feeling of trust and understand each other's cultural and working values. During these visits they attend training together as well as engage with informal activities to better understand each other. This helps build a bond between the team members, which results in good team coordination
6.	Applicability	Use visit onshore–offshore team when: • Team is distributed over different time zones
7.	Participants	Distributed onshore and offshore agile team members
8.	Collaboration	The onshore and offshore team members visit each other to improve team coordination
9.	Consequences	The visit onshore–offshore Team pattern has the following benefits and limitations: 1. It allows onshore and offshore team members to exchange cultural values with each other and work ethics. This helps overcome socio-cultural and communication and coordination challenges 2. It helps team members to feel they are part of one team, which develops trust among onshore and offshore team members. This helps overcome trust and knowledge transfer challenges 3. The travelling adds additional cost to the project budget
10.	Known uses	Ericsson is a Swedish multinational provider of communications technology and services. To build a XaaS platform and a set of services they used agile software development methodologies. The development team was distributed over 5 sites located in 3 countries. Four of the sites were located in Europe and one was located in Asia. They conducted workshops, which were attended by team members from different locations. The purpose of these workshops was to create a common vision for the whole organisation by setting common values as well also to improve the collaboration between the sites, thus build trust [14]
11.	Related patterns	Visit onshore–offshore team pattern is often used with collective project planning pattern as planning is better done when the whole team is co-located

References

1. Agile Requirements Change Management [Accessed on: 24th Oct 2016] http://agilemodeling. com/essays/changeManagement.htm.
2. Beck, K., Beedle, M., Van Bennekum, A., Cockburn, A., Cunningham, W., Fowler, M., ... & Thomas, D. (2001). Manifesto for agile software development.
3. Abrahamsson, Pekka, Juhani Warsta, Mikko T. Siponen, and Jussi Ronkainen (2003). "New directions on agile methods: a comparative analysis." In *Software Engineering, 2003. Proceedings. 25th International Conference on*, pp. 244–254. IEEE.
4. Taylor, Philip S., Des Greer, Paul Sage, Gerry Coleman, Kevin McDaid, and Frank Keenan (2006). "Do agile GSD experience reports help the practitioner?." In *Proceedings of the 2006 international workshop on Global software development for the practitioner*, pp. 87–93. ACM.
5. Šmite, Darja, Nils Brede Moe, and Pär J. Ågerfalk (2010). "Fundamentals of Agile Distributed Software Development." In *Agility Across Time and Space*, pp. 3–7. Springer Berlin Heidelberg.
6. Gamma, E., Helm, R., Johnson, R., & Vlissides, J. (1994). *Design patterns: elements of reusable object-oriented software*. Pearson Education.
7. Kausar, Maryam and *Adil Al-Yasiri*. "Distributed Agile Patterns for Offshore Software Development" 12th International Joint Conference on Computer Science and Software Engineering (JCSSE), IEEE 2015.
8. Distributed Agile Patterns. [Accessed on: 24th Oct 2016] http://stp872.edu.csesalford.com/ distributedagilepatterns.html.
9. Cottmeyer, Mike. "The good and bad of Agile offshore development." In *Agile, 2008. AGILE'08. Conference*, pp. 362–367. IEEE, 2008.
10. Berczuk, Steve. "Back to basics: The role of agile principles in success with an distributed scrum team." In *Agile Conference (AGILE), 2007*, pp. 382–388. IEEE, 2007.
11. Danait, Ajay. "Agile offshore techniques-a case study." In *Agile Conference, 2005. Proceedings*, pp. 214–217. IEEE, 2005.
12. Ramesh, Balasubramaniam, Lan Cao, Kannan Mohan, and Peng Xu. "Can distributed software development be agile?." *Communications of the ACM* 49, no. 10 (2006): 41–46.
13. Summers, Mark. "Insights into an Agile adventure with offshore partners." In *Agile, 2008. AGILE'08. Conference*, pp. 333–338. IEEE, 2008.
14. Paasivaara, Maria, Sandra Durasiewicz, and Casper Lassenius. "Using scrum in distributed agile development: A multiple case study." In *Global Software Engineering, 2009. ICGSE 2009. Fourth IEEE International Conference on*, pp. 195–204. IEEE, 2009.
15. Therrien, Elaine. "Overcoming the Challenges of Building a Distributed Agile Organization." In *AGILE*, pp. 368–372. 2008.
16. Kerth, Norm. "Project Retrospectives: A Handbook for Reviews." *Dorset House Publishing* (2001).
17. Poole, Charles J. "Distributed product development using extreme programming." In *Extreme Programming and Agile Processes in Software Engineering*, pp. 60–67. Springer Berlin Heidelberg, 2004.
18. Brown, Alan W. "A case study in agile-at-scale delivery." In *Agile Processes in Software Engineering and Extreme Programming*, pp. 266–281. Springer Berlin Heidelberg, 2011.
19. Avritzer, Alberto, and Daniel J. Paulish. "A comparison of commonly used processes for multi-site software development." In *Collaborative Software Engineering*, pp. 285–302. Springer Berlin Heidelberg, 2010.
20. Avritzer, Alberto, William Hasling, and Daniel Paulish. "Process investigations for the global studio project version 3.0." In *Global Software Engineering, 2007. ICGSE 2007. Second IEEE International Conference on*, pp. 247–251. IEEE, 2007.

21. Avritzer, Alberto, Francois Bronsard, and Gilberto Matos. "Improving Global Development Using Agile." In *Agility Across Time and Space*, pp. 133–148. Springer Berlin Heidelberg, 2010.

22. Wildt, Daniel, and Rafael Prikladnicki. "Transitioning from Distributed and Traditional to Distributed and Agile: An Experience Report." In *Agility Across Time and Space*, pp. 31–46. Springer Berlin Heidelberg, 2010.

23. Massol, Vincent. "Case Study: Distributed Agile Development." TheServerSide.com (2004).

24. Armour, Phillip G. "Agile… and offshore." *Communications of the ACM* 50, no. 1 (2007): 13–16.

25. Sutherland, Jeff, Anton Viktorov, Jack Blount, and Nikolai Puntikov. "Distributed scrum: Agile project management with outsourced development teams." In *System Sciences, 2007. HICSS 2007. 40th Annual Hawaii International Conference on*, pp. 274a–274a. IEEE, 2007.

26. Räty, Petteri, Benjamin Behm, Kim-Karol Dikert, Maria Paasivaara, Casper Lassenius, and Daniela Damian. "Communication Practices in a Distributed Scrum Project." *CoRR* (2013).

27. Yap, Monica. "Follow the sun: distributed extreme programming development." In *Agile Conference, 2005. Proceedings*, pp. 218–224. IEEE, 2005.

28. Kussmaul, Clifton, Roger Jack, and Barry Sponsler. "Outsourcing and offshoring with agility: A case study." In *Extreme Programming and Agile Methods-XP/Agile Universe 2004*, pp. 147–154. Springer Berlin Heidelberg, 2004.

29. Bose, Indranil. "Lessons learned from distributed agile software projects: A case-based analysis." *Communications of the Association for Information Systems* 23, no. 1 (2008): 34.

30. Modi, Sunila, Pamela Abbott, and Steve Counsell. "Negotiating common ground in distributed agile development: A case study perspective." In *Global Software Engineering (ICGSE), 2013 IEEE 8th International Conference on*, pp. 80–89. IEEE, 2013.

31. Vax, Michael, Stephen Michaud, "Distributed Agile: Growing a Practice Together," AGILE Conference, pp. 310–314, Agile 2008, 2008.

32. Korkala, Mikko, Minna Pikkarainen, and Kieran Conboy. "Combining agile and traditional: Customer communication in distributed environment." In *Agility Across Time and Space*, pp. 201–216. Springer Berlin Heidelberg, 2010.

33. Cristal, Mauricio, Daniel Wildt, and Rafael Prikladnicki (2008). "Usage of Scrum practices within a global company." In Global Software Engineering, 2008. ICGSE 2008. IEEE International Conference on, pp. 222-226. IEEE, 2008.

Index

A
Access control, 33, 40, 53, 55, 58, 187
Access rate, 74
Accountability, 37
Actors, 126
Adaptability requirements, 189
Agile, 291–296, 298–305
API security, 186
Architectural elements (process-level)
    (AEpc's), 251–256, 258, 260, 261
Architecturally significant requirements
    (ASRs), 184
Architecture
    minimum viable, 17
    partitioning, 251, 260
    requirements and, 16
ARSM approach, 67, 71, 79, 80, 83, 85
ASR classification, 191
ASRs' change impact analysis, 195
Assurance, 37
Asynchronous information transfer pattern,
    302, 311
Attackers and threats, 215
Automated security validation based on
    specific security test patterns, 226
Automotive embedded control unit (ECU), 218
Autonomic requirements, 55
Availability, 37, 75, 84
    constraints, 186
    requirements, 186

B
Behavioral analysis, 122, 124, 144
Billing
    account, 29, 39
    frequency, 29
    requirements, 189
Bounce access rate, 74

Boundedness, 121, 123, 131, 133, 135, 138,
    146
Business process model and notation (BPMN),
    152, 153, 156, 166, 168, 169, 174, 176,
    177, 236
Business paradigm, 48
Business process execution language
    (WS-BPEL), 237

C
Central code repository pattern, 302, 310
Centralized repository, 273
Change management, 155
Cloud
    agent (CA), 125, 129
    bus (CB), 125, 127
    checklist, 115
    computing, 91, 92, 94, 100, 121–123, 248,
        264, 267
    computing community, 49
    -enabled software application, 92, 99, 108
    enterprise service bus (CESB), 125
    -hosted services interoperability, 188
    infrastructure management, 95, 113
    -native software application, 92, 108
    requirements, 46–50, 53, 54, 57, 60
    resources, 182
    systems management requirements, 191
    universal description discovery and
        integration (CUDDI), 125, 127–130,
        133, 137
Collaborative planning poker pattern, 301, 308
Collective project planning pattern, 299, 306
Communication and collaboration
    requirements, 194
Communication and coordination, 294, 295
Compliance dimension, 27, 29, 31–33, 40, 41,
    58, 60
Consumers, 65–71, 73, 76, 77, 80, 83, 85

© Springer International Publishing AG 2017   317
M. Ramachandran and Z. Mahmood (eds.), *Requirements Engineering
for Service and Cloud Computing*, DOI 10.1007/978-3-319-51310-2

Consumer's perspective, 66, 68, 69
Containerization, 93, 97, 99, 109, 110
Context-free grammar, 158, 160
Contractual dimension, 27, 28, 39, 41, 57, 60
Cyber security analysis process, 215

D
Data and services isolation requirements, 190
Data location, 33
Data security, 186
Default priority constraints, 65, 71, 85
Different workflow patterns, 279
Distributed agile patterns, 291, 294, 295, 298,
    299, 303–305
Dotcom-monitor
    network latency, 281
Dynamic
    composition, 272
    requirements, 47, 60
    service choreography, 152, 155, 169, 177

E
EARS, 152, 154, 156, 158, 160, 161
Effective service access time, 76
Elasticity, 35, 38, 40, 42
    requirements, 185
Emergent architecture, 8
Enterprise cloud bus petri-net (ECBP), 124,
    131
Enterprise cloud bus system (ECBS), 121, 125,
    126
Enterprise service bus (ESB), 125, 152, 170,
    156, 170, 172
Enterprise software applications, 122, 123
Execution
    duration, 67
    trace, 280
External quality, 12

F
Failure access rate, 74
Feasibility study, 303
Feature creep, 19
Financial dimension, 27, 29–31, 39, 41, 58, 60
Flowgeneration algorithm, 168
Four-Step-Rule-Set (4SRS), 249, 250, 252,
    259, 262, 265
Functional requirements (FR), 111, 113, 230

G
Gap filling, 252
Global scrum board pattern, 301, 309

H
Hierarchical task network (HTN), 235
Hierarchical universal description discovery
    and integration (HUDDI), 125, 127–130
High-level Enterprise Cloud Bus Petri-net
    (HECBP), 121, 124, 131, 133, 145
Human communication, 16
Hypervisors, 99

I
Identity management, 33
Incident management, 35
Information system logical architecture, 248,
    249, 251, 259, 260, 266
Infrastructure as a Service, 46, 48
Internal quality, 12
Interoperability requirements, 188

J
Jurisdiction, 33, 35, 40, 58

K
Knowledge transfer, 294, 295

L
Legal compliance, 31, 33
Life span of a CWS, 274
Listening, 19
Liveness, 121, 123, 131, 133, 136, 138, 146
Local sprint planning meeting pattern, 301, 307
LOGGER, 125, 127, 129, 130, 133

M
MAPPER, 125, 127, 129, 130
Markov decision process (MDP), 231, 236,
    239, 242, 243
Mashed UCs, 250, 253, 255, 258, 261
Measurement, 37
Model
    generator, 162
    transformations, 249
Monitoring
    metrics, 185
    requirements, 189, 195
Multi-agent system (MAS), 123, 126, 128, 141
Multi-cloud architecture, 121, 122
Multi-CloudEnv, 126, 127
Multi-tenancy requirements, 190

N
Negative QoS attribute, 278
Non-functional

parameters, 65–69, 71, 73, 76–80, 83, 85
properties, 272
requirements (NFR), 90, 111, 113, 114,
    230, 236, 240

O

One time query, 274
Operational dimension, 27, 34, 35, 40, 41, 58,
    60
Organization's culture, 15
Original actors inclusion, 252, 254, 261
Overall aggregated effective quality of service,
    65, 76

P

Payment type, 30
PCB-QoS classification, 65–67, 71, 79, 85
PCB-QoS parameters, 74, 77
Performance, 37, 38
Performance metrics, 272
Persistence layer interoperability, 188
Planning domain definition language (PDDL),
    235
Platform as a service, 46, 48, 54
Policy-centred metamodel, 68
Premium registries, 273
Privacy, 48, 51, 53, 55, 58
Privacy requirements, 187
Probability score formula, 198
Process-level architectural elements (AEpc's),
    251–253, 255–257, 260, 267
Process-level requirements, 248, 249, 252, 259,
    262, 265
Product-level requirements, 248, 249, 252,
    261, 265, 266
Product-level use cases (UCpt's), 251, 253
Project charter pattern, 297, 299, 300
Provider agent (PA), 125, 128

Q

Quality of service (QoS), 65, 230–233,
    237–240, 243
    -aware middleware, 67
    -aware optimal solution, 275
    broker, 67
    classification, 65–67, 69, 71, 73, 74, 79, 85
    evaluation and monitoring, 69
    model extendibility, 69, 70
    parameters, 65–69, 71, 73, 77–79, 81, 83,
        85
Quality attribute, 212
Query/View/Transformation (QVT), 249, 255,
    261, 262, 264, 266, 267

R

Ranking, 65–67, 69–71, 73, 79, 80, 83, 85
Reachability, 133, 135, 139
Reactive adaptation, 231, 236
Redundancy elimination, 252, 253
Reinforcement learning (RL), 231, 239
Relation, 126
Reliability, 75, 84
Reputation, 67, 70, 73, 83
Request for
    information, 7
    for proposal, 7
    for quotation, 7
Requirement
    ambiguous, 6
    analysis, 48
    architecturally significant, 8
    assumptions in, 8
    classification, 158
    domain or system specific, 6
    elicitation, 11, 89–92
    elicitation and analysis, 305
    engineering (RE), 230, 231, 233, 234, 248,
        264, 267, 294, 295, 299, 303, 305
    functional and nonfunctional, 6
    IEEE 830 format, 7
    main problem areas, 10
    management, 48
    parser, 153, 156, 158, 161
    parser and analyser, 152, 158
    specification, 48, 305
    true, 6
    validation, 48, 305
    volatility, 11
Resource (RES), 125
    monitoring requirements, 190
    termination safety requirements, 190
Response time, 75
Risk analysis, 35
Runtime property, 35
Runtime QoS aggregation, 69, 70

S

SaaS, 3, 4, 6, 8, 10, 14, 15
Safeness, 121, 123, 131, 133, 136, 139, 146
Scalability, 35, 38
Scalability requirements, 185
Scheduling agent (SA), 125, 130
Search for an optimal solution
    exact algorithms, 275
Search space, 272
Security
    compliance, 31, 32

liabilities, 186
requirements, 55, 186
validation, 225
Selective query approach, 276
Self-adaptation (self-*), 232
Self-adaptation Software (SAS), 231, 234, 236, 240
Service
    broker's perspective, 73
    composition requirements, 189
    contract, 29, 37
    description, 29, 34–36, 40
    discovery module, 273
    layer interoperability, 188
    level agreement, 29, 35, 36, 39
    level agreement requirements, 189
    -oriented architecture (SOA), 73, 122, 230, 248, 249, 264, 267
    -oriented computing, 122
    -oriented logical architecture, 249, 250, 262–264, 267
    -oriented requirements engineering (SORE), 229–231
    providers' perspective, 73
    registry/broker, 276
    version database, 152, 154, 156, 157, 170, 172, 176
    version discovery, 170, 174
SLA, 66
Small and medium-sized enterprises, 48
Socio-cultural, 294, 295
Software
    -as-a-Service (SaaS), 46, 48, 54, 121, 122, 140, 248, 249, 259, 260
    -defined data center (SDDC), 93
    -defined environments (SDEs), 98, 99, 107, 117
    -defined infrastructures (SDI), 98, 99
    -defined networking (SDN), 102–104, 110, 115
    -defined storage (SDS), 104–107
Static composition, 272
Successful access rate, 75
Support for forensic, 33

Synchronous communication pattern, 302, 306, 312

T
Technical dimension, 27, 36, 40, 41, 59
Traceability, 152, 155, 157, 174, 176
    graph, 174
    rules, 174
Transition (between perspectives), 249, 265, 266
    rules, 251, 252, 255, 256
    steps, 251, 260, 261, 266
    use cases (UCtr's), 253–257, 267
Trust, 294, 295
Tukey fences, 278

U
UDDI registry, 152, 154, 157
Unified modeling language (UML), 236, 237, 248, 265–267
Usability, 38
Use case
    (diagrams), 249, 250, 266
    (Product-level) (UCpt's), 250–253
    (Transition) (UCtr's), 252, 261
    transformation, 251, 254
Utility function, 66

V
V+V Model, 249
Variability of QoS (vQoS), 237, 241
Virtualization, 93, 94, 97–101, 104, 105, 109, 110, 116
Visit onshore–offshore team pattern, 303
V-Model, 248–251, 259–261, 267
Vulnerabilities, 224
VxBPEL, 237, 238

W
Weakest link, 272
Web service, 65–69, 71, 74, 77, 78, 81, 83, 229–232, 235
Web service composition (WSC), 67, 230–233, 235–243

Printed in the United States
By Bookmasters